Digital Collections Worldwide:
An Annotated Directory

MICHAEL J. ALOI
MARJORIE FUSCO
SUSAN E. KETCHAM

Neal-Schuman Publishers

New York   **London**

Don't miss this book's companion website!
http://www.neal-schuman.com/digitalcollections
Username = reader
Password = 20digcol10

Published by Neal-Schuman Publishers, Inc.
100 William St., Suite 2004
New York, NY 10038

Printed and bound in the United States of America.

The paper used in this publication meets the minimum requirements of American National Standard for Information Sciences—Permanence of Paper for Printed Library Materials, ANSI Z39.48-1992.

Library of Congress Cataloging-in-Publication Data

Aloi, Michael J., 1974-
   Digital collections worldwide : an annotated directory / Michael J. Aloi, Marjorie Fusco, Susan E. Ketcham.
      p. cm.
   Includes bibliographical references and indexes.
   ISBN 978-1-55570-701-9 (alk. paper)
   1. Scholarly web sites—Directories. 2. Computer network resources—Directories. 3. Digital libraries—Directories. 4. Internet addresses—Directories. I. Fusco, Marjorie, 1941- II. Ketcham, Susan E., 1956- III. Title.

ZA4225.A44 2011
025.0422—dc22
                                                                                    2011000445

I dedicate this to my friend and companion Dr. William Thierfelder,
for his amazing encouragement and support.
—Michael Aloi

I dedicate this to my family and friends.
—Marjorie Fusco

I dedicate this to my mom, for a lifetime of love and support,
and in memory of my dad, for his love and inspiration.
—Susan E. Ketcham

Contents

Foreword xiii
Cheryl LaGuardia

Preface xv

Acknowledgments xxi

Chapter 1. World Initiatives 1
  Introduction 1
  World Initiative Sites 1

Chapter 2. Africa 17
  Introduction 17
  Continent 18
  Algeria 20
  Angola 21
  Benin 21
  Botswana 21
  Burkina Faso 22
  Burundi 22
  Cameroon 23
  Cape Verde 23
  Central African Republic 23
  Chad 24
  Comoros 24
  Congo Republic (Brazzaville) 24
  Congo Democratic Republic (Zaire) 25
  Côte d'Ivoire (Ivory Coast) 25
  Djibouti 25
  Egypt 25
  Equatorial Guinea 32
  Eritrea 32
  Ethiopia 33
  Gabon 33
  Gambia 33
  Ghana 34
  Guinea 34
  Guinea-Bissau 35
  Kenya 35
  Lesotho 35

Liberia 36
Libya 36
Madagascar 36
Malawi 37
Mali 37
Mauritania 38
Mauritius 38
Morocco 38
Mozambique 38
Namibia 40
Niger 40
Nigeria 40
Rwanda 41
São Tomé and Príncipe 41
Senegal 41
Seychelles 42
Sierra Leone 42
Somalia 42
South Africa 42
Sudan 44
Swaziland 45
Tanzania 45
Togo 45
Tunisia 46
Uganda 46
Western Sahara 46
Zambia 46
Zimbabwe 47

Chapter 3. Antarctica 49
Introduction 49
Continent 51
Antarctica 52

Chapter 4. Asia 57
Introduction 57
Continent 60
Afghanistan 67
Armenia 68
Azerbaijan 69
Bahrain 69
Bangladesh 70
Bhutan 71
Brunei Darussalam 72
Burma—*See* MYANMAR 72
Cambodia 73
China (People's Republic of China) 73
    Hong Kong (People's Republic of China) 77
    Macau (People's Republic of China) 77

Mongolia (People's Republic of China) 77
Tibet (People's Republic of China) 79
Cyprus 80
East Timor (Timor-Leste) 81
Hong Kong—*See* CHINA 82
India 82
Indonesia 84
Iran 84
Iraq 85
Israel 86
Japan 90
Jordan 96
Kazakhstan 97
Kuwait 97
Kyrgyzstan 98
Lao People's Democratic Republic (Laos) 98
Lebanon 98
Macau—*See* CHINA 99
Malaysia 99
The Maldives 101
Mongolia—*See* CHINA 101
Myanmar (Burma) 101
Nepal 102
North Korea 102
Oman 103
Pakistan 103
Palestinian Territories 103
    Gaza Strip 103
    West Bank 103
Philippines 104
Qatar 104
Russia 104
Saudi Arabia 107
Singapore 107
South Korea 108
Sri Lanka 108
Syria 108
Taiwan (Republic of China) 108
Tajikistan 108
Thailand 109
Tibet—*See* CHINA 109
Turkey 109
Turkmenistan 111
United Arab Emirates 111
Uzbekistan 111
Vietnam 111
Yemen 112

Chapter 5. Europe 113
  Introduction 113
  Continent 115
  Albania 117
  Andorra 117
  Austria 117
  Belarus 118
  Belgium 118
  Bosnia and Herzegovina 119
  Bulgaria 119
  Croatia 120
  Czech Republic 121
  Denmark 121
  Estonia 122
  Faroe Islands 122
  Finland 123
  France 123
  Germany 126
  Greece 128
  Hungary 129
  Iceland 130
  Ireland 131
  Italy 132
  Jan Mayen Islands—*See* NORWAY 135
  Latvia 135
  Liechtenstein 135
  Lithuania 136
  Luxembourg 136
  Macedonia 136
  Malta 137
  Moldova 137
  Monaco 137
  Montenegro 138
  Netherlands 138
  Norway 140
  Poland 141
  Portugal 142
  Romania 142
  San Marino 144
  Serbia 145
  Slovakia 145
  Slovenia 145
  Spain 146
  Sweden 148
  Switzerland 151
  Ukraine 152
  United Kingdom 153
    England 155

     Northern Ireland 155

     Scotland 155

     Wales 157

  Vatican City 158

Chapter 6. North America 161

  Introduction 161

  Continent 163

  Antigua and Barbuda 165

  Bahamas 165

  Barbados 165

  Belize 165

  Canada 166

  Costa Rica 168

  Cuba 168

  Dominica 170

  Dominican Republic 170

  El Salvador 171

  Greenland 171

  Grenada 171

  Guatemala 171

  Haiti 172

  Honduras 172

  Jamaica 173

  Mexico 173

  Nicaragua 174

  Panama 175

  St. Kitts and Nevis 175

  St. Lucia 175

  St. Vincent and the Grenadines 176

  Trinidad and Tobago 176

  United States 176

     Alabama 204

     Alaska 206

     Arizona 207

     Arkansas 209

     California 210

     Colorado 213

     Connecticut 215

     Delaware 216

     Florida 216

     Georgia 221

     Hawaii 223

     Idaho 224

     Illinois 225

     Indiana 226

     Iowa 227

     Kansas 227

Kentucky 228
Louisiana 229
Maine 230
Maryland 231
Massachusetts 233
Michigan 234
Minnesota 241
Mississippi 243
Missouri 245
Montana 247
Nebraska 249
Nevada 250
New Hampshire 252
New Jersey 252
New Mexico 253
New York 253
North Carolina 258
North Dakota 261
Ohio 261
Oklahoma 263
Oregon 264
Pennsylvania 267
Rhode Island 268
South Carolina 269
South Dakota 270
Tennessee 270
Texas 271
Utah 273
Vermont 274
Virginia 275
Washington 277
Washington, DC 280
West Virginia 280
Wisconsin 282
Wyoming 282

Chapter 7. Oceania 285
Introduction 285
Continent 287
Australia 287
Fiji 290
Micronesia 291
Guam 291
Kiribati 291
Marshall Islands 292
Nauru 292
Palau 292

New Zealand 293
Papua New Guinea 296
Samoa and Western Samoa 297
Solomon Islands 297
Tonga 298
Tuvalu 298
Vanuatu 299

Chapter 8. South America 301
Introduction 301
Continent 302
Argentina 303
Bolivia 304
Brazil 305
Chile 306
Colombia 307
Ecuador 307
Guyana 308
Paraguay 308
Peru 308
Suriname 309
Uruguay 309
Venezuela 310

Index of Reference Resources Described 311

Index of Names, Subjects, and Titles 329

About the Authors 345

Foreword

I get asked to read a fair number of manuscripts by various folks on various library-related subjects. Depending on the subject matter, the scope of the manuscript, and the author's skill and expertise, it can range from a deadly boring experience to being mildly interesting to being an absolute pleasure, because the book enlightens me and offers me material I can use in my work.

The experience of reading this manuscript fell into the category of absolute pleasure, because the authors have covered their subject quite exhaustively and they've done such an excellent job of describing digital collections around the world. Given the rate at which such collections are coming online, this must necessarily be an exercise in "sticking a hand in the river" of digital collections—and they've done that superbly. The listings here, accompanied as they are by rich annotations, will inform librarians and researchers alike; instead of searching Google for hours to uncover subsections of what's here, users can quickly and easily find pertinent information about digital collections around the globe and access them immediately. It's a time-saving and informative tool and one on which I'll depend in my work in support of courses and professional writing. I suspect it will become a standard resource for those of us involved in digital research and scholarship, and I'm delighted to have this opportunity to commend it to you.

Cheryl LaGuardia
Research Librarian
Widener Library
Harvard University
Cambridge, MA

Preface

We live in an increasingly digital world . . . the potential of digital projects to present information in new and important ways seems limitless,

—Trevor Jones (2001)

The Internet is full of interesting facts, figures, famous personalities, places of interest, and historical events and exploration spanning time from the historical to the present. Libraries, museums, archives, and other institutions have already digitized amazing collections of cultural, historical, and prized artifacts and are adding more every day. Through the use of digital technology, mankind is exposed to the "raw materials of history" from "the paintings on the walls of caves and drawings in the sand, to clay tablets and videotaped speeches" (Smith, 1999). The digital conversion of nearly every type of resource, from photographs to virtual tours to maps on almost any subject, provides researchers with extraordinary access to digital materials that are spread out around the world.

Digital collections enable anyone to access resources quickly and independently from anywhere—24/7. This is an unprecedented advancement in scholarship and research, enabling a high school student in Kenya to view the Dead Sea Scrolls in the exact same detail as a full professor at Oxford. But, with so much content available and so much more being added all the time, finding useful resources becomes more challenging each day. Using search engines like Google to comb the Internet has become the default accepted way of searching. But even after entering the search term(s), sifting through the resulting paid advertisements and other links of minimal value to researchers, finding valuable online resources on a specific topic is a painstaking process.

With luck, one can come across an online pathfinder or other page with a collection of well-chosen links on a topic. However, even many of these are not maintained, have broken links, or contain outdated information. Pathfinders do not always inform users whether sites are authoritative, what they are for, how to use them, or how extensive they are.

Digital Collections Worldwide: An Annotated Directory is designed to make identifying and using the best digital collections pain-free; the companion website at http://www.neal-schuman.com/digitalcollections (username = reader; password = 20digcol10) will eliminate the problem of broken links and make newer collections as accessible as older ones.

PURPOSE AND AUDIENCE

The authors of *Digital Collections Worldwide* have selected, organized, and described authoritative, useful, and permanent worldwide digital collections so researchers can easily locate and utilize whatever resources are available for any individual country. They have examined sites with valuable content about a country, both those promoted and maintained from within a country itself as well as those housed in another place.

The directory that follows organizes the sites geographically to provide users as strong a base of research tools as possible to examine the available resources for or about any country. The authors will periodically update this book's companion website to eliminate problems resulting from outdated URLs.

The primary audience of *Digital Collections Worldwide* is skilled researchers, but the scope is not limited to them alone. Anyone, whether a researcher, scientist, teacher, student, or even a layperson simply interested in the topic, will find the collections interesting, informative, and of value to their own particular needs. Humankind's own knowledge about our world has expanded without the boundaries of time and space. Anyone seeking information on the history or culture of a country may find it through the publicly accessible digital creations developed by its people. Those looking to create a new digital library of material will discover a myriad of examples of existing and diverse digital projects successfully highlighting collections around the world. The professional should view the collections referenced here as windows to other peoples, places, and times.

HOW TO USE THIS GUIDE

There are two primary ways to use *Digital Collections Worldwide*:

1. Those researching a specific continent or country may find it easily through either the table of contents or the subject index.
2. Those researching a specific subject or topic may find it by using the subject index.

Organization

Digital Collections Worldwide is organized geographically by continent, then alphabetically by country within. Sorting the sites by country is logical because a country's government, museums, and educational institutions themselves create many of the most authoritative and fruitful sites. Many countries have recognized that creating digital collections is a way of preserving their rich and unique histories. They can share their traditional stories while at the same time demonstrate their emergence into a technological age. In fact, this is often the motivating factor in creating a digital collection. Many countries' governments have not only approved but also initiated and funded some of the projects.

The book begins with Chapter 1, "World Initiatives," which introduces sites whose subject and geographical contexts are broad and far-reaching. These sites apply either to the whole world of nations as a group or to multiple countries from more than one continent.

"World Initiatives" is followed by chapters for each of the seven continents: Africa (Chapter 2), Antarctica (Chapter 3), Asia (Chapter 4), Europe (Chapter 5), North America (Chapter 6), Oceania (Chapter 7), and South America (Chapter 8). Each of the seven continent chapters begins with an introduction followed by annotated entries for general resources that cover the continent as a whole. Sites in the "continent" section of each chapter apply to whole subcontinental regions or multiple countries within a continent. Researchers looking for one specific country may want to look through these sites as well for relevant information. After the continent sites comes the alphabetical listing of each country and its specific entries. Entries are cross-referenced if they apply to multiple countries, and entries whose subject matter is a different country than that of its host institution are listed with the relevant country rather than with the host country, as the authors deemed this most useful to researchers.

Each annotation describes what the collector has digitized (e.g., images, photographs, documents of historical interest, maps, illustrations, or videos). The host institution is named along with the most current URL or web address for the collection and other pertinent information, such as copyright. Each digital collection discussed will be accompanied by details of the scope of the site and the intent of the creator, as in the following sample entry. The goal of each annotation is to highlight why a collection is online, what it covers, who is responsible for it, and how to explore it. Extremely large sites with many collections have annotations for a sample of the collections, with the intent of providing enough information for the researcher to decide whether to investigate further.

SAMPLE ENTRY

The National Museum of Contemporary History
http://www.muzej-nz.si/slo/zbirke.html

Translate the page into English using an online tool, and click "Collections" in the left menu. The focus of the National Museum of Contemporary History is on the First and Second World Wars, the First and Second Yugoslavias, and independent Slovenia. The museum offers a limited selection of images to highlight their many collections, among which are weapons and military equipment, photographs and negatives, fine arts, textiles, badges and signs, philatelics, postcards, medals and decorations, plaques, and numismatics. There are also three special Second World War collections. Choose a collection, and then click the sample images on the right or click "Gallery" to tour through the content. Content descriptions are available in English.

SELECTION CRITERIA

Over 1,400 entries were selected for inclusion in this directory. The types of digital collections included are as varied as the intents of their creators.

To be included here, the digital collection must have originated from one of the following types of organizations: educational institution, governmental body, museum, corporate site, library (including national libraries), archives, or a scholar's personal website. Included sites must also have had:

- a clearly identified author or responsible party and
- a clearly identified purpose making it worthy of viewing by a researcher.

Online pathfinders and webpages with collections of links were not included, as they were not deemed digital collections themselves. To preserve the focus of universal access to information, digital collections created by corporations to promote products (e.g., online photography sites with prints available for purchase) or any collections that require a fee to access (e.g., subscription databases or university sites that restrict access to registered students) were deemed ineligible for inclusion. An occasional exception to this last criterion was a for-profit site that had valuable sample documents accessible for free.

Although English is the primary language of most digital collections in the book, digital collections that are non-English have also been included. With so many free resources for translating online documents, foreign language sites with digital collections that were easy enough to use when translated were included. English-language sites with foreign language content are prominent for many countries, and language restrictions for part or all of a collection are noted in the annotations.

Once considered one of the Seven Wonders of the World, the ancient library of Alexandria and its treasures were forever lost to the world. Its new hope is that "the new Bibliotheca Alexandrina will be a lighthouse of knowledge to the whole world" (Schwartz, 2002). Its director, Ismail Serageldin, describes the future of libraries in the digital world: "Libraries are going to be the portals through which people will go on that marvelous journey of discovery whether it be to imaginary lands, to the historical past, or to understand the marvels of cutting edge science; it will be organized by libraries but available online" (Kniffel, 2007). The new technologies of digitization and the efforts of many will ensure that the cultural heritage of a country will not be lost to future generations.

Since the digital age began, digital collections have existed. From the first scanned book to the first download of family photos, digital objects have been organized, categorized, and classified to create like sets of materials. The creation of a digital collection is often the result of a person's or organization's desire to show off both what they have as well as the fact that they can do it. As the technology continues to develop, more and more institutions worldwide will join in this effort to record the history of mankind and his development, as well as the history and mystery of our planet Earth and beyond into the universe. It surely is an exciting time in this technological age to try to grasp the length, breadth, and depth of this venture. Exploring the web for digital collections around the world is a challenge worthy of exploration itself. You might say that, in a sense, this is the new exploration.

This is merely the first step of a wonderful journey.

REFERENCES

Jones, Trevor. 2001. "An Introduction to Digital Projects for Libraries, Museums and Archives." University Library, University of Illinois at Urbana-Champaign, May. http://images.library.uiuc.edu/resources/introduction.htm.

Kniffel, Leonard. 2007. "The Long Route to the Bibliotheca Alexandrina." *A CentenniAL Blog*, July 2. http://blogs.ala.org/AL100.php?title=the_long_route_to_the_bibliotheca_alexan&more=1&c=1&tb=1&pb=1.

Schwartz, Amy E. 2002. "Rebirth of a Notion" *Wilson Quarterly* 26, no. 2. http://proquest.umi.com/pqdweb?index=21&did=116918422&SrchMode=3&sid=1&Fmt=4&VInst=PROD&VType=PQD&RQT=309&VName=PQD&TS=1212436749&clientId=18091&aid=1.

Smith, Abby. 1999. "Why Digitize?" Council on Library and Information Resources (CLIR), February. http://www.clir.org/pubs/reports/pub80-smith/pub80.html.

Acknowledgments

We would like to acknowledge everyone around the world who has created or helped to create a digital collection and for being so dedicated to the pursuit of knowledge that they shared what they have learned with the world.

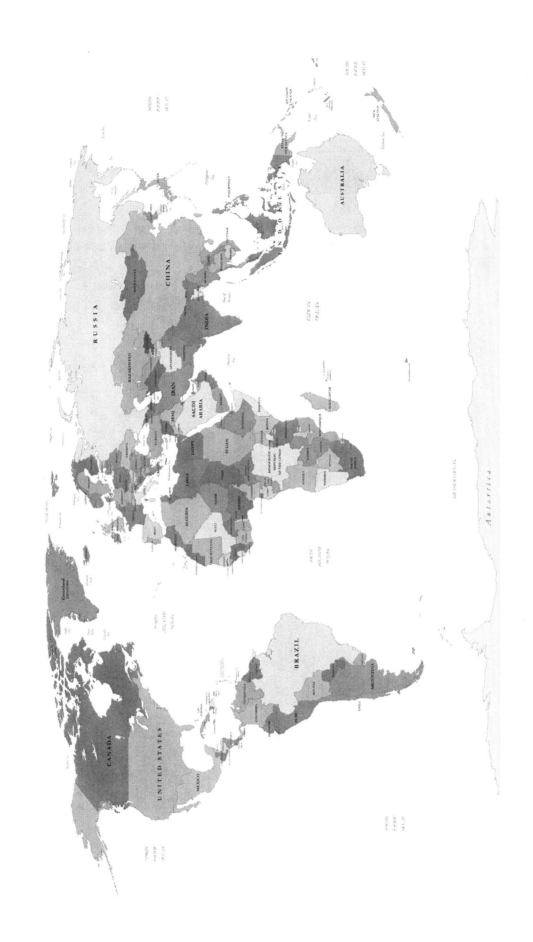

Chapter 1

World Initiatives

INTRODUCTION

Behind the impetus for creating an environment and presence for digital collections on the web there exists a united effort by major libraries, organizations, and agencies. Without the advancement of modern technology and digital communications such a presence would not be possible. Without the expertise and dedicated endeavors of this band of players the cultural heritage of countries from around the world would be lost in time forever. These players develop the infrastructure and the standards for digitization. They are involved in the research and planning methods for preservation of all kinds of materials, digitization of historical objects, and various types of formats and the technology for making collections available on the web. It is worth mentioning who they are and what they are doing to help bring man's cultural heritage one footstep closer in discovery of himself and his neighbors from around the world and to preserve this cultural heritage for future generations. These organizations are leaders in the field of digitization and models of what can be accomplished. They are great resources of information on the creation, development, and preservation of collections themselves. Some of these organizations are covered in this chapter. Other organizations, such as UNESCO, aid in promoting access to the digitized collections representing individual countries worldwide or, like the Library of Congress, build collections to represent the culture of various countries. These organizations provide the technology to work with groups in a country or act as portals to collections that otherwise would not be available online. The list in this chapter is not meant to be a comprehensive one. Rather, it is meant to help the reader understand the scope of what is being accomplished to bring the cultural heritage of any country to the forefront.

WORLD INITIATIVE SITES

Art Libraries Society of North America (ARLIS/NA)
http://www.arlisna.org/

ARLIS/NA plays a major role in the development of standards as they relate to art and is affiliated with art organizations worldwide. Annual conferences bring together professionals dealing with all aspects of art and products and services of suppliers of electronic data and visual materials. The ARLIS/NA site lists conferences and workshops. ARLIS/NA brings together the latest information from around the world on new technological developments, cataloging standards, and intellectual property rights. Each is important in developing and making digital collections accessible online. Publications and reports appear in PDF format. Although ARLIS/NA does not provide access to digital collections, it does provide valuable information for researchers about its affiliated organizations and art institutions and museums worldwide.

The Clark
http://maca.cdmhost.com/cdm4/about.php

This website is maintained by the Sterling and Francine Clark Art Institute, an organization dedicated to public education about the arts. Based in Williamstown, Massachusetts, this institute collects different forms of European and American art and has put together a number of digital collections to be viewed online. The link above provides access to four digital collections. One collection contains photographs and digital scans of each page of a field notebook relating to an early twentieth-century expedition to northern China. Another collection describes the history of photomechanical reproduction and includes hundreds of examples of different kinds of printed materials and how they can be illustrated with photographs. Images are accompanied by full bibliographic description, and a favorites option allows for up to 100 images to be saved into a personal "collection." The site provides an advanced search tool and an extensive help page to assist in using all functions of the site.

Coalition for Networked Information (CNI)
http://www.cni.org/organization.html

CNI is an organization made up of over 200 institutions representing higher education, publishing, network and communications, information technologies, and libraries and library organizations. CNI develops and manages content, builds technology, and creates standards and infrastructure for networked information. CNI's research, policies, and procedures contribute to emerging projects for digital preservation and Internet technologies.

Digital Library Federation (DLF)
http://clir.org/dlf.html

The DLF is a consortium of digital libraries and agencies in the United States and of sites around the world designed to encourage the development of and access to digital collections for teaching and learning and as a resource for scholars. The DLF helps to develop the structure, standards, preservation, and use of materials to make them available on the web. The numerous participants include such libraries as the British Library, Bibliotheca Alexandrina, the Library of Congress, OCLC, and a host of university libraries in the United States (e.g., Cornell, New York Public Library, Harvard University, Johns Hopkins University, University of Pennsylvania, the U.S. National Archives and Records Administration, the U.S. National Library of Medicine, and Yale University).

Don Quixote Iconography Digital Archive
http://www.csdl.tamu.edu:8080/dqiDisplayInterface/doSearchEditions.jsp?ftMode=
    phrase&ftFields=publisher&freeText=&year1=1500&year2=2100&places=All&
    languages=All&volumes=all&sizes=all&libraries=all&page=1&orderBy=1

Selections from the archive collection include over 1,100 images of "textual iconography of the *Quixote*." In addition to the images, the online collection also contains editions and facsimiles, collected solely to showcase the pictorial history of the *Quixote*, in Spanish, French, Italian, Dutch, English, and German dating as early as the mid-sixteenth century.

European Film Gateway (EFG)
http://www.europeanfilmgateway.eu/related_links.php

The EFG portal contains links to the Europeana portal that is creating a European digital library, museum, and archive. The EFG provides access to digital treasures from museums, archives, audiovisual archives, and libraries from across Europe. One can search various media from the EFG, which is composed of 21 partners from 15 European countries. Under the "Audio-Visual Portals and Projects" is a link to "Europa Film Treasures," listing a number of films, some dating back to the late-nineteenth century, from various countries that can be viewed online. Each film entry includes a description of the movie. It is a wonderful and interesting site to explore, and the list of films gives a glance into the culture of countries and the types of films being made in those countries at a particular time.

The Getty Research Institute (GRI)
http://www.getty.edu/research/index.html

J. Paul Getty founded the J. Paul Getty Foundation and dedicated it to preservation of the visual arts regionally and throughout the world through the collaborative efforts of the J. Paul Getty Museum, the GRI, and the Getty Conservation Institute. This is a wonderful site for learning about visual art projects around the world through the efforts of the GRI. There are special collections of rare materials from a Research Library for an international community of scholars and the public. Read about programs, institutional collaborations, GRI publications, digital services, and a scholars program. Current and back issues of Getty Conservation Institute newsletters are available online (e.g., the article "New Technologies in the Service of Cultural Heritage" by David Carson and Giacomo Chiari). There is also a Multimedia section with online videos, audio, and images of Getty Conservation Institute projects and lectures. In addition to its foundation work, the Getty Museum provides online access to its exhibitions and slide presentations of artworks and objects. Two tabs at the top of Getty's webpage, "Museum" and "Research," provide links to these materials. Select the "Research" tab, then select "Exhibitions," and then click on "See Also" for a link to current exhibitions (e.g., *Illuminated Manuscripts from Belgium and the Netherlands* and *New Galleries for Medieval and Renaissance Sculpture and Decorative Arts*). Each individual exhibition provides images and text describing that collection. Selecting the tab "Museum" at the top of the Getty webpage and clicking on "Explore Art" brings up this listing: "Artists" (browse by artist's name), "Types of Art" (browse by type or medium of art), and "Subject" (browse by theme or topic). Other selections are "Collection Overview," "Acquisitions," or "Video Gallery." Each link provides images and information about the selection. For example, view the beautiful painting *Hagar Weeping* by Dutch painter Gerbrand van der Eeckhout in the 1640s, which can be found under "Artists." Explore other links on the Getty site for items currently available, including video, sound recordings, and other formats.

Gutenberg Digital
http://www.gutenbergdigital.de/gudi/start.htm

The year 2000 marked the 600th anniversary of the birth of Johan Gutenberg, inventor of letterpress printing. The 1282 pages comprising the two volumes of the Bible printed in 1454 have been scanned and are online for the world to see. In addition to the Bible, this site also hosts the *Göttingen Model Book*, containing patterns for painting illuminations in the Bible, and the *Helmasperger's Notarial Instrument,* which recounts the dispute between Gutenberg and Johannes Fust, providing that Gutenberg was the inventor of printing with movable types. Additional links on the webpage lead to educational information on the topics of illumination, letterpress printing, and the Bible compared to the original Hebrew and Greek texts and translations. An accompanying CD can be purchased. Noted on the site are restrictions on the use of online materials.

Gutenberg-e
http://www.gutenberg-e.org/index.html

Gutenberg-e is a program of the American Historical Association and Columbia University Press. Prize-winning books written by historians are digitized and made available on this site. Books offer examples of primary sources, maps, photographs, and oral histories covering a wide range of subjects. The latest releases are listed. The electronic versions of the monographs contain hyperlinks to ancillary literature, images, music, video, and related websites. Financial support for this project comes from The Andrew W. Mellon Foundation.

HyperHistory
http://www.hyperhistory.com/online_n2/History_n2/a.html

Andreas Nothiger, a Swiss architect, is the author of the HyperHistory project, which covers 3,000 years of world history and contains an interactive chart of lifelines (brief biographies of "important persons in specialized categories"), timelines, and maps. Nothiger set out on a journey with friend in 1964 that took him across the Middle East, Afghanistan, Pakistan, India, Thailand, Laos, Cambodia, Borneo, China, Siberia, and Japan. While traveling he wrote the articles about the histories of Asian countries that became the basis for his World History project. The site begins with David and Solomon and stops with Einstein, Picasso, Roosevelt, and Churchill. Major events, empires and invasions, inventions and achievements, rulers and leaders, writers, philosophers, and scientists are covered among the topics. The information is linked from the history section to the text of a book on world history. View images and read background information on over 460 of the world's most influential people; over 3,000 facts about science, culture, and politics; and over 20 historical maps covering 3,000 years of world history. There are also charts and information about scientists, culture (artists, music, and writers), well-known religious persons, names in politics, and world religions. This great educational site is easily navigated and packed with information giving a glimpse back into the history of mankind.

International Federation of Library Associations and Institutions (IFLA)
http://www.ifla.org/

IFLA is a global voice for libraries and the information profession. The organization encourages national digitization strategies and partnership initiatives among groups to create virtual collections across continents. IFLA runs conferences, produces publications, and educates libraries on bringing together collections, preservation techniques, and access to collections. A search on the IFLA site for "digital collections" retrieves articles and information on the latest news and recommendations for digitization efforts. Read the "IFLA Manifesto for Digital Libraries, Bridging the Digital Divide: Making the World's Cultural and Scientific Heritage Accessible to All," reporting on the importance of digital libraries in opening up a universe of knowledge and information and "connecting cultures across geographical and social boundaries."

The Internet Archive
http://www.archive.org/index.php

The Internet Archive is a nonprofit digital library that offers free access to historians, scholars, researchers, and the general public. This is an excellent site that brings together a host of online formats, including "All Media Types"; "Moving Images" for art and music, news and public affairs, ephemeral films, cultural and academic films, animation and cartoons, and religion and spirituality; "Text" (lists library types); "Software"; "Education"; and "Forums." The search results provide an icon next to the collection to show whether the item is audio, a movie, a video, a podcast, a radio program, or another format. Support for the site comes from Alexa Internet, HP Computer, the Kahle/Austin Foundation, Prelinger Archives, the National Science Foundation, the Library of Congress, LizardTech, Sloan Foundation, and individual contributors.

ipl2—Internet Public Library (IPL) Newspapers and Magazines
http://www.ipl.org/div/news/

The Internet Public Library (IPL) and the Librarians' Internet Index (LII) merger produced this listing of worldwide newspapers and magazines maintained by library and information science professionals. Search for newspapers by country and magazines by subject. Some publications provide full-text stories or articles. Some magazine articles provide either current full-text articles or simply an abstract, and some provide back issues. This site is a valuable source of information allowing the online user to explore publications produced both locally and around the world. It is also a valuable resource for someone wanting to identify magazines in a particular subject field. Exposure to worldwide publications holds the potential for fostering better understanding, tolerance, and appreciation of other peoples and cultures. The site is hosted by Drexel University's College of Information Science and Technology.

Library & Information Technology Association (LITA)
http://www.ala.org/ala/mgrps/divs/lita/litahome.cfm

The Library & Information Technology Association (LITA) is a professional library organization dedicated to systems librarians, library administrators, library schools, vendors, and others involved in technology and applications for librarians. Similar to other professional library organizations, LITA conducts workshops, hosts an annual National Forum, and publishes materials for the profession. LITA's Digital Libraries Interest Technology Group addresses the technical issues surrounding digitization, creating standards and formats, archiving, and infrastructure for the web, and its Internet Resources and Services Interest Group is a forum for sharing information on the development, use, presentation, and integration of resources and services on the Internet.

Library of Congress—Global Gateway: World Culture and Resources
http://international.loc.gov/intldl/intldlhome.html

The Global Gateway provides links to two distinct avenues for finding international collections. The first link is to Collaborative Digital Libraries. View a list of the collaborative efforts of the Library of Congress and libraries or related organizations of other countries in the creation of the collection. One example of a collaborative effort is France in America/France en Amérique, a bilingual digital library exploring the history of the French presence in North America from the first decades of the sixteenth century. This collection offers manuscripts, video, sound, maps, and books online. Another collaboration, The Atlantic World: America and the Netherlands, offers manuscripts, books, photographs, and prints. The second link from the Global Gateway is to Individual Digital Collections. These collections appear in the Library of Congress collections and other sources focusing on history and cultures around the world. For example, the Islamic Manuscripts from Mali features 32 manuscripts dating from the sixteenth to eighteenth centuries from the Mamma Haidara Commemorative Library and the Cheick Zayni Bey Library in Timbuktu, Mali.

Library of Congress—Portals to the World
http://www.loc.gov/rr/international/portals.html

The Library of Congress hosts Portals to the World, links to websites through an alphabetical list of world countries. A country's website provides basic information taken from the World Factbook on such topics as culture, embassies, genealogy, government, health, language and literature, libraries and archives, listservs, newsgroups, economy, history, culture, education, media and communications, organizations, religion and philosophy, science and technology, recreation and travel, and search engines. Under each topic are links to additional sites for that topic. The annotated collection of websites is organized and maintained by the Humanities and Social Sciences Division. There is a disclaimer on this site stating that the links they provide are for informational purposes only; they do not constitute an endorsement or approval by the Library of Congress. To identify digital collections for a specific country, click on the country's name from the list. In the "Search" box that appears at the top right of the page, above "Portals to the World Web Pages," type in the words "digital collections." A list of collections will be generated. To limit to a specific topic, select a country, then select a topic under that country, and then type the words "digital collections" above the "Portals to the World Web Pages" selection.

The Margarita S. Studemeister Digital Collections in International Conflict Management
http://www.usip.org/resources-tools/digital-collections

In 2003, the digital library of the United States Institute of Peace was named after Margarita S. Studemeister, its creator. As director of the Jeannette Rankin Library Program from 1993 to 2003, she developed resources dealing with prevention, management, and international conflict resolution. Its collections, The Peace Agreements Digital Collection (full-text agreements to conflicts dating back to 1989), The Truth Agreements Digital Collection (reports), an Oral Histories Project, and documents from the Center for Post-Conflict Peace and Stability Operations, are all available online along with links to additional resources designed to help peace-building efforts around the world.

Museum Computer Network (MCN)
http://www.mcn.edu/

MCN, a nonprofit organization of information specialists from cultural heritage institutions and museums around the world, is involved in the latest developments in digital media, metadata standards, collection management, development of the web, and intellectual property issues. Of interest to those developing digitization projects and for the researcher is the Resources link at the top of the homepage. It provides access to the MCN-L Listserv, tools and research, online museums, organizations, and funding sources. There are also links to online newsletters and journals. Here one can read about the latest research and news in digitization efforts. *Ariadne*, a quarterly journal, reports on digital library initiatives and related topics. The *D-Lib Magazine*, a monthly, provides news about digital libraries and collections. For example, read about a Chinese project in the article "The National Digital Library Project" by Wei Dawei and Sun Yigang, from the National Library of China. Another article describes (with images) "The Hedda Morrison Photographs of China, 1933–1946," held by the Harvard-Yenching Library. Both articles are from the May/June 2010 issue. Other online journals and newsletters include *Current Cites* (IT literature for libraries, archives, and museums), *DigiCULT* (series on cultural heritage and society), *The Filter* (topics related to Internet law and society), *First Monday* (topics related to digital and cultural work), In the Know (news on intellectual property), *JoDI* (managing information in digital environments), *NISO Newsline* (articles on information standards), and *RLG DigiNews* (newsletter on digitization and digital preservation).

NASA—Our Earth as Art
http://earthasart.gsfc.nasa.gov/index.htm

View major areas of Earth through the beautiful and colorful pictures taken by the Landsat 7 satellite and the Terra Satellite's Advanced Spaceborne Thermal Emission and Reflection Radiometer (ASTER). View a gallery of images of our changing planet through the lens of the satellites. The images are named and listed alphabetically. View images by geographic regions: North & Central America, South America, Europe, Africa, Asia & the Middle East, Australia, and Antarctica.

National Geographic
http://photography.nationalgeographic.com/photography/photo-of-the-day/people
-culture/

Although National Geographic is a commercial site it does contain wonderful photographs within its collections of peoples and cultures from around the world. The link provided here goes directly to Photo of the Day: People & Culture. Clicking on the individual photographs reveals information on the photo.

National Information Standards Organization (NISO)
http://www.niso.org/

NISO, a nonprofit association accredited by the American National Standards Institute (ANSI), is involved in developing and publishing technical standards to manage information in the digital environment. This includes both traditional and new technologies related to information retrieval, storage, metadata, and preservation. NISO serves libraries, IT, media, and the publishing fields through workshops and through the cooperation of its committees to develop standards that will meet global needs to connect the international community. Its end goal is to serve the professional and student needs of colleges, universities, libraries, government agencies, and corporations from around the world. NISO publishes *A Framework of Guidance for Building Good Digital Collections* (available on the NISO website), which establishes principles for creating, managing, and preserving digital collections, digital objects, metadata, and projects for libraries and cultural heritage organizations planning their own digital collections. Read articles and the latest news on digital collections by typing in "digital collections" in the search task bar or review the various links on the webpage.

National Library Websites
http://www.library.uq.edu.au/natlibs/websites.html

This site, maintained by the University of Queensland, Australia, provides links to national libraries throughout the world. It is a logical resource for finding online collections. Unfortunately, at the present time, not all national libraries have digital collections. Depending on the country, the national library may (or may not) be in the process of digitization and building a website to include such collections. It is worth checking out these sites occasionally to determine if such collections have been scanned and made available online. It is expected that over time more national libraries will provide valuable digital collections, giving the world a glimpse into their country's history and culture.

National Oceanic and Atmospheric Administration (NOAA) Photo Library
http://www.photolib.noaa.gov/collections.html

The Earth has been home to mankind and all its creatures for millions of years. It continues to support life and the environment in which man lives. It seems fitting to include the work of NOAA and its scientific heritage. The NOAA Photo Library contains over 32,000 digitized images showing the work of scientists and others who study the Earth's environment by land, sea, air, and satellite. NOAA's photographic essay spans the world's oceans and atmosphere to solve environmental problems and encourage people to be the stewards for future generations. View images from these collections: Paths Less Taken—NOAA at the Ends of the Earth Collection (containing more than 1,800 images, ranging from Antarctica to the Arctic); NOAA In Space Collection (a pictorial history of NOAA's satellite program, including remarkable satellite imagery of storms, weather systems and other weather phenomena, and satellites and their launches); National Severe Storms Laboratory (NSSL) Collection (images of tornadoes and other severe storms); Historic Fisheries Collection (etchings, colored plates, and photographs of marine mammals, fish, and shellfish); It's a Small World Collection (images of foreign locations, such as the People's Republic of China, the Red Sea region, and the catacombs of Lima); Coral Kingdom Collection (photos of Northwestern Hawaiian Islands, the Caribbean, and the Red Sea reefs); National Estuarine Research Reserve System (NERR) Collection (images of estuaries); Geodesy Collection (images of the whole Earth); and Treasures of the Library Collection (images of works of art, early scientific instruments, nautical charts from the nineteenth century, mythical and real beasts of land and sea, and views of the Earth as first seen by European explorers).

National Science Foundation—Digital Libraries—Access to Human Knowledge
http://www.nsf.gov/news/special_reports/cyber/digitallibraries.jsp

The National Science Foundation (NSF) conducts digital libraries research. Together with the International Digital Libraries Collaborative Research program and other groups, the NSF is building a network of learning environment resources (maps, lesson plans, images, data sets, assessment activities, curriculum, and online courses) for technology, science, engineering, and mathematics education. This site has a link to the International Children's Digital Library, the goal of which is to make available about 10,000 children's books from 100 cultures as part of a research project to develop new technology to serve young readers. Another link goes to the Archeological Sites and Relics collection where UCLA researchers are creating an online, real-time computer model of the Roman Forum. Read about the work of the NSF and its partners and the work being done to build specialized collections and bring them online.

New York Public Library Digital Gallery
http://digitalgallery.nypl.org/nypldigital/index.cfm

This New York Public Library website offers an interesting number of collections representing the United States and countries from around the world. This webpage contains a list of major subject headings. By selecting one, for example, "Culture and Society," a listing of individual collections is retrieved with a digital image and description for each collection. One can also use the search bar to enter a search, for example, for a particular country, or follow the "Subjects A to Z" link. Browsing that list is useful for identifying a subject of one's choice. For example, by selecting the letter "C" and browsing the choices one will find the subject "Castles and Palaces" with the name of a country. Selecting this subject will bring up a gallery of images for that collection.

The Online Books Page
http://onlinebooks.library.upenn.edu/lists.html

The Online Books Page is hosted by the University of Pennsylvania. John Ockerbloom founded, edits, and is responsible for the content of this site. Over 40,000 books appear online. One can search by author and title or browse by new listings, author, title, subject, or serial archives (the best way to see what is available). The subject list is organized by Library of Congress subject headings. Here one can select from one of the categories. For example, "General Works" provides a link to the 50 volumes of The Harvard Classics at Bartley.com, where one can read *The Confessions of St. Augustine*. This is a marvelous opportunity to easily connect with great books in history and the present in various genres. Explore some of the links on the site for other options. The "archives and indexes" link, for example, leads to additional "major sources and indexes for free online texts, in all languages, both general and specialized."

Online Computer Library Center (OCLC)
http://www.oclc.org/worldcat/catalog/national/worldmap/default.htm

OCLC was created more than 40 years ago as a nonprofit membership organization committed to creating a global network of bibliographic databases and institutional metadata based on standards to be shared with all its members. As a cooperative service, OCLC's global catalog WorldCat makes library resources more visible on the Internet by distributing data across a growing number of partner services and web technologies. OCLC's achievements now make it possible in the digital age for libraries, archives, and museums worldwide to share their knowledge, collections, and information with each other. WorldCat includes records for all types of formats, including books, videos, serials, music, cultural artifacts, digital objects, and websites. Items represent more than 470 languages from over 100 countries. OCLC forms partnerships with the national libraries of many countries. The link provided leads to an interactive world map that reveals the names of the national libraries. The library icon will link to that library (if it is available online) where one can search for digital collections by simply typing in the words "digital collections" in the site's search box. A "translate" link at the top of the webpage provides English text for foreign languages.

The Open Video Project
http://www.open-video.org/index.php

The Open Video Project is a repository of digitized videos fashioned for other research communities to study a variety of problems related to the creation and evaluation of video content, the study of interfaces and systems, storage, and other aspects of the development of video collections. It is meant for education and research for the Internet 2 community. The Open Video repository provides video clips from a number of U.S. government agencies, including NASA. It contains a comprehensive list of videos hosted on this site for viewing by researchers, teachers, students, and laypersons to capture the imagination while being educated. One can search by genre (e.g., education, lecture, historical, documentary), by format (color or black and white), or by collection. This is an eclectic partial list of collections available on the site: NASASciFiles—History of Flight, History of Communication, Moon, International Space Station, and Shuttle. One can also select from a list of popular videos: *Bunjee* (people bunjee jumping from a bridge in New Zealand), *News Parade: Bombing of Pearl Harbor* (1942), or *A Is for Atom* (1953) (an animated classic about the atom, atomic energy, and nuclear fission). Participating organizations in the Open Video Project include the University of Maryland HCIL Open House Video Reports, the Informedia Project at Carnegie Mellon University, the Digital Himalaya Project, NASA K–16 Science Education Programs, and the William R. Ferris Collection. A complete list and other information on the project reside on the website. The Open Video Project is managed at the Interaction Design Laboratory of the School of Information and Library Science, University of North Carolina at Chapel Hill.

Scholars Resource
http://www.scholarsresource.com/

Scholars Resource is a great site for viewing art from around the world and is a wonderful resource for teaching art history for colleges and universities. Over 116,000 digital images are available for viewing, ranging from Ancient Art; Early Egyptian, Greek, and Roman Art; Non-Western, Early Christian, Medieval, Renaissance, Baroque, Nineteenth-Century, Impressionism, and American Art; to Art of the Americas and Contemporary Art and Architecture. The images of great art works can be searched by museum (e.g., Rijksmuseum in the Netherlands or the Pergamon Museum in Germany), by artist, by country, by the type of art, the period in art history, or by vendor. In addition to viewing the art, textbook sets are available from various sources by linking to vendors.

Smithsonian: Exhibitions
http://www.si.edu/exhibitions/

The Smithsonian: Exhibitions is a portal to search the collections of the Smithsonian, the world's largest museum complex and research organization. The Smithsonian: Exhibitions site links to a number of interesting online collections reflecting American culture as well as the cultures and histories of other nations.

▶ ### "Human Origins: What Does It Mean to Be Human?"
http://humanorigins.si.edu/

View the Smithsonian's well-illustrated and interesting website and follow its links to explore such major themes as Human Evolution Evidence (behavior, art and music, footprints, and tools), Human Evolution Research (climate and human evolution), the East African Research Project, the Asian Project, Fossil Forensics (images of various bones with descriptions), and Human Characteristics (tools and food, bodies, and social life). Follow the "Exhibit" link to view the Exhibit Floorplan Interactive (links on the floorplan to parts of the exhibit for images and information about the object). The exhibition is packed with wonderful photographs, images, and text with links to lesson plans (grades 9 through 12), a teachers' forum, and an education network.

Society of American Archivists
http://www2.archivists.org/search/luceneapi_node/digital%20collections

The Society of American Archivists develops standards for appraising, preserving, and providing access to digital records of historical value for the archives community. It also provides training and educational workshops and fosters communication among its members as they learn to collect and manage their historical documents and other objects or materials. The site provides access to publications (e.g., the *American Archivist*, *Archival Outlook*, and *In the Loop*) and many books and pamphlets of various archives topics. A search for "digital collections" on the site leads to documents, articles, reports, and other sources that may link to individual collections at sites of origin.

UNESCO World Heritage
http://whc.unesco.org/en/list

The United Nations Educational, Scientific and Cultural Organization (UNESCO) World Heritage program is responsible for preserving the cultural and natural heritages of places of importance throughout the world. The UNESCO World Heritage site offers a wonderful view of each country's cultural sites where one can learn and appreciate that country's heritage. The World Heritage List includes more than 900 properties considered of value by the World Heritage Committee for their cultural and natural heritages. Countries are listed alphabetically, with sublists of their distinguished sites. Select a site to view a description of it, its history, a gallery of pictures, an interactive map, and a video if available. For example, by selecting "Czech Republic," one can view information and pictures of one of its cultural sites, the Litomyšl Castle. It is a

"Renaissance arcade-castle of the type first developed in Italy and then adopted and greatly developed in central Europe in the 16th century." There are several other cultural sites listed under the Czech Republic. Of special interest to the world's community and to the countries involved is the link in the left column of the page titled "World Heritage in Danger," which leads to a list of endangered cultural sites around the world and the reasons why these sites may disappear or be destroyed for future generations. They may be threatened by "conflict and war, earthquakes or other natural disasters, pollution, poaching, urbanization, or unchecked tourism development." For example, many ancient Buddhist monasteries and other religious sites in the Bamiyan Valley in Afghanistan have been destroyed by the Taliban. This raises important considerations for those wanting to preserve the world's cultural heritage.

United States National Library of Medicine (NLM) National Institutes of Health—Online Exhibitions and Digital Projects
http://www.nlm.nih.gov/onlineexhibitions.html

The NLM is located on the campus of the National Institutes of Health in Bethesda, Maryland, in the United States. It is the largest medical library in the world and a provider of information on research in the areas of biomedicine and health care. The homepage has links to a number of exhibits, many of which have worldwide content. Viewers can access full lists by choosing "All Exhibitions by Subject" or "All Exhibitions by Date." Following is a sampling of the exhibits. *See also* UNITED STATES NATIONAL LIBRARY OF MEDICINE (NLM) *under* NORTH AMERICA: UNITED STATES.

▶ **Digital Repository: Cholera Online**
http://collections.nlm.nih.gov/muradora/browse.action?parentId=nlm%3Ahmdchol
   -coll&type=1

View monographs dating from 1817 to 1900 on various cholera pandemics.

▶ **Historical Anatomies on the Web**
http://www.nlm.nih.gov/exhibition/historicalanatomies/home.html

Historical Anatomies on the Web is a digital project featuring quality images from significant anatomical atlases in the NLM's collection. The focus is on the images rather than on text. For example, a number of images are from *Tabulae sceleti et musculorum corporis humani*, written by Bernhard Siegfried Albinus (1697–1770) and published in London by H. Woodfall and J. & P. Knapton in 1749; and *Isagogae breues, perlucidae ac uberrimae, in anatomiam humani corporis a communi medicorum academia usitatam* by Jacopo Berengario da Carpi (ca. 1460–1530) and published in Bologna by Beneditcus Hector in 1523.

▶ **Islamic Medical Manuscripts**
http://www.nlm.nih.gov/hmd/arabic/arabichome.html

Study the history of Islamic medicine and science during the Middle Ages and its influence in Europe's history. Follow the link "Medieval Islam" for a brief history of Islam. Select "Catalog" for galleries of images on a number of topics. Select "Bio-Bibliographies" for information on important figures in Islamic history. Select "Concordances" by its numbers to view important manuscripts, some beautifully illustrated or illuminated.

University of Wisconsin Digital Collections
http://uwdc.library.wisc.edu/Collections.shtml

The University of Wisconsin offers a great site containing digital collections reflecting numerous countries and cultures in addition to the United States. The collections are listed in alphabetical order, with descriptions. One can also browse through the list by clicking through the letters of the alphabet. The collection Africa Focus: Sights and Sounds of a Continent, for example, links to more than 3,000 slides, 500 photographs, and 50 hours of sounds from 45 different countries. Another collection title found under the letter "E" links to the East Asian Collection, a visual archive of twentieth-century East Asian cultural heritage, including images of China and the Sino-Japanese Conflict (1937–1945).

Visual Resources Association (VRA)
http://www.vraweb.org

The mission of VRA is similar to that of the other organizations included in this chapter in that it, too, plays a major role in research and development of standards and tools for educational purposes in the digital world of image management. In collaboration with other associations and organizations, its major concerns involve preservation, access to digital and analog images for visual culture, and intellectual property issues. As stated in its mission, "the Association actively supports the primacy of visual information in documenting and understanding humanity's shared cultural experience." Its international membership includes information and digital image specialists, including librarians and curators (art, architecture, film, and video), digital archivists (slides, photographs, and microfilm), architectural firms, galleries, art historians, artists, and photographers. The site offers access to publications and other resources related to its mission.

The Web Gallery of Art
http://www.wga.hu/index1.html

The Web Gallery of Art is a wonderful resource of art history covering European painting and sculpture from the eleventh to the mid-nineteenth centuries for students and teachers, including art from the Renaissance, Baroque and Rococo, Neoclassicism, Romanticism, and Realism periods. The site can be searched by a particular artist's name, nationality, period of art, or time frame or by selecting an artist from an alphabetical list of artists' names. One of the tours, The Art of Giotto, explores the works of this Renaissance painter. Other tours highlight art in Siena, art in Spain, Flemish altarpieces, French art, British art, German art, Italian painters, and European sculptures. There is also a link to music from these periods. The site was created by Emil Kren and Daniel Marx.

Wellcome Library—Collections
http://library.wellcome.ac.uk/collections.html

The Wellcome Library of London holds the world's leading collection of rare books, archives, films, pictures, and manuscripts relating to the history of medicine. By partnering with the Bibliotheca Alexandrina (BA), the Wellcome Library's Egyptian and Arabic collections are now available in BA's digital library, and the BA collection has been added to the World Digital Library. The Wellcome Library's online collections give an historical perspective into medicine throughout the world. Visit this site to view selected images of books, short films, and manuscripts. Two of its online collections are

Paintings, Prints and Drawings and Moving Image and Sound Collection. The online collection Wellcome Images provides images grouped into categories, including Highlights, Life, Culture, Nature, Illness and Wellness, and War. Each image is described.

"What a Piece of Work Is a Man"—Reading the Body in Medieval Manuscripts
http://libraries.slu.edu/archives/digcoll/manuscripta08/index.html

This is an online version of an exhibition in 2008 sponsored by the Vatican Film Library, Saint Louis University. View faithfully reproduced medieval manuscripts for depictions of medieval society and how the human body was viewed. Select "Related Links" to find a list of digitized collections of sacred texts and medieval and Renaissance manuscripts at other institutions from around the world.

World Civilizations Image Repository (WCIR)
http://content.wsulibs.wsu.edu/cdm-world_civ/

The WCIR presents a series of photographs donated by Washington State University professors for Turkey, Japan, India, Thailand, Asia, and Europe. There is also a link to images of "historical engravings from the rare book collections in Manuscripts, Archives, and Special Collections." The site can be easily searched by linking on the list of countries or by using the "Predefined Search" (click on the down arrow to see a list of countries). Washington State University Libraries, like many libraries, employ the services of OCLC CONTENTdm digital collection software by DiMeMa to develop visual collections free from copyright restrictions and to help manage the collections.

World Digital Library
http://www.wdl.org/en/

This unique site offers easy access to many online digital collections containing important primary materials from countries and cultures around the world. One can search by "Place" and browse by continent or select from a list of countries; by "Time" to select a period of time (from 8,000 BC to the present); by "Topic" to select from a list of topics (e.g., philosophy, social sciences, the arts, technology, and literature and rhetoric); by "Type of Item" to search for books, journals, manuscripts, maps, motion pictures, or sound; and by "Institution" to select from a number of institutions (e.g., Bibliotheca Alexandrina, Brown University Library, the Library of Congress, and Iraqi National Library and Archives). The World Digital Library is supported by the United Nations Educational and Cultural Organization.

World Monuments Fund
http://www.wmf.org/watch/project-map

This interactive map lists the world's 100 most endangered cultural heritage sites as chosen every two years by the World Monuments Fund. This organization is involved in raising awareness about the importance of heritage preservation. It helps to build infrastructures for cultural heritage sites around the world and is active in saving the world's architectural masterpiece sites from destruction. The organization responds to natural and man-made disasters to assess damage and initiates emergency conservation and long-term recovery assistance. Click on an area of the world map and one of the icons shown to identify monuments or historical sites in that country. Monuments listed on the site range from stone carvings and ancient temples to medieval churches and modern city districts. Each listing includes a picture and brief description of the monument's history and its significance.

World Treasures of the Library of Congress: Beginnings
http://www.loc.gov/exhibits/world/

This site examines how various cultures explained the beginning of the world and how they viewed the heavens and the earth evidenced through the writings of historical figures. The Library of Congress's collections of world treasures includes works written in more than 450 languages. The link "Exhibitions Overview" provides a checklist of the important works representing various cultures and faiths. Examples include *The Koran*; *The English Bible, Containing the Old Testament and the New* (London: The Doves Press 1903–1905); an image of a rare book by Bernard de Montfaucon, *Les monumens de la monarchie francoise, qui comprennent l'histoire de France . . .* (*The Monuments of the French Monarchy*; Paris: J.-M. Gandouin and P.F. Goffart, 1729–1733); and an image of a book by Galileo Galilei, *Syderevs nuncios*, Volume 2 (Bologna: 1655). Select "Introduction" to view images and explanations of the items in the exhibition.

Chapter 2

Africa

INTRODUCTION

Africa has been often referred to as the "Dark Continent" because of its long history of political misrule, poverty, and illiteracy. The African nations of Uganda, Ghana, Egypt, Libya, Ethiopia, Togo, and Burkina Faso are only a few of the areas that suffered many years of political and reckless military interventions (Omekwu, 2006). These factors greatly impacted both African culture and African libraries. Despite its many hardships, Africa has experienced growth in computer and technological communications. Africa stands at a crossroads in this information age and desires to take its rightful place as a member of the virtual community or global village. Africa has a rich cultural heritage and many wonderful national treasures to share with the world. A major barrier for African countries is a serious deficiency in the technology infrastructure. African public and national libraries lack the resources to meet the challenges to enter into the digital revolution. Great strides are being met from both within and outside of Africa to digitize and to share these treasures. Museums, organizations, universities, and government initiatives are making remarkable progress in digitizing ancient manuscripts, images, maps, books, artworks, photographs, newspapers, and other types of materials, ensuring Africa's place on the web.

Organizations outside of Africa, such as UNESCO (through its Memory of the World Programme), the Library of Congress, and the World Digital Library, are partnering with African institutions to assist in the digitization projects themselves and/or to become a portal for accessing African collections. One such example involves the ancient and great library of antiquity, Bibliotheca Alexandrina in Egypt and its individual collections of manuscripts, lectures, books, and images. With the help of UNESCO and libraries worldwide it has collected thousands of books and manuscripts from around the world in its attempt to preserve Islamic and Egyptian history. A second example is the Wellcome Library in London and its partnership with Bibliotheca Alexandrina in 2008 to bring rare papyri and Arabic medical manuscripts from ancient and modern Egypt together (Ashling, 2008). A third notable example is the Digital Imaging South Africa (DISA) project funded by the Andrew W. Mellon Foundation (Saunders, 2005) to digitize documents, oral histories, music, videos, articles, and other materials relevant to the political and social turbulence of the apartheid period.

This chapter reviews the digital collections of individual African countries hosted by Africa's own national libraries, museums, organizations, and governments. Websites with worldwide content, such as UNESCO's Memory of the World, the Library of Congress, and the World Digital Library, that also contain digital collections relevant to African culture and heritage are included. Some of these organizations and other institutions outside of Africa collaborate with African institutions to digitize their collections, and others act as a portal for a collection that resides in Africa. Some do both. Some African collections physically reside in institutions outside of Africa. At present some African countries lack a cultural presence on the web.

Two things are important to the African heritage with regard to digitized collections. One is that no matter where the collection resides, Africa will take its place globally in preserving and sharing its history with the world. The second is that, collectively, all mankind will be enriched with a knowledge and appreciation of Africa's history and its culture.

References

Ashling, Jim. 2008. "International Report: New Projects Boost Digital Library Content." *Information Today* 25, no. 10 (November 1): 26–27.

Omekwu, Charles O. 2006. "African Culture and Libraries: The Information Technology Challenge." *The Electronic Library* 24, no. 2: 243–264. http://www.emeraldinsight.com/journals.htm?issn=0264-0473&volume=24&issue=2&articleid=1558112&show=html.

Saunders, Christopher. 2005. "Digital Imaging South Africa (DIS): A Case Study." *Program: Electronic Library and Information Systems (UK)* 39, no. 4. http://www.emeraldinsight.com/journals.htm?issn=0033-0337&volume=39&issue=4&articleid=1528718&show=html.

CONTINENT

Africa Focus: Sights and Sounds of a Continent
http://digicoll.library.wisc.edu/AfricaFocus/

Hosted by the University of Wisconsin Digital Collections, this is a digital collection of texts, photographs, slides, and audio clips from many countries of Africa. The collection can be browsed by subject or searched by keyword. There is also a limiting link to search only the full-text information. This collection's intent is to both highlight the university's rare holdings and to make primary and secondary source materials available to scholars and teachers. Individual image subgroups, such as Rites & Ceremonies, Artisans, Drums, and Buildings & Structures, help searchers find materials. There are also individual digitized items specific to the smaller African countries of Ethiopia, Cape Verde, Sierra Leone, and Guinea.

African Activist Archive
http://africanactivist.msu.edu/

This online archive contains materials related to U.S. movements supporting the liberation struggles of the peoples of various African nations. It is housed at Michigan State University. The content goes beyond just anti-apartheid paraphernalia. Images of photographs, posters, and buttons are available, as well as other documents in PDF format. The site contains several audio and video recordings of interviews with notable figures, which require Adobe Flash Player to view. The content can be searched by keyword or browsed by media type, creating organization, or the subject country.

African Book Bank Online—Abbol
http://www.abbol.com/

This Dutch site hosts an online collection of African scholarly publications. The content is limited in scope to items in the social sciences from sub-Saharan Africa prior to 1960. The documents are predominantly English, French, and German.

African Digital Library
http://africaeducation.org/adl/Default.htm

This online library offers free access to more than 8,000 full-text books for anyone who lives in Africa. Those living outside of Africa can subscribe through NetLibrary, a service of EBSCO.

African Studies Center
http://www.africa.upenn.edu/Home_Page/GIF_Images.html

The African Studies Center of the University of Pennsylvania maintains a multimedia archive containing a number of small digital collections. Individual category links yield images of African city maps, country flags, sculptures, tribal masks, and many other items associated with African nations. There is no accompanying text, caption, or descriptions.

Aluka
http://www.aluka.org/action/doBrowse?searchText=clippings&sa=xst&br=tax-collections |part-of|collection-major

Aluka is a standalone worldwide digital collection of African scholarly materials. Its content is available through the JSTOR database to "not-for-profit institutions of higher education secondary schools, public libraries, museums, and other research or cultural institutions" that have an institutional license. Access is currently not available to individual users. Content includes textual materials and maps as well as visual and audio materials. The content is broken down into groups, including topical themes as well as more structured collections like Zimbabwe serials and Namibia posters. As with all Aluka content, thumbnail images can be viewed free over the web, but only subscribers can view more detailed images and download full text.

Ancient Manuscripts: From the Desert Libraries of Timbuktu
http://www.loc.gov/exhibits/mali/

View ancient manuscripts related to West Africans from the sixteenth to the eighteenth centuries. Thirty-two Arabic manuscripts on various subjects from the Mama Haidara Commemorative Library and the Library of Cheick Zayni Baye of Boujbeda, in Timbuktu, Mali, are displayed in their entirety. Select "Enter Collection" to view individual manuscripts (with textual explanations), such as *Structure of the Heavens*, *A Poem on Islamic Law*, *Islamic Saints*.

International Mission Photography Archive
http://digitallibrary.usc.edu/search/controller/collection/impa-m1.html

This archive contains photograph collections created during several evangelical missions to Africa, India, and the Far East. Each link is for the archive of a different missionary organization. The actual photographs are from various places around the world, but their digital versions are collectively hosted by the University of Southern California Libraries. Each photograph entry has a complete catalog record, including subject analysis and a brief description translated into English, when necessary.

16th–Early 20th Century Maps of Africa
http://www.library.northwestern.edu/govinfo/collections/mapsofafrica/

This is a digitized collection of over 100 maps of various African locations that are housed at the Northwestern University Library in Evanston, Illinois. The collection can be searched by title, date, subject area, place of publication, or cartographer, or the entire collection can be viewed as a list. Each entry has full bibliographic information, including a description.

The University of Southern California (USC) Digital Library
http://digitallibrary.usc.edu/search/controller/index.htm

The USC Digital Library is a wonderful site for viewing thousands of photographs showing the life, cultures, and histories of a host of countries. View a wide range of other media as well, such as drawings, illuminated manuscripts, oral histories, sound recordings, moving images, maps, posters, objects, and rare illustrated books. Materials come from the USC libraries and are a major contribution to the digitization of cultural heritage projects that are representative of the world. To locate materials on Africa, one can search by "Places" by selecting from a list of countries (e.g., Congo, South Africa). One can also search via a search box located at the top of the USC webpage by typing in the name of a specific country. For example, a search for "Egypt" revealed 246 images; "Congo" retrieved over 1,000 images; "South Africa" retrieved over 3,000 images; and "Africa" revealed over 12,000 images. By selecting "Advanced Search" at the top of the webpage, a search can be further narrowed to locate sound, video, maps, and other formats.

West Africa Online Digital Library
http://www.aodl.org/westafrica/index.php

This resource is a group of online collections relating to the West Africa nations of Mauritania, Senegal, and the Ivory Coast. Content includes photographs, digitized texts, and recorded oral histories of prominent persons. The site was constructed from 2000 to 2003. Technical assistance to create the digital collection was provided through a partnership between the Michigan State University African Studies Center and several African organizations. An interesting addition to this site is the "Build Your Own Gallery" feature, which allows users to take content from the various collections and make their own personalized "gallery."

ALGERIA

Forced Migration Online (FMO)
http://repository.forcedmigration.org/?search=algeria&start=0&rows=10

FMO provides access to a wide range of resources that illustrate "the movements of refugees and internally displaced people (people displaced by conflicts) as well as people displaced by natural or environmental disasters, chemical or nuclear disasters, famine, or development projects." A search for "Algeria" located 655 content items.

Musée National Cirta de Constantine
http://www.cirtamuseum.org.dz/

The Musée National Cirta is considered one of the oldest museums in Algeria. Highlights through text and photos of the Fine Arts section (Histoire due Musée), the Salles due Musée, and the Jardin Épigraphique hints at all the museum has to offer. The website is accessible in Arabic and French.

ANGOLA

Forced Migration Online (FMO)
http://repository.forcedmigration.org/?search=angola&start=0&rows=10

FMO provides access to a wide range of resources that illustrate "the movements of refugees and internally displaced people (people displaced by conflicts) as well as people displaced by natural or environmental disasters, chemical or nuclear disasters, famine, or development projects." A search for "Angola" located 1,043 content items.

New York Public Library Digital Gallery
http://digitalgallery.nypl.org/nypldigital/index.cfm

A search for "Angola" retrieved 76 photos. Most are images of people and places; others are maps and a selection of Portuguese decrees, laws, and edicts.

BENIN

Benin—Kings and Rituals: Court Arts from Nigeria
http://www.artic.edu/aic/collections/exhibitions/benin/index

This is an online exhibit highlighting 39 items from the original exhibit held July 10 through September 21, 2008, at the Art Institute of Chicago. To view the exhibit choose "Selected Works" from the right menu bar. The exhibit contains photos of brass plaques and statues, brass altar heads, ivory tusks, coral regalia and ivory arm cuffs, and waist pendants, some of which date as far back as the twelfth century. The website also provides access to "Additional Resources" (from the right menu bar) such as videos, charts and tables, a glossary, and a recommended reading list of texts about Benin.

BOTSWANA

Aluka
http://www.aluka.org/action/doBrowse?searchText=clippings&sa=xst&br=tax-collections
   |part-of|collection-major

Aluka is a standalone worldwide digital collection of African scholarly materials. Its content is available through the JSTOR database to "not-for-profit institutions of higher education secondary schools, public libraries, museums, and other research or cultural institutions" that have an institutional license. Access is currently not available to individual users. *See also* ALUKA *under* AFRICA: CONTINENT.

▶ **Botswana Historical Documents**
http://www.aluka.org/action/showCompilationPage?doi=10.5555/AL.SFF
.COMPILATION.COLLECTION-MAJOR.BOTHIS

The historical documents are part of the Melville J. Herskovits Library of African Studies collection at Northwestern University (Illinois). Among the documents are Botswana Democratic Party publications and the "Report of the Select Committee on Racial Discrimination of the Bechuanaland Legislative Council."

▶ **Botswana Serials**
http://www.aluka.org/action/showCompilationPage?doi=10.5555/AL.SFF
.COMPILATION.COLLECTION-MAJOR.BOTSER

This collection is in the Melville J. Herskovits Library of African Studies collection maintained at Northwestern University (Illinois). It contains over 30 volumes of minutes from African Advisory Council, European Advisory Council, and Joint Advisory Council discussions held between 1948 and 1960.

BURKINA FASO

Manéga—Musée de la Bendrologie
http://www.musee-manega.bf/

The Manéga is a private museum located in West Africa and was founded by Frédéric Pacéré Titinga. This website provides an introduction to Burkina culture and religion by offering brief glimpses through texts and photos of museum pieces, such as wood and brass art objects and instruments and Karinse, Bobo, and Nuni masks. Links include "The Dogons," "The Hunters," "The Yakouga or tombstones," and "The Youyounse pavilion." The habitats of the Fulani, Bobo, and Senoufo peoples are illustrated as well. The website is accessible in both French and English.

BURUNDI

University of Wisconsin Digital Collections
http://uwdc.library.wisc.edu/index.shtml

To access material about Burundi, use the search box on the homepage. A search for "Burundi" returned 18 results, the majority of which are views of the landscape.

World Digital Library
http://www.wdl.org/en/search/gallery?ql=eng&c=BI&s=burundi

There are two items classified under "Burundi" in this collection. The first is a book titled *Explorations in Africa, by Dr. David Livingstone, and Others, Giving a Full Account of the Stanley-Livingstone Expedition of Search, under the Patronage of the New York 'Herald', as Furnished by Dr. Livingstone and Mr. Stanley*, which describes Stanley and Livingstone's journey across the African continent between 1853 and 1856.

The second item is an 1884 map in color titled *Sketch of Equatorial Africa: Containing the Latest Information Collected by Agents of the International Society of the Congo.*

CAMEROON

New York Public Library Digital Gallery
http://digitalgallery.nypl.org/nypldigital/dgkeysearchresult.cfm?keyword=Cameroon

A search for "Cameroon" retrieved 25 photos. Most are images of people and places plus several maps.

University of Wisconsin Digital Collections
http://uwdc.library.wisc.edu/index.shtml

A search for "Cameroon" returned 74 results, a mixture of native peoples, villages, and several species of primates.

CAPE VERDE

New York Public Library Digital Gallery
http://digitalgallery.nypl.org/nypldigital/dgkeysearchresult.cfm?keyword=%22cape+verde%22

A search for "Cape Verde" retrieved 15 photos, the majority of which are maps and charts of the area. There are also a couple of landscapes and native peoples.

World Digital Library
http://www.wdl.org/en/search/gallery?ql=eng&s=cape+verde&view_type=gallery

There are three images classified under "Cape Verde" in this collection. *Map of Cape Verde* is a very detailed French map, circa 1700–1750. *The Voyage of the Sieur Le Maire, to the Canary Islands, Cape-Verde, Senegal, and Gambia* (1695) is Jacques-Joseph Le Maire's description of his voyage to West Africa and the Atlantic islands off the coast of Africa. In *The Guinean Campaign (1908)* Luis Monteiro Nunes da Ponte describes what the Portuguese would face in their attempts to colonize Guinea.

CENTRAL AFRICAN REPUBLIC

New York Public Library Digital Gallery
http://digitalgallery.nypl.org/nypldigital/dgkeysearchresult.cfm?keyword=%22Central+African+Republic%22

A search for "Central African Republic" retrieved six photos, the majority of which come from the book *L'Afrique Équatoriale Française: le pays, les habitants, la colonisation, les pouvoirs publics* (French Equatorial Africa: The Country, the Inhabitants, Colonization, the Government) by Georges Bruel (1918).

University of Wisconsin Digital Collections
http://uwdc.library.wisc.edu/index.shtml

A search for "Central African Republic" returned nine results, a combination of images of the Ubangi River, local villages, and landscapes.

CHAD

New York Public Library Digital Gallery
http://digitalgallery.nypl.org/nypldigital/dgkeysearchresult.cfm?keyword=chad

A search for "Chad" retrieved 27 photos, most of which depict native peoples of the country. There is also a map of Lake Chad and a chart of the rock formation called Hager Teous.

World Digital Library
http://www.wdl.org/en/search/gallery?ql=eng&s=chad

There are four items for "Chad" in this collection, one of which is Henry Carbou's 1912 book titled *La région du Tchad et du Oudaï; études ethnographiques, dialecte Toubou* (The Region of Chad and the Oudai; Ethnographic Studies, Toubou Dialect). The two volumes in one are written in French and Dazaga. Among the ethnic groups discussed are the Kanembou, the Toubou, and the Ouaddai.

COMOROS

World Digital Library
http://www.wdl.org/en/search/gallery?ql=eng&s=comoros

One item is classified under "Comoros" in this collection, two volumes by B.F. Leguével de Lacombe titled *Voyage à Madagascar et aux îles Comores (1823 à 1830)* (Voyage to Madagascar and the Comoros Islands, 1823–1830). Although the main focus of the book is on the social life and customs of Madagascar, the book also contains Lacombe's description of the traditions of Mohilla, one of the Comoro Islands.

CONGO REPUBLIC (BRAZZAVILLE)

New York Public Library Digital Gallery
http://www.wdl.org/en/item/2532?ql=eng&s=Brazzaville&view_type=gallery

When "Congo Republic (Brazzaville)" is searched, one item is retrieved, a booklet titled *L'indépendance de la République du Congo: textes des discours prononcés à la Session solennelle de l'Assemblée Nationale et à la Proclamation publique de l'Indépendance* (The Independence of the Republic of Congo: Texts of the Speeches Given at the Official Session of the National Assembly and During the Public Proclamation of Independence). The booklet was issued in 1960 by the Ministry of Information of the Republic of the Congo in honor of their independence from France.

The University of Southern California Digital Library
http://digitallibrary.usc.edu/search/controller/simplesearch.htm

When "Congo Republic (Brazzaville)" is searched, 37 images are retrieved. The photos, which are all part of the Yale Divinity School Library collection, are mostly of missionary buildings, churches, and clergy ca. 1885–1930.

CONGO DEMOCRATIC REPUBLIC (ZAIRE)

American Museum Congo Expedition 1909–1915
http://diglib1.amnh.org/

Between 1909 and 1915, Herbert Lang and James P. Chapin went on an American Museum of Natural History–sponsored expedition to the Belgian Congo. An extensive amount of their material has been digitized, including over 2,200 photographs from Lang's collection of 9,890 photos, photos of anthropological objects, Chapin's watercolor sketches, and their field notes and specimen data. The notes and data are searchable through this site. In addition, there are 160 publications relating to the expedition or the Congo region and a collection of African exploration maps. A five-minute slide introduces the Lang Chapin Congo Expedition; it requires the Flash 5 plug-in and is best viewed on a high-speed (DSL) connection. The introduction narrative is in English, but French, English, and Spanish subtitles are available.

CÔTE D'IVOIRE (IVORY COAST)

World Digital Library
http://www.wdl.org/en/search/gallery?ql=eng&c=CI&s=C%C3%B4te%20d%E2%80%99Ivoire

Two images are classified under "Côte d'Ivoire" in this collection. The first is the speech given by Felix Houphouet-Boigny prior to the September 1958 vote that would lead to the country becoming an independent republic. The second item is a 1743 map of western Africa. On the map Côte d'Ivoire is labeled as Cote d'Or.

DJIBOUTI

New York Public Library Digital Gallery
http://digitalgallery.nypl.org/nypldigital/dgkeysearchresult.cfm?keyword=Djibouti

Two images are classified under "Djibouti" in this collection. The photo of an indigenous marketplace and one of a Somali woman are both taken from *Les colonies françaises; petite encyclopédie coloniale publiée*, edited by M. Maxime Petit (ca. 1902).

The University of Southern California Digital Library
http://digitallibrary.usc.edu/search/controller/simplesearch.htm

When "Djibouti" is searched, 15 images are retrieved. The images are a mix of photos and postcards from the Yale Divinity Library Special Collections/Missionary Postcard Collection, the Mission Archives at the School of Mission and Theology in Stavanger collection, or the Historical Photographs from the Basel Mission collection.

EGYPT

The Agriculture Museum
http://www.touregypt.net/featurestories/agriculturalmuseum.htm

The Agriculture Museum, located in Cairo, exhibits the role of agriculture in Egyptian history, extending from prehistoric times to the present. Egypt draws its rich agricultural history from its water source—the Nile. Here one has access to illustrations, paintings, and pictures of peasants involved in various agricultural roles, including harvesting wheat, making bread and pastry (the Meshaltet patty), and growing fruits and vegetables. How they grew and used medicinal and aromatic plants are illustrated as well. The content and illustrations are provided by Tour Egypt, a travel agency website intended to be "the top online travel and history portal" for Egypt. *See also* TOUR EGYPT *under* EGYPT.

Bibliotheca Alexandrina
http://www.bibalex.org

October 17, 2002, marked the official opening of the $230 million dollar Bibliotheca Alexandrina in Egypt. The 11-story building bears a resemblance to a giant tilted disc. It is partially submerged in a pool of water, which is intended to evoke the sun that illuminates the world and human civilization. It is recognized as a symbol of the ancient Egyptian sun god Ra. This magnificent building won the Aga Khan Award for design. In its vision, as the reincarnation of the ancient and great library of antiquity, Bibliotheca Alexandrina with the help of UNESCO and libraries worldwide is collecting thousands of books and manuscripts from around the world in its attempt to bring together and to preserve Islamic and Egyptian history. Following are links to each project.

▶ **Bibliotheca Alexandrina—The Digital Assets Repository (DAR)**
   http://dar.bibalex.org

   The DAR system was developed to create and maintain the Bibliotheca Alexandrina's digital collections. It provides access to all types of digital materials. One can search over 150,000 books and 35,000 book images. View books by flipping or scrolling pages. Information describing the book is in English. Researchers can browse 5 percent of a book in Arabic. Many books have illustrations. Subjects include philosophy, psychology, social sciences, languages, natural sciences, mathematics, technology, the arts, literature and rhetoric, geography, and history. The database is searchable by title, author, subject, ISBN, keyword for books, images, videos, and audio materials.

▶ **Bibliotheca Alexandrina—Eternal Egypt**
   http://www.eternalegypt.org/EternalEgyptWebsiteWeb/HomeServlet

   The Eternal Egypt digital website takes the viewer on a multimedia trip through time, covering over 5,000 years of Egyptian culture. The digital project, funded by a $2.5 million grant, allows the viewer to see such artifacts as the Gold Mask of Tutankhamen, the unfinished head of Nefertiti, and the Icon of the Holy Family. Icons in the left menu provide links to multiple ways of exploring. For example, the "Map" page provides a geographic view to cities and places of interest. Each contains its own photographs and text-to-speech for listening. The "Timeline" feature helps one to discover how an artifact is related to a character, how that character is related to a place, and so on. Through "Sites & Museums" viewers can go on a number of virtual tours to re-creations of famous Egyptian sites as they were thousands of years ago and as they are today. Through these digital windows or webcams one can link to three-dimensional views of artifacts or view 360° interactive panoramic breathtaking views of locations in Egypt. A zoom tool allows viewing over 2,000 high-resolution pictures showing the exquisite details of artifacts. The site is sponsored by the Supreme Council of Antiquities, the Center for Documentation of Cultural and Natural Heritage, and the IBM Corporation.

▶ **Bibliotheca Alexandrina—The Supercourse**
http://www.bibalex.org/Libraries/Presentation/Static/12600.aspx?d=0

Through partnerships with cultural and academic institutions, governments, and corporations, Bibliotheca Alexandrina is creating a digital project featuring the theme of public health. More than 1,500 free lectures by scientists from 175 countries are available through the web, with the goal of increasing the number to one million. It maintains a mirror site that makes lectures available in 26 languages. Search for lectures on epidemiology, special diseases, and public health issues. One can download the whole Supercourse (or just one lecture or two) free of charge.

▶ **Eternal Egypt—Sites & Museums**
http://www.eternalegypt.org/EternalEgyptWebsiteWeb/HomeServlet?ee
_website_action_key=action.display.sites&language_id=1&text=text

Eternal Egypt, through its "Sites & Museums" link, provides access to digitized images, pictures, and multimedia experiences of Egyptian sites and museums. Travel back into history by listening to a description of each site or museum and get a virtual 360° view of what the site would look like during the Pharaonic, Byzantine, or Greco-Roman periods and what it looks like today. View a detailed map of each site. View Egypt's artifacts, such as clothing, furniture, games, implements, jewelry, artists, mosaics, writing equipment, tombs, the Palace of Prince Mustafa Fade, sculptures and antiquities from such sites as the Egyptian Museum, Giza, Islamic Ceramic Museum, Kom Ushim Museum, Luxor Temple, National Library and Archives, the Roman Auditorium, the Museum of Archeology in Tanta, Roman Auditorium, Coptic Museum, the Greco-Roman Museum, and the Museum of Islamic Art. A small number of these are highlighted here.

▶ **Eternal Egypt—The Coptic Museum**
http://www.eternalegypt.org/EternalEgyptWebsiteWeb/HomeServlet?ee_
website_action_key=action.display.site.details&language_id=1&element_
id=1028&text=text

The museum holds a collection of Coptic artifacts viewable online, such as the "The Wall Painting of Three Saints." Marcus Simaika Pasha founded the museum in 1910 to collect material necessary to study the history of Christianity in Egypt in art to fill in a gap.

▶ **Eternal Egypt—Giza**
http://www.eternalegypt.org/EternalEgyptWebsiteWeb/HomeServlet?ee_
website_action_key=action.display.site.details&language_id=1&element_
id=30625&text=text

Giza was chosen by Kings Khufu, Khafra, and Menkaure as their funerary complexes. Also located in Giza are the three Great Pyramids, the funerary boats of Khufu, the Sphinx, and the tombs of the courtiers of the Fourth Dynasty.

▶ **Eternal Egypt—The Graeco-Roman Museum**
http://www.eternalegypt.org/EternalEgyptWebsiteWeb/HomeServlet?ee_
website_action_key=action.display.site.details&language_id=1&element_
id=1029

The Graeco-Roman Museum of Alexandria was founded in 1892. The collections are donations from wealthy Alexandrians and organizations as well as from excavations.

▶ **Eternal Egypt—Islamic Ceramic Museum**
http://www.eternalegypt.org/EternalEgyptWebsiteWeb/HomeServlet?ee_
website_action_key=action.display.site.details&language_id=1&element_
id=1033

This website features masterpieces of Islamic ceramics throughout the centuries from prehistoric times to the present. Link to Egypt's Fatimid style (tenth to twelfth centuries), Umayyad style (eighth century), Ayyubid style (thirteenth century), and Mamluk style (fourteenth and fifteenth centuries) and to the Turkish style (sixteenth to eighteenth centuries).

▶ **Eternal Egypt—The Luxor Temple**
http://www.eternalegypt.org/EternalEgyptWebsiteWeb/HomeServlet?ee_
website_action_key=action.display.site.details&language_id=1&element_
id=1003&text=text

"Ipet resyt" was dedicated to the Theban Triad of Amun-Re, his wife Mut, and his son Khonsu.

The British Museum
http://www.ancientegypt.co.uk/menu.html

The British Museum of London, England, provides a great website on ancient Egypt. Although it is meant as a resource for teaching children, it is of interest to anyone seeking images of ancient Egypt. The site is divided into ten chapters that address themes or topics relevant to ancient Egypt. Links include "Egyptian Life," "Gods & Goddesses," "Mummification," "Pharaoh," "Temples," "Trades," and "Writing." Within each chapter are three sections: "Story," the presentation, and "Explore" and "Challenge," exercises for student learning.

Egypt State Information Service
http://www.us.sis.gov.eg/En/Cover01.aspx?Category_ID=722

This site introduces the viewer to several individual museums with samplings of photos, illustrations, and artworks and background information that provides insight into other facets of Egyptian history, important political figures, people, palaces, and geological features. Click "Links" in the left menu, and scroll down to "Museums" to access a number of websites to other museums, including The Agricultural Museum, The Nubia Museum, The Military Museum, The Graeco-Roman Museum, The Coptic Museum, and The Grand Egyptian Museum.

▶ **Egypt State Information Service—Egyptian Obelisks**
http://www.us.sis.gov.eg/En/Story.aspx?sid=1245

The story of Egyptian obelisks is told with photographs and text. There are only 27 Egyptian obelisks in the world, with only six still remaining in Egypt. There are 13 in Rome and Italy and one each in Paris, London, New York, Istanbul, Florence, Urbino, Wimborne (England), and Cesarea (Israel).

▶ **Egypt State Information Service—Egypt's Monuments**
http://www.sis.gov.eg/VR/photo/Monuments/img0201.htm

View a photo album of the Pharonic, Coptic, Roman, and Islamic monuments.

▶ **Egypt State Information Service—The Life of Ancient Egyptians**
http://www.sis.gov.eg/VR/pharo/html/front.htm

Learn about Egyptian culture, for example, the status of marriage, use of adornment, the role of science and education, immortality, and the bounty of the earth. Through the talents of draughtsman, painters, sculptors, and relief carvers what emerges is a human accounting of ancient Egyptian life. View colorful paintings inside ancient temples, inscriptions drawn on the monuments of pharaohs, obelisks, and the murals found on tombs. One topic explored is how animals (including goats, sheep, pigs, donkeys, boars, and crocodiles) were used for breeding, herding, transportation, and consumption.

▶ **Egypt State Information Service—The Pyramids**
http://www.sis.gov.eg/VR/pyramid/html/res00.htm

View the history of the three pyramids at Giza, including their prehistory, the Step Pyramid, and inside the pyramids through a series of photographs, reliefs from the tombs, and photos and illustrations of their excavations.

▶ **Egypt State Information Service—Your Gateway to Egypt**
http://www.sis.gov.eg/VR/nefer/html/intro.htm

The Egypt State Information Service website links viewers to a wealth of information on ancient Egypt. Like looking through the lens of a telescope back into ancient times, one can envision this wonderful and rich era in human history. This site maintains numerous webpages and links for learning about Egyptian culture through text, images, and photographs on such topics as Nefertari, Egyptian literature, folklore, the fine arts, cultural institutions, theater, and music.

▶ **Egypt State Information Service—Your Gateway to Egypt—History**
http://www.sis.gov.eg/En/History/

Learn about the history of the Pharonic, Greek, Roman, Coptic, Islamic, and Modern eras and about ancient Egyptian rulers through text and digital images.

Egyptian Geological Museum
http://www.touregypt.net/geo

The Egyptian Geological Museum was established and opened for the public in 1904 as part of the Egyptian Geological Survey (EGS) begun in 1896. The museum introduces visitors to Egyptian geology and history. The museum is located near Maadi,

Cairo. Highlighted text on the webpage links to topics such as predynastic times, showing the discovery of gold and copper in the Sinai. The links retrieve photographs illustrating the history of minerals and rocks, invertebrate fossils, Egyptian ores, and gemstones found during different eras in Egypt.

Egyptian National Agricultural Library (ENAL)
http://nile.enal.sci.eg

Located in Giza, ENAL's goal is to make agricultural research information accessible to all of Egypt and to international networks. The information on this site is strictly textual. The site's value lies in its acknowledgment of Egypt's increasing use of electronic resources as it makes available its latest research to the world. The "Online References" page links to commercial reference resources, including almanacs, atlases, encyclopedias, handbooks, conferences, books in print, and directories. "Online Books" links to commercial and free sources for e-books on a wide variety of subjects, including great authors and their texts.

▶ ### Egyptian National Agricultural Library—Online Books
   http://nile.enal.sci.eg/OBP.aspx

   In keeping with the topic of agriculture, Online Books is a valuable resource pulling together an ample amount of the published literature focusing on such topics as the conservation of soil. The publications are from various world organizations as well as other sources. Some titles appear in full text and are free. Others are advertised on commercial sites and require a fee for viewing or purchase.

Egyptian National Library and Archives
http://www.eternalegypt.org/EternalEgyptWebsiteWeb/HomeServlet?ee_website_
    action_key=action.display.site.details&language_id=1&element_id=1034&text=text

The National Library and Archives was established in AH 1286 (AD 1870) by decree and was originally housed in the Palace of Prince Mustafa Fadel. Currently its location overlooks the Nile at Ramlet Boulak. The National Library and Archives of Egypt opened a digitization facility at the National Library. Although this facility currently does not have a website, it is worth noting for its expected outcomes as items become digitized and made available online. The physical library itself contains over 57,000 of the most valuable manuscripts in the world. About 3,000 Arabic papyri manuscripts dating back to AD 705 were discovered in Kom Ashgow in Upper Egypt. The manuscripts record marriages, tax accounts, dowry payments, and medicine; some manuscripts are official documents. One planned project is a collaborative effort with the National Library of Congress, which maintains an acquisitions office in Cairo. Links at the bottom of the page (including "Manuscript of Shifà Al-Asqaam" by Shifii, who died in AH 1159 (AD 1746); and "Manuscript from the Book of Treating the Diseases by Food and Drugs") provide images from a number of historical texts.

Nag Hammadi Library
http://www.gnosis.org/naghamm/nhl.html

The Gnostic Society Library's Nag Hammadi Library provides access to a number of important ancient religious texts discovered in Palestine and Egypt. The first discovery was the Nag Hammadi collection of 13 ancient codices (leather-bound books) with more than 50 texts discovered in Egypt in 1945. The Nag Hammadi Library includes The Gospel of Thomas, The Gospel of Philip, and The Gospel of Truth; a number of other Gnostic scriptures are believed to have been destroyed. In the 1970s the translations were completed, allowing scripture scholars an opportunity to do further study on the nature of Gnosticism (believed to be a heresy during the second and third centuries AD). (Follow the link to "The Gnostic Society Library" to access other collections, including the Patristic Polemical Works Against the Gnostics, Christian Apocrypha and Early Christian Literature, Manichaean Writings, the Corpus Hermeticum, Cathar Writings, and Modern Gnostic Texts.) The second discovery was the Dead Sea Scrolls in 1947 in a series of caves near Qumran and the Dead Sea. These are 800 separate texts (250 BCE to 100 CE), and each has been translated. There are some pictures of the documents and a few images interspersed throughout the webpages. This collection is a great resource for researchers. The site also includes a series of online lectures by Dr. Stephan Hoeller, available for downloading for a nominal fee. The Gnostic Society sponsors the website.

National Archives of Egypt (NAE)
http://www.nationalarchives.gov.eg/nae/home.jsp

The NAE provides access to digitized documents relating to the political, economic, social, and cultural history of Egypt. The site is sponsored by Egypt's Ministry of Communications and Information Technology and Ministry of Culture. Documents are in Arabic or French, and they are a good source for historians. The NAE is the only place where the documents issued by the divans, ministries, and institutions of the state for various historical eras are kept. There is an image library, but documents are in Arabic. Link on "Collections" to access a description (with a limited number of links to selected images) of what the NAE describes as its most important collections. One collection, the Deeds of Sultans and Princes, reviews legal transactions, including land endowments and real estate. Other important archival collections review the history of the Sudan, the history of Greater Syria, the Egyptian Army, history of the Arabian Peninsula (e.g., the Al-Hijaz documents), and documents relating to Crete and Greece during the Mora wars. Other documents are a divorce document dated 22-7-934 and an agreement on prohibiting slave trade between the Egyptian and the British governments dated 1877.

Nubia Museum
http://www.numibia.net/nubia/collections.asp

Egyptologists and archaeologists and more than 60 expeditions were involved in the Nubian Rescue Campaign, which involved the excavation and recording of hundreds of sites, recovery of thousands of objects, and relocation of a number of important temples that were threatened by the rising waters of Lake Nasser in the early 1960s. With the help of UNESCO, a museum was constructed to house these valuable artifacts. One can search artifacts by type (e.g., basketry, jewelry, metal work, pottery, and sculpture) or by historic periods from prehistory up to the Islamic and Modern Nubia. The Museum won the Agha-Khan Award of Architecture in 2001. The area now called Nubia extends along the Nile from the South of Aswan to the town of Dabba, near the Fourth Cataract, linking Egypt (i.e., the northern part of the Nile valley) to the Sudan in the South. The name "Nubia" is first mentioned in Strabo's *Geographica*; the Greek author is believed to have visited Egypt ca. 29 BC.

Theban Mapping Project
http://www.thebanmappingproject.com

The goal of the Theban Mapping Project (now based at the American University in Cairo) is to contain a detailed map and database of every archaeological, geological, and ethnographic feature in Thebes. Thebes is one of the world's most important archaeological zones, with 62 numbered royal and private tombs in the Valley of the Kings, including the tombs of the sons of Ramesses II. Modern surveying techniques were used to measure the tombs. From the data collected, the Project is preparing three-dimensional computer models of the tombs. The site includes maps of the Valley of the Kings, a digital movie of the land, and a description of the land.

Tour Egypt
http://www.touregypt.net/edestinations.htm

The Tour Egypt website is a resource for schools and universities in teaching students about Egypt. Links on a map of Egypt provide written descriptions of many cities, towns, important sites, and bodies of water as well as directions for traveling to them. Learn important facts about such places as Alexandria, the Nile Valley, the Red Sea, and Sinai. Link to "Egypt Travel Articles" in the left menu and read about Egypt's history, culture, and other topics.

EQUATORIAL GUINEA

New York Public Library Digital Gallery
http://digitalgallery.nypl.org/nypldigital/dgkeysearchresult.cfm?keyword=Equatorial
+Guinea

A search for "Equatorial Guinea" retrieved 20 photos, most of which come from the book *España en el África occidental Río de Oro y Guinea Con dibujos y fotografías de M. G. de Enciso* (1910) and depict native peoples of the country.

World Digital Library
http://www.wdl.org/en/search/gallery?ql=eng&c=GQ&s=Equatorial%20Guinea

Three images are classified under "Equatorial Guinea" in this collection. Two are maps of the area, and the third is a book by Luis Ramos-Izquierdo y Vivar titled *Descripción geográfica y gobierno, administración y colonización de las colonias españolas del golfo de Guinea* (Geographical Description and Governmental Administration and Settlement of the Spanish Colonies in the Gulf of Guinea), which describes the early twentieth-century Equatorial Guinea colony.

ERITREA

New York Public Library Digital Gallery
http://digitalgallery.nypl.org/nypldigital/dgkeysearchresult.cfm?keyword=eritrea

A search for "Eritrea" retrieved two photos. The first is a color print of Eritrean askari (local military soldiers) and the second is an 1887 map of Eritrea and surrounding countries.

World Digital Library
http://www.wdl.org/en/search/gallery?ql=eng&c=ER&s=Eritrea

Three images are classified under "Eritrea" in this collection. The first is a set of 34 topographical maps created between 1909 and 1934 by the Italian military. The next two images are also maps, a 1675 portolan chart by Frederick de Wit followed by an 1896 topographical map of Eritrea.

ETHIOPIA

Ethiopian Manuscript Imaging Project (EMIP) Collection of Ethiopian Manuscripts
http://www.hmml.org/Vivarium/sgd.htm

EMIP is part of the online digital collections of Saint John's University (MN) and the College of Saint Benedict (MN). The collection was begun by Steve Delamarter in February 2005 and contains digitized images from collections in the United States, England, Israel, and Kenya. The EMIP collection consists of over 300 codices and 340 magic scrolls. Browse the codices or magic scrolls by date (sixteenth to twentieth centuries), search by keyword or exact phrase, or browse the entire EMIP collection.

GABON

New York Public Library Digital Gallery
http://digitalgallery.nypl.org/nypldigital/dgkeysearchresult.cfm?keyword=gabon

A search for "Gabon" retrieved 20 photos. Most of the photos depict native peoples, but there are also views of local housing and a map and a chart of the area.

The University of Southern California Digital Library
http://digitallibrary.usc.edu/search/controller/simplesearch.htm

A search for "Gabon" retrieved 83 images. The images are a mix of photos taken of native peoples, missionaries, and activities along the Ogooue and the Abanaga Rivers.

GAMBIA

Ethnographic Video for Instruction & Analysis (EVIA) Digital Archive
http://www.eviada.org/mainCat.cfm?mc=7

The EVIA Digital Archive is a collaborative project of Indiana University and the University of Michigan, with support from the Andrew W. Mellon Foundation, designed to provide anthropological scholars with video footage of traditional behaviors from around the world. For content on Gambia, look for the collection titled Music of the

Jalis (Griots) and Drum and Dance Events in Mali, Senegal, and the Gambia (1989–2003).

New York Public Library Digital Gallery
http://digitalgallery.nypl.org/nypldigital/index.cfm

A search for "Gambia" retrieved 58 photos, many of which from one of the four volumes of *Africa: Containing a Description of the Manners and Customs, with Some Historical Particulars of the Moors of the Zahara, and of the Negro Nations between the Rivers Senegal and Gambia: Illustrated with Two Maps, and Forty-Five Coloured Engravings* by Frederic Shoberl (1821). Other images include native peoples and places in Gambia as well as a several maps of the area.

GHANA

Ethnographic Video for Instruction & Analysis (EVIA) Digital Archive
http://www.eviada.org/mainCat.cfm?mc=7

The EVIA Digital Archive is a collaborative project of Indiana University and the University of Michigan, with support from the Andrew W. Mellon Foundation, designed to provide anthropological scholars with video footage of traditional behaviors from around the world. For content on Ghana, look for the collections titled Music of Urban Communities in Ghana and African Extensions (2000–2006) and Music, Song, and Dance on Mexico's Costa Chica (1989–1996).

The James Koetting Ghana Field Recordings Collection
http://dl.lib.brown.edu/koetting/

This collection, which is a project of the Graduate Program in Ethnomusicology of the Department of Music at Brown University (RI), contains James Koetting's field audio reel tapes (142) of musical performances taped during the 1970s at various festival and musical events throughout Ghana. In addition to the audiotapes, the website has a small gallery of photos, two essays, and a list of resources. It also provides access to Koetting's field notebooks, which consist of a project log and two recording logs that contain details about each tape and his activities, as well as newspaper clippings, concert programs, and occasionally a hand-drawn map.

GUINEA

Ethnographic Video for Instruction & Analysis (EVIA) Digital Archive
http://www.eviada.org/mainCat.cfm?mc=7

The EVIA Digital Archive is a collaborative project of Indiana University and the University of Michigan, with support from the Andrew W. Mellon Foundation, designed to provide anthropological scholars with video footage of traditional behaviors from around the world. For content on Guinea, look for the collections titled Music, Culture, and Rituals among the Vai, Gola, Mende, and Dei people in Liberia (1977–1978, 1987–1988) and Vodou Rites in Port-au-Prince, Haiti (1995).

World Digital Library
http://www.wdl.org/en/item/652/?ql=eng&s=Republic+of+Guinea&view_type=
    gallery

One image is classified under "Guinea" in this collection, which is from a book titled *La Guinée* (Guinea) by Fernand Rouget. This 1906 study, which is over 450 pages long, discusses the history, geography, population, administration, and economy of French Guinea. Click on "Open" on the image to read the entire book (written in French) and view other images.

GUINEA-BISSAU

Instituto Nacional de Estudos e Pesquisa
http://www.inep-bissau.org/Arquivos/Galerias/tabid/119/Default.aspx

The archives of the Instituto Nacional de Estudos e Pesquisa (Public Library of the National Institute of Study and Research) contains many old photos. The photographs are accessible from a drop-down menu of themes such as ethnicity, indigenous art, sports, and Portuguese population and social life. The site and description of photos are entirely in Portuguese, but one can use a webpage translator tool such as Google.

KENYA

Ethnographic Video for Instruction & Analysis (EVIA) Digital Archive
http://www.eviada.org/mainCat.cfm?mc=7

The EVIA Digital Archive is a collaborative project of Indiana University and the University of Michigan, with support from the Andrew W. Mellon Foundation, designed to provide anthropological scholars with video footage of traditional behaviors from around the world. For content on Kenya, look for the collection titled *Musical Labor Performance from the Sukuma Region of Western Tanzania* (1994–1995).

Friends United Meeting: Kenya
http://www.earlham.edu/archivesphotos/friends_united_meeting.html

This small collection of 20 photographs is one of several subcollections within the Earlham Digital Archives. The collection exemplifies the Friends United Meeting Quaker mission in Kenya, Africa. The photographs are a mix of subjects, including various construction projects and a newlywed couple.

LESOTHO

New York Public Library Digital Gallery
http://digitalgallery.nypl.org/nypldigital/dgkeysearchresult.cfm?keyword=Lesotho+

Seventy-four images are classified under "Lesotho" in this collection, all of which come from Frédéric Christol's book *Au sud de l'Afrique* (1897). The images are a mix of landscapes, native peoples, local villages, and buildings.

The University of Southern California Digital Library
http://digitallibrary.usc.edu/search/controller/simplesearch.htm

A search for "Lesotho" retrieved 82 images. The photos are part of two collections: DM-Échange et Mission and the Yale Divinity Library Special Collections, Missionary Postcard Collection. Taken ca. 1901–1940, photos include images of buildings, landscapes, housing, clergy, native peoples, agriculture, and churches.

LIBERIA

Ethnographic Video for Instruction & Analysis (EVIA) Digital Archive
http://www.eviada.org/mainCat.cfm?mc=7

The EVIA Digital Archive is a collaborative project of Indiana University and the University of Michigan, with support from the Andrew W. Mellon Foundation, designed to provide anthropological scholars with video footage of traditional behaviors from around the world. For content on Liberia, look for the collections titled Kpelle Music Events in Monrovia and Sanoyea Liberia (1988–1989), Music, Culture, and Rituals among the Vai, Gola, Mende, and Dei people in Liberia (1977–1978, 1987–1988), and Gospel Music Performance in Indiana and Texas, USA (1979–1982).

New York Public Library Digital Gallery
http://digitalgallery.nypl.org/nypldigital/dgkeysearchresult.cfm?keyword=liberia

A search for "Liberia" retrieved 423 images in this collection. Most are images of people and places; there are also maps, Liberian postage stamps, artifacts from the area, and drawings of local flora.

LIBYA

Libyan Art Galleries
http://www.temehu.com/libyan-art-galleries.htm

The Libyan Art Galleries website is a unique digital collection of drawings and photographs interspersed with information about chronology, styles, mythological themes, and vandalism of the rock art; Libya's main archaeological and tourist sites; traditional crafts; and Tuareg jewelry. The close-up photos, especially of the rock art, are a real plus.

MADAGASCAR

Gifts and Blessings: The Textile Arts of Madagascar
http://www.nmafa.si.edu/exhibits/malagasy/index.html

This is an online companion website of a previous exhibition at the Smithsonian Institution. It includes numerous images of Madagascar cloth and discussion of its cultural uses. One page contains samples of the music of Madagascar.

International Mission Photography Archive
http://digitallibrary.usc.edu/search/controller/collection/impa-m559.html

The collection of the School of Mission and Theology in Stavanger (Norway) in this archive contains images from Madagascar and South Africa. *See also* INTERNATIONAL MISSION PHOTOGRAPHY ARCHIVE *under* AFRICA: CONTINENT.

MALAWI

Cultural & Museum Centre, Karonga
http://www.palaeo.net/cmck/

Although the website is primarily about the museum itself, once you enter the site there is a "Photos" link in the top menu bar that provides access to nine different "galleries" of images, many of which are about local history and culture.

Ethnographic Video for Instruction & Analysis (EVIA) Digital Archive
http://www.eviada.org/mainCat.cfm?mc=7

The EVIA Digital Archive is a collaborative project of Indiana University and the University of Michigan, with support from the Andrew W. Mellon Foundation, designed to provide anthropological scholars with video footage of traditional behaviors from around the world. For content on Malawi, click on the "Collections" link and look for the ones titled Dance Forms in Malawi, Nkhata Bay, Tonga, Tumbuka and Ngonde; Mvano Women's Guild Music and Dance in Malawi; and Rap and Ragga Performance in Malawi.

MALI

Islamic Manuscripts from Mali
http://international.loc.gov/intldl/malihtml/

This collection is part of the Library of Congress's National Digital Library Program. It currently includes 32 complete manuscripts. They were written in Arabic and collected from multiple library collections in Mali. They can be browsed by title and subject or searched by keyword. The titles are translated into English, and brief English "notes" synopsize the content.

Slavery and Manumission Manuscripts of Timbuktu
http://ecollections.crl.edu/cdm4/index_timbuktu.php?CISOROOT=/timbuktu

Hosted by the Center for Research Libraries, this is a digitized collection of over 200 Arabic manuscripts detailing the slavery of African citizens in Muslim society, specifically in the city of Timbuktu, Mali. The manuscripts can be searched by subject or viewed as a complete list. Individual entries have information in English. The manuscripts themselves are in Arabic.

MAURITANIA

New York Public Library Digital Gallery
http://digitalgallery.nypl.org/nypldigital/dgkeysearchresult.cfm?keyword=mauritania

A search for "Mauritania" retrieved ten images, most of which depict native peoples of the country. There are also several maps and charts of the area.

University of Wisconsin Digital Collections
http://uwdc.library.wisc.edu/index.shtml

A search for "Mauritania" returned 28 search results, mostly aerial views of the landscape and of native peoples involved in daily activities.

MAURITIUS

New York Public Library Digital Gallery
http://digitalgallery.nypl.org/nypldigital/dgkeysearchresult.cfm?keyword=mauritius

A search for "Mauritius" retrieved 25 images, most of which depict drawings of places. There are also several versions of the country's flag, as well as an illustration of an extinct native parrot.

World Digital Library
http://www.wdl.org/en/search/gallery?ql=eng&s=mauritius

Six items are classified under "Mauritius" in this collection. The most relevant item is a map of the city of Port Louis, a port city on the island during the eighteenth century. Other items include a larger map of Africa and a text, both created by explorers who had visited the island.

MOROCCO

Genthe Collection
http://www.loc.gov/pictures/search?q=morocco&co=agc

This collection, housed by the Library of Congress, contains around 16,000 images taken by internationally renowned photographer Arnold Genthe in the late nineteenth and early twentieth centuries. There are approximately 100 images from Morocco in this collection. All images have the supplied title "Travel views of Morocco" and have limited accompanying information.

MOZAMBIQUE

Aluka
http://www.Aluka.org

Aluka is a standalone worldwide digital collection of African scholarly materials. Its content is available through the JSTOR database to "not-for-profit institutions of higher education secondary schools, public libraries, museums, and other research or cultural institutions" that have an institutional license. Access is currently not available to individual users. The collections listed below all have content related to Mozambique. The descriptive information for each collection comes from the "Collections Info" tab associated with that collection.

▶ **Isaacman Interviews (Mozambique)**
http://www.aluka.org/action/showCompilationPage?doi=10.5555/AL.SFF
    .COMPILATION.COLLECTION-MAJOR.ISAAC

This collection contains interviews performed by Allen Isaacman with both the country's first President, Samora Machel, as well as with native peasants who were segregated from the white population, forced to do menial and dangerous labor, and even relocated to facilitate the building of a dam that was to provide electrical power for South Africa, the country's neighbor to the south.

▶ **Lunstrum Interviews (Mozambique)**
http://www.aluka.org/action/showCompilationPage?doi=10.5555/AL.SFF
    .COMPILATION.COLLECTION-MAJOR.LUNSTR

These interviews were conducted over an 11-month period during 2004 and 2005 in several villages in Mozambique's Massingir District, which is located on the South African border adjacent to Kruger National Park. The interviews were part of Elizabeth Lunstrum's doctoral dissertation research, which focused on the politics of territory in that district, in particular the impact that the newly built Limpopo National Park was having on territorial relations. Interviews were conducted in the native language of Shangaana, and a portion of the content was translated into English.

▶ **Mozambique Liberation Documents**
http://www.aluka.org/action/showCompilationPage?doi=10.5555/AL.SFF
    .COMPILATION.COLLECTION-MAJOR.PWMOZ

This collection contains publications by the Liberation Front of Mozambique (FRELIMO) and the Mozambique Institute; programs and speeches from the memorial services for Dr. Eduardo Mondlane; and documents contributed from the private collection of Peter Weiss, "an American Human Rights lawyer and long-time friend and supporter of Mozambican liberation."

▶ **Mozambique Revolution**
http://www.aluka.org/action/showCompilationPage?doi=10.5555/AL.SFF
    .COMPILATION.COLLECTION-MAJOR.MOZREV

This collection contains issues from the *Mozambique Revolution* (formerly *Mozambican Revolution*), "an English-language periodical of the Mozambique Liberation Front (FRELIMO)." Published in Tanzania from 1963 to 1975, the periodical focused on drawing international support and attention to the country's struggle for freedom from Portuguese rule.

▶ **Penvenne Interviews (Mozambique)**
http://www.aluka.org/action/showCompilationPage?doi=10.5555/AL.SFF
    .COMPILATION.COLLECTION-MAJOR.PENVEN

The Penvenne Interviews were conducted during Jeanne Penvenne's doctoral dissertation research for *A History of African Labor in Lourenço Marques, Mozam-*

bique, 1877 to 1950. Penvenne's goal was to gather direct testimony from Mozambicans themselves about what life was like living and working in this particular city.

International Mission Photography Archive
http://digitallibrary.usc.edu/search/controller/collection/impa-m15498.html

The collection of the DM-Échange et Mission (Lausenne, Switzerland) in this archive contains images from Mozambique. *See also* INTERNATIONAL MISSION PHOTOGRAPHY ARCHIVE *under* AFRICA: CONTINENT.

NAMIBIA

Aluka—Namibia Poster Collection
http://www.aluka.org/action/doBrowse?sa=xst&t=431603&br=tax-collections|part-of
   |collection-minor

Aluka is a standalone worldwide digital collection of African scholarly materials. Its content is available through the JSTOR database to "not-for-profit institutions of higher education secondary schools, public libraries, museums, and other research or cultural institutions" that have an institutional license. Access is currently not available to individual users. National Archives of Namibia has contributed to Aluka a batch of posters related to the country's liberation movement.

NIGER

New York Public Library Digital Gallery
http://digitalgallery.nypl.org/nypldigital/dgkeysearchresult.cfm?keyword=niger

A search for "Niger" retrieved 246 images. Many of these images are from the country of Niger, but many also refer to the Niger River, which travels through a number of countries, or to the river's delta, which is actually in Nigeria. The results are easy to scan and dissect, as the site defaults to showing 20 images per page (which can be set to display up to 60 by clicking "Change Display" in the top menu bar).

University of Wisconsin Digital Collections
http://uwdc.library.wisc.edu/index.shtml

A search for "Niger" returned over 100 search results, referring both to the country and to the Niger River. A separate search for "Niamey" (the country's largest city) returned 13 color images, primarily candid shots of people and places in the city.

NIGERIA

New York Public Library Digital Gallery
http://digitalgallery.nypl.org/nypldigital/dgkeysearchresult.cfm?keyword=nigeria

A search for "Nigeria" retrieved 131 images. The vast majority of these images are of people, places, and maps of the vicinity.

University of Wisconsin Digital Collections
http://uwdc.library.wisc.edu/index.shtml

A search for "Nigeria" returned over 250 search results, mostly color images of people, places, and activities. Close-up views of structures and rivers are also included. Some of the search results are audio files containing samples of native music.

RWANDA

Rwanda's National HIV/AIDS Digital Library
http://www.payson.tulane.edu/gsdl-2.80/main-RNHDL/first.htm

This collection contains full-text resources covering Rwanda's approach to dealing with HIV/AIDS. The collection contains over 600 documents searchable by title, text, or contributing organization. The documents are all in PDF format and include research papers as well as government publications and statistics. Design and technical assistance is provided by Tulane University.

SÃO TOMÉ AND PRÍNCIPE

New York Public Library Digital Gallery
http://digitalgallery.nypl.org/nypldigital/dgkeysearchresult.cfm?keyword=sao+tome
+principe

A search for "São Tomé Príncipe" retrieved one image, showing an engraving of a boat leaving an island off the coast of Africa.

World Digital Library
http://www.wdl.org/en/search/gallery?ql=eng&s=sao+tome+principe

Two items are classified under "São Tomé and Príncipe" in this collection. One is a lengthy PDF file of a French-language book detailing the travels of a Franciscan friar who visited many places in Africa, including islands along the coastline. The other is an eighteenth-century map of West Africa that includes the islands off the coast.

SENEGAL

Beautiful and Diverse, Senegal, Through the Eyes of a Retiree
http://www.senegalview.com/

This small collection from the personal website of a Peace Corps volunteer contains 13 photographs taken during her last visit to the country.

Saint-Louis: Religious Pluralism in the Heart of Senegal
http://westafricanislam.matrix.msu.edu/saintlouis/unit.php?unit=1

This collection is part of the Africa Online Digital Library (http://www.aodl.org/), a collaborative project between Michigan State University and various scholarly and cultural organizations in Africa. This particular collection focuses on the interaction and mixing of the French Catholic and Muslim faiths in the city of Saint-Louis, in the heart of Senegal. It is set up in chapter format with narrative pages, accentuated by digitized photographs, maps, and interviews.

SEYCHELLES

New York Public Library Digital Gallery
http://digitalgallery.nypl.org/nypldigital/dgkeysearchresult.cfm?keyword=seychelles

A search for "Seychelles" retrieved six images. Some are artists' renderings of the environment, and two show the country's flag. There is also one image detailing the anatomy of the Seychelles gecko and comparing it to geckos from other countries.

World Digital Library
http://www.wdl.org/en/search/gallery?ql=eng&s=seychelles

One image is classified under "Seychelles" in this collection, which is a book detailing an Indian Ocean voyage from 1789 to 1790 by French army officer Louis de Grandpre. The text is nearly 300 pages long (translated into English from the original French) and includes the author's visit to the Seychelles.

SIERRA LEONE

UIC Sierra Leone (University of Illinois at Chicago)
http://collections.carli.illinois.edu/cdm4/index_uic_sierra.php?CISOROOT=/uic_sierra

This collection, housed at the University of Illinois at Chicago, contains 11 documents related to the British control of the colony of Sierra Leone, which expanded greatly when former slaves were relocated there. Documents include personal correspondence of British officials as well as hand-drawn diagrams of a slave ship.

SOMALIA

The Digital Somali Library
http://www.indiana.edu/~libsalc/african/Digital_Somali_Library/digibks.html

As part of a larger project to collect and preserve the history and culture of Somalia, the University of Indiana at Bloomington Library digitized the full texts of 137 Somali books and made them open to all. The works are not translated.

SOUTH AFRICA

African National Congress—South Africa's National Liberation Movement
http://www.anc.org.za/index.php

This website contains fully transcribed texts of many speeches and addresses related to the country's struggle to end apartheid. Scroll over "Documents" in the top menu bar and then "Collections" in the drop-down list to see a sublist of 13 categories. The content is grouped into categories, including famous speeches, women's struggles, and transition to democracy. Within each category list, the overarching theme of that list is described on the right side of the page, while the titles and dates of the speeches it contains are listed by date on the left. Several famous speeches from Nelson Mandela are included, such as his 1993 speech to the United Nations and his 1994 statement at his inauguration as the country's president.

African Orthodox Church
http://www.pitts.emory.edu/collections/exhibits/africanorthodox/index.cfm

This is an online collection of photographs interwoven with background information about the African Orthodox Church since its founding in South Africa in 1924. All items are listed on one page in blog format. The site is maintained by the Pitts Theology Library of the Candler School of Theology at Emory University in Atlanta, Georgia. Direct hyperlinking does not appear to work; cut and paste the above link into a browser to access the site.

Campbell Collections
http://campbell.ukzn.ac.za/

This online collection of digital resources is made available through the University of KwaZulu-Natal. The original items are from the private collection of the African collector Ms. Killie Campbell and her family, which was bequeathed to the university. The university has digitized thousands of items, including rare photographs, as well as images of art and other objects. The site is free, but new users must create an account first.

Community Video Education Trust
http://www.cvet.org.za/index.php

Part of the Michigan State University South Africa Film and Video Project, this is a collection of documentary-style video clips from South Africa related to the struggle against apartheid. The content can be browsed by category (e.g., speeches, demonstrations), and each clip is accompanied by contextual information, including the date, names of people, and organizations when possible.

Digital Innovation South Africa
http://www.disa.ukzn.ac.za/

This collection of digitized materials relates to the political history of South Africa from 1950 to 1994. The collection is aimed at researchers, and the goal is to create as much online content as possible. Click on "Browse Collection" in the top menu bar to link to digital content in over 30 types of formats, including text documents and oral histories.

Posters from the Melville J. Herskovits Library of African Studies
http://digital.library.northwestern.edu/africana-posters/index.html

The Melville J. Herskovits Library at Northwestern University has digitized a portion of its poster collection and made over 350 items available online. Many of these African posters deal with social issues and liberation struggles. However, the collection contains items produced by both governmental agencies as well as political, social, and cultural organizations. The collection can be searched by keyword or sorted by subject. Full bibliographic records are linked to each item.

South Africa.info—Gallery—Nelson Mandela
http://www.southafrica.info/pls/cms/show_gallery_sa_info?p_gid=4783&p_site_id=38

View over 50 pictures of Nelson Mandela, a Nobel Peace Prize winner and former president of the country. The photo gallery was compiled by Mary Alexander from the Nelson Mandela National Museum. SouthAfrica.info does not hold copyright on these photos. Permission for reuse should be sought from the copyright holder indicated below each photograph.

South Africa.info—Gallery—The Rock Art of South Africa
http://www.southafrica.info/pls/cms/show_gallery_sa_info?p_gid=2306&p_site_id=38

This site displays about 28 images of rock art dating from the Stone Age to the nineteenth century. Click on each image to see a larger view as well as a description and the copyright holder.

University of Pretoria, South Africa—Africana Books Collection
https://www.up.ac.za/dspace/handle/2263/4911

This website provides access to a collection of rare books housed in the Special Collections Unit in the Merensky Library, University of Pretoria. Works in this collection are in the public domain.

University of Pretoria, South Africa—Van Warmelo Collection
https://www.up.ac.za/dspace/handle/2263/89

Van Warmelo was a scholar and expert in South African indigenous languages. The materials he collected are housed in the Special Collections Unit of the Academic Information Service, University of Pretoria. Digitized photographs of tribal life form part of the Academic Information Service's African Heritage Digital Collection. Search the collection by keyword; browse the collection by title, author, subject, or date; or click on a recent submission in the right menu of the page. The records are provided for educational purposes only. They cannot be downloaded, reproduced, or distributed in any format without written permission of the University of Pretoria, Academic Information Service.

University of Pretoria, South Africa—Woodhouse Rock Art Collection
https://www.up.ac.za/dspace/handle/2263/595

Herbert (Bert) C. Woodhouse collected over 20,000 slides, maps, and tracings of southern African rock art. His digitized slides of rock art can be viewed online and browsed by title, author, subject, or date. These records are provided for educational purposes only. They cannot be downloaded, reproduced, or distributed in any format without written permission of the University of Pretoria, Academic Information Service.

SUDAN

New York Public Library Digital Gallery
http://digitalgallery.nypl.org/nypldigital/dgkeysearchresult.cfm?keyword=sudan

A search for "Sudan" retrieved 184 images. Most are images of people and places; there are also a few drawings of sculpture and artifacts from the area.

University of Wisconsin Digital Collections
http://uwdc.library.wisc.edu/index.shtml

A search for "Sudan" returned 184 search results, mostly aerial views of the landscape and of native peoples involved in daily activities.

SWAZILAND

Swaziland Digital Archives
http://www.sntc.org.sz/sdphotos/

This private website contains nearly 500 images related to the country's history. They are browseable by decade or searchable by title, date, caption, or photographer's name. Images are presented with as much description as possible and are available for free use. A contact e-mail address is located on the homepage.

TANZANIA

Ethnographic Video for Instruction & Analysis (EVIA) Digital Archive
http://www.eviada.org/mainCat.cfm?mc=7

The EVIA Digital Archive is a collaborative project of Indiana University and the University of Michigan, with support from the Andrew W. Mellon Foundation, designed to provide anthropological scholars with video footage of traditional behaviors from around the world. For content on Tanzania, look for the collections Generations of Sound: Popular Music, Genre, and Performance in Dar es Salaam, Tanzania; Musical Labor Performance from the Sukuma Region of Western Tanzania; and Taarab, Ngoma, and Dansi Performances in Tanzania.

The Sukuma Museum
http://philip.greenspun.com/sukuma/

This simple website contains significant information about the museum and its collection, with a representative sampling of images of some of its artifacts. The majority of images can be found by viewing "A Tour of the Sukuma Museum" located in the middle of the page. Contact information and a "Q&A Forum," which is similar to an FAQ, are also available.

TOGO

New York Public Library Digital Gallery
http://digitalgallery.nypl.org/nypldigital/dgkeysearchresult.cfm?keyword=togo+africa

A search for "Togo" retrieved results that are associated with other countries (e.g., Russia, Japan) whose languages include this word. A search for "Togo Africa," however, returned four results, including images of people and one primitive map, ca. 1600.

World Digital Library
http://www.wdl.org/en/search/gallery?ql=eng&c=TG&s=togo

Three items are classified under "Togo" in this collection, one of which is a 32-page digital file of the country's constitution, written in French and dated May 3, 1963. There is also a lengthy early twentieth-century book about Germany and its colonies, which included Togo at the time.

TUNISIA

National Library of Tunisia
http://www.bibliotheque.nat.tn/en/default.aspx

The National Library of Tunisia's online catalog includes digital scans of printed materials. The materials can be searched by keyword, and the results can be limited by material type. Content is viewable free of charge; however, the site is difficult to navigate as it is entirely in French.

UGANDA

Global Music Archive—Digital Collection of East African Recordings
http://diglib.library.vanderbilt.edu/ama-search.pl

This archive contains over 1,600 audio recordings of songs from Africa and North and South America but chiefly from Uganda and other East African countries. It is maintained by the Wilson Music Library at Vanderbilt University in Tennessee. The content can be searched by keyword, title, or performer and can also be browsed by location, language, ethnic group, and musical instrument. The files are MP3 format and require RealPlayer in order to download and play them.

WESTERN SAHARA

Forced Migration Online (FMO)
http://repository.forcedmigration.org/?search=western+sahara&start=0&rows=10

FMO provides access to a wide range of resources that illustrate "the movements of refugees and internally displaced people (people displaced by conflicts) as well as people displaced by natural or environmental disasters, chemical or nuclear disasters, famine, or development projects." A search for "Western Sahara" located over 250 items.

ZAMBIA

National Archives of Zambia
http://www.zambiarchives.org/library.htm

The National Archives of Zambia contains many physical materials, both governmental and privately donated. The archive also has a small web presence at the link provided.

One map, two stamps, two newspaper issues, and a handful of photographs represent the currently available content on the site. Although the amount of content is currently miniscule, the diversity of it indicates that the Archives is prepared to grow and expand in the future.

ZIMBABWE

Aluka—Zimbabwe Serials
http://www.aluka.org/action/doBrowse?sa=xst&t=2086&br=tax-collections|part-of
  |collection-minor

Aluka is a standalone worldwide digital collection of African scholarly materials. Its content is available through the JSTOR database to "not-for-profit institutions of higher education secondary schools, public libraries, museums, and other research or cultural institutions" that have an institutional license. Access is currently not available to individual users. This collection includes a run of issues of the *Zimbabwe African National Union*, a Zimbabwean magazine provided to the Aluka database by the Northwestern University Libraries.

Chapter 3

Antarctica

INTRODUCTION

One of the fascinating facts about Antarctica is its inhospitable climate. This frozen area of the Earth, although rich in sea life and some animal life, has not been inhabited for any length of time by humans. Consequently, the absence of inhabitation by man and the inability to develop a history over a long period of time places Antarctica in an inimitable circumstance. Antarctica did not follow the model of developing a cultural legacy of its own. The courageous labors of the early explorers of this desolate continent are followed today by the enduring efforts at research and scientific discovery of various organizations around the world. This fact makes Antarctica stand out as a unique entity.

What we do have is a history of the expeditions to Antarctica by explorers from various nations. There are also preservation efforts of original campsites, such as Captain Scott's base at Cape Evans, Sir Ernest Shackleton's 1907–1909 expedition to Cape Royds, and the 1899 Norwegian-led expedition at Cape Adare by the Antarctic Heritage Trust's Ross Sea Heritage Restoration Project (Antarctic Heritage Trust, 2009). Preservation and conservation of the first buildings to be erected and their artifacts by these explorers is funded by both private individuals and organizations, including The Getty Foundation and the New Zealand Government. There is even an *Antarctic Blog* that follows the efforts of the conservation teams sponsored by the Natural History Museum of London (Antarctic Heritage Trust, 2010).

Scientific discovery and current exploration of Antarctica is an ongoing challenge for this frozen continent. A good illustration of this comes from the Scientific Committee on Antarctic Research (SCAR) program that studies global change and sea ice conditions. Under ASPeCt (Antarctic Sea Ice Processes and Climate) protocols, digital images are captured from video of sea ice during the inbound and outbound transits of the icebreaker NB Palmer during the 2007 SIMBA—Sea Ice Mass Balance in Antarctic cruise to measure ice types and floe sizes and to gather other scientific data (Weissling et al., 2009). View photos, maps, and research from the website of the Scientific Committee on Antarctic Research (SCAR, 2010).

Another important site for scientific data on Antarctica is the U.S. Antarctic Resource Center (USARC) depository for Antarctic maps, charts, geodetic ground control, satellite images, aerial photographs, publications, slides, and videotapes. The resources are brought together by the Antarctic Treaty nations to exchange information and are maintained through an interagency cooperative agreement between the U.S.

Geological Survey (USGS) and the National Science Foundation (NSF) (USARC, 2001).

For the most recent research on glaciology and climate changes for Antarctica, visit the USGS's Scott Polar Research Institute website (Scott Polar Research Institute, 2005), which provides images, a three-dimensional movie, and views of Antarctic ice-streams; or the Byrd Polar Research Center website (Byrd Polar Research Center, 2010), which provides data and images. Authors Kim, Jezek, and Liu (2007) provide an in-depth explanation of the satellite state-of-the-art digital imaging technology that gives us the various images taken of the Pine Island Glacier through Google (Google Search, 2010), the Northern Larsen Ice Shelf (Scott Polar Research Institute, 2006), Filchner Ice Shelf (Campbell, 1998), and Whillans Ice Stream (Scott Polar Research Institute, 2007) found on these sites.

Whether interested in the history of the early expeditions to Antarctica, life that exists on this ice continent, or the latest scientific research learned by recent expeditions and satellite, a visit to many of the sites in this chapter will satisfy one's imagination.

References

Antarctic Heritage Trust. 2009. "Major Conservation Work at Cape Evans." *Antarctic Heritage Trust* 44: e-newsletter. http://www.heritage-antarctica.org/content/library/E_Newsletter_June_2009.pdf.

Antarctic Heritage Trust. 2010. "Antarctic Explorers and Heritage Preservation." Antarctica Heritage Trust (New Zealand). Accessed August 23. http://www.nzaht.org/AHT/.

Byrd Polar Research Center. 2010. "Welcome to BPRC!" Ohio State University. Accessed August 31. http://bprc.osu.edu.

Campbell, Robert Wellman, ed. 1998. "Filchner Ice Shelf, Antarctica: 1973, 1986." Earthshots: Satellite Images of Environmental Change, U.S. Geological Survey. http://earthshots.usgs.gov/Filchner/Filchner.

Google Search. 2010. "Pine Island Glacier." Google. Accessed August 23. http://images.google.com/images?hl=en&q=Pine+Island+Glacier&um=1&ie=UTF-8&ei=q25fSowPkc4zgvq0rgI&sa=X&oi=image_result_group&ct=title&resnum=4.

Kim, K., K.C. Jezek, and H. Liu. 2007. "Orthorectified Image Mosaic of Antarctica from 1963 Argon Satellite Photography: Image Processing and Glaciological Applications." *International Journal of Remote Sensing* 28, no. 23: 5357–5373. http://www.tandf.co.uk/journals.

SCAR (Scientific Committee on Antarctic Research). 2010. "Welcome to SCAR." Last saved August 18. http://www.scar.org/.

Scott Polar Research Institute. 2005. "Inland Thinning of Pine Island Glacier, West Antarctica." University of Cambridge. Last saved September 20. http://www.spri.cam.ac.uk/research/projects/pineislandglacier/.

Scott Polar Research Institute. 2006. "Larsen Ice Shelf Has Progressively Thinned." University of Cambridge. Last saved December 14. Available: http://www.spri.cam.ac.uk/research/projects/larseniceshelf/.

Scott Polar Research Institute. 2007. "Assessing the Role of Subglacial Hydrology on the Flow of West Antarctic Ice Streams: A Numerical Modelling Approach." University of Cambridge. Last saved May 24. Available: http://www.spri.cam.ac.uk/research/projects/wasubglacialhydrology/.

USARC (United States Antarctic Resource Center). 2001, May. *USGS Fact Sheet 051-01*. http://usarc.usgs.gov/downloads/FS_0051_01_ND.pdf.

Weissling, B., S. Ackley, P. Wagner, and H. Xie. 2009. "EISCAM—Digital Image Acquisition and Processing for Sea Ice Parameters from Ships." *Cold Regions Science and Technology* 57: 49–60. http://www.sciencedirect.com/science?_ob=ArticleURL &_udi=B6V86-4VDS87W-2&_user=10&_coverDate=06%2F30%2F2009&_rdoc =1&_fmt=high&_orig=search&_origin=search&_sort=d&_docanchor=&view=c& _acct=C000050221&_version=1&_urlVersion=0&_userid=10&md5=c76f5dc6c33 8ee5fcd3be9465cf6bda0&searchtype=a.

CONTINENT

Antarctic Heritage Trust—New Zealand, United Kingdom
http://www.heritage-antarctica.org/aht.htm

The Antarctic Heritage Trust is a nonprofit organization responsible for the care of the expedition bases associated with the first explorer expeditions of Captain Robert Falcon Scott (1901–1904), Sir Ernest Shackleton (1907–1909, 1914–1917), and Carsten Borchgrevink (1898–1900) of the Ross Sea region of Antarctica. Links on the site take visitors to the history of the expeditions, YouTube videos on the race to the Pole and the Project Architect Pip Cheshire about Captain Scott's base at Cape Evans, published scientific papers, and a gallery of historic and modern photographs of Cape Adare, Hut Point, Cape Royds, and Cape Evans and of historical artifacts.

An Antarctica Time Line: 1519–1959
http://www.south-pole.com/p0000052.htm

This site provides the history of the exploration of the Antarctica region dating from 1519 to 1959, listing major historical events. Embedded in the text are links to information about important explorers, including Jean-Baptiste Charles Bouvet de Lozier, James Cook, and James Clark Ross, along with pictures of their ships. Images of Operation Deep Freeze (1955–1998) and the expeditions of Wilkes, Byrd, and Paul Siple are included. The site is sponsored by the American Society of Polar Philatelists.

Maps of Antarctica—Described by R.V. Tooley and Illustrated
http://www.antarctic-circle.org/tooley.htm

Posted on this site is an interesting paper by the famous carto-historian R.V. Toole. It is one of the few efforts to describe how Antarctica has been depicted by cartographers over the centuries. It is hosted on the Antarctic Circle website. Tooley is deceased, and at present the holder of the rights is unknown.

Scott Polar Research Institute—Picture Library
http://www.spri.cam.ac.uk/library/pictures/

The Scott Polar Research Institute was founded in 1920, in Cambridge, England, as a memorial to Captain Robert Falcon Scott, RN, and his four companions, who died returning from the South Pole in 1912. The Institute is an international center for research and reference in a variety of fields related to polar environments—historical, scientific, and social. The SPRI Picture Library houses one of the world's most comprehensive collections of historical photographs of the Polar Regions. Freeze Frame, a digitization project, brings together photographs from Arctic and Antarctic expeditions of explorers and scientists. It also has a marvelous collection of modern photographs taken by scientists and researchers working in the field. The site offers links to a searchable database of images and photographs of interest, including biographical images, historical photographs, people and places of Antarctica, and images of the historical expeditions.

Scott Polar Research Institute—Polar Museum
http://www.spri.cam.ac.uk/museum

Polar Museum holds a unique collection of artifacts, journals, paintings, photographs, clothing, equipment, maps, and other materials illustrating polar exploration and polar science. The museum contains over 600 objects, including hunting implements, domestic utensils, and art, dating from the eighteenth century to the 1980s.

ANTARCTICA

Alfred Wegener Institute
http://www.awi.de/en/news/images_video_audio/image_galleries

The Alfred Wegener Institute for Polar and Marine Research holds a comprehensive video archive covering most fields of its main research topics. Most of the material was filmed by researchers on expedition. There is also a gallery of photos (e.g., *Life Below Ice Shelves*) and pictures of the New and the Current German Antarctic Research Station. Explore the site for other pictures of ships, stations, and aircraft and for audio interviews (although in German).

Australian Antarctic Division
http://www.aad.gov.au/default.asp

The Australian Antarctic Division leads Australia's Antarctic program. This site contains links to research and photos on topics such as the environment, marine ecosystems, the ocean, animals, geology, icebergs, plants, and weather. Read articles of interest in *The Australian Antarctica Magazine* online. Articles are embedded with links to photos. View live webcams, exhibitions, whale research, and a picture gallery. There is also a link to information about the British, Australian, and New Zealand Antarctic Research Expedition (1929–1931).

Boreal Wilderness Institute
http://boreal.net/BorealLinks/arctic-antarctic-links.shtml

This is an educational site for wilderness training. However, within the site one can learn about the history of Antarctic exploration. A bibliography of books provides a synopsis of each book as well as publication information. There are also links to additional resources, such as Shackleton's book *South*, which can be read online: under "Arctic and Antarctic Explorer Articles," select the "Ernest Shackleton" link and then under "Additional Resources" click on "South; The Story of the Shackleton Expedition." One can also view photographs and information on other explorers, such as Roald Amundsen, by selecting the appropriate link on the main webpage.

Byrd Polar Research Center Archival Program
http://library.osu.edu/sites/archives/polar/byrd/byrd.php

The Ohio State University maintains the Byrd Polar Research Center Archival Program, which contains the papers of Admiral Richard E. Byrd. The "Go to Online Exhibits" link provides access to exhibits such as *Under the North Pole: The Voyage of the Nautilus (75th Anniversary of the Wilkins-Ellsworth Trans-Arctic Submarine Expedition)*; *Conquering the Ice (75th Anniversary of Admiral Richard E. Byrd's South Pole Flight November 1929)*; *Echoes in the Ice (Exploration and Science in Antarctica)*; and *Admiral Byrd's 1926 North Pole Flight (A Commemoration of the 75th Anniversary of Admiral Richard E. Byrd's North Pole Flight May 9, 1926–May 9, 2001)*. The link "Richardson Films Preserved" provides access to two films from the Harrison H. Richardson Collection (the meteorological observer on Byrd's third expedition to Antarctica (U.S. Antarctic Service Expedition, 1939–1941) believed to be some of the first color footage shot in Antarctica. From this site one can also link to the university's digital repository *The Knowledge Bank* for photographs and information on the 1925–1935 and 1939–1956 expeditions.

Ice Station POLarstern (ISPOL)—6 November 2004–19 January 2005
http://www.ispol.de/index.html

ISPOL was a multinational, interdisciplinary study organized by the Alfred Wegener Institute for Polar and Marine Research, Germany, involving glaciologists, biologists, oceanographers, and meteorologists from different institutes and nations. It was a "field experiment designed to improve our understanding of the role of early summer physical and biological atmosphere–ice–ocean interactions in the western Weddell Sea." View the Cruise Diary and many photographs of life on the ice, including penguins and seals, and of the crew at work. Link to the history of the second German Antarctic Expedition (1911–1913) and the Trans-Antarctic Expedition (1914–1916) led by Sir Ernest Henry Shackleton.

NASA Goddard Space Flight Center—Global Observatory—Image of the Day
http://earthobservatory.nasa.gov/IOTD/view.php?id=36736

Earth Observatory is part of the EOS Project Science Office located at NASA Goddard Space Flight Center. View a photo of Antarctic Warming Trends (posted January 23, 2009). There is a search box for finding other photographs related to Antarctica. Additional search options are to browse by topic (e.g., atmosphere, snow, and ice) or by date, spanning 1999 to 2010. The webmaster is Goran Halusa.

National Library of Australia
http://catalogue.nla.gov.au/Search/Home?lookfor=Antarctica&filter[]=format:AllDigi

The National Library of Australia's coverage of Antarctica includes over 1,048 great pictures, maps, manuscript images, books, and audio recordings. This well-constructed website allows one to narrow a search to a particular format (e.g., pictures, maps, manuscripts, books, and audio). One can also search by subject area, such as Australasian Antarctic Expedition (1911–1914) or the British Antarctic Expedition (1907–

1909), or narrow a search to a series of private collections, such as the Sir Douglas Mawson Collection of Antarctic Photography. The site also contains reading materials about the items in several languages.

National Library of New Zealand
http://www.natlib.govt.nz/about-us/search?SearchableText+antarctica

Enter "Antarctica" in the search box to retrieve a number of items in various formats specific to Antarctica. There are digital books, maps, drawings, paintings, prints, cartoons, government publications, manuscripts, newspapers, photographs, and more to explore.

NOVA—Warnings from the Ice
http://www.pbs.org/wgbh/nova/warnings

NOVA, one of the highest rated science series on television, originally broadcast "Warnings from the Ice" on April 21, 1998. Through text and images, scientists explain the threat of disappearing coastal ice to the world's coastlines. This is an educational site for teachers as well as for laymen. The site features an Antarctic Almanac, Ice Timeline, and a Teacher's Guide. Also on the NOVA site one can access other related programs, including "Arctic Dinosaurs," "Extreme Ice," and "Fastest Glacier." This website was produced for PBS Online by WGBH Educational Foundation.

Royal Geographical Society
http://images.rgs.org

The Royal Geographical Society's Antarctic Collection, accessible from this website, contains over 1,500 images. There are maps and photographs of explorers, their ships, camps, artifacts, an ice cavern, glaciers, and more. Each item is identified. Copies of images can be ordered.

Scientific Committee on Antarctic Research (SCAR)
http://www.scar.org

SCAR provides information about the Antarctic Treaty, including reports and articles about the Antarctic (many in PDF format), links to maps, statistics, photographs, and background on research groups. View such items as the *Atlas of Antarctic Sea Ice Drift* and the *Map of Stations in Antarctica* by clicking on "Antarctic Information."

United States Antarctic Program—Antarctic Photo Library
http://photolibrary.usap.gov/

This website of the National Science Foundation's Office of Polar Program contains a photo archive with categories such as "Science," "Transportation," "Historical" (which contains a photo of a letter from Dwight D. Eisenhower to Amundsen and Scott), and "Wildlife" in Antarctica. Access to *The Antarctic Sun,* a newspaper "published during the austral summer at McMurdo Station, Antarctica," as well as video clips, maps, and webcams, is also provided.

United States Antarctic Resource Center (USARC)
http://www.usgs.gov/

The USARC, located at the U.S. Geological Survey (USGS) in Reston, Virginia, maintains the nation's most comprehensive collection of Antarctic aerial photography, maps, charts, satellite imagery, and technical reports. The USGS is a multidisciplinary science organization focused on biology, geography, geology, geospatial information, and water and devoted to the study of the landscape, natural resources, and the natural hazards that threaten man. Tabs at the top of the webpage provide the links to research, photographs, and other resources. Select "Maps, Imagery, and Publications" to access "Maps," "Aerial Photography and Satellite Imagery," "Publications," "Related Data," and a video and image gallery that includes video, audio, and podcasts. This is a great site for scientific study and for educational purposes. Select the tab "Hazards" to view, for example, "Earthquake Hazards," "Volcano Hazards," and "Coastal and Marine Geology." Other tabs include "Newsroom," "Education," and "Library."

Virtual Antarctica
http://www.doc.ic.ac.uk/~kpt/terraquest/antarctica/

The TerraQuest Expedition to Antarctica was launched in December 1995. This site archives the scientists' journals, photos, and routes and includes intriguing information on the history and science of Antarctica. Review the ship's log, a history of expeditions, and issues in ecology, maps of Antarctica, and the Antarctica Treaty. TerraQuest is a Joint Adventure of Mountain Travel-Sobek and WorldTravel Partners.

Chapter 4

Asia

INTRODUCTION

The continent of Asia covers about 30 percent of the world's landmass and includes 44 countries, islands, and dependencies. China and India are the most inhabited countries. Opinions differ as to what countries today make up Asia and the Middle East. The Russian landmass west of the Ural Mountains is considered a part of Asia. It is referred to as "European Russia" because of its culture, politics, and proximity to Europe. Turkey and Taiwan are also considered to be part of the Asian continent. This chapter reviews the development of digitization efforts broadly for the countries of Asia and the issues related to its development.

There is a wide range of differences among the digitization efforts of the major Asian countries. Digital collections that reflect the cultures and history of Asia depend on many factors. To begin digitization projects, institutions must have sufficient technology, computers, scanners and other equipment, preservation materials, trained personnel, and financial support. The less developed countries need to create a community of specialized people to do this work and to build an infrastructure to link them together (Shoaf, 2007). A report in *The Economist* in 2007 on technology in India and China stated, "India has only 24 personal computers for every 1,000 people and fewer than three broadband connections" (Cox, 2007). Most information professionals are ready to make the transition with the new technologies but need the opportunity to learn and to connect with the rest of the world. For example, in the South Asian region a barrier to the development of digital collections exists within the information profession itself. Insufficient experience, lack of technological skills, outdated training for library professionals, and government infrastructures that ban or inhibit the development of library networks block the way for developing new services and resources (Goswami and Jain, 2008).

The ability to develop wonderful digitized collections requires cultural and historical materials. A look at Asian history reveals that many of its countries do not have a library or an institution holding such items. Valuable artifacts, documents, and other materials have been destroyed, and some types were never even produced during some cultural periods. For example, Indonesia, like several other Asian countries, historically did not have a dominant written tradition and had a poor appreciation of these resources. Some records and documents were in the possession of the ruling or intellectual branches of society and therefore may no longer exist.

More recently other issues have prevented the development of collections. These surround the political and social structures that impact the role of librarians. In Indonesia, the National Library of Indonesia, a branch of the government, experienced a repressive spirit going back to the 1940s of the New Order regime until more recently. However, in this country change is taking place as democracy grows, empowering new local societies (Tjieka, 2008). Conversely, there even exists a lack of support from the government in China, a country with rich digital collections. In a survey distributed to libraries, archives, and information centers in 14 of the provinces in China, two distinct problems were identified. First, the government has not fully recognized the importance of preserving digital resources, leaving a gap in training and in the management of digital preservation. Second, government departments lack any guidelines for such projects (Liu and Yang, 2007). In the 2008 World Olympics opening ceremonies held in Beijing, the Chinese displayed a magnificent use of technology and their capabilities. Hopefully, the same skills and desire to display their capabilities will be carried over into supporting digitization projects for their ancient cultures and heritage and they will come to appreciate their heritage and share it with the world.

The past few years have witnessed a rapid development in information technologies, especially in the areas of digitization and digital libraries, as a way to improve the conditions in Indonesia and other developing countries. An example of this is the Desa Informasi (Information Village) website, a model for preserving and disseminating indigenous knowledge. Instituted at Petra Christian University, it is an institutional repository in the form of a digital library containing student and faculty published works for research and teaching that show the intellectual life of the institution (Tjieka, 2007). Online are student theses, scientific journals published by the various academic departments, and the Petra@rt Gallery: Works of Art by the Campus Communities (Tjieka, 2007). This project led to the Surabaya Memory Collection, documenting the historical and cultural heritage of this city. Another major development in Indonesia is the Ganesha Digital Library (GDL), which became the Indonesian Digital Library Network (IDLN), the first digital library network in Indonesia. It links to digitized documents in 20 Indonesian academic libraries (Sulistyo-Basuki, 2004). A rare instance of a privately funded smaller cultural institution in Thailand is the Ban Jalae Hill Life Tribe and Culture Center (Russo and Watkins, 2005). Its website provides short videos and pictures of the native culture, daily life, the tribes, and their people. It features digital storytelling, folk music, community interviews, and documentation of traditional festivals. These are examples of change. Many of the countries in Asia are still in the early years of digitization projects. Slowly librarians' attitudes are changing, and they are beginning to understanding how important it is to identify and preserve items related to their national heritages. Recent focus is on existing libraries and institutions to develop digital collections to preserve regional history and culture. Asian countries that are backed by governmental support for technology, training, and building of the necessary infrastructure are gaining opportunities to take their rightful place on the web.

Developments in U.S. libraries devoted to East Asian countries are also noteworthy. In the United States over 80 North American prestigious universities have East Asian libraries or collections in Chinese, Japanese, and Korean languages. Collectively they contain 17 million print items and 1 million nonprint items, and about 350,000 items are being added each year. Items include rare books, manuscripts, and specialized materials. The pressure on these libraries and collections to keep up with twenty-first-century trends is motivating them to move from a print tradition to a digital and networked future through mass digitization so that Asians on both continents and around the world will have access to Asian history, culture, and life (Zhou, 2009). This effort broadens man's ability to access Asian materials from anywhere.

At present, worldwide institutions like UNESCO (United Nations Educational Scientific and Cultural Organization), with its Memory of the World Programme, encourage Asian countries to preserve their cultural and natural heritage and provide venues for making their heritage available online. Through UNESCO's Memory of the World Programme one can learn about many of the Asian countries, including Korea, Malaysia, Mongolia, Nepal, Japan, Iran, India, China, and Afghanistan, online. Other institutions, such as the Library of Congress, the University of Wisconsin Digital Collections, and various national libraries, around the world have also compiled digital collections containing photographs, images, documents, and videos illustrating various Asian cultures. This chapter lists many of these individual projects.

References

Cox, S. 2007. "High-Tech Hopefuls: A Special Report on Technology in India and China." *The Economist* 385: 3881.

Goswami, P.R., and P.K. Jain. 2008. "Information Professionals in the South Asian Region: The Challenges Ahead." *Bulletin of the American Society for Information Science and Technology* 34, no. 3: 26–29. http://www.asis.org/Bulletin/Feb-08/FebMar08_GoswamiJain.html.

Liu, J.Z., and D.L. Yang. 2007. "Status of the Preservation of Digital Resources in China: Results of a Survey." *Program: Electronic Library and Information Systems* 41, no. 1: 35–46. http://www.emeraldinsight.com/Insight/ViewContentServlet?contentType=Article&Filename=Published/EmeraldFullTextArticle/Articles/2800410103.html.

Russo, Angelina, and Jerry Watkins. 2005. "Digital Cultural Communication: Enabling New Media and Co-creation in South-East Asia." *International Journal of Education and Development Using Information and Communication Technology* 1, no. 4 (December): 4–17. http://0-www.proquest.com.library.dowling.edu/.

Shoaf, Eric C. 2007. "A Global View of Sharing Digitized Information: An Interview with Ching-chih Chen." *Library Administration and Management* 21, no. 4: 169–171.

Sulistyo-Basuki, L. 2004. "Digitization of Collections in Indonesian Academic Libraries." *Program: Electronic Library and Information Systems* 38, no. 3: 194–200. http://www.emeraldinsight.com/0033-0337.htm.

Tjieka, L. (Aditya Nugraha). 2007. "Desa Informasi: The Role of Digital Libraries in the Preservation and Dissemination of Indigenous Knowledge." *Bulletin of the American Society for Information Science and Technology*, June: 37–42. http://0-www.proquest.com.library.dowling.edu/.

————. 2008. "Glancing at the Rearview Mirror, Focusing on the Road Ahead: Library and Information Professionals in Indonesia." *Bulletin of the American Society for Information Science and Technology*, February: 43–46. http://0-www.proquest.com .library.dowling.edu/.

Zhou, Peter X. 2009. "Managing Change: East Asian Libraries in Transition." *Library Management* 30, no. 6/7 (February/March): 383–392. http://www.emeraldinsight .com/0143-5124.htm.

CONTINENT

Arnold Arboretum of Harvard University
http://nrs.harvard.edu/urn-3:hul.eresource:bciedigi

The Botanical and Cultural Images of Eastern Asia, 1907–1927, collection contains over 4,500 images of plant life, people, and scenery in Eastern Asia created by early twentieth-century plant collectors such as John George Jack, Ernest Henry Wilson, Frank Nicholas Meyer, William Purdom, Joseph Hers, and Joseph Charles Francis Rock.

Asian & Pacific Studies—Historical Photographs
http://coombs.anu.edu.au/WWWVLPages/AsianPages/Asian-Historical-Photographs .html

Begun in 2008 and edited by Dr. T. Matthew Ciolek, Canberra Research School of Pacific and Asian Studies (RSPAS), Australian National University, this webpage is a portal to over 80 online collections of Asian and Pacific images from the Asian Studies WWW Virtual Library and the Pacific Studies WWW Virtual Library.

Asian Historical Architecture
http://www.orientalarchitecture.com/index.php

This is a wonderful photographic journey for anyone with an interest in Oriental architecture. Many have contributed to this collection of photographs that can be searched individually by country. There are almost 15,000 photographs from over 700 sites in 21 countries (Afghanistan, Bhutan, Cambodia, China, India, Indonesia, Iran, Japan, North Korea, South Korea, Laos, Malaysia, Myanmar, Nepal, Pakistan, Philippines, Singapore, Sri Lanka, Taiwan, Thailand, and Vietnam). Some virtual tours are included. First select a country, and then select a city within that country. This will lead to a visual index of photographs taken in that city. Each city collection provides information about the contributors.

Calisphere—California Cultures: Asian Americans
http://www.calisphere.universityofcalifornia.edu/calcultures/ethnic_groups/ethnic2 .html

Calisphere, a project of the California Digital Library (CDL), provides access to over 150,000 items, which include but are not limited to photographs, documents, newspaper pages, political cartoons, works of art, and diaries. Within this project are selected primary California Asian American (Chinese, Filipino, Japanese, Korean, Cambodian, Hmong, Laotian, Southeast Asian, and Vietnamese) resources. A sampling of the wide range of topics covered include the Gold Rush Era, the Chinese Exclusion Act of 1882, opera and theater, and social conditions and customs. Also available are links to newspapers and to lesson plans for grades 4–12.

Center for South Asian Studies
http://artsandsciences.virginia.edu/soasia/resources/other.html

This webpage links to dozens of digital collections. The content comes from many institutions, including the University of Virginia, while the infrastructure is supported solely by the University of Virginia. For example, follow the link to the Tibetan and Himalayan Digital Library to access one of the first digital libraries to cover the geographical, cultural, and linguistic regions associated with Tibetan and Himalayan cultures. Other links to South Asia resources at the University of Virginia provide access to electronic newspapers, journals, newsletters, films, and videos. View a video of Romilar Thapar's lecture "Somanatha" (in October 2003), a sacred temple of the ninth and tenth centuries. Somanatha endured raids and destruction of its idol by Mamu. The event is associated with the rift between the Hindus and the Muslims that persists today.

Central Intelligence Agency—World Factbook
https://www.cia.gov/library/publications/the-world-factbook/index.html

The CIA World Factbook provides good background information on countries throughout the world, including cultural and historic points of interest. View a country's flag, map, images, and photographs of historical sites. Click on a region in Asia on the interactive map to access links related to countries in that region.

Digital South Asia Library
http://dsal.uchicago.edu/images/

The Digital South Asia Library is a consortium of universities and colleges in the United States at which scholars actively engage in teaching and research about India. The site is hosted by the University of Chicago and currently lists five collections. The Hensley Photo Library, Keagle Photograph Library, and Bond Photograph Library collections contain images taken by WWII servicemen. The focus of the American Institute of Indian Studies collection is primarily art and architecture. The images maintained in the collection of the Government College of Arts and Crafts (Chennai) are primarily of people, places, and artifacts from different parts of India. The site is continuing to expand, with a new collection under development.

East and Southeast Asian Sources
http://libguides.miami.edu/eastandsoutheastasia

This guide is a portal to selected East and Southeast Asian (Brunei, Cambodia, China, East Timor [Timor-Leste], Indonesia, Japan, Laos, Malaysia, Myanmar [Burma], North Korea, Philippines, Singapore, South Korea, Taiwan, Thailand, and Vietnam) print and electronic resources. Click on a country's tab to view a host of resources, including art, drawings, prints, maps, slides, videos, virtual histories, reports, and documents, depending on what resources are available for a particular country. This site was compiled by Chella Vaidyanathan, a University of Miami Libraries subject librarian.

East Asian Collection
http://digicoll.library.wisc.edu/EastAsian/

The East Asian Collection contains historical images of early twentieth-century China. This website, part of the larger University of Wisconsin Digital Collections, contains several subcollections, each with a unique focus.

▶ **Ainu Komonjo (18th & 19th Century Records)—Ohnuki Collection**
http://digicoll.library.wisc.edu/EastAsian/subcollections/JapanRiceAbout.html

The books in this collection depict the Ainu hunting–gathering way of life. The books were authored by explorers and scholars ordered to do so by the Japanese government. They were written on rice paper and contain original illustrations and wood block prints. Select "Browse Ainu Komonjo" to view over 40 listings in the collections. There is a Japanese description and an English translation for each item. To view a book, select one of the Japanese titles and then select the link under "Contents" at the bottom of the book's page. The book can be viewed page by page by clicking on "Page" at the top and following the arrows to each successive page. Text is in Japanese.

▶ **The China in the 1930s Collection/Tianjin Collection**
http://digital.library.wisc.edu/1711.dl/EastAsian.China1930s

This collection contains predominantly military photographs depicting such periods as the Sino-Japanese Conflict (1937–1945) and the WWII theater in China. It also includes photos of both city and rural life and architecture. A description of each photo is obtained by clicking on the photo.

▶ **The William Hervie Dobson Collection**
http://digital.library.wisc.edu/1711.dl/EastAsian.Dobson

Dr. William Hervie Dobson, a Presbyterian missionary, doctor, and resident of the Yeungkong area in southern China, documented the life of the people he lived among. Click "Search the Collection" to access over 200 photographs.

Forced Migration Online (FMO)
http://www.forcedmigration.org/

FMO provides access to a wide range of resources documenting "the movements of refugees and internally displaced people (people displaced by conflicts) as well as people displaced by natural or environmental disasters, chemical or nuclear disasters, famine, or development projects." Click on the "Digital Library" link and then type in a particular Asian country, such as China or India, to access texts (reports, papers, documents), videos, podcasts, and images.

Gertrude Bell Archive
http://www.gerty.ncl.ac.uk/

Gertrude Bell (1868–1926) photographed Middle Eastern archaeological sites (many of which have now disappeared) as she traveled throughout the Middle East as a British Intelligence person during the First World War. Later she was a key political figure for Iraq. Her huge collection of photographs includes Syria, Turkey, Iraq, India, Korea, Japan, and Saudi Arabia. Click on the links at the top of the webpage to view photographs, diaries, and letters.

Libraries of Asia Pacific Directory
http://www.nla.gov.au/apps/lapsdir?action=LapsBrowse

This website provides an alphabetical list of libraries for countries in the Asia and Pacific region. The basic services, collections, and contact personnel are described for each library. A limited number of libraries have online digital collections. This is an initiative of the Conference of Directors of National Libraries of Asia and Oceania (CDNLAO) and is supported by the National Library of Australia. Two libraries with digital collections are listed here.

▶ **Manuskrip Malayu Pusaka Gemilang**
　http://www.pnm.my/manuskrip/default.htm

　This is a great website to study the glorious Malay civilization. View historical manuscripts produced from the fourteenth to the twentieth centuries. Select the "English Version" tab at the top left of the page for a description of the website. Then click "Collection" and then one of the sublinks—"Folk Literature," "Malay Poetry (Syair)," "Malay Poetry (Nazam)," "Islamic Text," "Medicine," "Beliefs and Amulet," "Laws," "History," or "Custom"—to view individual works. Most writings are in Malaysian.

▶ **MyLib**
　http://mylib.pnm.my/

　The MyLib portal is a pilot project of the National Digital Library Initiative (PERDANA) in an effort to promote community knowledge sharing. It is a great site with links to "e-books" (many are free); "e-newspapers" (in English, Malaysian, Chinese, and Tamil); "e-reports" (on such topics as business and the economy, health, science, and environment and nature); "e-maps"; "Multimedia" (Malaysian resources, including a photo gallery, video, and global radio and television resources such as CNN, Discovery.com, Canadian news, and BBC Online); "Theses and Dissertations"; "Conferences and Proceedings"; and "Institutional Repositories." MyLib was inaugurated on June 27, 2000, by Deputy Prime Minister Dato' Seri Abdullah Ahmad Badawi, at Cyberview Lodge, MDC, Cyberjaya.

The Margarita S. Studemeister Digital Collections in International Conflict Management
http://www.usip.org/resources-tools/digital-collections

The United States Institute of Peace (USIP) digital library is a collection of peace agreements and truth commission documents gathered with the intention of providing worldwide access to resources dealing with prevention, management, and resolution of international conflict. In addition to audio files and video links for presentations on specific countries such as Afghanistan, Sri Lanka, North Korea, and Iran, there are interviews (available as full texts) with individuals who are involved in stability operations in Iraq, the Sudan, and Afghanistan.

Military Education Research Library Network (MERLN)
http://merln.ndu.edu/

The MERLN website, maintained by the National Defense University Library in Washington, DC, provides access to U.S. policy statements on selected topics, digitized full-text papers, lectures and legislation, and links to other military resources. Regions covered include East Asia and the Pacific, Near East and North Africa, and South and Central Asia. Links within the regions go to recent documents and information about the region; U.S. policies and current news; human rights and refugees; oil, energy, and natural resources; politics and governments; security, terrorism, and extremism; news sources and online journals; and web resources.

Portal to Asian Internet Resources
http://digicoll.library.wisc.edu/PAIR/

This gateway to online resources is organized by broad-ranging topics such as agriculture, business and industry, demography and population, development, economy, education, history, human rights, and popular culture. Search by "Featured Resources," "Keyword," or "Atlas." Records retrieved are text descriptions along with an icon to connect to the webpage for that record. Depending on the items, there may be photographs, illustrations, and other resources. Some foreign-language websites may provide the option to translate the text into English through a Google toolbar feature.

South Asian Studies
http://libguides.miami.edu/southasia

This guide is a portal to selected South Asian (Afghanistan, Bangladesh, Bhutan, India, the Maldives, Nepal, Pakistan, and Sri Lanka) print and electronic resources. It was compiled by Chella Vaidyanathan, a University of Miami Libraries subject librarian. Search by either country or type of resource to view wonderful photographs of historical buildings and sites. Click on a country's tab at the top of the webpage to view resources for that country. For example, "Afghanistan" links to the Afghanistan Digital Library and its collections and to an Afghanistan Old Photos collection with images of Afghan kings, historical engravings, Buddhas, and ancient banknotes. Sources for the collections are provided.

Southeast Asia Digital Library
http://sea.lib.niu.edu/rescountry.html

This digital library, which is maintained and continually updated by the Northern Illinois University Libraries, contains items such as photographs, videos, books, indexes, manuscripts and reference materials, and general information about and Internet links for Brunei, Cambodia, East Timor, Indonesia, Laos, Malaysia, Myanmar (Burma), Philippines, Singapore, Thailand, and Vietnam. Library materials are organized by country, language, project, and institution.

UNESCO—Underwater Cultural Heritage in Asia-Pacific Waters
http://www.unescobkk.org/culture/our-projects/underwater-cultural-heritage-movable
    -heritage-and-museums/underwater-cultural-heritage-in-asia-pacific-waters/

UNESCO is a major player in the international effort to protect the underwater cultural heritage being looted in Asia-Pacific waters. Read about these efforts and view images of some rare archaeological finds buried beneath the sea.

University of Hawai'i at Manoa Libraries—Asia Collection
http://www.hawaii.edu/asiaref/

The Asia Collection, which is housed at the Hamilton Library of the University of Hawai'i at Manoa, contains materials that date back to 1920. Within this collection are several subcollections featuring Asia, China and Taiwan, Japan, Korea, Philippines, and South Asia, including the countries of Afghanistan, Bangladesh, India, Nepal, Pakistan, and Sri Lanka. New digital collections are highlighted at the bottom of the homepage. When searching by a country, such as China, the webpage retrieved will list a number of resources. Some of these are restricted. However, a link to the Lian Huan Hua Collection leads to a site displaying a number of Chinese picture storybooks beautifully illustrated. Searching through the selections listed is necessary in order to find that gem of a collection.

▶ **Asia at Work: A Collection of Digital Images**
http://libweb.hawaii.edu/libdept/asia/books/

With photographs, drawings, and paintings from books published in the early twentieth century, this digitized collection illustrates the occupations of the peoples of Asia and the environments in which they live. Countries included are Burma, Cambodia, China, India, Indonesia, Japan, Korea, Laos, Malaysia, Singapore, Thailand, and Vietnam.

▶ **Opium in Asia**
http://libweb.hawaii.edu/libdept/asia/opium/

View photographs and maps illustrating the control, cultivation, distribution, processing, reform, social effects, and users of opium and the impact opium usage has had on Asia. Several articles and a number of books (in PDF format), for example, *Drugging a Nation* (Samuel Merwin, 1908), have been digitized and made available here.

University of Washington—History: Asia
http://guides.lib.washington.edu/history-asia

To view maps, photographs, and images, select "East Asia," "South Asia," or "Southeast Asia." This site, hosted by the University of Washington, is a portal to resources including but not limited to teaching guides, interactive maps, translated works, ceremonial writings, and photographs. There are also tabs to access resources by format—articles, books, and encyclopedias.

University of Washington—International Collections Database
http://content.lib.washington.edu/icweb/index.html

This digital database contains hundreds of selected photographs and postcards dating from the 1870s to the 1930s illustrating Asia and South America, with particular emphasis on China, India, Japan, and other Southeast Asian countries. The images depict historical events, typical street scenes, and native peoples in traditional dress.

University of Wisconsin-Milwaukee Libraries—Digital Collections
http://www4.uwm.edu/Library/digilib/

Currently the University of Wisconsin-Milwaukee Libraries (UWM) provides access to 16 digital collections containing almost 50,000 photographic images, maps, and books that come initially from the American Geographical Society Library, the Archives, Special Collections, and the Curriculum Library collections. With the exception of the Peck School of the Arts Slide Collection, which can be accessed only by UWM students, faculty, and staff, the collections are accessible online.

▶ **American Geographical Society Library Photo Archive**
http://www.uwm.edu/Libraries/digilib/agsphoto/html/about.html

View a selection of mid-nineteenth-century historical photos of Afghanistan, Egypt, Jordan, Korea, Thailand, and Nepal drawn from the American Geographical Society Library Print Collection, Harrison Forman Collection, Robert W. McColl Collection, and the Edna Schaus Sorensen and Clarence W. Sorensen Collections. Select "Browse" to view almost 8,000 photographs. To limit photographs to a specific country click on "Advanced Search" and type in the name of the country, for example, "Korea." To the left of the photographs is a list of subjects within the photos to limit further results. For example, searching for "North Korea" retrieved over 100 photos, and limiting it to the subject of "Mountains" retrieved around 20 photographs of mountains in Korea.

▶ **Cities**
http://www.uwm.edu/Libraries/digilib/cities/

The Cities Collection contains over 6,000 photographic slides focusing on architecture, city life, people, transportation, and urban development. They feature both present-day and ancient cities and deserted settlements. The photographs were taken between 1942 and 1994 by Harrison Forman and Harold Mayer and are drawn from their respective collections.

▶ **Tibet**
http://www.uwm.edu/Library/digilib/tibet/index.html

The collection consists of photos drawn from the Harrison Forman Collection (1932–1937) as well as 50 taken of central Tibet and Lhasa by two Mongolian Buddhists. The collection also includes four plans of the city of Lhasa and six historical maps of Tibet.

▶ **Transportation Around the World: 1911–1993**
http://www.uwm.edu/Library/digilib/transport/records/about.html#content

This collection contains 650 images depicting various means of transportation in 79 countries. The photographs originate from three collections: the Harrison Forman Collection, Harold Mayer Collection, and American Geographical Society Library Print Collection.

World Digital Library
http://www.wdl.org/en/

The World Digital Library's homepage displays a map of the world, including links to "Central and South Asia," "East Asia," and "Southeast Asia." The links provide access to prints, photographs, digitized images of manuscripts, books, and maps. Searching can be limited to place (specific country), time period, type of format, or institution providing the image. A search bar on each region's main page allows narrowing items to specific countries in the regions.

AFGHANISTAN

Afghanistan Digital Library
http://afghanistandl.nyu.edu/about.html

In 2005, the Afghanistan Digital Library began to recover and restore rare and disappearing Afghan publications from the years 1871 to 1930. The time period will be extended to include publications up through 1950. The publications, many of which reside in private collections, are being digitized and made available on the website. About 400 books have been completed. Ultimately the collection will include serials, documents, pamphlets, and manuals. The Afghanistan Digital Library is a project of New York University Libraries with the support of the National Endowment for the Humanities, the Reed Foundation, and the W.L.S. Spencer Foundation. The website is in English, but the materials are in Arabic.

Afghanistan: Images from the Harrison Forman Collection
http://www.uwm.edu/Library/digilib/afghan/

Harrison Forman (1904–1978) was a photographer who specialized in photographing the peoples, landscapes, and cultures of Asia, Indochina, the Middle East, South Pacific, Africa, and South America. This University of Wisconsin-Milwaukee Libraries collection focuses on Afghanistan in the late 1960s, the turbulent 1970s and 1980s, the Soviet invasion, and the Taliban rule. The almost 200 images are searchable by six topical categories: architecture, history, land, people, settlements, and transportation. Follow the "Map of Afghanistan" link at the top of the homepage to see images of Kabul, Hindu Kush, Mazar-e Shari, and other cities and regions.

Afghanistan Old Photos
http://www.afghanistan-photos.com/

View a collection of late nineteenth-century to early twentieth-century photographs. The photographs are of the Afghan cities Kabul, Kandahar, Bamiyan, and Jalalabad as well as Afghan royalty, monuments, and historic events.

Preserving and Creating Access to Unique Afghan Records
http://www.afghandata.org/

Documents related to the history, social history, economics, and culture of Afghanistan are accessible through this collection. The documents are primarily in Pashto and Dari. The project, which is funded by the National Endowment for the Humanities, is a collaboration between the University of Arizona Libraries and the Afghanistan Centre at Kabul University.

Revolutionary Association of the Women of Afghanistan (RAWA)
http://www.rawa.org/index.php

RAWA, the oldest political/social organization of Afghan women who have struggled for freedom and women's rights in Afghanistan since 1977, produced this wonderful site. There are hundreds of photographs of women and children; many links to images dealing with poverty, human rights violations, and atrocities aimed at women; movie clips, some of which are disturbing; and a photo album of the martyred Meena. This website offers a comprehensive view of human rights violations in this area of the world and will especially interest researchers who study women's rights issues.

ARMENIA

Armenian Historical Sources of the 5–15th Centuries
http://rbedrosian.com/hsrces.html

This personal webpage of an American contains criticisms and interpretations, as well as actual text translations, of selected Armenian historical sources. The site also contains links to maps, chronologies of Armenian history, and other selected writings. The creator has designated his personal work as freely available and distributable to the public.

Azad-Hye (Middle East Armenian Portal)
http://www.azad-hye.net/photos/photos.asp

This website was designed as an online meeting place and information exchange for Armenian people living in the Middle East. The link provided is to the photographic section of the website, where contributors can post groups of photos as albums for others to see. The content ranges from people at activities or events to locations, settings, and scenery.

BibliOdyssey—Armenian Manuscript
http://bibliodyssey.blogspot.com/2007/09/armenian-manuscript.html

This link is to full-page scans of a complete, ornate, twelfth-century Armenian manuscript titled *Ewangeliarz ze Skewry* (*Ewangeliarz lwowski*). The digital images actually reside at the National Digital Library of Poland; however, the manuscript was selected, highlighted, and described extensively in English on this blog, BibliOdyssey. BibliOdyssey highlights wonderful examples of print art, and a September 11, 2007, entry includes the illuminated Armenian manuscript. Users who prefer the Polish site can access it near the bottom of the BibliOdyssey blog entry, which also includes brief descriptions of the illustrations.

Goodspeed Manuscript Collection
http://goodspeed.lib.uchicago.edu/

The Goodspeed Collection encompasses 68 early Greek, Syriac, Ethiopic, Armenian, Arabic, and Latin manuscripts dating from the fifth to the nineteenth centuries. In addition to the manuscripts, 114 papyri fragments will also be digitized. The collection is searchable through several avenues. "Browse the Collection" by selecting the link "All Digitized Manuscripts" and then select a manuscript from the list. Click on "Thumbnails" to view images of pages, "Description" for information about the manuscript, and "Zoomable" to view larger images. Additional "Browse" links include "Title or

Type of Text," "Common Names of Manuscripts," "Places of Origin or Association," "Dates of Origin," "Languages," "Names of Individuals or Organizations," "Materials of Construction," "Imagery," and "Books of the Bible."

National Library of Australia—Stanford's "Treaty Map" of South Eastern Europe and Armenia
http://nla.gov.au/nla.map-rm3513

The National Library of Australia has digitized Edward Stanford's 1878 colored "Treaty Map" of South Eastern Europe and Armenia. The map displays the then-existing boundaries as well as the boundaries proposed in the Treaty of San Stefano between the Ottoman Empire and Russia after the Russo-Turkish War (1877–1878). Stanford was an important cartographer who published atlases for countries around the world in the latter 1800s.

AZERBAIJAN

Azerbaijan National Library
http://www.anl.az/index_e.php

View a collection of books online, such as *Heydar Aliev and National-Spiritual Values* by Adil Abdullah Al-Falah (in English) by clicking on the image of the book on the main webpage. Select "Electron Library" on the webpage for a list of digitized books or essays (in PDF format) that may be available in English, Russian, Persian, or Azeri. Some books are "forbidden" and not available online.

Central Intelligence Agency—World Factbook
https://www.cia.gov/library/publications/the-world-factbook/geos/aj.html

View the flag, a map, images, photographs, and information about Azerbaijan from the Central Intelligence Agency.

Forced Migration Online
http://repository.forcedmigration.org/?search=azerbaijan&start=0&rows=10

Access over 300 resources dealing with the conditions of Azerbaijan displacement and migration. Items include book chapters, evaluation reports, journal articles, field and research reports, case studies, occasional papers, discussion papers, conference reports, journal issues, bibliographies, and country reports. There are also links to online journals, photographs, audio podcasts (e.g., *Sahrawi Disappeared* and *Rwanda and the Great Lakes: A Personal View from the Oxfam Archive*), and a collection of videos (e.g., *Yemen: Refugees Crossing the Gulf of Aden* and *Iraqis in Egypt: Time Is Running Out*).

BAHRAIN

Bahrain House of Photography
http://www.gvpedia.com/Bahrain/Bahrain-House-of-Photography-Top-Photographic-Museum.aspx

View photographs and interesting information about the country of Bahrain. This website was developed by the Global Village Publishing Company, and the photography is by Mr. Abdulla Al Khan. This is a commercial site with links to various topics about Bahrain. For example, the link "Arts and Culture" retrieves photographs of important sites in Bahrain with full descriptions.

Central Intelligence Agency—World Factbook
https://www.cia.gov/library/publications/the-world-factbook/geos/ba.html

View a map, images, and facts about Bahrain provided by the Central Intelligence Agency.

New York Public Library Digital Gallery
http://digitalgallery.nypl.org/nypldigital/dgkeysearchresult.cfm?keyword=bahrain

View portraits of pilgrims from Bahrain and photographs of Sheikh Mohamed bin Isa signing the guestbook at the New York World's Fair (1939–1940). Photographs and descriptions are provided by the New York Public Library Digital Gallery.

BANGLADESH

Central Intelligence Agency—World Factbook
https://www.cia.gov/library/publications/the-world-factbook/geos/bg.html

View a map, images, and facts about Bangladesh provided by the Central Intelligence Agency.

National Library of Australia—Bangladesh Envoy Hossain Ali Presents Letters of Credence in Canberra, 1972
http://nla.gov.au/nla.pic-an22676741

View photos of Bangladesh envoy Hossain Ali's 1972 meeting with Australian Governor-General Sir Paul Hasluck.

New York Public Library Digital Gallery
http://digitalgallery.nypl.org/nypldigital/dgkeysearchresult.cfm?keyword=bangladesh

View colored lithographs illustrating Brahmins saying their daily prayers, an eighteenth-century map of the Ganges River showing how it empties into the Bay of Bengal, and photographs depicting cremation or funeral rites on the Ganges River. This collection was found by typing in "Bangladesh" in the search box. Similar collections of photographs, maps, and illustrations can be found for other countries as well.

UNESCO World Heritage
http://whc.unesco.org/en/statesparties/bd

UNESCO plays an important role in preserving the cultural heritage of Bangladesh. The tab "Description" provides a number of historical sites for Bangladesh, with background information and images (e.g., the Historic Mosque City of Bagerhat, the Ruins of the Buddhist Vihara at Paharur, the Lalmai-Mainamati group of monuments, and the Lalbagh Fort). The tab "Documents" provides access to documents and publications related to the preservation of Bangladesh culture and history. At the top of the webpage select the tab "The List" to view an "Interactive Map" to more than 900 properties worldwide that UNESCO identifies as historical sites.

University of Wisconsin Digital Collections
http://uwdc.library.wisc.edu/index.shtml

This website has over 740 links to descriptions of a wide range of periodicals and annual reports. To view them, type in "Bangladesh" in the search box at the top of the webpage.

University of Wisconsin-Milwaukee Libraries—Digital Collections
http://collections.lib.uwm.edu/

View primarily black-and-white photographs of life in Dhaka, Bangladesh, circa 1950, plus several color photos of Chittagong and Dhaka taken during the 1960s. To view this collection, type in "Bangladesh" in the search box.

World Digital Library
http://www.wdl.org/en/search/gallery?ql=eng&s=bangladesh

A search for "Bangladesh" retrieved three items. View an early twentieth-century colored map depicting the British Empire presence in India prior to the creation of Pakistan; a 1760 work by William Watts titled *Memoirs of the Revolution in Bengal*, which is an account of the Battle of Plassey (1757); and the third edition (1772) of *A Voyage to the East Indies*, by author John Henry Grose. Included in the third edition is John Carmichael's narrative of his journey from Aleppo, Syria, to Basra, Iraq. Each work has both a written and an audio (click "Listen to this page") description.

BHUTAN

Central Intelligence Agency—World Factbook
https://www.cia.gov/library/publications/the-world-factbook/geos/bt.html

View a map, images, and facts about Bhutan provided by the U.S. Central Intelligence Agency.

Collection of Francoise Pommaret (Photos)
http://www.himalayanart.org/search/set.cfm?setID=185

The collection contains images of Himalayan art related to Bhutan. The images are provided by the Himalayan Art Resources Website (HAR), which is supported by the Shelley and Donald Rubin Foundation.

National Museum of Bhutan
http://www.nationalmuseum.gov.bt/museum-galleries.html

View images and descriptions of items reflecting the culture of Bhutan now online from the National Museum of Bhutan. Collections include Tshogshing lhakhang or "Tree of Life," a three-dimensional mandala reflecting the four schools of Buddhism; thangka paintings used in ceremonies or rituals; and *Arms and Armour*, an exhibit of traditional weapons (guns, cannons, swords, and bows and arrows).

World Digital Library
http://www.wdl.org/en/search/gallery?ql=eng&s=bhutan&x=0&y=0

A search for "Bhutan" retrieved two items. One is *Bhotan and the Story of the Dooar War* (1866) by David Field Rennie, a military surgeon who witnessed the attempt to appropriate Duârs from Bhutan. The other is a 1903 colored map of the British Empire rule in India. Both works have a written and an audio (click "Listen to this page") description.

BRUNEI DARUSSALAM

Southeast Asia Digital Library—Brunei
http://sea.lib.niu.edu/rescountry.html#brunei

The Southeast Asia Digital Library, maintained by the Northern Illinois University Libraries, provides access to digital library materials, Internet links, and general information about countries in Southeast Asia. There are two links for Brunei. The first provides information about Brunei, and the second provides further links to additional sites containing information and collections related to Brunei. The links are organized by subject and format, including government; political and social issues; news; history, culture, and religion; journals; and digital collections. Photographs, videos, books, manuscripts, and other resources are contained within the sites themselves.

University of Miami Libraries—East and Southeast Asian Studies
http://libguides.miami.edu/content.php?pid=22480&sid=220811

Access selected print and electronic resources in East and Southeast Asian Studies available through the University of Miami Libraries and collaborating open-access websites. Clicking the tab for Brunei leads to photographs of a stained-glass window and of the Sultan Omar Ali Saiffudin mosque in Brunei. There is also a list of places where additional information on Brunei can be found.

University of Wisconsin Digital Collections
http://uwdc.library.wisc.edu/index.shtml

Search for "Brunei" to access a list of digital resources, such as text-based materials (books, journal series, and manuscript collections), photographic images, slides, maps, prints, posters, and audio and video links. Select from the list by clicking on the URL icon to link to host sites. Each resource has a brief description.

World Digital Library
http://www.wdl.org/en/search/gallery?ql=eng&s=brunei

A search for "Brunei" retrieved two color maps of Borneo, the third largest island in the world. Brunei occupies part of the island along the northern coast. One map is dated 1881 and titled "Map of North Borneo." It depicts how the island was divided up between the Dutch, the Sultan of Sulu, the Sultan of Brunei, and the North Borneo Company. The second map, "Borneo," focuses on infrastructure developments in 1919. View images of the maps, and read or listen to a description of each.

BURMA—*SEE* MYANMAR

CAMBODIA

Southeast Asia Digital Library
http://sea.lib.niu.edu/rescountry.html#cambodia

Link to digital library materials, photographs, and Internet links, and learn general information about Cambodia.

University of Hawai'i at Manoa Libraries
http://libweb.hawaii.edu/libdept/asia/books/cambodia/cambodia1.htm

View late eighteenth- and early nineteenth-century black-and-white drawings that depict everyday life.

University of Southern Mississippi Libraries Digital Collection
http://digilib.usm.edu/cdm4/results.php?CISOOP1=all&CISOBOX1=cambodia&
    CISOFIELD1=CISOSEARCHALL&CISOOP2=exact&CISOBOX2=& CISOFIELD2=
    CISOSEARCHALL&CISOOP3=any&CISOBOX3=&CISOFIELD3=CISOSEARCHALL
    &CISOOP4=none&CISOBOX4=&CISOFIELD4=CISOSEARCHALL&CISOROOT=/
    cartoon&t=a

View political cartoon images in the AAEC (Association of American Editorial Cartoonists) Editorial Cartoon Collection. The cartoons appeared in the late 1960s through the mid-1970s. Subjects include Richard M. Nixon and the Republican National Committee (USA).

University of Wisconsin Digital Collections
http://uwdc.library.wisc.edu/index.shtml

Search for "Cambodia" to access 260 digital resources such as text-based materials (books, journal series, and manuscript collections), photographic images, slides, maps, prints, posters, and audio and video links.

University of Wisconsin-Milwaukee—Digital Collections
http://www4.uwm.edu/Library/digilib/

Search for "Cambodia" to view photographs of Angkor Wat (Angkor, Cambodia) and Phnum Pénh, a Buddhist high priest (ca. 1958); color maps of Indochina from 1892 to 1928; and photos of protests against the invasion of Cambodia taken in 1970 at the University of Wisconsin-Milwaukee campus.

CHINA (PEOPLE'S REPUBLIC OF CHINA)

Block Prints of the Chinese Revolution
http://diglib.princeton.edu/xquery?_xq=getCollection&_xsl=collection&_pid=
    chineseprints

This small collection of 30 poster-like block prints depicts the 1911 struggle between the Han Chinese and the Manchus. The prints are in both color and black and white and were donated by Princeton alumnus Donald Roberts. Select "Page Images" to view the first print, and scroll through the rest by clicking the "next" arrow icon. The images are maintained by the Princeton University Library Digital Collections.

Cartoons: British Cartoon Archive
http://www.cartoons.ac.uk/search/cartoon_item/China

View over 2,300 black-and-white cartoons related to China preserved in the British Cartoon Archive, University of Kent. Searches can be narrowed by artist (e.g., David Low, Keith Waite, Michael Cummings, Vicky [Victor Weisz], or Nicholas Garland), publications in which the cartoons appeared, what important figure is being depicted, and specific countries.

Cartoons of Thomas Nast: Reconstruction, Chinese Immigration, Native Americans, Gilded Era
http://www.csub.edu/~gsantos/cat15.html

View cartoons on Chinese immigration to the United States created between 1868 and 1883. These images are on the California State University-Bakersfield website.

China Christian Colleges and Universities Image Database
http://research.yale.edu:8084/ydlchina/index.jsp

This is a gateway to more than 7,500 photographs and films from the Yale Divinity Library archives of the United Board for Christian Higher Education in Asia and the Lingnan University Board of Trustees. Scholars will find this collection a unique source of information on education, medical work, architecture, and society in early twentieth-century China. Click on "list of subject headings" to view a list of search terms you can use. Type a term (for example, "museums") in "Keyword" and then click on "Search" to retrieve images. Each image contains a brief description, the date collected, and a source.

The Chinese in California, 1850–1925
http://lcweb2.loc.gov/ammem/award99/cubhtml/

Through thousands of photographs, original art, cartoons, letters, diary excerpts, business records, legal documents, pamphlets, broadsides, speeches, and sheet music, the history, personal experiences, and contributions of Chinese immigrants in California have been brought to life. The Bancroft Library (University of California Berkeley), the Ethnic Studies Library (University of California Berkeley), and the California Historical Society (San Francisco) have all contributed resources to this online collection.

Chinese Paper Gods
http://www.columbia.edu/cu/lweb/digital/collections/eastasian/paper_gods/index
.html

View a collection of paper god prints donated by Anne S. Goodrich (1895–2005), a one-time Christian missionary in Peking. The colorful paper images represent deities and were displayed on various occasions and used in ceremonies.

Chinese Public Health Posters
http://www.nlm.nih.gov/hmd/chineseposters/index.html

View an online exhibition of colored posters created between 1933 and 1974. The wording on the posters is in Chinese, but they are briefly described in English. The posters are organized into five categories: understanding the human body, hygiene education for children, public health movement, prevention of diseases, and pharmaceutical advertisements.

East Asian Collection
http://digital.library.wisc.edu/1711.dl/EastAsian.China1930s

The majority of images in the East Asian Collection come from the University of Wisconsin Digital Collections. Most are connected with the military, including the Chinese 19th Route Army, the U.S. 15th Infantry Regiment at China Service, and the Japanese Army. Many depict scenes of the Japanese invasion and Chinese defense during the Sino-Japanese Conflict (1937–1945) and the World War II theater in China. Other images portray village and city life, street scenes, and Chinese architecture.

The East Asian Collection—Holmes Welch Collection
http://digital.library.wisc.edu/1711.dl/EastAsian.HolmesWelchCollection

Holmes Hinkley Welch (1921–1981) was an eminent twentieth-century scholar on modern Chinese religions, especially Buddhism. After Welch's death, his family donated his library collection to Memorial Library, the University of Wisconsin-Madison. This collection includes different materials and media, among which are hundreds of photographs most of which have never been published or circulated. In an effort to make these photographs more accessible, a digitization project is underway. The digitized photographs are mostly about religious life in China and Hong Kong between the 1930s and 1960s. The images capture different aspects of the Chinese Buddhist monastic life as well as Chinese Buddhist architecture. Other images portray village and city life, street scenes, and Chinese architecture.

Haldore Hanson's China Collection (1937–1938)
http://apps.carleton.edu/digitalcollections/haldore_hanson/

Haldore Hanson took over 140 photographs while he was in China in 1937 and 1938. Featured in this collection are early photographs of Chinese Communist Party leaders Mao Zedong (Tse-tung), Lin Piao (Lin Biao), and Chu Teh (Zhū Dé) as well as guerilla troop members. A second set of negatives of these photographs are housed in the Beijing Military Museum, China. The photographs are maintained and made available through the Digital Collections of Carleton College in Northfield, Minnesota.

The Hedda Morrison Photographs of China, 1933–1946
http://hcl.harvard.edu/libraries/harvard-yenching/collections/morrison/

German photographer Hedda Hammer Morrison (1908–1991) took more than 5,000 photographs during her time in Beijing. Through her eyes we see the lifestyles, trades, handicrafts, landscapes, religious practices, and architectural structures prevalent between 1933 and 1946. In addition to the photographs, the Harvard Yenching Library also holds thousands of her negatives.

Historical Photographs of China
http://chp.ish-lyon.cnrs.fr/index.php

The photographs in this collection were taken between the years 1870 and 1950 by both professional and nonprofessional photographers and contain a broad range of subjects. The photographs are parts of the private collections of a Chinese diplomat, foreign businessmen, staffs of the administrations in the Chinese treaty ports, missionaries, and officials of the Chinese Maritime Customs Service and are organized into four categories, for example, Chinese Maritime Customs. This project came about through the partnership of the University of Bristol, the University of Lincoln, and the Institut d'Asie Orientale (Institute of East Asian Studies). The University of Bristol in the United Kingdom maintains the site.

Little Journeys to the Great War
http://www.greatwardifferent.com/Great_War/Chinese_Laborers/Chinese_Laborers_01.htm

This webpage contains excerpts from the July 27, 1918, issue of *The War Illustrated*, a British war magazine published during the 1914–1918 conflict. It is a pictorial record of the great war of nations.

Old China Hands Archive
http://digital-library.csun.edu/cdm4/browse.php?CISOROOT=%2Foldchinahands

The goal of the Old China Hands Archive (part of the Special Collections and Archives Department of the University Library at California State University, Northridge) is to safeguard yet make known the rich heritage of the people who have served China through commerce, civil service, or as missionaries through sharing their written, printed, graphic, audio, and video materials.

Robert Henry Chandless Photographs of China, 1898–1908
http://content.lib.washington.edu/chandlessweb/index.html

View an eclectic collection of photographs from the Robert Henry Chandless Collection (part of the University of Washington Libraries Digital Collections) that were taken between 1898 and 1908. They range in subject from the Boxer Rebellion in 1900 to political and commercial life to picturesque views of Peking and Tietsin.

Sidney D. Gamble Photographs
http://library.duke.edu/digitalcollections/gamble/

View an online collection of Sidney Gamble's (1890–1968) photographs taken during his visits to China between 1917 and 1932. His photos feature boats, Buddha, children, funerals, gorges, pagodas, students, temples, The Great Wall, and women. Photographs from earlier visits are being digitized and will be added. This is just one collection in the Duke University Libraries' Archive of Documentary Arts.

Stefan Landsberger's Chinese Propaganda Poster Pages
http://www.iisg.nl/landsberger/

This is a collection of over 2,000 Chinese propaganda posters covering a period of over 50 years, beginning in 1935. The posters are presented in 32 diverse online exhibitions.

Tseng Family Collection of Chinese Antiquities
http://library.csun.edu/Collections/SCA/SC/Tseng

View a sampling of Chinese relics that were donated to the California State University, Northridge. Relics include an ancient stone axe blade and bronze pieces.

The William Hervie Dobson Collection
http://digicoll.library.wisc.edu/WebZ/AugmentedQuery?sessionid=01-42274
   -2021875994

Dr. William Hervie Dobson, a missionary and doctor, built a missionary and hospital compound and school in the early twentieth century in the Yeungkong area, which survived civil wars, hostility from local inhabitants, the Boxer Rebellion, and changes in the local government. View over 200 photographs taken by Dobson.

Hong Kong (People's Republic of China)

Hong Kong University Libraries Digital Initiatives
http://lib.hku.hk/database/

This is a portal to local collections containing documents, archival materials, historical images, sketches, maps, books, newspaper clippings, and more. Additional digitizing projects are being continuously developed.

Macau (People's Republic of China)

Macau: A Selection of Cartographic Images
http://memory.loc.gov/ammem/gmdhtml/macau/macau.html

This attractive online presentation is based on the one-day symposium "Macau: A Cultural Dialogue toward a New Millennium," held September 21, 1999. The symposium, which was cosponsored by the Library of Congress and the Instituto Cultural de Macau, was held in acknowledgment of the transfer of Macau from Portugal to China. The selected maps and views come from the Library of Congress Geography and Map Division collections and cover the time periods of 1655–1764, 1787–1806, 1834–1952, and 1988–1991.

Sidney D. Gamble Photographs
http://library.duke.edu/digitalcollections/search/results?t=macau

View 20 black-and-white photos taken between 1917 and 1919 by Sidney D. Gamble, a noted sociologist and China scholar. The site is maintained by Duke University Libraries Digital Collections.

Mongolia (People's Republic of China)

The Bogd Khaan Winter Palace Museum
http://www.legendtour.ru/eng/mongolia/ulaanbaatar/bogd-khaan-winter-palace
   .shtml

View some photographs of the Bogd Khaan Winter Palace Museum and its contents. Built in 1924, this was one of the first museums in Mongolia. The palace was the winter residence of the last Bogd Khaan of Mongolia, Javzandamba. The palace compound was built between 1893 and 1903 and includes the Gate of Peace, a Temple, and the personal library of Bogd Khaan. View images such as the Andi Men Peace Gate constructed between 1912 and 1919 in commemoration of the eighth Bogd's coronation as absolute monarchy. Note that although this site is a commercial site, it does provide information reflecting the history and culture of Mongolia.

The Choijin Lama Temple Museum
http://www.legendtour.ru/eng/mongolia/ulaanbaatar/choijin-lama-museum.shtml

The images in this collection show five Buddhist temples and five arched gates. There are works by the national masters of painting and sculpture. In the main temple are the sculpture of Choijin Lama and an embalmed mummy. Note that although this site is a commercial site, it does provide information reflecting the history and culture of Mongolia.

Gandan Monastery
http://www.legendtour.ru/eng/mongolia/ulaanbaatar/gandan-monastery.shtml

Built in 1838, the Gandan Monastery grew in importance as a center for learning and practicing Buddha's teachings throughout the Mahayana Buddhist community. View photographs of the monastery and read about its history. Note that although this site is a commercial site, it does provide information reflecting the history and culture of Mongolia.

Monasteries in Ulaanbaatar
http://www.legendtour.ru/eng/mongolia/ulaanbaatar/ulaanbaatar_monasteries.shtml

Read the history about the temples (*sum*), monasteries (*khiid*), and monks and nuns who served Ulaanbaatar. In the 1930s most of the monasteries and temples were destroyed during Stalinist purges, including the murdering of thousands of the religious Buddhists. The site contains images and links to Mongolia monasteries, some including a diagram. Note that although this site is a commercial site, it does provide information reflecting the history and culture of Mongolia.

Mongolia Natural History Museum—Pictures
http://www.legendtour.ru/eng/mongolia/ulaanbaatar/ulaanbaatar-natural-history
-museum_pictures.shtml

View photographs of the museum and its contents. This site provides additional links to collections.

Mongolian Military Museum
http://www.legendtour.ru/eng/mongolia/ulaanbaatar/mongolian_military_museum_
pictures.shtml

The Mongolian Military Museum has approximately 8,000 possessions related to the history of the Mongolian army. Several images are displayed on the site.

The National Museum of Mongolian History, Ulaanbaatar
http://depts.washington.edu/silkroad/museums/ubhist/ubhist.html

This is a great site for learning about Mongolian history. There are images from prehistory, the Xiongnu Period, Early Turk Empire, the Qidan/Liao Period, the Mongol Empire of Chingis Khan and his successors, and the Period of Manchu/Qing Rule. There are also cultural and ethnographic images.

Selected Mongolian Laws and Regulations, 1917–1940
http://www.mongoliacenter.org/library/digitalbooks/index.html

This is a collection of 36 books (1580 pages) containing Mongolian laws and regulations written from 1917 to 1940, an important time in the history of Mongolian independence. The Library of Congress received the books from the American Center for Mongolian Studies. Selections from the books written in Mongol script can be viewed online. There is metadata providing information on each title.

UNESCO World Heritage
http://whc.unesco.org/en/statesparties/mn

View a map and a description of the Uvs Nuur Basine, a large, shallow, and very saline lake. There is also a link to the Orkhon Valley Cultural Landscape—an extensive area of pastureland on the banks of the Orkhon River. Archaeological remains date back to the sixth century. The Orkhon Valley also includes the thirteenth- and fourteenth-century capital of Chingis (Genghis) Khan's vast empire. Read about its history and view an image and map.

Zanabazar Museum of Mongolian Fine Arts
http://www.zanabazarfam.mn/web_eng/index.php

View images of paintings, carvings, and sculptures, many by the honored sculptor and artist Zanabazar. The museum also contains rare religious artifacts, such as scroll paintings (thangka) and Buddhist statues.

Tibet (People's Republic of China)

Tibet Album: British Photography in Central Tibet, 1920–1950
http://tibet.prm.ox.ac.uk/index.php

Access over 6,000 photographs of Tibetan culture spanning 30 years from two British museum collections: the Pitt Rivers Museum (Oxford) and the British Museum (London). In addition to individual photos, the website also contains photo albums created by three of the photographers, interactive maps, diaries, and documents.

The Tibetan and Himalayan Library (THL)
http://www.thlib.org/

The THL infrastructure is supported by the University of Virginia's Library and by the Institute for Advanced Technology in the Humanities. The THL hosts a number of web projects that involve collaborations among individuals, institutions, and communities to create a number of resources—maps, images, audios, videos, texts, and more. Click on "Projects" at the top of the page. Three examples are the Sera Monastery Website, the Meru Nyingpa Monastery Website, and the Drepung Monastery Website. All three websites provide a glimpse into the richness of Tibetan culture and society.

▶ **Drepung Monastery**
http://www.thlib.org/places/monasteries/drepung/

The Drepung Monastery Project provides information, images, an interactive map, essays, and a video of the largest monastery in the history of Tibet. Drepung Monastery is one of the most important religious institutions in Tibet and provides a glimpse of many aspects of Tibetan life.

▶ **Meru Nyingpa Monastery**
http://www.thlib.org/places/monasteries/meru-nyingpa/

From this site explore the link to "Detailed Images of Paintings," images of murals of the Meru Nyingpa Dukhang. One link focuses on the monastery's architecture, including blueprints of the floors of the temple and a three-dimensional model of the complex. Meru Nyingpa Monastery holds many qualities that make it unique. The complex is located within the center of Lhasa, the holiest of Tibetan Buddhist cities.

▶ **Sera Monastery**
http://www.thlib.org/places/monasteries/sera/

The Sera Monastery Project provides an all-encompassing view of a Tibetan Buddhist monastery through state-of-the-art digital technology. Since the early fifteenth century Sera Monastery has been Tibet's most important monastic educational institution. According to tradition, TsongkhapaTsong kha pa (1357–1419), the founder of the GelukDge lugs school, composed his commentary on Nāgārjuna's *Mūlamadhyamakakārikā*, titled *The Ocean of Reasoning* (Rikpé Gyatso rigs pa'i rgya mtsho). His writings foreshadowed the founding of this monastery. Read the full story and view virtual panoramas of Sera Monastery. The website also includes an interactive map and an online book of essays, *Sera Hermitages*.

CYPRUS

Council of Historical Memory of the Liberation Struggle of EOKA 1955–1959 (SIMAE)
http://library.ucy.ac.cy/digital_library/english/simae_en/eoka_en.htm

The University of Cyprus Library has an extensive digital archive of the EOKA, the National Organization of Cypriot Fighters. According to the homepage, the members of this organization were Greek-Cypriots whose goal was to end British rule of Cyprus and reunite with Greece. The collection has four main parts. Select the icon "Interviews of Fighters Collection" for audio interviews with participants and radio broadcasts, which are available as MP3 files. Select the icon "Photographic Collection" to view a collection of photographs depicting persons, places, and events during the struggle. Select the icon "Videos" for videos of interviews, television broadcasts, documentaries, and speeches (Microsoft Internet Explorer must be used to view). Select the icon "Publications" for printed publications of the organization containing firsthand accounts and opinions of members. Each of these sections can be searched by keyword or browsed by subject or title.

The Cypriot Museum
http://www.cs.ucy.ac.cy/museums/team6/dig_exhib.php?langId=2

The Cypriot Museum website, maintained by the University of Cyprus, has links to ten digital collections containing images of art objects grouped by time period. Images can be browsed and clicked on to increase the viewing size and are accompanied by brief descriptions.

The Cyprus Folk Art Museum
http://www.cs.ucy.ac.cy/museums/team3/dig_exhib.php?langId=2

The Folk Art Museum, which is housed in the old Gothic Archbishopric Palace, has digitized images from several collections of weaving, pottery, embroidery, lace, costumes, metalwork, woodcarving, basketry, leatherwork, native painting, agricultural and weaving tools. The photos are displayed in numbered floor collections, and the image titles are translated into English. The website's Virtual Tour shows the artifacts as displayed in the museum exhibits.

The Cyprus Museum Digital Collections
http://www.cs.ucy.ac.cy/museums/team6/dig_exhib.php?langId=2

View photographs of artifacts from the Neolithic through the Roman periods. Select from a list of the collections provided.

Kouriun
http://www.limassolmunicipal.com.cy/kourion/en/buton3-2.html

Read about the history and the monuments of Kouriun. Links to sites of interest are listed on the left. View photographs of such historical places as the Forum Complex, excavated in 1975–1997; the ancient Hellenistic Theatre with a circular orchestra, constructed probably around the late second century AD; and the Roman Nymphaeum, a sacred place devoted to the nymphs, the daughters of Poseidon, constructed in the first century AD and destroyed in the seventh century during a period of Arabian raids. Another important site is the Sanctuary of Apollo Hylates, one of the most famous sanctuaries on the island. Maps are also included.

Museum of the History of Cypriot Coinage
http://www.boccf.org/main/default.aspx?tabid=46

Read about the history of the museum and the coin collection of the Bank of Cyprus Cultural Foundation, which also maintains the website. The valuable coin collection traces over 2,000 years of Cypriot history. A drop-down box on the right of the homepage allows the coin collection to be searched by categories: city states and mints, chronological time periods, rulers, coins in cases, portraits on the coins, Christian settings, and subjects on the coins, such as animals and plants. On the left are links to view other special collections, such as "Rare and Historical Documents Collection," "Cyprus Map Collection," "Engravings, Old Photographs and Watercolours," and "Art Collections of Cypriot Artists."

The Sydney Cyprus Survey Project: Digital Archive
http://ads.ahds.ac.uk/catalogue/projArch/scsp_var_2001/index.cfm

This is an online archive of documents from an archaeological survey done on the island of Cyprus from 1992 to 1997. It was initiated by Macquarie University in Sydney and then taken over by the University of Glasgow's Department of Archaeology. The archive contains overviews, descriptions, and data downloads of the Cyprus project and is housed, along with other archaeology projects, in the larger website called the Archaeology Data Service maintained by the University of York.

EAST TIMOR (TIMOR-LESTE)

Charles Darwin University—East Timor Special Collection
http://arada.cdu.edu.au/cgi-bin/library

The East Timor Collection, which is part of the Arafura Digital Archive (AraDA) project, consists of 36 books and articles. The website is in English, but the documents are predominantly in Portuguese. Some texts can be viewed online and downloaded by clicking on the images of the book covers. The site is maintained by the Charles Darwin Library, Darwin, Australia.

National Library of Australia Digital Collection
http://catalogue.nla.gov.au/Search/Home?lookfor=east+timor&filter%5B%5D=pi%3Anla.pic*&type=all

This mixed collection of images contains principally military photographs but also includes comic strips and some portraits. The photographs were taken from 1945 to 2007.

Southeast Asia Digital Library
http://sea.lib.niu.edu/rescountry.html#easttimor

This digital library contains over 4,000 images as well as videos and selected Internet links for a number of countries in Southeast Asia.

World Digital Library
http://www.wdl.org/en/search/gallery?ql=eng&s=east+timor

This webpage contains publication information and a description of the 1867 book *Portuguese Possessions in Oceania* by Affonso de Castro. The book, in Portuguese, can be read online or downloaded.

HONG KONG—*See* CHINA

INDIA

Digital South Asia Library
http://dsal.uchicago.edu/images/

The Digital South Asia Library is the project of a consortium of universities and colleges around the world at which scholars actively engage in teaching and research about India. Four of the major collections maintained at this site are highlighted.

▶ **American Institute of Indian Studies (AIIS)**
http://dsal.uchicago.edu/images/aiis/

The AIIS collection from the Center for Art and Archaeology in Gurgaon, Haryana, India, contains over 125,000 photographs. The images fall into the broad categories of architecture, sculpture, terracotta, painting, and numismatics. To search the collection, click on "Search Tips" and follow the directions. Suggested search terms, such as architecture, temple, women, children, gods, and caves, are provided. Search terms will retrieve a list of related images. Click in the check box called "Add to details list" next to all images of interest, click on the "Get Details" button, and obtain information on the selected images.

▶ **Bond Photograph Library**
http://dsal.uchicago.edu/images/bond/

According to the website, "The Bond collection consists of photographs taken during World War II by Frank Bond while serving in the Army Air Corps, 40th Photographic Reconnaissance Squadron, stationed in India and Burma. . . . Bond was a specialist in the development of film from aerial photography that provided essential intelligence to the Allied forces during their advance through central Burma . . . and his personal photographs [document] aspects of daily life in India. Working at a time when access to quality cameras and film were limited, Bond's photographs are a vital and compelling historical resource. This photographic collection is dedicated as a memorial to his service and artistry." There is a "List of Subjects" link at the top of the page to select from, or search by typing in a term in the "Subject" box.

▶ Hensley Photo Library
http://dsal.uchicago.edu/images/hensley/

The Hensley Collection contains almost 600 photographs taken during World War II by American serviceman Glenn S. Hensley, who gave the photographs to the University of Chicago Library. According to the website, "Mr. Hensley [was] a professional photographer participating in the surveillance of the Japanese in Burma for the U.S. Army. During his off-duty time Mr. Hensley used his ethnographer's eye to capture daily life in a number of locations around India. The majority of the images are from Calcutta and its environs. Other locations in this collection are Madras, Kharagpur, Agra, and Burma. The photographs and notes were prepared by Hensley for his wife to use in teaching world history courses in Missouri during World War II." There is a "List of Subjects" link at the top of the page to select from, or search by typing in a term in the "Subject" box.

▶ Keagle Photograph Library
http://dsal.uchicago.edu/images/keagle/

This collection showcases photographs taken during World War II by American serviceman Robert Keagle. There is a "List of Subjects" link at the top of the page to select from, or search by typing in a term in the "Subject" box.

GandhiServe Online Image Archive
http://www.gandhiserve.org/information/photo_library.html

Here is a wonderful site filled with images and other items related to Gandhi, including his diary. The almost 6,000 images are divided into numerous categories, including art, cartoons, correspondence, publications, documents, photographs of historical personalities, personal photos, family, and places associated with Gandhi. Truly a wonderful treasure of images reflecting Gandhi's life and his contributions, this website is maintained by the GandhiServe Foundation of Germany.

Indian Raj British Indian Photography, 1845–1947
http://www.harappa.com/photo3/index.html

The link provided is to the Photograph section of the larger Harappa.com website, produced by Omar Khan and filled with media images, sounds, photos, and movies about South Asia's past, including. the Raj period in the ancient Indus Valley. There are over 1,000 images of postcards, lithographs, and photographs in such collections as "Hawkshaw's India: From Lahore to Gwalior"; "Magic Lantern India 1895," featuring William Henry Jackson's 21 images from his 1895 tour of India; "Bremner's India: 1883–1923," with images of Baluchistan, Sindh, and Punjab; and century-old maps of India and Pakistan.

University of Hawai'i at Manoa Libraries—Asia at Work Collection
http://libweb.hawaii.edu/libdept/asia/books/india/india1.htm

View 42 black-and-white etchings from two books: *Picturesque India* by W.S. Caine (1891) and *Rural Life in Bengal* by Grant Colesworthy (1860).

INDONESIA

Aceh Books
http://www.acehbooks.org/

This website provides access to over 1,200 books (in PDF format) about Aceh. The books, which date from the seventeenth century through the present, are written in a variety of languages, including Indonesian, Acehnese, English, and Dutch. Some books are large files and take a few minutes to open.

Cornell Modern Indonesia Collection
http://cmip.library.cornell.edu/

View a collection of 75 digitized documents about Indonesian politics, history, and social systems. The documents, which date from 1956 onward, are divided into four groups: interim reports, translations, monographs, and bibliographies. The collection can be searched by keyword or browsed by title or author. The "Browse" tab lists all the titles of the documents with author and date.

Indonesia Independent—Photographs 1947–1953
http://www.geheugenvannederland.nl/?/en/collecties/indonesie_onafhankelijk_-_
    fotos_1947-1953

On December 27, 1949, Indonesia's independence from the Netherlands was officially recognized. Photographers Cas Oorthuys and Charles Breijer, working independently of each other, recorded the decolonization progression. There are over 4,500 images in this online collection, a project of the Nederlands Fotomuseum (Netherlands Museum for Photography). Click on "View theme: History and society" to access five subject areas: economy, colonies, war, religion, and politics and royals. Click on a subject area to view related photographs.

Perpustakaan Nasional Republik Indonesia (National Library of the Republic of Indonesia)
http://www.pnri.go.id/default.aspx

The homepage is in Indonesian but can be translated into English. The digitized collections include articles, manuscripts, photos, government policies, standards and manuals, and a dance video. These materials are in Indonesian and cannot be translated into English.

IRAN

Institute for Iranian Contemporary Historical Studies
http://www.iichs.org/index_en.asp

The site is in Iranian but can be translated into English. There is a photo gallery, a document gallery, statesmen's photographs, an oral history, and links to publications.

National Library of Iran
http://www.nli.ir/

The National Library's website, which can be translated into English, has four digitized collections: Book Caricature, Memorial Note, Library Photos, and Archives Photos. Neither descriptions of the collections (such as the number of images in each collection) nor descriptions of the individual images are provided. Items in the Memorial Note collection are in Iranian.

New York Public Library Digital Gallery
http://digitalgallery.nypl.org/nypldigital/dgkeysearchresult.cfm?keyword=iran

Here is a wonderful group of photographs representing Iran. Photos include Polish soldiers and children, prints of costumes, lithographs, and etchings and maps taken from the book *Voyage en Perse* by Eugène Flandin. Other photographs and items, including engravings of archaeological sites and ancient warfare, photos of Iranian stage actors, and prints, come from *A New General Collection of Voyages and Travels; Consisting of the Most Esteemed Relations, Which Have Been Hitherto Published in Any Language; Comprehending Everything Remarkable in its Kind, in Europe, Asia, Africa, and America* by John Green. There are over 500 items in this collection. The site is hosted by the New York Public Library.

World Digital Library
http://www.wdl.org/en/search/gallery?ql=eng&s=iran

A search for "Iran" retrieved an eclectic digital collection that includes maps, seventeenth-century drawings, a sixteenth-century Persian dictionary, calligraphic fragments, manuscripts and sheets, *The Constellations* (fifteenth century) by Abd al-Rahman ibn 'Umar al-Sufi, an early twentieth-century colored photograph, and manuscripts of poetry. Items are in Arabic, English, Persian, Portuguese, and Russian. Click on an image to retrieve a description of it, including its creator, date or time period, language, place, and related subjects.

IRAQ

AGSL Digital Photo Archive—Asia and Middle East
http://collections.lib.uwm.edu/cdm4/results.php?CISOOP1=any&CISOFIELD1=title&
    CISOROOT=/agsphoto&CISOBOX1=Iraq

A search for "Iraq" retrieved over 100 color photos taken by photographers Clarence W. Sorensen, Francis C. Tucker, and Eugene V. Harris between 1950 and 1973 of everyday Iraqi life and archaeological sites. All the images are taken from the American Geographical Society Library Digital Photo Archive: Asia and Middle East Collection, and the website is maintained by the University of Wisconsin-Milwaukee Libraries Digital Collection.

Europeana: Think Culture
http://www.europeana.eu/portal/brief-doc.html?start=1&view=table&query=iraq

A search for "Iraq" retrieved over 1,200 items on a wide range of subjects. The vast majority of the collection is images, but links to texts and videos are included as well. Image descriptions are predominantly in French, and English translation is not available. The videos are done in multiple languages.

New York Public Library Digital Gallery
http://digitalgallery.nypl.org/nypldigital/dgkeysearchresult.cfm?keyword=iraq

View bas-relief images from *A Second Series of the Monuments of Nineveh; Including Bas-Reliefs from the Palace of Sennacherib and Bronzes from the Ruins of Nimroud* by Austen Henry Layard; photographs of people, including some taken at the New York World's Fair in 1939–1940; and a small selection of plates from *The Monuments of Nineveh, from Drawings Made on the Spot* by Austen Henry Layard.

World Digital Library
http://www.wdl.org/en/search/gallery?ql=eng&s=iraq

A search for "Iraq" retrieved 19 issues of *Layla* (1923–1925), the first women's magazine to be published in Iraq; Qur'anic verses from the ninth century; maps; and photographs of the 1921 meetings between Arab and British officials at Amir Abdullah ibn Hussein's camp at Amma. Click on an image to retrieve a description of it, including its creator, date or time period, language, place, and related subjects.

ISRAEL

The American Colony in Jerusalem
http://www.loc.gov/exhibits/americancolony/

This exhibition offers a glance into the extraordinary history of the Christian American Colony that formed in Jerusalem in 1881. View photographs, documents, letters, manuscripts, and artifacts that record the history of Jerusalem and the Middle East from the last years of the Ottoman Empire into the twenty-first century. Exhibition sections include "World War I," "The Locust Plague," "Wartime Aid," and "Family Tragedy"—a personal account of the drowning of a man's four children in a ship disaster.

Israel Museum
http://www.english.imjnet.org.il/HTMLs/Home.aspx

The Israel Museum offers access to digitized resources. Follow the links to collections of art, photography, and galleries. Individual collections are listed here.

▶ **The Vera and Arturo Schwarz Collection of Dada and Surrealist Art**
http://www.imj.org.il/Imagine/dada_surrealism/index.asp

This collection includes paintings, readymades, and photographs plus contemporary works in a variety of mediums. Browse "Highlights of the Collection" or search the collection by keyword, artist, or checklist. Access to the Arturo Schwarz Library is provided as well.

▶ **World War II Provenance Research Online**
http://www.imj.org.il/Imagine/irso/index.asp

After World War II, the Jewish Restitution Successor Organization (JRSO) and the Jewish Cultural Reconstruction (JCR) were created in part "to distribute heirless and unclaimed property." Many of the works displayed came from Jewish synagogues that did not survive the war and are under the care of the Museum. The large collection of paintings of landscapes, portraits, and other works is divided into three sections: Paintings, Prints and Drawings, and Judaica. Artists' names are given when known, but many works are anonymous. The Paintings collection and the Prints and Drawings collection can be searched by either artist or collection. The Judaica collection can be searched by subject or collection.

Jerusalem Virtual Library
http://www.jerusalem-library.org/frameset.php

Historical materials and primary sources about Jerusalem have been gathered from the archives of the Jewish National Library, the Israel Antiquities Authority, and the collections of al-Quds University. Clicking on different icons provides access to a wealth of materials. Select "Documents" to view documents (organized by author; in multiple languages), for example, *The Bible: The Authorized King James Version*; select "Photos" to view photos of places and people (organized by album title; predominantly in French, English, and German); select "Plans" (in English and French), to view, for example, *Plans of the Sacred Edifices of the Holy Lands*; select "Maps" to view maps (organized by author; in multiple languages); select "Illustrations" (organized by author; in multiple languages), to view for example, *Jehoshaphat*; and select "Inscriptions" to view those found on buildings and other places, for example, "Inscription a la mosque de la citadelle" (French).

Jewish National and University Library
http://jnul.huji.ac.il/eng/

Click on "Online Heritage" at the top of the webpage to access a list of links to the digitized collections. For example, "Ancient Maps" leads to colorful images of "Ancient Maps of Jerusalem," "Ancient Maps of the Holy Land," and "Historical Maps of the World," with descriptions. These are some of the notable individual collections.

▶ **Ancient Maps of Jerusalem**
http://maps-of-jerusalem.huji.ac.il/

Maps are accessible by gallery, persons, or date. Links to other maps of Jerusalem are included.

▶ **The David and Fela Shapell Family Digitization Project—Ketubbot Collection**
http://jnul.huji.ac.il/dl/ketubbot/

Researchers of Jewish history, law, and art will find this site a major resource for studying the custom of ketubbot, a Jewish prenuptial agreement. This digitization project aims to create a worldwide registry of ketubbot, gathered from public and private collections. The collection currently contains 1,600 ketubbot originating from different countries and some dating back 900 years. They can be viewed by clicking on "Virtual Exhibition: Jerusalem in Ketubba Illuminations." The collection is browseable by clicking on "Textual List" to search by country, city, and year. The bibliographic record information is not in English.

▶ **Digitized Manuscripts**
http://jnul.huji.ac.il/dl/mss/index_eng.html

From the collection of the National Library of Israel and other institutions, a select group of digitized manuscripts are now accessible through this site. The manuscripts are divided into the following categories: Bible (e.g., "Bible: Spain 1341"); Ketubbot; Talmudic Literature (e.g., "Online Treasure of Talmudic Manuscripts"); Liturgy (e.g., "Mahzor Worms"); Persons (e.g., "Writings of Maimonides"); Communal Documents (e.g., "The Frankfurt Memorbuch"); and Miscellaneous.

▶ **Early Hebrew Newspapers**
http://jnul.huji.ac.il/dl/newspapers/eng.html

The aim of this website, which is entirely in Hebrew, is to provide open access to nineteenth- and twentieth-century Hebrew newspapers. They include *Halevanon* (1863–1886), *Hamagid* (1856–1903), *Havazelet* (1863–1911), *Hazefirah* (1862–1931), *Hameliz* (1860–1904), and *Hazevi/Haor/Hashkafa* (1884–1914). Some newspapers are indexed by common era date, Jewish calendar date, and volume and issue numbers. There are no comprehensive indexes to *Hazevi*, *Hazefirah*, and *Hameliz*.

▶ **Einstein Archives Online**
http://www.alberteinstein.info/

This website provides access to Albert Einstein's scientific and nonscientific manuscripts and travel diaries in the Albert Einstein Archives housed at the Hebrew University of Jerusalem. Click on "Archival Database" to search approximately 43,000 items, such as writings and professional and personal correspondence. Click on "Gallery" to view a selection of manuscripts from the Einstein Archives: "scientific manuscripts relating to Einstein's special and general theories of relativity; an example of one of his lecture notebooks; non-scientific manuscripts relating to his interest in Jewish affairs and to his world-wide fame; and a sample from his personal material—one of his travel diaries."

▶ **Historic Cities**
http://historic-cities.huji.ac.il/

The Historic Cities Center of the Department of Geography, the Hebrew University of Jerusalem, and the Jewish National and University Library have teamed up to create this site that contains maps (including ancient maps of Jerusalem and the Holy Land), literature, documents, and books. Search alphabetically by letters A–Z or by year or by map maker. A Historic Cities screensaver for Windows is available for downloading. The screensaver is a compilation of selected images from the website.

▶ **Holy Land Maps from the Eran Laor Cartographic Collection**
http://www.jnul.huji.ac.il/dl/maps/pal/html/

This collection of ancient maps of the Holy Land is part of a much larger collection of ancient maps of the world, early printed atlases, and travel books. The entire collection was donated by Eran Laor, author of *Maps of the Holy Land* (1986). The collection is searchable by person, date, and site and includes links to other map collections worldwide.

▶ **Israeli Internet Sites Archive**
http://www.jnul.huji.ac.il/IA/ArchivedSites/IA/firstpage.html

As part of an "experiment in the preservation of Israeli Internet sites," The Jewish National and University Library created two collections: Collection of Sites for the 17th Knesset Elections 2006 and Selection of Sites Dealing with the Israeli-Arab Conflict. Some technical difficulties remain unresolved, causing some viewing problems. The collections contain many images, texts, and sounds of the cities, prayers, religions, homes, and markets that reflect the rich cultural heritage of Israel.

▶ **JNUL Digitized Book Repository**
http://www.jnul.huji.ac.il/eng/digibook.html

The Jewish National and University Library is digitizing selected rare and out-of-print monographs ranging from fifteenth-century incunabula to early twentieth-century works in its collection. Over 1,000 volumes have been digitized with the support of the Dorot Foundation. Most of the bibliographic information is in Hebrew.

▶ **Mahzor Nuremberg**
http://jnul.huji.ac.il/dl/mss-pr/mahzor-nuremberg/index.html

View the Nuremberg Mahzor, a fourteenth-century manuscript of the sidur, or Jewish prayer book, which contains a set order of daily prayers according to the Ashkenazi rite, the five Megillot, and the Haftarot. There are commentaries written in the margins on the piyyutim (liturgical hymns) and prayers. Read about the history of this important manuscript written on parchment in calligraphic script in 1331. Because of the size of the manuscript, over 1,000 pages, it was necessary to digitize it in three parts: Shabbat Bereshit to Shavuot?, Shabbat following Shavuot to Erev Yom Kippur?, and Yom Kippur to Shmini Atseret, Haftarot. To view these images it is necessary to download DjVu, a free viewer program.

▶ **Newton's Secrets**
http://www.jnul.huji.ac.il/dl/mss/newton/

This is an exhibition of Isaac Newton's nonscientific papers. His alchemical and theological manuscripts "discuss Biblical interpretation, the architecture of the Jewish Temple, ancient history, alchemy and the Apocalypse." Click "Enter" to view the exhibit and to access other links to information on Newton, the collection, and the works and to a gallery of images.

▶ **Online Treasury of Talmudic Manuscripts**
http://jnul.huji.ac.il/dl/talmud/intro_eng.htm

The Jewish National and University Library, the David and Fela Shapell Family Digitization Project, and the Hebrew University Department of Talmud have joined together to provide online access to Talmudic manuscripts. The manuscripts are entirely in Hebrew and Aramaic. The Talmud Bavli is indexed by tractate, daf, and amud, and the Mishna is indexed by tractate, chapter, and mishna. Navigation through the site is only in Hebrew.

▶ **The Second Nuremberg Haggada**
http://jnul.huji.ac.il/dl/mss-pr/mss_d_0076/index.html

From the collection of David Sofer, a digitized version of the Second Nuremberg Haggada is now accessible. The fifteenth-century illuminated Haggada contains striking illustrations depicting Passover motifs, Biblical stories of the Exodus, the lives of the patriarchs Abraham, Isaac, and Jacob, as well as later Biblical figures. The illustrations are based on rabbinic literature commentary also known as Midrash. Viewers must first download the free DjVu plug-in.

Picturing Golda Meir
http://www4.uwm.edu/libraries/digilib/Golda/index.cfm

This website is a University of Wisconsin-Milwaukee Libraries online collection of selected images from its Golda Meir Collection (1904–1987). The photographs trace her life beginning with her childhood in Russia and subsequent years in the United States, her years in Palestine, and onward to her time as Prime Minister of Israel. Also included are photographs of her private life and oral history interviews. There is a link at the top of the webpage to her "Biography."

JAPAN

Digital Silk Road in Photographs
http://dsr.nii.ac.jp/photograph/

The Silk Road, regarded as the first great East–West trade route going back to 206 BC, is considered the information superhighway of its age. It served as an agent for the spreading of knowledge and ideas between the East and the West. It was the desire, especially among Persians and Romans, for silk that initiated trade. The Silk Road has a long political history as well. The photographs on this site open the door of discovery to its history and culture. "Digital Archive of Toyo Bunko Rare Books" links to over 100 rare books fully digitized. Other links to wonderful photos include "Citadel of Bam, Iran: Keeping Memories and Gathering Information for Post-earthquake Reconstruction," "Silk Road Narratives," and "Silk Road Maps." A must-see is also the link "NII Imagery Museum DSR." Select English or Japanese to view this virtual tour, and explore the links at the top of the page to the "Museum" to see the archaeological site of Bamiyan and Buddhist remains; to the "Library" to see images of rare books; to "Cinema" for short videos of Bamiyan heritage; and to "Panoramic Photos" to see the Bamiyan Valley. Links on the left of the Imagery Museum homepage offer a "Silk Road Tour" and a "Chronological Map," which provides icons to select to view videos about each trade route, music of the area, and photographs of sites and objects. The website also offers short videos and a live panoramic view of the Silk Road landscapes. The Silk Road Project is sponsored by the National Institute of Informatics.

Ehon: The Artist and the Book in Japan
http://digitalgallery.nypl.org/nypldigital/explore/dgexplore.cfm?col_id=443

This is a rich source of information for researchers of ehon (Japanese for "picture books"). Access is available to over 1,000 images spanning 1,200 years of Japanese book art, which includes Buddhist sutras, painted manuscripts, portraits, landscapes, calligraphic verse, and photographic books. The site is maintained by the New York Public Library Digital Gallery.

The Floating World of Ukiyo-e: Shadows, Dreams, and Substance
http://www.loc.gov/exhibits/ukiyo-e/

This wonderful exhibit of prints, books, and drawings illustrates the talents of Japanese and Western artists from the seventeenth to nineteenth centuries who pursued the Japanese art form of Ukiyo-e. The exhibition sections are "The Early Masters"; "Major Genres: Beauties, Actors & Landscapes"; "Images and Literary Sources" (depicting history, legends, and myths); "Realia and Reportage"; "Japan and the West: Artistic Cross-Fertilization"; and "Beyond Ukiyo-e." Select "Object Checklist" for a complete list of items. View beautiful woodblock prints and images from each category, such as "Hairdressing," an early eighteenth-century woodblock print; Utagawa Hiroshige II's "Whale Hunting at Gotô in Hizen Province" from the series *One Hundred Views of Famous Places in the Provinces*, 1859; the color woodblock print "Picture of Prosperous America," 1861; and "Views and Costumes of Japan by Stillfried & Andersen," circa 1877, a silver albumen photograph with hand-applied watercolor.

Japanese and Chinese Prints and Drawings Donated by Gillett G. Griffin
http://diglib.princeton.edu/xquery?_xq=getCollection&_xsl=collection&_pid=pudl0026

View a collection of Japanese (Edo Period, 1600–1868) and Chinese prints and drawings, sketchbooks, and eighteenth- and nineteenth-century drawings. The collection is maintained by Princeton University Library.

JARDA: Japanese American Relocation Digital Archives
http://www.calisphere.universityofcalifornia.edu/jarda/

In 1942 approximately 110,000 Japanese Americans and Japanese people living in the United States were forcibly moved to "war relocation camps." This site provides insight into the daily lives of these people through personal and official photographs, letters and diaries, transcribed oral histories, and art. This is a great site for primary source material, photographs, and lesson plans. Links are highlighted within their descriptions.

Joseph Berry Keenan Digital Collection
http://www.law.harvard.edu/library/special/exhibits/digital/jbkcollection.html

This site offers digitized manuscripts and photographs about the Japanese War Crimes Trial (1945). The website's content is organized into two collections.

▶ **Joseph Berry Keenan Papers**
  http://pds.lib.harvard.edu/pds/view/11916053

  This link provides access to Keenan's personal letters written during his tenure as the Chief Counsel in the International Prosecution Section. Much of the correspondence is directly related to the International Military Tribunal for the Far East

(IMTFE), commonly called the "Tokyo trial." Supplemental to this correspondence are such items as materials concerning the court-martial of Major Walter V. Radovich; a 1946 transcript of a Madame Chiang-Kai-Shek interview; letters from Japanese and American citizens regarding the war and war crime trials; and candid notes by Keenan. Newspaper clippings, photographs, business cards, and notes are also a part of this collection.

▶ **Joseph Berry Keenan Visual Materials Collection**
http://via.lib.harvard.edu/via/deliver/deepLinkResults?kw1=forms%20part%20of
    %20Joseph%20Berry%20Keenan&index1=Anywhere

The collection consists chiefly of black-and-white photographs collected by Keenan between the years 1945 and 1947. The photographs are of Keenan himself, military ceremonies and figures in Japan, banquets and celebrations, portraits of Japanese people, and aerial views of the Japanese landscape following the atomic bomb drops of 1945.

Nagasaki University Digital Collection
http://www.lb.nagasaki-u.ac.jp/search/ecolle/index-e.html

Access images, photographs, and books digitized from individual collections at the Nagasaki University. The collections are described here. Some collections appear in both English and Japanese. The Japanese collections can easily be translated via the Google Toolbar feature automatically available at the tops of the homepages (on computers running Google).

▶ **Bauduin Collection: Photographic Albums of Japan Around the End of the Shogunate Period**
http://oldphoto.lb.nagasaki-u.ac.jp/bauduins/

View the personal photo albums of Dr. A.F. Bauduin and his brother A.J. Bauduin taken between 1862 and 1870.

▶ **Catalogue of Early Japanese and Chinese Medical Books**
http://www.lb.nagasaki-u.ac.jp/search/ecolle/wakan/index.html

View Japanese texts and images from early medical books.

▶ **Economic Branch Library Muto Collection**
http://www.lb.nagasaki-u.ac.jp/search/ecolle/muto/index.html

View a painting, images of books, and images of objects on this site by clicking on various links.

▶ **Full Text Image Database of Translations of Western Books in the Dawn of Modern Japan**
http://gallery.lb.nagasaki-u.ac.jp/dawnb/

Click on the highlighted Japanese text to view digital images of books.

▶ **Galapagos Islands Image Database**
http://gallery.lb.nagasaki-u.ac.jp/galapagos/

Ecologist Syuzo Itow (Shuzo Ito) took close to 1,300 photographic slides during field investigations of plants and vegetation in the Galapagos archipelago over 38 years beginning in 1964. Links lead to information and facts about the Galapagos Islands as well as to pictures.

▶ **Glover Atlas—Fishes of Southern and Western Japan**
http://oldphoto.lb.nagasaki-u.ac.jp/GloverAtlas/index.php

Follow the icons and highlighted Japanese text to view this atlas.

▶ **High-Definition Image Database of Old Photographs of Japan**
http://zoomphoto.lb.nagasaki-u.ac.jp/

This database contains almost 500 high-definition images taken of Nagasaki and other parts of Japan during the Late Edo and Meiji Periods. The captions and explanations are in both Japanese and English. Searching can be done using keywords or from two interactive maps.

▶ **Japanese Old Photographs in Bakumatsu-Meiji Period**
http://oldphoto.lb.nagasaki-u.ac.jp/en/

View close to 6,000 photographs and images of Japan beginning with Bakumatsu (1853–1867, the final years of the Edo Era) through the Meiji Period (1868–1912). The collection can be searched by photographer, category, keyword, or location.

▶ **Modern Medicine Historical Materials**
http://www.lb.nagasaki-u.ac.jp/search/ecolle/igakushi/index2.html

Although the website is in Japanese, it is possible to view the individual collections listed by clicking on each of the titles. For example, one can view the rotating image of a human torso, illustrations of flowers used in medicine, photographs (including some of notable personalities), maps, and other digitized images.

▶ **Transcript of Bauduin's Lectures**
http://www.lb.nagasaki-u.ac.jp/search/ecolle/bkogi/

The digitized text of Bauduin's lectures on various subjects, including physiology, ophthalmology, syphilis, and surgery, is available online.

▶ **Virtual Exhibition of the Old Photographs**
http://www.lb.nagasaki-u.ac.jp/search/ecolle/kaso/index.html

View a series of old photographs of Nagasaki by clicking on the Japanese titles.

National Diet Library (NDL)
http://www.ndl.go.jp/en/gallery/index.html

The NDL is the only national library in Japan and was established in 1948 by the National Diet Library Law. The "Online Gallery" tab at the top of the page lists the individual collections included. The site is in Japanese but can be translated into English. Some of the collections are described here.

▶ **Fauna and Flora in Illustrations—Natural History of the Edo Era**
http://www.ndl.go.jp/nature/index.html

Based on a 2005 special exhibition, this collection of digital materials showcases the natural history of the Edo Era (1603–1868). View colorful illustrations of birds, sea life, and other animals, including man. The text is in Japanese.

▶ **Incunabula—Dawn of Western Printing**
http://www.ndl.go.jp/incunabula/e/index.html

This website, based on *Inkyunabura no Sekai* (*The World of Incunabula*) by Hiroharu Orita, shows images of 13 incunabula (European books that were printed through the year 1500) and 55 incunabula leaves (pages). The incunabula were printed in Germany and Italy. The incunabula leaves were printed in Germany, Italy, France, the Low Countries, England, Spain, and Portugal.

▶ **The Japanese Calendar**
http://www.ndl.go.jp/koyomi/e/index.html

This page offers an introduction to the history of the Japanese calendar with digital images of the Daisho-reki calendar, which was popular in the Edo Era (1603–1867).

▶ **Japanese Ex-libris Stamps**
http://www.ndl.go.jp/zoshoin/e/index_e.html

View a selection of 30 ex-libris ownership stamps imprinted in books to indicate ownership. They were used by the privileged class and in shrines and temples. At the top of the webpage click on "next" to scroll through the illustrations and explanations of the stamps.

▶ **The Meiji and Taisho Eras in Photographs**
http://www.ndl.go.jp/scenery_top/e/index.html

View selected photographs of famous buildings and sights from the end of the nineteenth century to the beginning of the twentieth century. Information about the photographs is given in a combination of Japanese and English. Search through photographs of Tokyo and Kansai by clicking on the title box "Tokyo" or "Kansai."

▶ **Modern Japan in Archives**
http://www.ndl.go.jp/modern/e/index.html

Primary historical sources such as letters, diaries, documents, and manuscripts linked to Japan's contemporary political history can be found on this site. Items are in Japanese, but each document has an explanation in English. The collection is accessed by the links on the left of the webpage. The site also contains photographs, a slide show, and a map.

▶ **Nippon in the World**
http://www.ndl.go.jp/site_nippon/e/default.html

Japanese history, culture, and international exchanges are a sample of the topics explored by clicking on "Scenic Mementos of Japan," "Vienna International Exposition" (1873), and "Modern Japanese Political History Materials." The site contains photographs and documents in Japanese with English descriptions.

▶ **100 años de imigração japonesa no Brasil**
http://www.ndl.go.jp/brasil/pt/index.html

This site is entirely in Portuguese and can be translated only into Japanese. The site provides documents, newspaper articles, and other materials related to Japanese immigration to Brazil.

▶ **The Picture Book Gallery**
http://www.kodomo.go.jp/gallery/index_e.html

This International Library of Children's Literature and National Diet Library exhibition follows the development of the picture book genre from the eighteenth century to the 1930s using picture books published in Japan, the United States, Germany, and elsewhere. View the history of children's books and well-known illustrated stories and listen to selected books being read aloud. Select "About Digital Gallery" at the top of the homepage to read a detailed description of the website, or select "Kodomo no kuni magazine article search" to search for picture book magazine articles by author or title. Links on the left of the homepage list various aspects of the collections chronologically. Spend time exploring each selection to view the wonderful illustrations or reading or listening to stories or songs on this delightful website. The books selected are in either English or Japanese.

▶ **Portraits of Modern Japanese Historical Figures**
http://www.ndl.go.jp/portrait/e/index.html

View selected portraits of statesmen, government officials, military officers, businessmen, scholars, cultural figures, and others who have contributed to contemporary Japanese society. A photograph, print, or painting and a brief biography are included for each person. The website is viewable in either English or Japanese.

▶ **Rare Books of the National Diet Library**
http://www.ndl.go.jp/exhibit/50/index.html

The contents of an exhibition held in 1998 to commemorate the fiftieth anniversary of the NDL have been digitized. The exhibition is searchable by indexes, maps, and chronological tables. The site is in Japanese only.

▶ **Rare Books of the National Diet Library—The 60th Anniversary**
http://www.ndl.go.jp/exhibit60/e/index.html

View an online exhibition of images of pages from rare books created for the 2008 commemoration of the National Diet Library's 60th anniversary. The materials are categorized into three themes: "Carrying on the Classics," "Intellectual Exchange," and "Varieties of 'ehon' Books." All items are in Japanese, but their descriptions are in English.

▶ **Small Electronic Exhibitions: "Kaleidoscope of Books"**
http://rnavi.ndl.go.jp/kaleido/

Books on various themes and topics and pamphlets from 2008 exhibits are accessible on this website, which is in Japanese only.

On the Cutting Edge: Contemporary Japanese Prints
http://www.loc.gov/exhibits/cwaj/

This is a wonderful exhibit of prints created predominantly by Japanese artists. View over 200 colorful and exciting works. Each print is identified by artist, date, and medium used, such as etching, woodblock, or lithograph. Superb examples are the "Biologist's Dream" by artist Kuniko Ishihara in 2004 and "Snow Moon" by artist Brian Williams in 2005.

Sokiku Nakatani Japanese Teaware Digital Collection
http://digital.lib.csus.edu/teaware/

View Sokiku Nakatani's personal collection of the ceramics, scrolls, and tea utensils that she used in her studies and as a teacher of Chado (the Way of Tea).

Topaz Japanese-American Relocation Center Digital Collection
http://digital.lib.usu.edu/topaz.php

View school yearbooks and literary magazines written and illustrated by some of the over 8,000 Japanese Americans held in Topaz between the years 1942 and 1945 for a glimpse into their daily lives, activities, and thoughts. Links to additional web resources about the Topaz Relocation Center are provided. This site is maintained by the Utah State University Digital Library.

The University of Tokyo Library System
http://www.lib.u-tokyo.ac.jp/koho/guide/coll/index-e.html

The main webpage describing the collections is in English; however, all the collection titles and text are in Japanese. By linking on the Japanese titles within the collections one can access images of books, texts, and photographs.

▶ **Digital Katei Collection**
   http://133.11.199.8/cgi-bin/KateiIndex/

   View Japanese writer Watanabe Katei's collection of Edo-Period novels and theater plays. The site is in Japanese. Follow Japanese caption links to find the JPEG digital images within the collection.

▶ **Digital Shizen Shin'eido**
   http://sizen.dl.itc.u-tokyo.ac.jp/sizen/

   View Japanese philosopher Ando Shoeki's eighteenth-century works. Select from a list of highlighted works in the left column of the webpage. To scroll through a book's pages, use the arrow icons at the top of the webpage. This collection is entirely in Japanese.

▶ **Ogai Collection and His Notes Database**
   http://rarebook.dl.itc.u-tokyo.ac.jp/ogai/

   View Japanese writer Mori Ogai's collection of history and literature works, biographies, Edo-Period maps, and Western books.

JORDAN

New York Public Library Digital Gallery
http://digitalgallery.nypl.org/nypldigital/dgkeysearchresult.cfm?keyword=jordan

A search for "Jordan" retrieved almost 300 images, including photographs, lithographs, maps, and over 200 prints.

Scrolls from the Dead Sea: The Ancient Library of Qumran and Modern Scholarship
http://www.loc.gov/exhibits/scrolls/toc.html

This is a superb exhibition for researchers interested in the Dead Sea Scrolls. A history of the late second Temple period (200 BCE to 70 CE) and the history of the relationship between Judaism and Christianity provides the background needed to understand the meaning of the scrolls. View images of artifacts related to the scrolls, such as the scroll jar, and images of the 12 scrolls themselves, including The Enoch Scroll (copied ca. 200–150 BCE), The Hosea Commentary Scroll (copied late first century BCE), and the Psalms Scroll (copied ca. 30–50 CE), each with translations. The Psalms Scroll touches on the geographical and religious contexts of the Qumran Community period and explores the scroll-bearing caves.

World Digital Library—Sixth Map of Asia
http://www.wdl.org/en/item/2702/

View this map of the Arabian Peninsula from the 1478 edition of Ptolemy's *Geographia*. Follow the "Middle East and North Africa > Jordan" link to view eight photographs from Jordan, including several photos taken in 1921 at Amir Abdullah in Hussein's camp at Amman. Click on an image to retrieve a description of it, including its creator, date or time period, language, place, and related subjects.

KAZAKHSTAN

University of Wisconsin-Milwaukee Libraries—Digital Collections
http://collections.lib.uwm.edu/cdm4/results.php?CISOOP1=any&CISOBOX1=
    Kazakhstan&CISOFIELD1=CISOSEARCHALL&CISOROOT=all

View color photos from the Harrison Forman Collection (June 1959) depicting everyday life in Kazakhstan from the digital collections at the University of Wisconsin-Milwaukee.

World Digital Library
http://www.wdl.org/en/search/gallery?ql=eng&s=KAZAKHSTAN+&x=0&y=0

Among the four images of Kazakhstan is a color photograph titled "Fabric Merchant Samarkand" taken by early twentieth-century photographer Sergei Mikhailovich Prokudin-Gorskii, best known for his pioneering work in color photography. This and three other images are accompanied by full descriptions of the images, creator, date or time period, language, place, and related subjects.

KUWAIT

World Digital Library
http://www.wdl.org/en/search/gallery?ql=eng&s=kuwait&x=0&y=0

A search for "Kuwait" retrieved 11 items, all maps created between 1478 and 1740, including one map from Ptolemy's *Geographia*. The maps mostly depict Ancient Arabia and are predominantly in Latin, while the rest are in French, Dutch, and English. Click on an image to retrieve a description of it, including its creator, date or time period, language, place, and related subjects.

KYRGYZSTAN

University of Washington Libraries
http://content.lib.washington.edu/cdm4/results.php?CISOOP1=all&CISOBOX1=
kyrgyzstan&CISOFIELD1=nation&CISOROOT=/buildings

A search for "Kyrgyzstan" retrieved 16 color photos of important landscapes plus Kyrgyz natives and everyday life.

World Digital Library
http://www.wdl.org/en/search/gallery?ql=eng&s=Kyrgyzstan

A search for "Kyrgyzstan" retrieved a portrait of a Kyrgyz woman in traditional dress and a Kyrgyz bridegroom. The photographs were taken from *Turkestan Album* (1871–1872). The Kyrgyz are Turkic inhabitants who live throughout eastern Turkestan. Click on an image to retrieve a description of it, including its creator, date or time period, language, place, and related subjects.

LAO PEOPLE'S DEMOCRATIC REPUBLIC (LAOS)

University of Hawai'i at Manoa Libraries—Asia at Work Collection
http://libweb.hawaii.edu/libdept/asia/books/index.htm

Click on "Laos" to view two 1885 drawings, "Musician, Masquerader or Mummer, and Two Hill People," and "Launching a Boat at Luang-Prabang, on the Mekong," plus an etching by M. Backus titled the "Coronation of a Lao King" (1884).

World Digital Library
http://www.wdl.org/en/search/gallery?ql=eng&c=LA&s=laos

A search for "Laos" retrieved two late nineteenth-century maps of Indochina, both in French, and a 1901 travel brochure for French Indochina in both English and French. Click on an image to retrieve a description of it, including its creator, date or time period, language, place, and related subjects.

LEBANON

Gibran Museum
http://www.lebanon.com/where/lebanonguide/gibranmuseum.htm

The Gibran Museum has a long and interesting history. The museum began as a cave dating back to the fifteenth century known then as the Hermitage for Saint Sarkis where many hermits found refuge. It was later a residence for the Papal Nuncio at the time of Mokaddam Rizhallah (1472) and became the core of the church. By the end of the seventeenth century, the notables of Bsharri offered the hermitage—its existing building erected during the sixteenth century—and the surrounding oak forest to the

Carmelite Fathers, who were then living in the Qadisha Valley and built the monastery in 1962. Kahlil Gibran, a Lebanese American artist, poet, and writer known for his book *The Prophet*, desired to own the monastery and surrounding woods for his burial place. His sister Mariana bought the monastery and the adjoining lands and thus fulfilled her brother's will to make the hermitage his burial place. The website offers a history of this prominent monastery, photographs of Gibran, and links to galleries of his art works.

The National Museum
http://www.lebanon.com/where/lebanonguide/nationalmuseum.htm

The National Museum also has an interesting history. Construction of the museum ended in 1937. However, it was not inaugurated because of the Second World War. It was during the war that the museum's artifacts, tombs, statues, mosaics, and mummies were photographed and hidden either underground, in stores, or in the Central Bank. The website tells the story of the difficulties experienced in obtaining funds to rebuild the museum and restore it to its former glory. Photographs of its treasures are included.

Nicolas Sursock Museum
http://www.lebanon.com/where/lebanonguide/sursock4.htm

The Nicolas Ibrahim Sursock Museum is known as the modern art museum of Lebanon. It was left to the city of Beirut by Sursock, an "aristocrat" of the golden age. He describes his mission: "I wish there would exist in Beirut, capital of the Republic of Lebanon, museums and exhibitions rooms open to everyone, where master-pieces and antiques would be preserved and displayed." Its main focus is its exhibitions of artists' paintings and sculptures. Follow the links to photographs and images. The desire for the museum to become a full-fledged cultural center is expressed on the website. It is worth checking the website periodically for future exhibitions.

MACAU—*See* CHINA

MALAYSIA

National Library of Malaysia (Perpustakaan Negara Malaysia)—List of Digital Initiative Websites
http://www.pnm.gov.my/index.php?id=129

The National Library of Malaysia lists several digital initiative websites. Those with digital collections are described here. A number of the sites can be viewed in English, but the information included is about what is available at the National Library, not online. Not all of the sites described appear in English, but they do contain images.

▶ **Denggi**
http://denggi.pnm.my/?lg=bm&fd=2&sfd=9

The Denggi website contains images of the mosquito responsible for Denggi fever found in Southeast Asia. The site contains links to an audio and a video describing the disease and to World Health Organization statistics on the disease.

▶ **International Islamic Digital Library**
http://www.iidl.net/

The International Islamic Digital Library is a portal to information concerning different aspects of Islam. This includes digitized books, manuscripts, rare books, articles, full-text conference proceedings, and three-dimensional displays of Islamic artifacts.

Oceania (Malaysia, Australasia, Polynesia)
http://nla.gov.au/nla.map-rm3303

View a historical map of Oceania, comprising Malaysia, Australasia, and Polynesia, This 1868 map was engraved and published by G.F. Cruchley, map seller and globe maker, 81 Fleet St., London.

Sejarah Melayu—A History of the Malay Peninsula
http://www.sabrizain.org/malaya/

According to the website, "The Sejarah Melayu Library is possibly the largest public on-line collection of books and other texts on the history of the Malay archipelago [group of islands] and its surrounding region." This collection of over 1,000 items includes travelogues, general histories, academic papers, encyclopedias, and dictionaries. In addition, "The Sejarah Melayu Gallery houses thousands of images of portraits, engravings and maps related to the history of the Malay archipelago. These range from ancient inscriptions and medieval engravings to 19th century colonial watercolours and photography. In addition, the collection features postcards, stamps and coins from the past 150 years. Click on any of the images . . . to visit the relevant image gallery."

Web Sirih Pinang (Betel Leaf and Betel Nut): Simbol Budaya Melayu (The Symbol of Malay Heritage)
http://www.pnm.my/sirihpinang/

This website was developed to be an information center on the betel leaf and betel nut, which are used in ceremonial events and other traditional customs. The website contains 1,835 images categorized into 28 different topics, such as history, folk tales, and ceremonial tools. The links from this site lead to individual pages that are not in English; however, many of the pages contain images that can be appreciated.

World Heritage Sites in Malaysia
http://www.thesalmons.org/lynn/wh-malaysia.html

This website contains information about three historical locations in Malaysia: The Gunung Mulu National Park, Kinabula Park, and Melaka and George Town. The Gunung Mulu National Park, on the island of Borneo in the State of Sarawak, is identified on the UNESCO World Heritage List as one of the most studied tropical limestone landscape caves in the world. The park contains 17 vegetation zones and 3,500 species of vascular plants and palm species. The spectacular caves are home to millions of cave swiftlets and bats. The Sarawak Chamber, 600 meters by 415 meters and 80 meters high, is the largest known cave chamber in the world and is accessible only by air or water. Click on "World Heritage Tour" and follow the links to see virtual panoramic shots of the forest, the caves, and the bats.

THE MALDIVES

Southeast Asian Studies
http://libguides.miami.edu/content.php?pid=21553&sid=187886

This guide to the Maldives was compiled by University of Miami Libraries librarian Chella Vaidyanathan. It is a portal to over 20 selected print and electronic resources. A list of topics about Maldives can be viewed. The website contains mostly texts about the area. However, some images can be found under various topics. Search by either country or type of resource.

MONGOLIA—*See* CHINA

MYANMAR (BURMA)

Myanmar.com—Arts & Literature
http://www.myanmar.com/artsandliterature/index.html

Following a general history of traditional dances in Myanmar are links (icons) to images and descriptions of other arts and crafts, musical instruments, dances, handicrafts, costumes, and paintings. Traditional arts and crafts began when gold and silver artifacts were brought back to Bagan from the Mons capital of Suvunna Boumi by King Anawrahta of Bagan. These included Buddha images, cattle bells, and gongs. Monasteries and pagodas are decorated with intricate patterns of stucco works. The artisans produced wood products using the turner's lathe. This craft also owed much to Mons of Suvunna Boumi. View a description with images of Pandain metalwork, the history of painting, and Myanmar dances, such as the Marionette dance duet, and listen to the harp music distinctive of Myanmar culture.

Online Burma/Myanmar Library
http://www.ibiblio.org/obl/

The Online Burma/Myanmar Library provides links to documents, articles, conference papers, theses, books, reports, archives, and directories such as the *Burma Press Summary* (1987–1996). The database can be searched by description, keyword, date, language, title, author, and publisher. The site is supported by the WWW Virtual Library.

Southeast Asia Digital Library
http://sea.lib.niu.edu/rescountry.html#burma

This is a portal to digital resources maintained by the Southeast Asia Digital Library at Northern Illinois University. Follow the links under "Myanmar/Burma" to books, manuscripts, images, a video, and other Internet sites related to Myanmar.

University of Hawai'i at Manoa Libraries—Asia at Work Collection
http://libweb.hawaii.edu/libdept/asia/books/burma/burma1.htm

View photographs, drawings, and paintings of people and everyday Myanmarian life.

NEPAL

Digital Himalaya Project
http://www.digitalhimalaya.com/collections/index.php

Digital Himalaya is a digital collection of anthropological information from the Himalayan regions, including Nepal. This is a wonderful website because it encompasses so many formats. Follow the links to view trailers for films, listen to audio about the culture, listen to songs in native tongues, and view journals (in PDF or text) and rare books and manuscripts (in PDF), maps, and photographs from various collections. View film clips from the Fürer-Haimendorf Collection. Christoph von Fürer-Haimendorf, an anthropologist, traveled throughout the Himalayas from the 1930s through the 1980s to study the Naga ethnic groups of the North Eastern Frontier Area of India and the Sherpa ethnic group of northeastern Nepal. He took over 100 hours of film throughout the region. Link to "Films" and then to "Punam" to view a 2005 film that won acclaim. Featuring nine-year-old Punam Tamang, a girl from Nepal, it depicts the harsh life and social conditions in which she lived. The Digital Himalaya Project is hosted by the University of Cambridge Museum of Archaeology and Anthropology.

Imaging Everest
http://imagingeverest.rgs.org/Concepts/Virtual_Everest/-1.html

The Royal Geographical Society (with the Institute of British Geographers) in collaboration with the British Council in Nepal created Imaging Everest from its collection of approximately 20,000 photographs taken on the nine Mount Everest Expeditions between 1921 and 1953. Link to a history of Everest; descriptions of expeditions in the 1920s, 1930s, and 1950s; images of the Tibetan people, Nepal in the 1950s, and Sherpas; biographies of expedition members (1921–1953); and a slide show of Everest.

Map of Nepal
http://nla.gov.au/nla.map-rm2777

View a map of Nepal with the routes of Captain Kirkpatrick and the Nepalese army in 1793. Relief is shown pictorially.

World Heritage Sites in Nepal
http://www.thesalmons.org/lynn/wh-nepal.html

View cultural and natural properties in Nepal on this World Heritage website. Link to a map, images, and a description of the Kathmandu Valley of Lumbini, the birthplace of the Lord Buddha. Other links lead to images of the Royal Chitwan National Park and the Sagarmatha National Park.

NORTH KOREA

Korea
http://libweb.hawaii.edu/libdept/asia/books/korea/korea1.htm

View drawings of everyday people and a photograph of a Korean cadet corps, all by Isabella Bird (1898). Images are part of the Asian Collection at the University of Hawai'i at Manoa Libraries.

OMAN

Middle Eastern Studies
http://libguides.miami.edu/content.php?pid=21390&sid=214112

Over 30 selected print and electronic resources about Oman are available through the University of Miami Libraries and collaborating open-access websites. Follow the links to images, photographs, and text about a wide range of subjects.

PAKISTAN

Early Postcards of India and Ceylon
http://www.harappa.com/post4/index.html

View postcards of India, Pakistan, and Sri Lanka from the "golden age" of postcards, 1900–1920. Views include Mumbai (Bombay), Kolkatta (Calcutta), and Lahore. Some postcards were created in Plate's art studio in Colombo, and others are by Karachi photographers. The site is maintained by Harappa.com.

Pakistan: Historic Karachi
http://www.worldisround.com/articles/104540/index.html

Karachi, the capital of the new Pakistan, has historically been linked to Alexander the Great, whose armies sailed from Krokola. Read about the history and view photographs of this historic city. Among the views are Elphinstone Street (1930), Empress Market (1889), Frere Hall (1918), Gandhi Gardens (1930), and Independence Day (August 14, 1947). This is a commercial site sponsored by Worldisround. It is valuable for its photographs and its historical information.

PALESTINIAN TERRITORIES

Gaza Strip

New York Public Library Digital Gallery—Middle East in Prints and Photographs
http://digitalgallery.nypl.org/nypldigital/dgkeysearchresult.cfm?keyword=gaza+strip

A search for "Gaza Strip" retrieved four prints and a photograph taken from three books: *Picturesque Palestine, Sinai and Egypt*, by Colonel Wilson (ed.); *The Holy Land, Syria, Idumea, Arabia, Egypt and Nubia* by David Roberts; and *Sinai and Palestine* by Francis Frith.

West Bank

Israel & Palestinian Territories
http://libguides.miami.edu/content.php?pid=21390&sid=214107

View selected print and electronic resources about the Palestinian Territories that are available through the University of Miami Libraries and collaborating open-access websites. Clicking on the titles listed will retrieve information, text, photographs, illustrations, and other items. For example, select "Central Zionist Archives" and then "Gallery" to view images of documents and photographs dating back to 1882. Other links within this site offer posters, photographs, and other resources of interest.

PHILIPPINES

University of Wisconsin Digital Collection—Philippines Image Collection
http://digicoll.library.wisc.edu/WebZ/initialize?sessionid=0&javascript=true&dbchoice=
  1&active=1&entityCurrentPage=Search1&dbname=SEAiT&style=SEAiT&next=
  NEXTCMD%7FSortedQuery?&context;&termsrch=ti%3D+%28%22Library+of+
  Congress+Philippines+Image+Collection%22%29&fmtclass=gallery&next=html/
  nfbrief.html&bad=error/badsearch.html&entitytoprecno=1&entitycurrecno=1&
  entitytempjds=TRUE&numrecs=12%7F

View over 600 images of aspects of life in the Philippines, including agriculture, children, military conflicts, elderly, handicrafts, and structures.

QATAR

Middle Eastern Studies
http://libguides.miami.edu/content.php?pid=21390&sid=214556

Over 20 selected print and electronic resources about Qatar are available through the University of Miami Libraries and collaborating open-access websites.

RUSSIA

The Empire That Was Russia: The Prokudin-Gorskii Photographic Record Recreated
http://www.loc.gov/exhibits/empire/

Sergei Mikhailovich Prokudin-Gorskii (1863–1944) was the photographer to the Tsar of Russia. His portraits are of the Russian Empire on the eve of World War I and the revolution. Link to his work by subject; for example, "Architecture" provides descriptions and photographs of medieval churches and monasteries of old Russia. "Transportation" shows Russia emerging as an industrial power. Other links include "People at Work" and "Making Color Images." The exhibit includes digital images, photographs, and prints made from glass plates, with accompanying information about each item and about Prokudin-Gorskii's travels across Russia.

Meeting of Frontiers
http://international.loc.gov/intldl/mtfhtml/mfsplash.html

"Meeting of Frontiers tells the story of the American exploration and settlement of the West, the parallel exploration and settlement of Siberia and the Russian Far East, and the meeting of the Russian-American frontier in Alaska and the Pacific Northwest." The website was created through a collaboration of the Library of Congress, the University of Alaska Fairbanks, the Russian State Library, the National Library of Russia, and Siberian and Russian Far East libraries, archives, and museums. The website can be viewed in either English or Russian.

The National Library of Russia
http://www.nlr.ru/eng/line/

The National Library of Russia is a treasure trove of Russian history and culture. A good portion of the online collection is in English and is full of images, maps, photographs, and descriptions. The "Exhibitions" link goes to an online gallery of more than 30 exhibitions. They are in English, and a sampling includes *Cultural Heritage of Europe in Collections of the National Library of Russia* and *950 Years of the Ostromir Gospel*, both featuring manuscripts; *A Mirror of the World: Five Centuries of Geographical Atlases* (maps); *Along the Banks of the Volga River* (photographs); *St. Petersburg on Russian Postcards* and *Postcards of the 1920s and 1930s* (postcards); *Glamour and Elegance of Past Centuries (Russian Woman in Engravings and Lithographs)* and *Pakhomov Alexey Fedorovich—For the Centenary of His Birth* (prints); and *Road to Victory—The Second World War Posters and Postcards* (posters). The "Online Collections" link goes to such collections as "Images of Saint-Petersburg (1900–1941)" and "Psalter Published by Ivan Fedorov, 1570." The link "Celebrate 300 Years of St. Petersburg" leads to wonderful maps, postcards, and albums of St. Petersburg. Many other digital collections are in Russian only but are still worth investigating for their materials.

Reflections: Russian Photographs, 1992–2002
http://www.loc.gov/exhibits/reflections/

This photograph exhibit represents an important era in Russian history following the collapse of the Soviet Union. The photos are taken from the first English-language daily newspaper, the *Moscow Times*, printed in Russia, which became a primary source of free news and commentary during this time of social and economic change. View photos taken by photographer Igor Tabakov, such as "U.S. Secretary of State Madeleine Albright Meets Russian Orthodox Patriarch Alexy II at the Danilov Monastery in Moscow" (February 1997) or the photo of "Russian Orthodox Patriarch Alexy II Comforts Children of Sailors Who Perished in the Kursk Nuclear Submarine Disaster" (August 2000).

Revelations from the Russian Archives
http://www.loc.gov/exhibits/archives/intro.html

Documents, photographs, and films from the Russian Archives present a "highly secret internal record of Soviet Communist rule" for the first time in a public venue. The documents are an important source of primary materials for twentieth-century history because they help us to understand one of the largest and "most powerful political machines of the modern era." The archives cover Soviet history from the October Revolution of 1917 to the failed coup of August 1991. Materials come from the Central Committee, the presidential archive, and the KGB.

Russian Archives Online
http://www.russianarchives.com/index.html

This Russian and Soviet-related archives website has links to films, photographs, documents, texts, and audio compiled by different sources in a collaborative effort to cover

Russian history and its culture. Some links from this site provide information about existing collections but not direct access to them; they reside in other institutions. The links to collections that do provide online access are listed here.

▶ **Oriental Art: Images of the East**
http://www.russianarchives.com/gallery/oriental/index.html

"The Russian State Museum of Oriental Art houses a wide range of paintings, graphics, sculpture, and handicrafts from the Far East and Middle Asia, including the countries of China, Japan, Vietnam, Burma, Laos, [and] Thailand. . . ." Link to such collections as "Yuri Gagarin: His Life in Pictures," about the first Russian cosmonaut in space; "Soviet Propaganda," a collection of posters and cartoons; "Oriental Art," including paintings and illustrations; "A Romanov Album," an online photo album; "The Listening Room," containing audio interviews with Russian scholars and scientists on various topics; and "RIA Novosti," a photo collection of the Russian Information Agency Novosti. Additional links include "Sergei Eisenstein," about an important Russian filmmaker; "Krasnogorsk?," an archive of film footage that dates back to Nicholas II's coronation and photographs and albums dating back to the 1850s; "The Last Tsar," the story and photos of Tsar Nicholas II; and "Red Army," which provides a brief outline of its history.

▶ **Russian History Online: The Khrushchev Years**
http://www.russianarchives.com/rho/index.html

This is an online course for Russian universities and contains photographs and film clips of the Khrushchev era. Follow the link "The Khrushchev Years" to Russian text, a song, and photographs.

▶ **Videos**
http://www.russianarchives.com/videos/index.html

View a growing number of video clips from the Russian Archives on a wide range of topics. Titles include *U.S. Propaganda*, *Women's Athletic Award Ceremony*, *Joseph McCarthy and Anti-Communist Arrests*, *Atomic Bomb*, *Korolyov's Story*, *Krasnogorsk Propaganda*, *Space Walk*, and *First Woman in Space*, to name a few.

Russian History Digital Library
http://www.academicinfo.net/russhistlibrary.html

Here you can access more than 50 Russian archival collections of photographs, films, audio clips, documents, and transcripts from the 15 republics of the former Soviet Union, including Russia, Ukraine, and Georgia.

Serge Diaghilev and His World: A Centennial Celebration of Diaghilev's Ballets Russes, 1909–1929
http://myloc.gov/exhibitions/balletsrusses/Pages/default.aspx

Nearly 50 photographs of musical scores, productions, costume designs, dance notation manuscripts, programs, and posters make up this exhibition featuring Serge Diaghilev's Ballets Russes, a famous dance company during the twentieth century. Items come from the collection of Bronislava Nijinska, sister of dancer and choreographer Vaslav Nijinsky.

State Historical Museum, Moscow
http://depts.washington.edu/silkroad/museums/gim/gim.html

The State Historical Museum's collections range across centuries of Eurasian history. Thumbnail photographs of selected artifacts are provided, which show larger pictures when clicked on. A sampling of collections include "Russia in the 17th Century," "Beginnings of Russian Portraiture," and "Peter the Great's Era and Beyond." Another collection is the "Turkic Peoples of the Steppe." The images show a number of objects from the Golden Horde (Simferopol hoard) and are accompanied by short descriptions. The collection dates back to the eleventh century and includes examples of silver dirhams, beads, stone statues, an arrowhead, silver ingots, jewelry, coins, ceramic ware, and pottery.

SAUDI ARABIA

Middle Eastern Studies
http://libguides.miami.edu/content.php?pid=21390&sid=214384

Over 30 selected print and electronic resources about Saudi Arabia are available through the University of Miami Libraries and collaborating open-access websites. They were compiled by Chella Vaidyanathan at the University of Miami Libraries.

SINGAPORE

Lin Hsin Hsin Art Museum
http://www.lhham.com.sg/

Experience a virtual museum that is distinctive in design. Images are links to artworks in various mediums, including sculpture, oil on canvas, and oil on paper, and are often associated with poetry. The site claims to be the world's first virtual museum and is over 15 years old. Lin Hsin Hsin is a pioneer in the genre of digital art, a composer, and a poet. She has had exhibitions in Asia, Europe, and the United States. She was also named one of the 200 cyber personalities in "24 Hours in Cyberspace."

National Library of Singapore—Singapore Pages
http://snap.nl.sg/

"The Singapore National Album of Pictures (SNAP) is a visual treat that allows the discovery of Singapore through images." Images are organized into such categories as commerce and industry, recreation, arts, geography, nature, ethnic communities, events, politics and government, personalities, and architecture and landscape.

SGCool—Singapore Collections Online
http://www.sgcool.sg/

View Singapore's treasures in this online repository. Artifacts and artworks are provided through the auspices of the National Heritage Board. Use the "Quick Find" feature on the left side of the webpage. The drop-down box provides choices based on types of items. For example, selecting "Bronze" retrieved over 100 items made in bronze; "Brass" retrieved nearly 100 brass items; "Documents & Paper" retrieved more than 18,600 items; "Paintings" retrieved more than 1,800; and "Prints," over 250. Each item includes a description. The "Highlights" button on the homepage provides a sample of 12 items.

SOUTH KOREA

University of Hawai'i at Manoa Libraries—Asia at Work Collection
http://libweb.hawaii.edu/libdept/asia/books/korea/korea1.htm

View drawings of everyday people and a photograph of a Korean cadet corps, all by Isabella Bird (1898).

SRI LANKA

World Digital Library
http://www.wdl.org/en/search/gallery?ql=eng&s=sri+lanka&x=0&y=0

A search for "Sri Lanka" retrieved nine images, all part of the George Grantham Bain Collection at the Library of Congress. Each image is accompanied by a description, including the creator, date created, and publication information. A sampling of items includes "India," "Weighing Tea: Ceylon," and "Journey to the East Indies and China, Undertaken at the King's Command, from 1774 until 1781." Sri Lanka became an independent country in 1948. In 1972 its name was changed from Ceylon to Sri Lanka, which means "resplendent land" in Sanskrit.

SYRIA

Middle Eastern Studies
http://libguides.miami.edu/content.php?pid=21390&sid=214385

View over 20 selected print and electronic resources about Syria made available through the University of Miami Libraries and collaborating open-access websites.

TAIWAN (REPUBLIC OF CHINA)

East and Southeast Asian Studies—Taiwan
http://libguides.miami.edu/content.php?pid=22480&sid=220802

Over 15 selected print and electronic resources about Taiwan are available through the University of Miami Libraries and collaborating open-access websites.

TAJIKISTAN

World Digital Library
http://www.wdl.org/en/search/gallery?ql=eng&s=Tajikistan+&x=0&y=0

A search for "Tajikistan" retrieved seven images portraying wedding rituals, religious ceremonies and customs, and other aspects of Tajikistan culture. Each image is accompanied by a description, including the creator, date created, and publication information. The images include "Syr Darya Oblast. Old District of Khodzhend," " Syr Darya Oblast. Orthodox Churches. One in Khodzhend," "Religious Ceremonies and Customs of Tajiks. Mosque Interior of the Holy Sheik Maslakhatdin in Khodzhend," "Tajik Wedding Rituals. Chimilig," "Women's Customs Among the Tajiks. Women's Tuesday, Bibi Seshambe," "Assault and Seige of the Fortified City of Khodzhend from May 17 to 24, 1866: Drawn by the Topographer NCO Filippov," and "Women's Customs Among the Tajiks: Fortune-Telling." The World Digital Library is supported by UNESCO.

THAILAND

Central Intelligence Agency—World Factbook
https://www.cia.gov/library/publications/the-world-factbook/geos/th.html

View the flag, a map, images, photographs, and information about Thailand from the Central Intelligence Agency.

Perry-Castañeda Library Map Collection—Thailand Maps
http://www.lib.utexas.edu/maps/thailand.html

View country maps, thematic maps (e.g., economic, ethnic groups, population, and vegetation), and historical maps (e.g., Indo-China, 1886; and Indo-China and Thailand, Series L506) of Thailand. Additional links retrieve city and country maps. Unless otherwise indicated, all maps were produced by the U.S. Central Intelligence Agency.

University of Hawai'i at Manoa Libraries—Asia at Work Collection
http://libweb.hawaii.edu/libdept/asia/books/thailand/thailand1.htm

View etchings and drawings created between 1875 and 1888 of people and everyday life in Thailand.

Welcome to the Land of Smiles—Thailand
http://www.mahidol.ac.th/thailand/thailand.html

Read and learn about Thailand, its history, religion, education, economic and political systems, resources, and especially about its land and its people. Dozens of links explore these topics and others. Within the webpages are descriptions, images, and photographs. The site's content comes from the Thai government and some commercial agencies and is maintained by Mahidol University.

TIBET—*See* CHINA

TURKEY

Gertrude Bell Archive
http://www.gerty.ncl.ac.uk/search_all.php

Click the "Search" tab at the top of the page, enter "Turkey," and access almost 3,000 photographs, 88 letters, and 34 diaries. The Gertrude Bell (1868–1926) Archives resides at Newcastle University in the Special Collections Department. It is of interest to travel, archaeology, history, and political enthusiasts.

Historic Camel Photos—Camels in Asia
http://www.camelphotos.com/camels_asia.html

For those who love camels, here are some superb photographs. The website is produced by Roger Berry, an American who traveled throughout the world photographing camels. Learn more about this amazing animal, which is linked to the life and culture of many, especially in Asia. This unique website contains historical photographs, full-screen virtual panoramas, slide shows, videos, and even a live webcam. It is packed with stories and legends about the camel. It is a great site for children, the curious, those who love adventure, and the researcher alike.

National Library of Turkey—Milli Kütüphane
http://www.mkutup.gov.tr/

Select "English" to view this site in English. The National Library of Turkey is made up of three libraries spread out over three blocks, and the website offers a wonderful introductory video of this magnificent library. It takes one on a journey into its history and describes its comprehensive collections of books, Arabic texts, manuscripts, and rare books. The visual images of manuscripts and texts are appealing to the intellect and foster a desire to know more about the Turkish culture. Links on the left side of the homepage include "Hacivat and Karagöz" (about traditional hand puppet shows), "Movie Posters," and "Paintings." Select "Manuscripts and Rare Books" from the drop-down "Manuscript" tab at the top of the homepage to view scanned images of manuscripts, selected handwritings, and rare books. One example is *Mesnevi* by Mevlana Celaleddin Rumi (1207–1279). Other examples include The Holy Quran, printed books such as *Cihannüma*, and volumes such as *Kafes semseli*. This website of the National Library of Turkey stands out as a model of what can be done to bring its literary history to the whole world. Access is limited, and there are restrictions for using the site.

▶ **Hacivat and Karagöz**
http://www.mkutup.gov.tr/menu/57

Read the history of this form of traditional hand puppet theater. The puppets are called "tasvir" in Turkish and portray humans, animals, or objects that move in front of a white screen. View wonderfully colored images depicting scenes in a number of plays by clicking on "Views from Karagöz and Hacivat Puppet Theater." View beautiful postcard images of the puppets by clicking on "Postcards from Karagöz and Hacivat Puppet Theater."

▶ **Movie Posters**
http://www.mkutup.gov.tr/sinema/

View a selection of movie posters from the National Library's collection. The posters are in Turkish.

▶ **Paintings**
http://www.mkutup.gov.tr/tablolar/ornekler

A number of selections from the paintings in the National Library of Turkey's collection represent Turkish art. The paintings are still lifes and landscapes.

TURKMENISTAN

World Digital Library
http://www.wdl.org/en/search/gallery?ql=eng&s=turkmenistan

A search for "Turkmenistan" retrieved three images. One photograph is "Village of Farab, Turkmenistan. Railroad Station and Tracks," by Sergei Mikhailovich Prokudin-Gorskii (1863–1944), a pioneer in the development of color photography. The train station in Farab, eastern Turkmenistan, is near the border of Uzbekistan. Another photograph, "Turkmen Man Posing with Camel Loaded with Sacks, Probably with Grain or Cotton, Central Asia," also by Prokudin-Gorskii, shows a Turkmen camel driver wearing traditional dress and headgear. The photographs were taken between 1905 and 1915.

UNITED ARAB EMIRATES

Middle Eastern Studies
http://libguides.miami.edu/content.php?pid=21390&sid=214113

View selected print and electronic resources about the United Arab Emirates available through the University of Miami Libraries and collaborating open-access websites.

UZBEKISTAN

World Digital Library
http://www.wdl.org/en/search/gallery?ql=eng&s=uzbekistan

A search for "Uzbekistan" retrieved four photographs created between 1905 and 1915 by Sergei Mikhailovich Prokudin-Gorskii (1863–1944). The photographs are titled "Fabric Merchant. Samarkand," "Melon Vendor. Samarkand," "Emir of Bukhara. Bukhara," and "Village of Farab, Turkmenistan. Railroad Station and Tracks." Other images include "The History of Persia"; "Three Bayts (Verses) to a Loved One," a calligraphic fragment of poetry; and "Portion of Shir-Dar Minaret and its Dome with Tillia-Kari. Samarkand," a Muslim theological academy and school constructed in 1619–1636 and now part of a complex of mosques. A description accompanies each image.

VIETNAM

Vets with a Vision
http://www.vwam.com/vets/photos.html

The Vietnam War (1965–1972), a painful period of American history, is portrayed by a number of photographs on this website of the group "Vets with a Vision." Photos portray the hardships endured by the soldiers who fought in the war. Photographic subjects include the NLF, the male and female Vietnam army, the Vietcong, the Tet Offensive, and Marble Mountain. The website includes photos from the AP Wire Service, *Life Magazine*, and Nin Loc Son.

Viet Nam Cultural Profile
http://www.culturalprofiles.net/viet_nam/Directories/Vi_ACYAlw-7879_ADs-t_Nam_ Cultural_Profile/-1497.html

Learn about the culture of Viet Nam by following links to photographs and text about its geography, history, government, population, languages, society, economy, religion, and educational system. This site was created through a partnership between Visiting Arts and the Ministry of Culture, Sports and Tourism (MCST) of Viet Nam, with financial support from the Rockefeller Foundation. It is one of three online cultural guides to the countries of the Greater Mekong Subregion. The other two, which can be linked to, are the Cambodia Cultural Profile and the Laos Cultural Profile. The targeted audience is both professionals and the general public.

YEMEN

World Digital Library
http://www.wdl.org/en/search/gallery?ql=eng&s=Yemen

A search for "Yemen" retrieved a number of digitized books, for example, *A Voyage in the Indian Ocean and to Bengal, undertaken in the Years 1789 and 1790: Containing an Account of the Sechelles Islands and Trincomale.* This illustrated 288-page book was created in 1803 by Louis de Grandpré (1761–1846), a French army officer who made an extensive tour of the Indian Ocean region in 1789–1790. Another book is *Voyages and Travels in India, Ceylon, the Red Sea, Abyssinia, and Egypt, in the Years 1802, 1803, 1804, 1805, and 1806.* It contains 566 pages of text and illustrations and was created in 1809 by George Annesley, Earl of Mountnorris (1764–1844). Both of these books are part of the Library of Congress's collection. To open a book, click on its index thumbnail image and then on the "+ Open" link on the larger image retrieved. A number of other images are photographs of maps. One example is the "Sixth Map of Asia," created by Ptolemy (second century) covering the Arabian Peninsula, including such features as the Red Sea and the Indian Ocean. This map is from the Central Library, Qatar Foundation. Each image is accompanied by a written description, including the creator, date created, and publication information, as well as the option to listen to the description being read.

Chapter 5

Europe

INTRODUCTION

Throughout Europe we find vast differences with regard to the internal development of libraries in general with regard to their collections, training, management, and services, not to mention the huge task of digitizing valuable collections for web access. This will impact a country's ability or inability to enter into the online environment and make its cultural heritage visible to the world. One such example is found in Italy's public libraries, which lack a sufficient amount of physical collection resources and funding to ensure basic access to its culture (Guerrini and Frigimelica, 2009). This is found to be true for other areas of the world as well. The difficulties experienced in Italy and in other countries have inspired leading universities, institutions, and organizations to take a leadership role in the digitization process. A number of institutions named in this chapter provide access to the cultural heritage of Italy.

Ceynowa (2009) addresses a major dilemma facing many countries—the funding of digitizing cultural materials and making them accessible for the web environment. Bavaria is one such country with this dilemma. The Bavarian State Library, one of the world's leading international research libraries, entered into a public–private partnership in 2007 with Google, a leading Internet search engine provider that absorbed the entire digitization costs. The Bavarian State Library copyright free collections (sixteenth to nineteenth centuries) include 91,000 manuscripts, 20,000 incunabula, and 130,000 prints. The digitization of these rare manuscripts and collections ensures the conservation of Bavaria's cultural heritage and offers the resources to the world through the web. This collaboration between the Bavarian State Library and Google (one of a number of similar partnerships with Google) is an example of what can be done to preserve the cultural heritage of a country. When visiting any website of a digitized collection it is not always apparent to the researcher what collaborations took place, what costs to digitize the collections were incurred, or how the collections became available online. Is it the work of the sponsoring library, organization, museum, or institution where the collection resides? Or, is the collection available through a portal (another institution making them available)? Samplings of such projects are referred to here and in this chapter.

One such collaboration is the European Digital Library Project (EDLP). In recent years there has been a great deal of collaboration in the digitization of content such as photographs and sound recordings to be made available online through the web. The number of institutions involved from European countries continued to grow through CENL (Conference of European National Librarians) under the name of "European Library: Gateway to Europe's Knowledge" and through the EDLP project

(EDLproject, 2010). The initial goal of the European Library in the 2001 was to act as a gateway or portal to the collections of the national libraries of Europe. By 2007, there was online access to the bibliographic catalog information of more than 150 valuable collections from 23 European countries (van der Meulen, 2007). Although this was a major development in gaining access to information about these collections, there was a limitation. This was the desire to view the actual objects (images, full-text documents, etc.) online as well. Much has been accomplished since van der Meulen's article. At present it is possible to search the European Library website's portal to national libraries for digital collections by format and country and to view online collections such as the Napoleonic Wars (1799–1815) for portraits, maps, and texts (European Library, 2010). This validates how rapidly digital collections are making their way to the web environment.

Other developments include the project of the British Library to digitize maps found in rare books. This came out of the need to preserve these valuable maps that were being torn out of rare books, a casualty for many historical manuscripts and documents. One such map preserved comes from the 1651 English text *Discovery of New Brittaine* (British Library Board, 2010c), whose map titled "a mappe of Virgina discovered to ye hills" (Kowal and Martyn, 2009), describes the discovery of New Brittaine. Maps now appear on the British Library Images Online pages (British Library Board, 2010a) and can be accessed by selecting the link "Maps and Landscapes." A visit to the British Library's Online Gallery opens an exciting door to 30,000 items in online exhibitions, historical documents (e.g., Magna Carta), virtual books (e.g., *Lewis Carroll's Alice's Adventures Under Ground*) with audio, and Leonardo da Vinci's Notebook (British Library Board, 2010b).

The Austrian National Library has an important historical background. It came into existence in medieval Europe when Emperor Frederick III in the fifteenth century took steps to collect objects d'art from the scattered Habsburg inheritance. This was carried on by Emperor Maximilian I when he commissioned the works of scholars (Mueller, 2002). Today the catalog records for these collections are online. The collections include manuscripts, printed books, maps, pictures, and papyruses (Austrian National Library, 2010).

Only a few of the more recent projects have been mentioned in this introduction. This chapter lists many of the digitized collections of national libraries, museums, and other institutions that reflect the history and culture of Europe's countries, although some European countries do lack an online presence for the reasons mentioned earlier. To bridge this gap, digitized collections for these countries that originate outside the country are included. Ongoing projects in various stages of the planning process will bring even more of these wonderful collections to the web and to the world.

References

Austrian National Library. 2010. "Papyrus Catalog" (in German). Austrian National Library. Accessed August 23. http://aleph.onb.ac.at/F?func=file&file_name=login&local_base=ONB08.

British Library Board. 2010a. "British Library Images Online." The British Library. Accessed August 23. http://www.imagesonline.bl.uk/.

British Library Board. 2010b. "Explore the British Library Here." The British Library. Accessed August 23. http://www.bl.uk/onlinegallery/index.html.

British Library Board. 2010c. "Picture Preview: Map of Virginia." The British Library. Accessed August 23, 2010. http://www.imagesonline.bl.uk/results.asp?image=063565 &imagex=9&searchnum=6.

Ceynowa, Klaus. 2009. "Mass Digitization for Research and Study: The Digitization Strategy of the Bavarian State Library." *INFL Journal* 35, no. 1: 17–24. http://www.sagepub.com/cgi/content/abstract/35/1/17.

EDLproject. 2010. "European Digital Library Project." EDLproject. Accessed August 23. http://www.theeuropeanlibrary.org/portal/organisation/cooperation/archive/edlproject/.

European Library. 2010. "The European Library 2.3." The European Library, Koninklijke Bibliotheek, the Netherlands. Accessed August 23. http://search.theeuropean library .org/portal/en/index.html.

Guerrini, Mauro, and Giovanna Frigimelica. 2009. "Libraries in Italy: A Brief Overview." *IFLA Journal* 35, no. 2: 94–116. http://www.sagepub.vcom/cgi/content/abstract/35/2/94.

Kowal, Kimberly C., and Christophe Martyn. 2009. "Descriptive Metadata for Digitization of Maps in Books: A British Library Project." *Library Resources and Technical Services* 53, no. 2: 108–120. http://nstl1.nstl.gov.cn/pages/2009/44/06/53(2).pdf.

Mueller, Christa. 2002. "The Austrian National Library's Card Image Catalog." *OCLC Systems and Services* 18, no. 3: 146–152. http://www.onb.ac.at/ev/index.php.

van der Meulen, Eric. 2007. "The European Library—History, Technique and User Expectations." *Interlending and Document Supply* 35, no. 3: 154–156. http://www .emeraldinsight.com/0264-1615.htm.

CONTINENT

The European Library
http://search.theeuropeanlibrary.org/portal/en/collections_all.html

The European Library is a completely virtual collection built by contributions from 48 national libraries of participating European countries. It is maintained by the Conference of European National Librarians (CENL), and the national library of any country in the Council of Europe is eligible to participate. Some content is digital, and some is the online bibliographical records for physical items. All online content is freely available to anyone worldwide. The top menu bar of the page has several links. Under the "Organisation" link is information typically found in an "About Us" page of a website. Under the "Libraries" link is a map of Europe and a complete list of links to the national libraries of all member nations. Under the "Collections" link the countries are listed again, with links to their digital collections that are available through the European Library site. Some national libraries, like those in Albania and Bosnia-Herzegovina, have provided no digital content yet, but links to their online catalogs are available. Other nations with more digital content have more extensive sections. It should be noted that because the content comes only from national libraries, this site should not be considered exhaustive of all digital resources from these European countries. The website's Central Index is also accessed through the "Collections" tab. Under the list of countries is a master list of links to the individual databases. Collections can be browsed by description, subject, or material type. Each individual database can also be selected or deselected from the list and searched as a group, similar to a federated search of aggregated databases. Other website features include a runner menu bar at the bottom of each page providing links to an extensive FAQs page, the site's policies about privacy and language usage (including what content is translatable into which languages), a site map, and contact information (the home base of the site is in The Hague, Netherlands). A corresponding runner menu bar at the top of each page has a "Help?" link to provide assistance in using all features of the site.

A Heavenly Craft: The Woodcut in Early Printed Books
http://www.loc.gov/exhibits/heavenlycraft/

View medieval and Renaissance woodcut-illustrated books from the Library of Congress's Rosenwald Collection via this site. The books were printed in Europe within the first century after Gutenberg mastered printing with moveable type. Images displayed are woodcuts created in the fifteenth and sixteenth centuries. Examples of rare books from the online exhibit are *Meditatione de la passione de Christo* (Magdeburg: Moritz Brandis, 1500) and *L'Art de bien vivre et de bien mourir* (Paris: Antoine Vérard for André Bocard, February 12, 1453).

Medieval Manuscripts of Syracuse University Library
http://library.syr.edu/digital/collections/m/MedievalManuscripts/mainpage/

The Syracuse University Library, Syracuse, New York, maintains a collection of ten Latin manuscripts from the thirteenth through the sixteenth centuries. These manuscripts are from various countries and are in several languages, but all are digitally reproduced for public use. Each manuscript is accompanied by a description and an index of selected images from that document.

Melvin C. Shaffer World War II Photographs
http://digitalcollections.smu.edu/all/cul/mcs/italyfrance.html

This set of 335 photographs is housed in the digital library of Southern Methodist University in Dallas, Texas. Schaffer was an Army photographer in Europe during the Second World War and gifted the collection to the university. The images are from Italy, France, Germany, and North Africa, and there is also a dedicated link on the homepage to a subset of 188 photos from just Italy and southern France. The collection can be searched by keyword to narrow the results. Click on the thumbnail images to see enlarged versions, along with full bibliographic information, including descriptions.

Timarit.is
http://www.timarit.is/search_init.jsp?navsel=0&lang=en

The national libraries of the Faroe Islands, Greenland, and Iceland have collaborated to create this database, which will ultimately include digital scans of the entire runs of all national newspapers in the three countries. The site also includes periodicals from Canada and Denmark and already boasts more than three million pages available online. Each item is only in its native language, while the site is translatable into the languages of the three host countries, as well as English and Danish. Although the content is freely accessible to all, many publishers have placed a two- to four-year embargo on adding the most current content to the collection. The collection can be browsed by title of publication, with each listing including the years covered and the home country.

ALBANIA

New York Public Library Digital Gallery
http://digitalgallery.nypl.org/nypldigital/dgkeysearchresult.cfm?keyword=albania

Fifteen images are classified under "Albania" in this collection, including images of persons (shepherds, soldiers, etc.) and places (such as a market in Tirana, Albania). Several of the images are from the late nineteenth and early twentieth centuries.

World Digital Library
http://www.wdl.org/en/search/gallery?ql=eng&a=-8000&b=2009&c=AL&r=Europe

Two images are classified under "Albania" in this collection. One is a 1923 photograph of two boys in native Albanian clothing. The other is an ethnographic map of the Balkan Peninsula as it stood in 1918, made by a professor at the University of Belgrade at the time.

ANDORRA

University of Wisconsin Digital Collections
http://uwdc.library.wisc.edu/index.shtml

To use this collection, follow the link provided here for the Digital Collections' homepage and use the search box. A search for "Andorra" retrieved 14 search results, including six images of a church and tower at Santa Coloma dating between 800 and 1200 AD.

World Digital Library
http://www.wdl.org/en/search/gallery?ql=eng&a=-8000&b=2009&c=AD&r=Europe

One image is classified under "Andorra" in this collection, which is of the Chapel of Saint Joan de Cassellas in Andorra. The image is from a book by an American author who wrote about some of the smallest countries in the world, including Andorra.

AUSTRIA

Austrian National Library (Osterreichische Nationalbibliothek)—Austrian Newspapers Online
http://anno.onb.ac.at/

This is an extensive digital database of Austrian newspapers dating from the eighteenth to twentieth centuries. The newspapers are all in German. The content can be browsed both by alphabetical title and by year, which currently ranges from 1716 to 1939.

Austrian National Library—Picture Archive
http://www.onb.ac.at/ev/collections/picturearchive.htm

The Austrian National Library has an extensive Picture Archive, which boasts more than 600,000 images of portraits, photos, drawings, paintings, art objects, and archive documents of previous royal families. While certain webpages can be translated into English, the actual archive and image descriptions are available only in German. Use an online translation tool (such as Google Translator) to see image descriptions in English. There is a fee to reproduce or in any way use the images from the archive.

Sigmund Freud: Conflict and Culture
http://www.loc.gov/exhibits/freud/

Freud's life and ideas and his impact on the twentieth century are examined. View Freud's birth certificate and photographs of Amalia Freud (1903) and other family members from his formative years. Study the life and career of Freud through photographs, manuscripts, and other materials that highlight the evolving influence of psychoanalysis on popular culture.

BELARUS

New York Public Library Digital Gallery
http://digitalgallery.nypl.org/nypldigital/dgkeysearchresult.cfm?keyword=belarus

Nine images are classified under "Belarus" in this collection illustrating military personnel and some of the damage done to the countryside during World War I. The images all come from the New York Public Library digital gallery collection titled World War I Photograph Albums and Postcards.

World Digital Library
http://www.wdl.org/en/search/gallery?ql=eng&a=-8000&b=2009&c=BY&r=Europe

Eleven images are classified under "Belarus" in this collection, some of which are scenic views of cathedrals and a river. There is also a map of the Minsk Province, from a book containing 61 maps of the Russian empire as it stood in 1821, which included the land now known as Belarus. Most of the images are of souvenir cards that were made of all the provinces of the Russian empire. Some of these cards, made in the 1850s, include parts of what is now Belarus.

BELGIUM

Belgian-American Research Collection
http://digicoll.library.wisc.edu/WI/subcollections/BelgAmrColAbout.html

This digital collection was started by the University of Wisconsin to help preserve the culture and history of the Walloon-speaking Belgian population that emigrated to the northeastern region of Wisconsin in the mid-1800s. The collection has over 3,000 image, sound, and text files. The regular advanced search page for all of the university's digital collections can be used to limit and browse any one collection, or the homepage link provided here has dedicated groupings of content, sorted by immigration histories, oral histories, architectural surveys, log structures, and survey maps. There is also a full-text search option to explore the PDF text documents.

Louvain Posters: German-Occupied Belgium during the First World War
http://digitalcollections.mcmaster.ca/node/37680

As part of a larger poster collection at McMaster University in Canada, the Louvain Posters are a group of 149 German propaganda posters that alternately begged, pleaded, demanded, and threatened the Belgian people to allow Germany access through Belgium to fight France in World War I. Louvain was one of the first major Belgian cities to fall during the war, as the small country was used as a major battleground for the conflict. The posters can be scrolled through and viewed, each with bibliographic information and a brief statement regarding the intent of the poster. The content can also be searched as part of the larger group of war posters in the university's collection.

BOSNIA AND HERZEGOVINA

New York Public Library Digital Gallery
http://digitalgallery.nypl.org/nypldigital/dgkeysearchresult.cfm?keyword=bosnia

Ten images are classified under "Bosnia" in this collection, and a search for "Herzegovina" found an additional one. The images include military scenes, as well as native portraits and examples of clothing and dress. The content comes from the Picture Collection of the New York Public Library.

World Digital Library
http://www.wdl.org/en/search/gallery?ql=eng&a=-8000&b=2009&c=BA&r=Europe

Sixteen images are classified under "Bosnia and Herzegovina" in this collection, many of which are from the collection created by Safvet beg Bašagić, a Bosnian scholar and patron of the arts. He developed an extensive collection of Arabic documents and manuscripts that detail the development of the Islamic civilization. The collection is now housed in the Slovakian capital city of Bratislava.

BULGARIA

The International Poster Collection
http://digital.library.colostate.edu/cgi-bin/pquery.exe?CISOROOT1= %2Fposter&
    CISOROOT2=%2Fposter9193&CISOOP=all&CISOFIELD1=CISOSEARCHALL&
    CISOBOX1=bulgaria&CISORESTMP=%2Fposter%2Fitems.html&CISOVIEWTMP=
    %2Fposter%2Fitem.html&CISOROWS=2&CISOCOLS=5&CISOSTART=11

This collection, housed at Colorado State University, contains hundreds of poster entries from around the world for the biennial Colorado International Invitational Poster Exhibition held at the university since 1991. A search for "Bulgaria" returned over 30 poster images submitted by entrants from the country on various topics.

CROATIA

Archaeological Museum, Split
http://www.mdc.hr/split-arheoloski/eng/FS-zbirke.html

This section of the museum's website contains images chosen to represent each of the museum's collections. The collections are Prehistoric, Graeco-Hellenistic, Roman-Provincial, Early Christian, Old Croatian, Epigraphic, Coin, and Submarine Archeological. Click on a collection name and then choose items in the left menu to see the content. Brief descriptions and other details of the objects shown are often included.

Croatian Academy of Sciences and Arts—Glyptotheque Sculpture Museum
http://mdc.hr/gliptoteka/permanent_display.aspx

The museum has several permanent collections and offers an online selection from each. On the homepage, choose "English" from the right and then scroll down to the list of nine linked collections near the bottom. They include collections of plaster casts, copies of frescoes, sculptures, drawings, and medals and plaques. Each collection link shows a map of the building where the collection is housed, along with sample images and descriptions of items on display

Croatian Cultural Heritage
http://www.kultura.hr/eng/About-us

The Croatian Cultural Heritage Project is an initiative promoting the archiving and preservation of library and museum cultural collections around the country. To see the collections currently included, scroll over "Collections" in the top menu bar. The collections can be sorted and browsed by theme, time period, region, or type of material. Choose a collection from the categories and click the link at the bottom to access the host institution and search that collection on its home site. Or, use the search box at the upper right of the Croatian Cultural Heritage page to search across all collections. For example, search "earthquake" in the box, and see one search result from the photo gallery of the destruction caused by an 1880 earthquake. Click into the one result, and there is access on the right side to 23 different related images.

Ivan Meštrović Museums
http://www.mdc.hr/mestrovic/fundacija/index-en.htm

In 1952, a Croatian sculptor named Ivan Meštrović donated to his native Croatia (at that time part of Yugoslavia) many of his works of art, as well as his four Croatian estates, which have become known as the Ivan Meštrović Museums: the Meštrović Atelier, the Ivan Meštrović Gallery, the Kaštelet-Crikvine, and The Most Holy Redeemer Church. An online selection of images from the permanent displays from each of the museums is available along with a virtual tour of each building. Once entering the site, click on any of the museum names at the top of the page. Then choose "Permanent Display" or "Virtual Walk" to access the sample content online. The main website also includes clips from the video *Indians, the Chicago Monument, 1926–1928* and The Roundtable, which is a list of links to the works of Ivan Meštrović in various other collections, museums, and galleries.

CZECH REPUBLIC

State Regional Archives—Litomerice
http://www.soalitomerice.cz/eng/fondy.php

This website is an archive of historical documents and photographs related to the northern and northwestern regions of the Czech Republic, including the town of Litomerice and its surrounding area. While much of the content is descriptions or inventories of physical collections, there are several selected digital scans of texts and photographs available for public viewing.

DENMARK

Det Kongelige Bibliotek (Royal Library of Denmark)—Nationalbibliotek og Kobenhavns Universitetsbibliotek (Copenhagen University Library)
http://dia-prod-mas-01.kb.dk/KBPresse/Site/index.jsp

The Copenhagen University Library collaborates with the Royal Library of Denmark on a variety of projects. One is an online image database of over 800 historical images, including photographs, drawings, and portraits, complete with bibliographic data, which can be searched by keyword. Click each image for a larger view, or click the "info" button for a caption or description if available.

Electronic Resources from The Royal Library
http://www.kb.dk/en/nb/materialer/e-ressourcer/index.html

This is the portal page to electronic resources from The Royal Library of Denmark. Content includes printed materials in both English and Danish, manuscripts from as far back as the Middle Ages, literature from writers such as Hans Christian Andersen and Soren Kierkegaard, as well as maps, prints, photographs, and portraits.

▷ ### The Danish National Digital Sheet Music Archive
http://www.kb.dk/en/nb/samling/ma/digmus/index.html

The Royal Library has a separate archive of digital scans of sheet music from the library's Music and Theatre Collection. An advanced tool is provided to search the content, or browse an author or title list if unsure how to spell something. The links to lists of citations of what was digitized each month may be easier for non-Danish-speaking users to navigate.

Roskilde University Digital Archive (RUDAR)
http://rudar.ruc.dk/community-list

Roskilde University's digital archive contains works created by people in the university community. The content is organized by category, with browse lists available to peruse through. Content is in either English or Danish and ranges from one-page posters to longer essays and other documents in PDF format. For a brief description of the scope of the collection, click the "About RUDAR at RU" link at the bottom of the left menu.

Timarit.is
http://www.timarit.is/listing_init.jsp?lang=en&order=country&filteron=&filterval=

The national libraries of the Faroe Islands, Greenland, and Iceland have collaborated to create this database, which includes periodicals from the three countries, as well as Denmark and Canada. Over 20 publications are from Denmark. *See also* TIMARIT.IS *under* EUROPE: CONTINENT.

ESTONIA

DIGAR (Digital Archives of the National Library of Estonia)—Eesti Rahvusraamatukogu
http://digar.nlib.ee/eelmine

The National Library of Estonia offers a handful of digital collections on this website. Viewers can translate the page from Estonian using an online web translator such as that on the Google Toolbar. Access the content through the "DEA digitized newspapers" link or the "Index" link in the left menu. The "Index" link provides access to both documents and maps; the documents are in PDF format and can be searched by keyword.

Red Book of Estonian Publications, 1535–1850
http://www.nlib.ee/PunaneRaamat/indexeng.html

This special collection on the National Library of Estonia website houses digital images from over 400 Estonian-language books. The books selected for this project are considered to be some of the most unique and rare texts in the history of the country; and the "Introduction" link provides more detailed information regarding selection criteria. The advanced search tool (click "Search" in the left menu) allows limiting by place of publication, location of the physical item, date range of publication, availability, and condition of the item. The limiting choices in the drop-down menus are in Estonian, as is all content and accompanying description; but a web tool such as Google's can be used to translate the information into English.

University of Tartu Library
http://dspace.utlib.ee/dspace/

This university library uses DSpace software to house and make available thousands of documents electronically. The DSpace setup sorts the content into "Communities," with a title and the number of items next to it. First choose a community, and then search the content by keyword. One can also search in the community by title, author, subject, or date. Most of the content is in Estonian, with some in English. Certain communities are available only to the University of Tartu community, but much is accessible for general use.

FAROE ISLANDS

Timarit.is
http://www.timarit.is/listing_init.jsp?lang=en&order=country&filteron=&filterval=

The national libraries of the Faroe Islands, Greenland, and Iceland have collaborated to create this database, which includes periodicals from the three countries, as well as

Denmark and Canada. Fifteen publications are from the Faroe Islands. *See also* TIMARIT.IS *under* EUROPE: CONTINENT.

FINLAND

National Library of Finland Digital Collections
http://digi.kansalliskirjasto.fi/index.html

The National Library of Finland has made a number of digital collections accessible through the link provided here. Three are highlighted.

▶ **Ephemera**
http://digi.kansalliskirjasto.fi/pienpainate/secure/main.html

The Ephemera Collection touts approximately three million items associated with the activities of various organizations. The content ranges from guidebooks and instructions, to membership lists and telephone directories, to brochures, time schedules, and calendars. It also includes industrial price lists and product catalogues from 1810 to 1944. The content can be browsed by publisher (creator) name or by individual year, the earliest being 1855 and the latest 1945. The "Frequently asked questions" link at the bottom of the page states that the content is not subject to copyright and may be used, provided credit is given to the collection.

▶ **Historical Newspaper Library**
http://digi.kansalliskirjasto.fi/sanomalehti/secure/main.html

The Historical Newspaper Library claims to have digital content from all newspapers published in Finland from 1771 to 1900, currently more than 1.7 million pages of text. The top menu bar provides several ways to examine the site, including "Browse" a list of publications by title and an "Article Index" in Swedish and Finnish. Traditional basic and advanced search capabilities are also available. According to the website, most of the content is in Swedish, because most of the country's publications were in Swedish during the covered time period.

▶ **Journals**
http://digi.kansalliskirjasto.fi/aikakausi/secure/main.html

The collection of digitized journals available is extensive. Some journals are out of copyright and are freely available, and others are not; consult the page itself for details. The publications can be browsed alphabetically by title or publisher, with basic and advanced search tools also available. The content is in either Swedish or Finnish.

FRANCE

Bibliotheque de la Sorbonne (Universite de Paris)
http://www.bibliotheque.sorbonne.fr/sid/

This university library has an entire section devoted to digital resources. Some information is available only to the library or university communities; however, some is available for public use over the Internet. The site is only in French, but once a webpage translator is used, browse the blue subject list in the left menu and look for items with the green "unlocked" icon. These items are accessible over the Internet.

Centre Pompidou—La Collection du Musee National d'Art Moderne
http://collection.centrepompidou.fr/Navigart/index.php?db=minter&qs=1

The Musee National d'Art Moderne is France's National Museum of Modern Art. Both simple and advanced search options can be used to view 60,000 images from the twentieth and twenty-first centuries. Other options allow users to create a "personal selection file" (basically a folder of images of interest) and to e-mail the images. While commercial or professional use is subject to copyright and royalty regulations, personal use is acceptable.

Creating French Culture: Treasures from the Bibliothèque Nationale de France
http://www.loc.gov/exhibits/bnf/bnf0001.html

This superb exhibition illustrates French culture. Displayed are manuscripts, liturgy books, bibles, art, music, maps, costumes, and coins. The sections are arranged chronologically to highlight different eras in French history and are titled "Monarchs and Monasteries," "Path to Royal Absolutism," "Rise and Fall of the Absolute Monarchy," and "From Empire to Democracy."

Devil's Island Paintings
http://digital.library.umsystem.edu/cgi/i/image/image-idx?page=index;c=devilic

Francis Lagrange, a prisoner on Devil's Island off the coast of French Guiana (South America), created 24 paintings that illustrate prison life on Royale, St. Joseph, and Devil's Islands. The paintings are part of the Museum of Art and Archaeology (University of Missouri-Columbia) Collection.

France in America
http://memory.loc.gov/intldl/fiahtml/fiahome.html

This is a collaborative project between the Library of Congress in the United States and the Bibliothèque nationale de France (National Library of France). It provides digital access to texts and images from the collections of both libraries that relate to French influence during the early years of American history through the end of the nineteenth century. The "Collections" tab in the top menu bar lists the contents (in both English and French), which are categorized by format (manuscripts, books and printed materials, maps, and audio and video files). Each collection has a "Browse" link to view the items and complete bibliographical information and a "Details" link to access a brief description of the collection as well as copyright and reproduction information. Several advanced search tools are also available.

Gallica—Bibliothèque Numèrique
http://gallica.bnf.fr/?&lang=EN

This is a digital library of materials made accessible from the National Library of France's website. The webpage can be translated into English, French, Spanish, and Portuguese, but some content is in additional languages as well, including German. Suggested works and featured collections are highlighted, and there is a search tool available to explore further. Scroll over the orange "Browse" bar to access a list of content sorted by format with the number of items in each group. Then choose a format and click. Results can be narrowed further at that point.

The Louvre—Databases
http://www.louvre.fr/llv/oeuvres/bdd_oeuvre.jsp?bmLocale=en

This page of the museum's website provides access to several online databases that will enrich the user's experience. Two of these are highlighted.

▶ **Atlas: Database of Exhibits**
http://cartelen.louvre.fr/cartelen/visite?srv=crt_frm_rs&langue=en&initCritere=true

Atlas allows remote users to view what is on display at the museum. Each entry contains an image accompanied by basic descriptive information about the work. Advanced searching allows users to limit their searches by a number of criteria, including by wing, floor, or department in the building. This can create the fluid experience of moving through the exhibits. Atlas is available in English and French.

▶ **La Fayette: Database of American Art**
http://musee.louvre.fr/bases/lafayette/?lng=1

La Fayette is another database on the Louvre website that contains representations of a very unique collection. All works of art in this set are productions from American artists but were found in or acquired by French museums or national collections from 1620 to 1940. The site is also in French and English and has basic and advanced search tools and a "Masterpieces" link that breaks down the collection by medium (paintings, sculptures, etc.).

Melvin C. Shaffer World War II Photographs
http://digitalcollections.smu.edu/all/cul/mcs/italyfrance.html

The photographs in this collection were taken by a World War II Army photographer and are housed at Southern Methodist University in Dallas, Texas. The images are from several European countries. This page has a dedicated link to a subset of 188 photos from just southern France and Italy. *See also* MELVIN C. SHAFFER WORLD WAR II PHOTOGRAPHS *under* EUROPE: CONTINENT.

Napoleonica.org
http://www.napoleonica.org/us/index.html

Maintained by Fondation Napoleon, this group of digital collections contains significant primary source material from France's Napoleonic era. Three collections are highlighted.

▶ **Drawings by Frederic Christophe de Houdetot [1797–1835]**
http://www.napoleonica.org/us/hou/index.html

This collection has over 250 sketches and drawings by Frederic Christophe de Houdetot who, as an Auditeur du Conseil d'Etat, had a ringside seat to draw candid portraits of members of the Conseil d'Etat.

▶ **Napoleon's Letters to Bigot de Preameneu [1800–1815]**
http://www.napoleonica.org/us/corbi/index.html

This collection contains the text of 145 letters of correspondence between Napoleon and his Ministre des Cultes, Bigot de Preameneu, which sheds light on Napoleon's attitudes and policies in certain matters of state.

▶ **Printed Working Documents of the Conseil d'Etat [1800–1814]**
http://www.napoleonica.org/us/ce/index.html

This collection includes a complete inventory of 4,620 printed documents and the full texts of 3,660 of these documents from this governing body under Napoleon's presidency.

Roman de la Rose Digital Library
http://romandelarose.org/#home

The poem *Roman de la Rose* is considered by many to be a staple of French historical literature. Thanks to a collaborative effort by Johns Hopkins University and the Bibliothèque nationale de France (National Library of France), this site is an attempt to make digital copies available of all known versions of the work, believed to number around 300. The homepage currently claims to have digital copies of 130 different versions as of 2009. From the menu on the left, the content can be accessed by nine different criteria, including place of origin, current location, common name, date, and transcription status. The site can be translated into both English and French.

GERMANY

Dresden: Treasures from the Saxon State Library
http://www.loc.gov/exhibits/dres/dresintr.html

This wonderful exhibit comes from the Saxon State Library in Dresden, Germany. The homepage is a hyperlinked table of contents, and the contents are arranged chronologically and cover major subjects and eras. Each section provides a history and displays rare sample images representing the cultural riches of Central Europe from the Middle Ages up to the nineteenth century. Click "The Bible" to view an image of a bible printed by Nikolaus Jenson in 1479 and "Luther's German translation of the Bible, 1534." Click "The Electoral Library" to view an image of the "Personal Bible of Elector Augustus"; "An early illustration of American tomato plants, entitled 'Red Apples from the New World'"; and "A treatise on horses, 1576," with pictures depicting various types of hunts staged in Dresden's Altmarkt. Select "Renaissance Fine Bindings" to view images of book bindings, such as "Binding by Urban Köblitz" and "An unusual heart-shaped binding by Caspar Meuser."

German Emblem Books
http://images.library.uiuc.edu/projects/emblems/index.asp

Emblem books are works that include elaborate images intermixed with text. The images are more than just pictures, however, as the presence of the image and its associated wording interplay with the traditional text and provide more meaning than just the text alone, provided the reader can identify the clues hidden in both the text and the emblems. The University of Illinois at Urbana-Champaign claims a collection of more than 600 emblem books written between 1540 and 1800 from Germany, France, Italy,

Spain, and England. They have chosen to digitize and make available the works of German origin, all 19 of which can be browsed in their entirety from this website. Click "Browse and search the Illinois collection" on the lower right of the page to see the books.

German History in Documents and Images
http://germanhistorydocs.ghi-dc.org/home.cfm?language=english

This website is maintained by the German Historical Institute and gathers together primary source documents, images, and maps detailing the history of Germany from 1500 to the present. The time frame is divided into ten separate periods, and expert researchers in these areas have accumulated the content for each section. The site itself is translatable into English and German, and all German content has English translations. Content exists for a wide range of topics, including government, economy, military, social life and customs, politics, literature, science, and culture. Tools are available to search by keyword, author, or subject, with the choice to limit by one time period if desired. Search results are automatically grouped by type: document, image, or map. All content is free for scholarly or educational purposes, and citation help is available. Click one of the ten time period blocks to start browsing, or click the "Search" icon at the bottom of the page to search all the content at once.

Germany Under Reconstruction
http://digital.library.wisc.edu/1711.dl/History.GerRecon

This website, hosted by the University of Wisconsin, contains English- and German-language resources from the time period following World War II. The content is focused on the political, economic, and social feelings of the times, much of it in firsthand accounts. All 516 documents in the collection can be browsed by title; many are complete scans of sequential periodical issues (both German and English) from the late 1940s. Full-text searching is available for some of the content, and a traditional keyword search tool is available as well. The content is free for educational or research purposes, and each item provides an exact link for citations.

Göttinger Digitalisierungszentrum (GDZ)
http://gdz.sub.uni-goettingen.de/en/gdz/

The GDZ (Center for Retrospective Digitization) is an organization based in the city of Göttingen whose goal is to digitize scholarly information for libraries and academic institutions. The website boasts over five million digitized pages, which are grouped by subject areas ranging from literature, autobiographies, and maps to travel information and zoological resources. Use the search box in the upper right of the webpage to perform a basic keyword search across all resources. Search results are only in German and include brief bibliographic information. Content is always being added, and RSS feeds for different collections are available on the lower right of the page.

Melvin C. Shaffer World War II Photographs
http://digitalcollections.smu.edu/all/cul/mcs/italyfrance.html

The photographs in this collection were taken by a World War II Army photographer and are housed at Southern Methodist University in Dallas, Texas. The images are from several European countries. A keyword search across all fields for "Germany" returned 49 images. *See also* MELVIN C. SHAFFER WORLD WAR II PHOTOGRAPHS *under* EUROPE: CONTINENT.

Munich Digitisation Centre (Munchener DigitalisierungsZentrum Digitale Bibliothek)
http://www.digital-collections.de/index.html?c=startseite&l=en

This is an online, free-access collection of over 380,000 digital items pulled from a number of institutions, most notably the Bavarian State Library. The content includes manuscripts, books, maps, photographs, and periodicals on various topics, such as history, music, and classical literature. Click "Digital Collections" on the left to access a search menu and two search boxes. Click "Browsing Index" to narrow the content by subject. The menu also contains a "Search" link to perform a basic search and a "Brief Overview" link to descriptions of individual collections and their completion status. The "Latest Additions" and "RSS Feeds" links will keep frequent users informed of new content.

GREECE

E-fimeris: National Library of Greece Digital Newspapers Collection
http://www.nlg.gr/english/dlefimerides.htm

This initiative by the National Library of Greece provides free access to over 200,000 pages of text from five newspapers published over nearly a century, from 1893 to 1983. The five newspapers are *Eleftheria*, *Empros*, *Rizospastis*, *Scrip*, and *Tahidromos* (Egyptian). The site has a Greek-only search tool that can limit by periodical title for narrower searches. The content is in PDF form and requires Adobe Acrobat to view.

Pandektis—Digital Thesaurus of Primary Sources for Greek History and Culture
http://pandektis.ekt.gr/dspace/

This website is a conglomeration of a number of digital collections maintained by the National Hellenic Research Foundation. The collections reflect all aspects of Greek history and culture and were created by other organizations, including the Institute of Neohellenic Research, the Institute of Byzantine Research, and the Institute of Greek and Roman Antiquity. Each collection shares a search tool to browse content by title, author, subject, or keyword. There is also an option to search all collections at one time. Click a collection title in the left menu to access the search tool and an informational page detailing scope, size, access, and copyright information regarding each collection. Some of the collections are highlighted here, along with brief descriptions.

▶ **Ancient Greek and Latin Inscriptions from Upper Macedonia, Aegean Thrace and Achaia**
   http://pandektis.ekt.gr/dspace/handle/123456789/326

   Some entries contain images of the inscriptions themselves and others just descriptive information.

▶ **Greek Cartography: The Documents**
   http://pandektis.ekt.gr/dspace/handle/123456789/23163

The collection contains maps and atlases from the fifteenth century to 1820. Manuscripts and other cartographic works are also included.

▶ **Greek Painters after the Fall of Constantinople**
http://pandektis.ekt.gr/dspace/handle/123456789/2079

The collection includes biographical information about Greek painters who lived between 1450 and 1830, along with images from and an index of their works.

▶ **Heraldic Database of Greece**
http://pandektis.ekt.gr/dspace/handle/123456789/1

The images illustrate monuments all over Greece created between the thirteenth and nineteenth centuries. Each image is accompanied by descriptive data, including location.

▶ **Industrial Establishments and Workshops in the Aegean**
http://pandektis.ekt.gr/dspace/handle/123456789/428

The collection contains images illustrating the industrial heritage of the region and includes some bibliographic data.

▶ **Modern Greek Visual Prosopography**
http://pandektis.ekt.gr/dspace/handle/123456789/14056

This digital collection contains more than 12,000 portraits of Greek men and women of note. The original items are in various collections around the world. Some of the images are copyright free.

▶ **Monastic Archives: Documents from Mount Athos and Patmos**
http://pandektis.ekt.gr/dspace/handle/123456789/9045

This collection contains digital scans of microfilmed archives from the monastic community of Mount Athos and the monastery of St. John the Theologian in Patmos. Descriptions and accompanying information are in Greek.

▶ **Name Changes of Settlements in Greece**
http://pandektis.ekt.gr/dspace/handle/123456789/4968

The records in this collection document geographic name changes between 1913 and 1962.

▶ **Travel Literature on Southeast Europe and the Eastern Mediterranean 15th–19th Centuries**
http://pandektis.ekt.gr/dspace/handle/123456789/23160

The collection includes rare travel literature located both in Greek collections and abroad.

HUNGARY

Hungarian Digital Archive of Pictures
http://keptar.oszk.hu/indexeng.phtml

This digital library was created and is maintained by the National Széchényi Library. Basic and advanced searching is available using the tools in the right menu, and the advanced search includes a limiter by "Type," which includes a drop-down menu with unusual choices such as blueprint, engraving, and family tree. Within the search results, each item is shown in a thumbnail image and accompanied by descriptive information, which is in Hungarian. The library also attempts to include large portions of noncopyrighted material from its collections. An extensive "About Us" link in the top menu bar explains the availability of the content, search capabilities, rights, and collection development procedures of the site.

Hungarian Digital Image Library
http://www.kepkonyvtar.hu/

This digital collection is a collaborative project between the National Széchényi Library and 48 other Hungarian libraries. It is designed to pull images from many different collections into one resource highlighting Hungarian history and culture. The website is translatable into English (the link provided here is to the Hungarian page; click the British flag icon in the upper right corner of the page to translate), but the search tools as well as the content and related descriptions are only in Hungarian. The content includes various formats, from posters and postcards to textual manuscripts, and is free for personal or academic use. Standard searching and browsing tools exist, and a "Collections" link in the top menu bar serves as a limiter by listing the individual collections from which the site draws its content.

National Audiovisual Archive of Hungary (NAVA)
http://nava.hu/english/nava/index.php

NAVA is a repository of audiovisual content about Hungary produced both in Hungary and outside of the country. It includes official broadcasts as well as audiovisual materials from nonofficial sources if they are deemed to have cultural or historical significance worthy of preservation. The archive is maintained by the John von Neumann Digital Library and Multimedia Centre. The site has two separate search tools: one for searching the footage of broadcasts of Hungarian television channels and the other for searching other special collections, such as Hungarian films and newsreels. The search results are in Hungarian, and videos can be opened and viewed using a simple RealOne player computer application.

ICELAND

Antique Maps of Iceland
http://kort.bok.hi.is/

The National and University Library of Iceland has made available in digital format many maps of Iceland from before the year 1900. The link provided defaults to the Icelandic page; click "English" in the upper right corner to translate the page. Each map entry has descriptive information that can be translated into both Icelandic and English. Search links are provided in the top menu bar. The "Maps" link allows users to choose a time period and browse lists of maps by title, creator, and approximate year. The "History" link expands on the background of each time period. The "Search" link provides a keyword search of the entire collection and the option to limit by year or country of origin. Currently the collection has over 250 maps.

Icelandic Online Dictionary and Reading
http://digicoll.library.wisc.edu/IcelOnline/About.html

The University of Wisconsin offers an online course that teaches Icelandic. While much of the course information requires users to log in, many reading selections (including Icelandic literature) and an online dictionary are accessible by anyone.

Sagnanet—Icelandic Medieval Literature
http://www.sagnanet.is/

This digital collection provides access to hundreds of thousands of pages of text from Icelandic history. It includes poetry, prose, medieval literature, contemporary sagas and tales, and mythologies, the original texts of which are housed in various collections at the National and University Library of Iceland, the Arni Magnusson Institute in Iceland, and Cornell University Library, which owns the Fiske Icelandic Collection. The purpose is to preserve and provide access to the core of Icelandic historical literature. Click the American flag to translate the site into English. Then click one of the links in the top section to get started, including "Search" to peruse the contents by title, author, and subject.

Timarit.is
http://www.timarit.is/listing_init.jsp?lang=en&order=country&filteron= &filterval=

The national libraries of the Faroe Islands, Greenland, and Iceland have collaborated to create this database, which includes periodicals from the three countries, as well as Denmark and Canada. Over 200 publications are from Iceland. *See also* Timarit.is *under* Europe: Continent.

IRELAND

Act of Union Virtual Library
http://www.actofunion.ac.uk/

This digital collection contains primary source material related to the 1800 Act of Union, which united Britain and Ireland. Original pamphlets, newspapers, manuscripts, and parliamentary papers have been accumulated from various public and private collections and have been digitally reproduced and presented together. The site is extremely easy to use, with standard searching and browsing capabilities, as well as a timeline and explanation of the Act for unfamiliar users. A complete history of the digitization project is also documented, and contact information is available for the host site, which is the Centre for Data Digitisation and Analysis at the Queen's University of Belfast. Mouse over the "About" link in the top menu bar and click "the project" to see the numerous partners that have contributed content to the site.

Fenian Brotherhood Collection
http://www.aladin0.wrlc.org/gsdl/collect/fenian/fenian.shtml

According to the homepage, the Fenians, also known as the Irish Republican Brotherhood, existed in the latter half of the nineteenth century for the purpose of overthrowing British rule in Ireland. Member groups were located in both the United States and Ireland, and this manuscript collection includes scanned images of their documents.

Many of the documents appear to be correspondence between members and leaders, including John O'Mahony, James Stephens, John Mitchel, and O'Donovan Rossa. The majority of the collection dates from the 1860s to the 1880s, when the organization was at the height of its activities, but some items date from as early as 1859 to as late as the first decade of the twentieth century. In addition to correspondence, the collection includes pamphlets, newsletters, account books and ledgers, and even legal records. The collection can be browsed by a number of different categories or searched using an advanced tool. The site is maintained by the American Catholic History Research Center and University Archives in Washington, DC, where the physical collection is kept.

National Library of Ireland
http://digital.nli.ie/cdm4/index_glassplates.php?CISOROOT=/glassplates

The National Library of Ireland's website currently has eight separate collections of photographs. Each collection has a title and a brief description of its focus, which ranges from portraits to political events, Dubliners to country folk, and still photos to the activities of daily life. Click an individual collection title to access its content, and then narrow a search using the tools provided in the right menu. Users can also click "Browse" at the top of any webpage to search all images at once, currently numbering over 38,000.

Whole Works of Sir James Ware concerning Ireland
http://digital.library.villanova.edu/Joseph%20McGarrity%20Collection/Joseph%
20McGarrity%20Books/Whole%20Works%20of%20Sir%20James%20Ware%
20concerning%20Ireland/

Included in the digital collections at the Falvey Memorial Library of Villanova University are the full-text scans of the two volumes of the *Whole Works of Sir James Ware concerning Ireland*, published in 1764 but written more than a century earlier, about the history and archaeology of Ireland. Images of plates and other illustrations in the work are included.

ITALY

Cinecitta Luce
http://www.luce.it/

This website, maintained by the Istituto Luce, contains an online archive of free-access visual materials, including videos and photographs. The site is completely in Italian but can be translated by a webpage translator. Choose the "Archive/Historical View" box in the lower portion of the page, and then choose "Archivio Cinematographico" (Movie Archive) or "Archivio Fotographico" (Photo Archive) in the right menu to see the content. A search page will be generated tailored to that collection, along with a description of what can be found.

Institute and Museum of the History of Science
http://fermi.imss.fi.it/rd/bd?lng=en

The website offers access to dozens of digital collections on a multitude of scientific themes categorized under "Thematic Collections," "Galilaean," "Scientists," and "Serials." The collections can be browsed individually, searched individually, or searched as a group. Simple, advanced, and index searching by name, author, location, or date options are available. Some of the smaller collections include Ancient Gardens from Babylon to Rome, the Vitrum Digital Collection about the history of glass, and online publications of the Proceedings of the Congresses of Italian Scientists. A number of collections are dedicated to various Italian scientists of note, including the extensive Galilean Digital Library. Most collection descriptions identify the organizations that contributed to their creation. Once an item is located, one can download a brief catalog record or an entire PDF file. All the collections highlighted here are in the "Thematic Collections" category except the Library of Galileo Galilei.

▶ **Ancient Mathematics**
http://fermi.imss.fi.it/rd/bd?lng=en

This collection contains approximately 1,000 original works of mathematicians of the past.

▶ **Cimento Academy**
http://fermi.imss.fi.it/rd/bd?lng=en

This collection contains certain editions and translations of the *Saggi di naturali esperienze* (*Essays on Natural Experiments*), published in 1667 by Lorenzo Magalotti.

▶ **The Library of Galileo Galilei**
http://fermi.imss.fi.it/rd/bd?lng=it&progetto=733

This collection is a separate, Italian-only collection of over 400 digital documents considered to be in part a Galilean bibliography. The entire set can be browsed as a list or narrowed down by author, title, location, or date.

▶ **Lincei Academy**
http://fermi.imss.fi.it/rd/bd?lng=en

This collection contains documents related to the first Accademia dei Lincei (1603–1630), the oldest Italian Academy, founded in 1603 by Federico Cesi.

▶ **Scientific Iconography**
http://fermi.imss.fi.it/rd/bd?lng=en

This collection contains digital images of "tecno-scientific illustrations mainly selected from works of the antique and rare books collection" of the museum's library.

▶ **Scientific Knowledge**
http://fermi.imss.fi.it/rd/bd?lng=en

This collection contains Italian texts on the history of science dating from the sixteenth to the eighteenth centuries.

▶ **Stanzino Matematiche**
http://fermi.imss.fi.it/rd/bd?lng=en

This collection contains virtual images of books from the antique collection of the Medici. The physical items are now housed in various Florentine collections.

Internet Culturale
http://www.internetculturale.it/genera.jsp?s=6&l=en

This website is maintained by the Ministry for Cultural Heritage and Activities in Italy and functions as a central clearinghouse for digital objects from many different organizations. Various libraries, museums, archives, and other cultural institutions around Italy have their digital content indexed in this one resource for public use. The homepage lists and describes the content of more than 25 different collections from subject areas such as music, literature, maps, and science. The page can be translated into English, Italian, French, and Spanish, but individual collections cannot be clicked on. The collections can be searched as a group by clicking on the "Digital Contents" link at the top of the page or in the left menu. Basic and advanced keyword searching is available, and the results can be viewed as a list or individually. Once a single item is chosen, a thumbnail image of the content is displayed, with the opportunity to "View" a larger image or "Download" the file. Accompanying bibliographic data include the name of the collection the item is drawn from, the sponsoring organization and project web address, along with the cost of accessing the item. The authors' sampling of items indicated many are free for personal use but are not available for commercial purposes.

Liber Liber
http://www.liberliber.it/comunicare/english/index.htm

This website offers free online access to a collection of translated books. It is run by a nonprofit organization that uses donations to acquire copyright-free materials to digitize, and it also accepts donated electronic versions of translated texts to add to its collection. The site is in Italian but is easy to use, and the homepage can be translated into English. The contents of the collection can currently be browsed alphabetically by author or title. Once a selection is made, the text can then be downloaded in PDF, RTF, and TXT formats. Subscribing to Liber Liber is possible although not required for access.

Melvin C. Shaffer World War II Photographs
http://digitalcollections.smu.edu/all/cul/mcs/italyfrance.html

The photographs in this collection were taken by a World War II Army photographer and are housed at Southern Methodist University in Dallas, Texas. The images are from several European countries. This page has a dedicated link to a subset of 188 photos from just southern France and Italy. *See also* MELVIN C. SHAFFER WORLD WAR II PHOTOGRAPHS *under* EUROPE: CONTINENT.

Share the Perspective of Genius: Leonardo's Study for the Adoration of the Magi
http://www.loc.gov/exhibits/leonardo/

Leonardo was commissioned to paint an altarpiece on the Adoration of the Magi in 1481, which he was unable to complete. His preliminary sketches are the subject of this wonderful online exhibition. They are studied and scientifically presented here for the serious researcher or artist. Various images of Leonardo's drawings are explained in detail through a multilayer presentation comparing images in visible and infrared light ranges. A movie, *Beyond the Visible: Rediscovering the Adoration*, by the Institute and

Museum of the History of Science in Florence, Italy, provides an exciting analysis of Leonardo's work.

JAN MAYEN ISLANDS—*See* NORWAY

LATVIA

Latvians.com
http://www.latvians.com/en/Reading/reading-history.php

This site is a portal to resources such as albums and pictures, articles, documents, books (both complete and excerpts), and biographies related to Latvia's history and culture. The link provided is to the "Digital Collection" tab in the top menu bar. Scroll down the page to see the resources available, or sort them by subject ("Culture"), time period ("Timeline"), or material type ("Materials") using the tabs in the middle of the page. Most resources are in English.

National Library of Latvia—Digital Library
http://www.lnb.lv/en/digital-library

For over ten years the National Library of Latvia has been digitizing parts of its collections, including newspapers, pictures, maps, books, sheet music, and audio recordings. Click on the links in the left menu to access the collections by format. Two collections are highlighted here.

▶ **Latvia in the 16th–18th Century Maps**
  http://data.lnb.lv/nba05/kartes/frame_anglu.htm

  The 130 maps in this collection of Livonia include Latvia and its historical regions, Poland-Lithuania, Scandinavia, Russia, Northern Europe, Europe, and the Baltic Sea. Find it under the "Maps" link in the left menu.

▶ **Latvian Song Celebration Festival (1864–1940)**
  http://dziesmusvetki.lndb.lv/

  The *History of Latvian Song Celebration Festivals, 1864–1940* by Valentīns Bērzkalns (1965) is the foundation of this collection, which consists of 17 posters, 19 books, as well as 35 postcards and photos. It can be found under the "Collections" link in the left menu.

LIECHTENSTEIN

Liechtenstein Museum
http://www.liechtensteinmuseum.at/en/pages/home.asp

The Liechtenstein Museum (Vienna, Austria) is named for the House of Liechtenstein. The museum houses the Princely Collections, whose contents date back to the seventeenth century and include works by such master artists as Mantegna, Raphael, Giambologna, Rubens, and Rembrandt. This site provides a sampling of the art hanging in the museum. Use the links in the left menu to explore the site and its content, some of which has accompanying brief descriptions.

LITHUANIA

New York Public Library Digital Gallery
http://digitalgallery.nypl.org/nypldigital/dgkeysearchresult.cfm?keyword=lithuania

A search for "Lithuania" retrieved 251 images. Most images are of crosses and icons published in the New York Public Library Digital Gallery's Collection Guides World War I Photograph Albums and Postcards; Russia and Eastern Europe in Rare Photographs, 1860–1945; and Icons and Images of Cultures: Plate Books from the Russian Empire, Early Soviet Russia, and Eastern Europe, 1730–1935.

World Digital Library
http://www.wdl.org/en/search/gallery?ql=eng&s=lithuania

Ten images are classified under "Lithuania" in this collection. Items include a 1770 Latin map of the Grand Duchy of Lithuania by cartographer Tobias Conrad Lotter, several 1856 souvenir illustrated cards from a set of cards made of all the provinces of the Russian empire, and a 1922 photograph of the old Jewish cemetery in Vilnius, Lithuania, which is part of the Frank and Frances Carpenter Collection at the Library of Congress.

LUXEMBOURG

Bibliothèque nationale de Luxembourg—Luxemburgensia Online
http://www.luxemburgensia.bnl.lu/cgi/luxonline1_2.pl?action=splash

The National Library of Luxembourg's website is in French but can be translated by an online tool (such as Google Translator). The site provides access to four digital collections: Daily and Weekly (periodicals), Literature, Reference Books, and Postcards. Each collection can be clicked and browsed separately. The textual content is in PDF format and in French, which is not altered by webpage translators.

MACEDONIA

Museum of the Macedonian Struggle
http://www.macedonian-heritage.gr/Museums/History_And_War/Mma_Thessalonikhs.html

In 1982 the Museum of the Macedonian Struggle, which is located in the former Consulate General of Greece in Thessaloniki, opened its doors. The museum houses relics and materials from the period of the Macedonian Struggle. The Photo Archive of the Macedonian Struggle is a collection of photographs of the military conflicts in Macedonia between 1904 and 1908 and the First Balkan War (1912), as well as cultural, social, and school activities. Thumbnail images of items in the museum collection are provided on the right and can be enlarged.

MALTA

New York Public Library Digital Gallery
http://digitalgallery.nypl.org/nypldigital/dgkeysearchresult.cfm?keyword=malta

One hundred nineteen items are classified under "Malta." The majority come from several collections, namely, The Middle East in Early Prints and Photographs, the Art and Architecture Collection, the Uniforms and Regimental Regalia: The Vinkhuijzen Collection of Military Costume Illustration, and the George Arents Collection.

World Digital Library
http://www.wdl.org/en/search/gallery?ql=eng&s=malta

Nineteen images are classified under "Malta." They are a mix of maps, illustrations, a photochrome print of the Piazza of San Marco (Venice, Italy), plus several books, including *Journal of Magellan's Voyage* (1522–1525) and *Two Quaint Republics, Andorra and San Marino* (1913). One map, called "The Austrian Circle," shows a subdivided Holy Roman Empire.

MOLDOVA

New York Public Library Digital Gallery
http://digitalgallery.nypl.org/nypldigital/dgkeysearchresult.cfm?keyword=Moldova

One hundred ten items are classified under "Moldova," most of which come from the Russia and Eastern Europe in Rare Photographs, 1860–1945, collection and include images of schools, churches, gymnasiums, gates, pavilions, flea markets, horse farms, and persons.

World Digital Library
http://www.wdl.org/en/search/gallery?ql=eng&s=Moldova

Thirty-two images are classified under "Moldova." They include several 1856 souvenir illustrated cards as well as some maps and photos by pioneer color photographer Sergei Mikhailovich Prokudin-Gorskii.

MONACO

Gallica—Bibliothèque Numerique
http://gallica.bnf.fr/Search?ArianeWireIndex=index&p=1&lang=EN&q=monaco

This database is a digital library of materials made accessible by the National Library of France. A search for "Monaco" in the "All Gallica" tab at the top of the page returned over 7,600 items. Most of the results are categorized as books; however, there are over 300 images as well as many periodical entries. The power of the database is evident, as the search results can be sorted in multiple ways using the choices in the left menu. These include type of document (book, image, etc.), language, author, and publication date. *See also* GALLICA—BIBLIOTHÈQUE NUMÈRIQUE *under* FRANCE.

MONTENEGRO

Narodni muzej Crne Gore (National Museum of Montenegro)
http://www.mnmuseum.org/txt_e.htm

This museum in Cetinje, which dates back to 1896, consists of five departments: King Nikola's Museum (former State Museum), Art Museum, Historical Museum, Ethnographic Museum, and the Museum of Petar II Petroviæ Njegoš. An overview of and sample images from each department are accessible from an interactive geographical map on the homepage showing the location of each building in Cetinje. Information and photos about old, new, and temporary exhibitions and a photo gallery with scenic shots of Cetinje (click "gallery" in the left menu) are among the website's offerings.

NETHERLANDS

Digital Library of the Royal Netherlands Academy of Arts and Sciences
http://www.digitallibrary.nl/

This digital library provides access to collections of resources, both single books and periodicals, previously published by the Royal Netherlands Academy of Arts and Sciences. The resources are grouped into three databases.

▶ **History of Science and Scholarship in the Netherlands**
   http://www.historyofscience.nl/

   This website is the entrée to the works of historical Dutch scientists and scholars ranging from the eighteenth to the twentieth centuries and covering many subjects. The database is organized by author. Each author entry includes a short biography, a list of related links, and sometimes information on individual works. Choose an author from the drop-down search box to access the content. Texts and biographies are in English, Latin, German, French, and Dutch.

▶ **Levensberichten & Herdenkingen**
   http://www.digitallibrary.nl/levensberichten/

   This collection contains "life messages" and tributes written after the deaths of Academy members. Choose a member by name from the drop-down list to access brief biographical information and the message. This resource is in Dutch only but can be translated using an online webpage translator.

▶ **Proceedings of the Royal Netherlands Academy of Arts and Sciences**
   http://www.digitallibrary.nl/proceedings/

   The *Proceedings* are scientific articles published by the Academy between 1898 and 1997. Currently, access is available to some complete volumes of the earlier years; however, the content is arranged by article author. Use the drop-down search box to choose an author by name, or enter search terms in the full-text search box.

National Library of the Netherlands (Koninklijke Bibliotheek)
http://www.kb.nl/menu/webexposities-en.html

The National Library currently has several web exhibitions on its "Expositions and Collections" page. A sampling includes the medieval manuscripts exhibition *Illuminated Manuscripts*, which showcases 11,000 illustrations from the Koninklijke Bibliotheek and the Museum Meermanno-Westreenianum; the book art exhibition *Koopman Collection*, which includes selections of French literary works of the twentieth century; the chess exhibition *Queen's Move; Women and Chess through the Ages*; the almanacs and calendars exhibition *A Matter of Time: Almanacs and Calendars of the Koninklijke Bibliotheek*; and the historical exhibition *The Memory of Netherlands*, which focuses on the cultural heritage of the Netherlands. Each exhibition has a link to its own webpage where it can be further examined.

Rijksmuseum Amsterdam
http://www.rijksmuseum.nl/collectie/?lang=en

The Rijksmuseum offers "webspecials" ("unique presentations of works of art, owned or loaned by the Rijksmuseum"), exhibits, and a number of digital collections, some of which are highlighted here.

▶ **Accessorize!**
http://www.rijksmuseum.nl/accessoires-webtentoonstelling?lang=en

This web exhibition showcases the museum's fashion accessory collection of gloves, shoes, hats, and various other clothing accessories. One can also play an online "Fan Game" as well as experience some other interactive links.

▶ **Early Netherlandish Paintings in the Rijksmuseum, Amsterdam. Volume I—Artists Born before 1500**
http://www.rijksmuseum.nl/early-netherlandish-paintings?lang=en

This online catalog provides access to nearly 160 early Netherlandish paintings by artists born before 1500. Click on an artist's name in the "index" to view the paintings.

▶ **Explore 1000 Major Exhibits**
http://www.rijksmuseum.nl/collectie/ontdekdecollectie?lang=en

Search through the Rijksmuseums's top exhibits by exploring this one collection. The content is efficiently organized and is browseable by artist, theme, and several other indices in the left menu. A keyword search tool is also available to search all of the exhibits at once.

▶ **The Masterpieces**
http://www.rijksmuseum.nl/meesterwerken?lang=en

According to this webpage, while the Rijksmuseum is under restoration, the best of its permanent collection is being displayed in the newly furnished Philips Wing. Three-dimensional interactive panoramas of the Philips Wing feature several rooms, including the Dutch Republic, World Power, Frans Hals, and Rembrandt and his pupils. Apple QuickTime is required to view the panoramas. The "Masterpieces special" link provides an online presentation of highlights of The Masterpieces collection, which can be viewed one by one, thematically, or chronologically.

NORWAY

Astrup Fearnley Museum of Modern Art
http://afmuseet.no/?top_menu=3

This museum in the capital city of Oslo is devoted to both Norwegian and international modern art, and selected artists are highlighted on the website. On "The Collection" page, choose an artist's name from the left menu to read information about the artist and views some of the artist's works by clicking through the photos in the lower right of the page.

Edvard Munch: Prints—The Complete Graphic Works
http://www.munch.museum.no/grafikk/english.asp

By using the advanced search tool on the lower right of the page and criteria such as title, date range, method, technique, and printer, The Munch Museum exhibition catalogue of over 700 graphic motifs by Edvard Munch will yield the researcher a detailed display of the individual works.

National Library of Norway
http://www.nb.no/english/digital-stories

The National Library of Norway has digitized a selection of its material and presents them as "Digital Stories." There are currently five.

▶ **George Morgenstierne**
http://www.nb.no/baser/morgenstierne/english/index.html

This archive contains audio, movie, and photographic content from Professor Morgenstierne's journeys to various South Asian countries.

▶ **Letter from the South Pole**
http://www.nb.no/southpole/

In December 1911 explorer Roald Amundsen left a letter for "Admiral His Majesty King Haakon VII of Norway" and a note for explorer Robert Falcon Scott at the South Pole. This is a digital story of the letter, using an interactive clickable timeline.

▶ **Promise of America**
http://www.nb.no/emigrasjon/emigration/

This is a portal to resources (articles, books, letters, photos, etc.) about Norwegian Americans, their history, and their emigration to the United States between 1825 and 2000. Enter the site, and then click on the different formats in the left menu to peruse the content.

▶ **This Month's Object**
http://www.nb.no/manedens/illuminasjon/

This Norwegian-only page highlights a different object from the collection each month.

▶ **Tiny Traces**
http://www.nb.no/sma_spor/index_content.html

The digital exhibits accessed from this page have one thing in common—children. *Through the Eyes of Children* is a collection of photographs taken by children at the dawn of the twenty-first century. *A Gifted Girl* showcases "The Four Seasons," a miniature book that Nobel Prize winner and novelist Sigrid Undset made as a child. *The One and Only* is a glimpse into the childhood of Crown Prince Olav (Olav V, King of Norway). *Children of the Eight Seasons* uses one photograph taken by Kåre Kivijärvi in 1964 to engage viewers to learn about the Sami people of Norway. *Magic Moments* is a photo slide show of people and landscapes taken by Kåre Kivijärvi.

POLAND

Memorial and Museum—Auschwitz-Birkenau
http://en.auschwitz.org.pl/m/index.php?option=com_ponygallery&Itemid=3

This photo gallery contains historical photographs and documents, contemporary photographs of the former Auschwitz-Birkenau Concentration and Extermination Camp (1940–1945), photographs from both the permanent and national exhibitions of the Auschwitz-Birkenau State Museum, and photos of art pieces that were created in secret by the prisoners of the concentration camp.

Museum of the Mazovian Countryside
http://www.mwmskansen.pl/en/index.php

The Museum of the Mazovian Countryside preserves historic monuments of folk culture. Take a virtual walking tour of the village of Sierpc and its surroundings. The tour and related information is in Polish or translatable into German.

National Museum in Poznan
http://www.mnp.art.pl/index_a.html

The National Museum in Poznan has nine collections: Gallery of Antique Art, Gallery of Medieval Art, Gallery of Polish Art of 16th–18th Centuries, Gallery of Polish Art of 18th–20th Centuries, Gallery of Contemporary Art, Gallery of Foreign Painting, Print Room, Gallery of Poster and Design, and Coin Room. Put the mouse on "Collections" in the middle of the page and choose one. Each collection includes some background information and thumbnail photographs that can be enlarged.

National Museum in Warsaw
http://www.mnw.art.pl/index.php/en/collections/

This website has two main areas of content. Click "Permanent Galleries" and then choose from seven separate areas of the museum collection, including Ancient Art, Medieval Art, Polish Art, and European Painting. Collections in the "Study Collections" link include Eastern Christianity Art, Oriental Art, Decorative Arts and Crafts, and Foreign Prints and Drawings. Each page contains an introduction to the collection and a slide show of photos that can be enlarged.

Wilanów Poster Museum
http://www.postermuseum.pl/en/exhibition

The Wilanów Poster Museum houses one of the world's largest collections of posters. The website offers a sampling of posters from the 2003–2007 exhibitions. Click on each year to see the content.

PORTUGAL

Biblioteca Nacional de Portugal
http://purl.pt/index/geral/PT/index.html

The National Library of Portugal has digitized images of items in several collections. First, translate the page using an online tool. Then choose one of the collections listed in the upper right, which are organized by format, such as text, image, map, and sound files. Browse or search each collection separately by author, title, date, or keyword using the links in the left menu on each collection page.

▶ ### Portuguese Culture
http://purl.pt/index/porCulture/EN/index.html

Portuguese Culture is a special digital library project maintained by the National Library and funded by the Luso-American Development Foundation. Its goal is to highlight and provide content concerning Portuguese culture and history from works that have been translated into English and thus are more easily used by the international community. Current content is grouped into three categories: books, iconography, and maps.

ROMANIA

Biblioteca Nationala a României
http://www.bibnat.ro/Colectii-digitale-s94-ro.htm

The National Library of Romania has begun to digitize various documents in its collection, such as manuscripts, rare books, and historical archives. Materials were selected for this project based on a number of criteria, most notably age and physical condition. Included are the *National Library Journal*, the *Journal of the History of the Book*, and items from the Information and Documentation collection. Translate the webpage into English using an online tool, and then choose "Manuscripts" or "Historical Archive" under "Digital Collections" in the left menu to start browsing.

Museums and Collections in Romania
http://ghidulmuzeelor.cimec.ro/selen.asp

This webpage is a portal to digital materials from museums and collections throughout Romania. Narrow a search by selecting items from the lists of "County," "Location," or "Museum main profile," or enter words into the "Search by expression" box. Highlight multiple selections in the lists for federated searching. Collections are also accessible from an alphabetical list of individual museums or by clicking on a letter from the A to

Z list. These links are at the bottom of the page. A map of all the museums in Bucharest is accessible as well.

Muzeul National de'Arta al Romaniei (National Museum of Art of Romania)
http://www.mnar.arts.ro/

Click on "English" (or "French" or "Romanian") in the lower portion of the page to enter the website. The website is organized into several galleries and collections, which are described here. Each has a separate page, with descriptive information and images that can be clicked and viewed.

▶ **Decorative Arts Collection**
http://www.mnar.arts.ro/Decorative-arts

This museum collection is a combination of tapestries, miniature paintings, ceramics and glassware, Art Nouveau works, furniture, jewelry, jade and ivory carvings, silver, bronze, tin, and seventeenth- to nineteenth-century clocks. The online collection provides access to 37 items from the collection, which are organized chronologically by object classification and country of origin (schools, workshops, and artists).

▶ **Drawings and Prints Collection**
http://www.mnar.arts.ro/Drawings-and-prints

This museum collection, which contains works by both Romanian and foreign artists, is a blend of drawings, watercolors, and prints. Highlights of the collection include Romanian contemporary art, including caricatures, poster designs, and Japanese prints. The online database presents 40 works from the Cabinet of Drawings and Prints, which are organized by school.

▶ **The European Art Gallery**
http://www.mnar.arts.ro/European-art

Sixty works from the museum's collection of European paintings and sculptures ranging in date from the fourteenth through the twentieth century are highlighted in this gallery. Scroll down to see all the content, or choose a named "School" from the middle of the page to limit the content.

▶ **Lapidarium**
http://www.mnar.arts.ro/Lapidarium

This is part of the stone sculpture collection of the Romanian Medieval Art Gallery and highlights the craftsmanship of the Wallachian stone masters from the fourteenth to the eighteenth centuries. The online exhibit consists of a selection of tombstones, inscriptions, decorative door and window frames, monumental columns, column bases, and capitals.

▶ **Oriental Art**
http://www.mnar.arts.ro/colectii/EN_arta-orientala.php

This collection is organized into "Islamic Art" (textiles, ceramics, metalwork, and embroideries), "Chinese Art" (paintings, jade carvings, ceramics and porcelain, costumes and embroideries, metalwork, cloisonné and ivories, and wood, bronze, and stone sculptures), and "Japanese Art" (paintings, ivory carvings, ceramics and porcelain, arms and armor pieces, liturgical textiles, metalwork, and sculptures). Follow one of the links and then click an image to enlarge and view it.

▶ **Romanian Medieval Art**
http://www.mnar.arts.ro/Romanian-Medieval-Art

Forty works representing Walachia, Moldavia, and Transylvania from the late fourteenth through the early nineteenth centuries are showcased. This gallery's content is grouped by format and accessed by the following links: "Fresco Fragments," "Embroideries and Textiles," "Manuscripts," "Woodcarvings," "Metalwork," and "Icons."

▶ **Romanian Modern Art**
http://www.mnar.arts.ro/Romanian-Modern-Art

Organized chronologically, the 40 works presented here are just a small representation of the many Romanian Modern Art paintings and sculptures that are part of the museum's collection.

Virtual Museum of the Ethnographical Monuments in the Romanian Open Air Museums
http://www.cimec.ro/Etnografie/aer/aeretnen.htm

According to the "Foreward" [*sic*] page, The Institute for Cultural Memory (CIMEC), in collaboration with 17 museums and museum open air sections and with support from the Romanian Ministry of Culture's Department of Museums and Collections, created the "Virtual Museum" project. Its aim is to showcase folk architecture monuments that are reflective of the different ethnic minorities living in Romania: Hungarians, Szecklers, Lippovans, Germans, Ukrainians, Turks, Tartars, etc. Some of the monuments have been preserved in museums, such as the Zapodeni House, which is housed in the Village Museum, while others remain in their original locations. The website is searchable by museum, ethnographic area, ethnical group, and county. Only parts of this site are available in English.

SAN MARINO

New York Public Library Digital Gallery
http://digitalgallery.nypl.org/nypldigital/dgkeysearchresult.cfm?keyword=san+marino

Seventy-nine images are classified under "San Marino" in this collection, the majority of which are part of Uniforms and Regimental Regalia: The Vinkhuijzen Collection of Military Costume Illustration.

World Digital Library
http://www.wdl.org/en/item/629/?ql=eng&s=san+marino&view_type=gallery

One item is classified under "San Marino" in this collection. It is a book titled *Two Quaint Republics, Andorra and San Marino*, by American writer Virginia Wales Johnson. This 1913 book describes the history, social life, customs, and economic resources of San Marino.

SERBIA

Digital National Library of Serbia
http://digital.nb.rs/eng/index.php

The National Library of Serbia website has a handful of accessible digital collections containing Cyrillic manuscripts, poetry, rare books, periodicals, maps, photographs, posters, music, and art. Use the search box on the homepage to search across all collections, or choose a collection in the left menu to browse one at a time. Individual collection pages have brief descriptions and tools to search within the collection. Descriptive information is in English, but the content is in Serbian.

The Museum of Applied Art
http://www.mpu.org.rs/english/index.htm

The Museum of Applied Art in Belgrade contains artwork created by both Serbians and artists worldwide. Click on "Departments with Collections" at the bottom of the page to see a list of the museum departments. Each department (Metal and Jewellery; Textile and Costume; Furniture; Photography and Applied Graphic Art; Ceramics, Glass and Porcelain; Contemporary Applied Art; and Architecture, Urbanism and Architectural Design) has digitized a select handful of items for viewing. Four photographs from the exhibit *Nikola Vučo's Legacy* are also available: "Man-Bicycle," "Jelka with Net," "We Don't Have Anyone to Persuade" and "The Wall of Agnosticism." Take a virtual tour of the museum by clicking "Virtual Visit" in the bottom bar.

SLOVAKIA

Slovak National Gallery
http://www.sng.sk/?id=1&loc=1&lang=1

The Slovak National Gallery provides an online sampling of objects in the current exhibition as well as highlights from past (2004–2010), foreign (2007–2009), and permanent (*16th–18th Century European Art, Gothic Art in Slovakia, Baroque Art in Slovakia,* and *19th Century Art in Slovakia*) exhibitions. Click on a choice under "Exhibitions" in the left menu. From within, choose a year if necessary, and then choose an exhibition from the blue section. Exhibitions are presented with descriptions and images that can be clicked on and enlarged.

SLOVENIA

National and University Library (Narodna in Univerzitetna Knjiznica)
http://www.nuk.uni-lj.si/

The Digital Library of Slovenia is a portal to digitized resources such as journals, books, manuscripts, maps, photographs, music, and reference material. All collections are freely accessible. Translate the site by clicking "English" near the top middle of the homepage, then click "Virtual Exhibition" under the "What's On" header at the right end of the red bar. Exhibition content changes periodically.

The National Museum of Contemporary History
http://www.muzej-nz.si/slo/zbirke.html

Translate the page into English using an online tool, and click "Collections" in the left menu. The focus of the National Museum of Contemporary History is on the First and Second World Wars, the First and Second Yugoslavias, and independent Slovenia. The museum offers a limited selection of images to highlight their many collections, among which are weapons and military equipment, photographs and negatives, fine arts, textiles, badges and signs, philatelics, postcards, medals and decorations, plaques, and numismatics. There are also three special Second World War collections. Choose a collection, and then click the sample images on the right or click "Gallery" to tour through the content. Content descriptions are available in English.

SPAIN

Biblioteca de Catalunya
http://www.bnc.es/digital/cercacat.php?categoria=FDIG

The digital collections of the Library of Catalonia include historical, cultural, and Catalan literature resources in the forms of documents, cartographic graphics, sound recordings, incunabula, manuscripts, musical scores, and magazines. This collections page presents the content by format. Click a "+" sign to expand a collection and browse the content.

Biblioteca Nacional de Espaòa (National Library of Spain)
http://www.bne.es/en/Catalogos/BibliotecaDigital/bibliotecadigitalhispanica.html

The online resources of the National Library of Spain are made available through the Hispanic Digital Library (Biblioteca Digital Hispánica). The digital library proffers access to books, manuscripts, drawings, prints, brochures, posters, photographs, newspapers, maps, and atlases by clicking on a theme or subtheme or by choosing a theme in the drop-down box near the top of the page, such as masterpieces, fine arts, pure sciences, science and culture in general, and literature. Click on "Collections" at the top to see an alphabetical list and descriptions of the collections. Two collections are highlighted here.

▶ **Collection of Drawings of Architecture and Decoration of the Eighteenth Century**
http://bibliotecadigitalhispanica.bne.es/R/9Y6ASA7P89A762B1H5LEQHP9X68PB
UDGE6JTQE683IYJ27PK6D-00709?func=collections-result&collection_id=1471

This is a collection of nearly 1,200 drawings of eighteenth-century European architecture and furniture.

▶ **Quixotes Collection**
http://bibliotecadigitalhispanica.bne.es/R/?func=search-advanced-go&find_code1=
COL&request1=quijotes

Just a small sampling of the items that can be found in the National Library Cervantes collection have been made available.

Fundación Eugenio Granell
http://www.fundacion-granell.org/colecciones/index.php

The Eugenio Granell Foundation owns works by the painter himself (oils, drawings, constructions, collages, found objects, photographs) but also works by other surrealist artists as well. A small sampling of Granell's artwork along with the artwork of Philip West and others is available here. Choose one of the collections in the left menu and click to see the content.

Fundación Gala-Salvador Dalí
http://www.salvador-dali.org/dali/coleccio/en_index.html

The Gala-Dalí Foundation oversees several collections of works by Salvador Dalí (paintings, drawings, sculptures, engravings, installations, jewelry, holograms, and photography). Click "Selected Works" to view 45 of his works done between 1918 and 1982 or "Catalogue Raisonné of Paintings 1910–1939," which is searchable by keyword, title, catalog number, chronologically, or by collection.

Fundación Picasso
http://fundacionpicasso.malaga.eu/opencms/opencms/fundacionpicasso/portal_en/
    menu/submenus/seccion0001/secciones/principal

Plaza de la Merced (Malaga) is Pablo Picasso's birthplace and also the location of the Foundation. The Foundation offers a selection of Picasso's works from its collection. Click on "Catalogue of Works of Art" to see all content, and then limit by type of work to narrow the focus.

Lazarus Foundation Galdiano
http://www.flg.es/colecciones.asp

The foundation is named for Jose Lazaro Galdiano, a financier, publisher, and collector of Spanish art. The images here are representative of the more than 12,000 pieces in the museum, and information about each item such as the author, title, chronology, school, subject, technique, and dimensions is provided. Some of the collections represented are Fans; Arms and Armor; Archeology; Bronze; Ceramics; Drawings; Sculpture; Enamels; Prints; Irons; Precision Instruments; Trappings; Jewelry; Ivory and Bone; Medals; Miniatures; Coins; Furniture; Hard Rock; Painting; Platelets; Silver; Watches; Textiles; and Glass and Crystal. Translate the page into English using an online tool, and then choose a collection from the list on the right. Then use the search tools provided to browse within that collection.

Letters of Philip II, King of Spain, 1592–1597
http://lib.byu.edu/dlib/phil2/

The Harold B. Lee Library at Brigham Young University is home to a collection of unpublished letters and documents dated between 1592 and 1597, many of which are signed by King Philip II and addressed to Diego de Orellana de Chaves, Corregidor of the Four Towns of the Sea on Spain's North Coast. Click a link under "Learn More" for more information, or "Browse the Collection" in the left menu to see the content, currently 176 items.

Museu de Prehistòria de València
http://www.museuprehistoriavalencia.es/listado_fotografia.html

The Museum of Prehistory of València's photographic archive contains thousands of images taken from glass plates, negatives and transparencies, slides, and digital photographs. Included are photographs from the excavations of El Tossal de Sant Miquel (Llíria, Valencia), La Cova Negra (Xàtiva, Valencia), La Cova del Parpalló (Gandía, Valencia), and La Bastida de les Alcusses (Moixent, Valencia). Translate the page using an online tool and click one of the five predetermined categories, or use the search box to get started.

Museo Nacional del Prado (Prado Museum)
http://www.museodelprado.es/en/the-collection/online-gallery/

The online database provides access to almost 1,000 images, which are representative of the Museum's collection of paintings, sculpture, prints, drawings, and decorative arts. The museum will continue to add content until the website contains images of the entire collection. The online collection is available in English; enter an artist or title in the search box, or choose "Advanced Search" for other options.

SWEDEN

Andrée Expeditionen
http://www.grennamuseum.se/info.aspx?visa=galleri

S.A. Andrée's polar expedition in 1897 is the focus of the *Andrée Expedition* exhibit, which is housed in the Polar Centre of the Grenna Museum. The photo gallery includes a selection of personal and expedition photos plus excerpts from a diary kept during the expedition. The site is in Swedish but can be translated by using an online tool (such as Google Translator).

Arkitekturmuseet
http://www.arkitekturmuseet.se/english/picture_bank/

The Museum of Architecture contains drawings, sketches, and items mainly from the 1850s onward about the history of Swedish building. The museum's picture bank contains nearly 8,000 drawings and photographs, most of which date from the twentieth century. Architect, project name, and photographer are just a few of the search terms that can be used to access this extensive database. Click "database" embedded in the text in the middle of the page to access the advanced search page. Translate the advanced search page separately using an online tool to more easily use the search criteria. The picture bank and the image descriptions are in Swedish.

Göteborgs Konstmuseum
http://www.konstmuseum.goteborg.se/

The Göteborg Museum of Art, known for its collection of Nordic Art, offers an online selection of images from a variety of collections, including art ranging from the fifteenth to the twentieth centuries. While information about the images is available in English, the left menu does not always translate from Swedish when the page is translated. Click "samlingar" in the left menu to access the collection categories. Then browse through these to see the content.

Jamtli
http://bildarkivet.jamtli.com/

Jamtli is a foundation whose museum contains a photo archive with over 100,000 photos focusing on the cultural history of Jämtland and Härjedalen. The collection is searchable by keywords, date, location, subject (person in the picture), the photographer, and the collection. All description information is in Swedish.

Kungliga Biblioteket (National Library of Sweden)
http://www.kb.se/samlingarna/digitala/

Since 1661, the National Library of Sweden has been collecting print materials from Sweden or in Swedish. Digitization of the library collections is ongoing. Translate the webpage using an online tool and look for links to the collections (titles in Swedish with English equivalents) in the left menu.

▶ **Affischer (Posters)**
http://www.kb.se/samlingarna/digitala/affischer/

This site includes digital exhibitions of Swedish posters that are arranged by author or theme.

▶ **Codex Gigas**
http://www.kb.se/samlingarna/digitala/codex-gigas/

Since 1649 the Codex Gigas, or Devil's Bible, has been a part of the National Library collection after it was taken by the Swedish army as plunder during the Thirty Years War.

▶ **Digitaliserad dagspress (Digitized Newspapers)**
http://www.kb.se/samlingarna/digitala/Digitaliserad-dagspress/

This site includes over 200,000 pages from newspapers.

▶ **Kartor (Maps)**
http://www.kb.se/samlingarna/digitala/kartor/

Here is a selection of digitized maps ranging from the mid-sixteenth century to the twentieth century.

▶ **Linnés nätverk (Linnaeus' Network)**
http://www.kb.se/samlingarna/digitala/Linnes-natverks/

This site highlights 26 friends and colleagues of Carl Linnaeus (1707–1778), who was a botanist, physician, and zoologist and considered the "Father of Taxonomy."

▶ **Resor genom tiderna (Travel through the Ages)**
http://www.kb.se/samlingarna/digitala/resor-tiderna/

This variety of resources on the subject of travel include travel in Sweden, Swedish emigration to America, photographs taken or purchased by researcher Arthur Thesleff while traveling through Europe and South America (including those he took of the Roma in Europe), and two journals that describe separate journeys taken in 1746 by the East India Company to the Far East.

▶ **Suecia antiqua . . .**
http://www.kb.se/samlingarna/digitala/suecia/

Suecia Antiqua et Hodierna or *Ancient and Modern Sweden*, is a collection of engravings that was compiled by Erik Dahlbergh during the mid-1600s.

Länsmuseet Gävleborg
http://sofie.xlm.se/

Gävleborg County Museum has a Swedish website, which can be translated using an online tool (such as Google Translator). The site has two online collections identified at the bottom of the page. Included among the thousands of photographs in the photo database are views of the county (city and rural), aerial photographs, postcards, and portraits. The objects ("lot") database contains photos of chairs, couches, cabinets, mirrors, and other items from the furniture warehouse. Folk art textiles from the Hedwig Ulfsparre collection are also searchable. Both databases are searchable by clicking the "Search" link at the base of each collection. An online wallpaper database is planned for 2011.

Moderna Museet
http://www.modernamuseet.se/en/The-Collection/The-collection1/

The Moderna Museet art collection is international in scope, with artworks spanning from 1900 to the present. The photograph collection contains works as far back as the 1840s. The online database, which is continuously updated, holds over 20,000 images and is a mix of paintings and sculptures, films and videos, drawings, graphic art, and photography. Click "Search the Collection" in the top menu bar to get started. Image descriptions are in Swedish.

Museum Gustavianum
http://www.gustavianum.uu.se/en/node2

Museum Gustavianum, which is part of the Uppsala University campus, has a number of collections containing nearly 150 objects, including the Augsburg Art Cabinet, a cabinet of curiosities that dates back to the early 1600s. Click on the individual collections in the left menu to see information and sample images of some museum exhibits. The Augsburg Art Cabinet link can be found under "Art Collections." Click the online option to see the virtual tour. A Flash Player is required to view the tour, and it is in Swedish.

Museum Kulenovic Collection
http://www.museumldv.com/slike/slike1.htm

This museum's online photo gallery is a selection from its extensive collection of paintings, drawings, etchings and prints, sculptures, artifacts, and ceramics. The reverse paintings on glass of Rizah Kulenovic, the custodian of the museum, are also highlighted. Click on one of the three categories in the main section of the page to see the selected images available. Move between categories using the links near the top of the page.

Nationalmuseum
http://www.nationalmuseum.se/sv/English-startpage/Collections/

The Nationalmuseum online collection is composed of paintings, sculptures, drawings and graphic art, furniture, and applied art and design. The collection is searchable by a number of criteria, including artist, nationality, title, and type of object. Image details are in Swedish and will contain information such as the title, artist, date of signature, materials and techniques, measurements, inventory number, and acquisition data. Click "Search the Collections—WebArt" in the left menu to access the advanced search page.

Råå Museum
http://www.raamuseum.se/index-eng.htm

The theme of this museum, located near the harbour of Råå, Helsingborg, Sweden, is fishermen and sailors. A model of the village of Öresund (The Sound), fishing tackle, a typical fisherman's home, navigation instruments, carpenters' tools, ship models, a re-creation of a boat captain's cabin from a sailing ship, and a wheelhouse and galley from a trawler are just some of the photos in the online gallery. Click on "Gallery" in the left margin and then choose the areas of the museum individually to see the sample content.

Rolf Bergendorff's Radio Museum
http://home1.swipnet.se/~w-12206/radio/main.htm

The Radio Museum's online exhibit displays radios from different time periods and by over 20 different manufacturers, including Philips, Blaupunkt, Grundig, Telefunken, and Luxor. Click a manufacturer and then an image within to see multiple views and some brief accompanying specs.

Spårvägsmuseet
http://sparvagsmuseet.sl.se/

The Stockholm Transport Museum's online collection contains digitized maps, press clippings, photographs, and drawings all dealing with the cultural and historical aspects of the local traffic of Stockholm. The items range in date from the first horse trams in 1877 through modern day. Translate the page using an online tool. Click on "Know More" in the left margin, and then choose "Collections" to see the categories.

SWITZERLAND

Sammlungen
http://www.landesmuseen.ch/e/sammlung/online_sammlungen/index.php

The Swiss National Museum illuminates the archaeology, history, artistry, and cultural legacy of Switzerland. The National Museum currently has three online collections.

▶ **Timemachine**
http://www.timemachine.ch/

This online collection has an exhibition titled *Switzerland in Motion*. Visitors can search the time machine of over 500 images by subject and/or decade or take the guided tour. The exhibit is in German only.

▶ **Virtuelle Transfer**
http://vtms.musee-suisse.ch/

This interactive collection tells stories about museum objects using historical and fictional characters to present their history. The site is available in English, German, French, and Italian.

▶ **Webcollection**
http://webcollection.landesmuseen.ch/

This online digital collection is reflective of the many museum collections. The text is available in German, French, and Italian.

Swiss National Library NL—Swiss Poster History
http://www.nb.admin.ch/themen/01417/index.html?lang=en

The posters available in this online collection are drawn from several collections in addition to the National Library's, including the Bibliothèque de Genève, the Bibliothèque publique et universitaire de Neuchâtel, the Médiathèque Valais, and the Museum of Transport. They were created by both Swiss and international artists and range in date from the late 1800s to the present. The posters cover such topics as tourism, exhibitions, publicity, cultural activities, sports, and political campaigns. Click the categories under "Swiss poster history" in the left menu to access the content.

UKRAINE

The Bohdan Medwidsky Ukrainian Folklore Archives
http://www.museums.ualberta.ca/dig/search/ukrn/

The Ukrainian Folklore Archives' online database is under the auspices of the Department of Modern Languages and Cultural Studies at the University of Alberta, Canada. The online collection contains over 23,000 records and can be searched or browsed. Click "Search the Collection" and choose to search by keyword, people, subject, or accession number. Search results include images that can be enlarged and a brief accompanying description.

▶ **Ukrainian Commercial Recording**
http://www.museums.ualberta.ca/dig/search/ukrn/

Commercial recordings of Ukrainian music and songs have been preserved. Search the collection of over 5,000 albums and 13,000 songs and musical pieces by album, song, title, performer, recording label, recording location, and date of recording. Click "Search the Collection" and choose "Commercial Recordings" in the left margin.

▶ **Ukrainian Folklore Sound Recordings**
http://projects.tapor.ualberta.ca/UkraineAudio/

Since 1998 Natalie Kononeko has been interviewing people in the villages of Central Ukraine. Poetry, illnesses and cures, folk narratives, songs, and discussions of folk beliefs and rituals are some of the subjects in these recordings. Click a topic from the English list on the right side of the page.

▶ **Ukrainian Wedding Exhibit**
http://www.museums.ualberta.ca/exhibits/ukrnwedding/r_intro.html

Ukrainian wedding traditions is the focus of this online collection. The site offers an overview of both traditional Ukrainian and Ukrainian Canadian wedding rituals, along with photographs, video clips, teaching resources, and a glossary. Select from the options in the left menu.

Pysanky—Easter Eggs
http://www.ukrainianmuseum.org/pysanky.html

The Ukrainian Museum presents an online exhibit of Ukrainian *pysanka* or painted Easter eggs. This page describes the traditional folk art of egg painting, and the images can be enlarged by clicking on them. Click "To the Pysanky Slide Show" to view 17 images of both actual *pysanka* and artwork that encompasses them. Choose "Collections" in the left menu to see other kinds of objects in the museum.

UNITED KINGDOM

The British Library
http://www.bl.uk/onlinegallery/index.html

The British Library is the national library of the United Kingdom and was created in 1973. Prior to this, the national library was part of the British Museum. The library contains books, journal and newspaper titles, patents, sound recordings, and much more. The online gallery features 30,000 items from the library collection through exhibitions, virtual books, and a selection of highlighted resources and personal galleries that users have chosen to share. The library uses its own Turning the Pages™ software, which allows viewers to peruse page by page through great works. The "Highlights tour" (a tab on the top menu bar) currently showcases 15 unique works from the library's collections, including the Gutenberg Bible and the Magna Carta. The "Online exhibitions" tab (on the top menu bar) brings to light popular online exhibitions, including three of the most viewed and three of the most recent additions. The "Online Gallery Home" offers eight major exhibitions, which are described here.

▶ **Black Europeans**
http://www.bl.uk/onlinegallery/features/blackeuro/homepage.html

Featured are the lives of Alexander Pushkin, Alexandre Dumas, George Polgreen Bridgetower, Samuel Coleridge-Taylor, and John Archer, all of whom are of African descent. The exhibition was guest-curated by Mike Phillips for the British Library Online Gallery.

▶ **Henry VIII: Man and Monarch**
http://www.bl.uk/onlinegallery/onlineex/henryviii/index.html

Created to mark the 500th anniversary of Henry VIII's accession to the throne, this exhibition features key documents such as personal and official correspondence and maps from the life and times of Henry VIII. Included also are video clips from Dr. David Starkey's television series *Henry VIII: The Mind of a Tyrant*.

▶ **Historical Texts**
http://www.bl.uk/onlinegallery/onlineex/histtexts/index.html

Famous historical documents are featured, such as the Anglo Saxon Chronicle, Nelson's Memorandum, and Florence Nightingale's letters.

▶ **Magna Carta**
http://www.bl.uk/treasures/magnacarta/index.html

Features of this exhibition include the ability to closely examine the Magna Carta and to get it translated from Latin into English as you go along. Short videos show the curator briefly answering "frequently asked questions" about the Magna Carta.

▶ **Points of View**
http://www.bl.uk/onlinegallery/onlineex/pointsofview/index.html

Explore eight exhibitions (*Art*, *Beginnings*, *Life*, *New Century*, *Portraits*, *Progress*, *Science*, and *Travel*) of nineteenth-century life documented in photographs. Videos about early photographic techniques are part of the exhibitions as well.

▶ **Sacred**
http://www.bl.uk/onlinegallery/features/sacred/homepage.html

This exhibition shows Jewish, Christian, and Muslim holy books. It also includes videos, such as a Sufi dancer performing a modern "whirling dervish" dance; podcasts, such as *Science vs Religion? The Atheists' View*; and interactive features, such as *Sacred Stories*.

▶ **Taking Liberties**
http://www.bl.uk/takingliberties

The struggle for Britain's freedoms and rights over a period of more than 900 years is the focus of this exhibition. Access documents such as the Magna Carta and the 1998 Belfast Agreement, take an interactive journey and see where your views on liberty and freedom stand with everyone else's, or listen to podcasts. The online interactive requires Flash.

▶ **Turn the Pages**
http://www.bl.uk/onlinegallery/virtualbooks/index.html

Watch a video that shows how to use the Turning the Pages™ software, or choose a volume to page through from the titles listed, such as the draft score of Handel's *Messiah*, a selection of Leonardo da Vinci's sketches, the Ramayana, or a seventeenth-century bible from Ethiopia.

Cornucopia
http://www.cornucopia.org.uk/

According to its homepage, Cornucopia, developed and managed by the Museums, Libraries and Archives Council, is an online database portal to over 6,000 collections in museums, galleries, archives, and libraries in the United Kingdom. Browse the database by several methods: using the categories time, people, place, subject, or culture;

entering a search term; combining a keyword and your postcode to search for collections near you; or searching across other websites using web services.

England

Victoria and Albert Museum
http://www.vam.ac.uk/collections/index.html

The Victoria and Albert Museum website provides access to over 1,000,000 works from its collections, including ceramics, fashion, furniture, glass, metalwork, paintings, photographs, prints, sculptures, and textiles. Choose a category from the grid on the main page and start exploring.

Northern Ireland

Murals of Northern Ireland
http://ccdl.libraries.claremont.edu/collection.php?alias=/mni

Housed in the Claremont Colleges Digital Library, created by the Claremont University Consortium in Southern California, the Murals of Northern Ireland collection contains images of murals that relate to the period of "Troubles," or the period of violence in Ireland from the late 1960s and the late 1990s. There are currently 597 images in the site, each with full bibliographic information and a textual description. There is a simple keyword search tool, or the entire collection can be browsed by subject. Images include murals representing both sides of the conflict and range from political statements to representations of violence.

Scotland

Aberdeen Art Gallery & Museums
http://www.aagm.co.uk/TheCollections/collections.aspx

The Art Gallery has several collections. Subjects include fine art, applied art, maritime history, science, technology and industry, archaeology, and coins, banknotes, medals, and tokens. The collections can be searched by artist/maker, title of works, keyword, specific collection, date range, or the Aberdeen Art Gallery & Museum's reference code. The collections are also accessible by doing an A to Z search of artists' names and subjects. Click "Basic Search," "Advanced Search," or "Artist Search" to peruse the collection. Click "Highlights from the Collection" to see the six special collections described here.

▶ **Archaeological and Numismatic**
   http://www.aagm.co.uk/TheCollections/Highlights/highlight-archaeological
      -numismatic.aspx?dosearch=y&exhibition=Archaeological+Allsorts

   Images show a small collection of artifacts, both household objects as well as coin currency found in Aberdeen and northeast Scotland.

▶ **Contemporary Metalwork**
   http://www.aagm.co.uk/TheCollections/Highlights/highlight-contemporary
      -metalwork.aspx?dosearch=y&exhibition=Contemporary+Metalwork

The collection contains jewelry, hollowware, and flatware made from precious and semiprecious materials by both local and foreign metalworkers.

▶ **David Allan—Dresses Mostly from Nature**
http://www.aagm.co.uk/TheCollections/Highlights/highlight-mostly-from-nature
.aspx?dosearch=y&exhibition=DAVID+ALLAN

This collection includes more than 60 watercolor drawings of traditional costume created by Scottish artist David Allan during the eighteenth century.

▶ **Maritime History**
http://www.aagm.co.uk/TheCollections/Highlights/highlight-maritime-history
.aspx?dosearch=y&exhibition=Maritime+Highlights

This small collection contains 30 images of a representative sample of the Maritime History Collection, mostly of ships, ship parts, and tools.

▶ **Portrait Collection**
http://www.aagm.co.uk/TheCollections/Highlights/highlight-portrait-collection
.aspx?dosearch=y&exhibition=ALEXANDERMACDONALDPORTRAIT+
COLLECTION

The collection contains over 90 portraits and self-portraits depicting different artists, which were collected by Alexander Macdonald, a nineteenth-century merchant and collector of art.

▶ **Science and Industry Collections**
http://www.aagm.co.uk/TheCollections/Highlights/highlight-science-and-industry
.aspx?dosearch=y&exhibition=S%26I+Collection+Highlights

This collection contains a hodge-podge of items from smaller collections of scientific interest, including engineering plans and photographs relating to Aberdeen's granite industry.

National Library of Scotland
http://www.nls.uk/digitallibrary/index.html

Before the National Library of Scotland there was the Library of the Faculty of Advocates, which opened in 1689. In 1925, the National Library of Scotland was formally constituted by an Act of Parliament. The National Library has an extensive collection of photographs, maps, music, books, posters, drawings, and manuscripts from its holdings that are accessible through the Digital Archive. The National Library's Scottish Screen Archive is a film and video collection of over 100 years of Scotland's history. The collection consists of documentaries, newsreels, educational material, television and public information films, industrial material, advertising and promotional material, and amateur footage. The National Library also has 28 special "web features," such as Scottish Science Hall of Fame, The Murthly Hours, Bartholomew Archive, Slezer's Scotland, The Spread of Scottish Printing, Experiences of War, Pencils of Light, Scottish History in Print, Churchill: The Evidence, Playbills of the Theatre Royal Edinburgh, Mary Queen of Scots, Propaganda—A Weapon of War, The Photographs of John Thomson, and The Union of the Crowns. These are briefly described at the link provided here. Click a collection to access its individual homepage.

Wales

Llyfrgell Genedlaethol Cymru—Digital Mirror
http://www.llgc.org.uk/index.php?id=122

The National Library of Wales has a number of digital collections accessible from its Digital Mirror website. They are listed in the left menu; click a title to access its homepage. The collections are described here.

▶ **Archives**
   http://www.llgc.org.uk/index.php?id=127

   Documents include medieval charters, a population survey, a vestry book, and an excerpt from the diary of David Lloyd George.

▶ **Exhibitions**
   http://www.llgc.org.uk/index.php?id=exhibitions

   Sixteen exhibitions are highlighted. Titles include *Architecture of Wales*, *Celtic Voices*, and *Welsh Legends*.

▶ **Manuscripts**
   http://www.llgc.org.uk/index.php?id=126

   The collection contains over 40 manuscripts, such as *Book of Taliesin*, *Chronicle of the Princes*, *Piers Plowman*, and *Dylan Thomas and the Map of Llareggub*.

▶ **Maps**
   http://www.llgc.org.uk/index.php?id=maps0

   This collection consists of *The Principality of Wales*, a volume of maps published by Thomas Taylor in 1718, and Lewis Morris and William Morris's sea charts.

▶ **Photography**
   http://www.llgc.org.uk/index.php?id=photographs0

   This collection is a mix of photographs, ambrotypes, daguerreotypes, and postcards and includes works by photographers Carleton E. Watkins, John Thomas, and Geoff Charles.

▶ **Pictures**
   http://www.llgc.org.uk/index.php?id=pictures

   This collection includes artwork by John Ingleby, Thomas Rowlandson, J.M.W. Turner, and other artists plus topographical prints of Welsh landscapes, framed works of art, and the cartoons of Leslie Illingworth.

▶ **Printed Material**
   http://www.llgc.org.uk/index.php?id=128

   This small collection includes books from the mid-sixteenth century, a pamphlet from 1773, a Welsh-language magazine, and access to the database Welsh Biography Online.

▶ **Sound and Video**
http://www.llgc.org.uk/index.php?id=129

Listen to Madge Breese singing the Welsh national anthem (1899) or an excerpt from one of the David Lloyd George speeches, or watch part of his funeral at Llanystumdwy (1945).

▶ **Welsh Biography**
http://wbo.llgc.org.uk/en/index.html

The Welsh Biography Online database contains nearly 5,000 biographies of prominent Welsh men and women who made significant contributions to Welsh life and who died before January 1, 1971.

VATICAN CITY

Rome Reborn: The Vatican Library and Renaissance Culture
http://www.loc.gov/exhibits/vatican/toc.html

Read about the history of Rome and the Vatican Library, and view materials that reflect the time the library was conceived by Pope Nicholas V. It was Sixtus IV who brought it to fruition. View images of Rome in the fourteenth century, illustrations, letters (including one from Henry VIII to Anne Boleyn), a parchment of Homer's *Iliad*, Galileo's sunspot observation, the Urbino Bible, as well as other bibles and manuscripts. Exhibition sections are "The Vatican Library," "Archaeology," "Humanism," "Mathematics," "Music," "Medicine," "Nature," "Orient to Rome," and "Rome to China." In "Nature," view an image of a Latin manuscript with engravings, *Metallotheca*. It is a comprehensive treatise on minerals written by Michele Mercati (1541–1593) the director of the Vatican botanic gardens and a keen collector of minerals. Also view images of handwritten Greek and Latin manuscripts that are classics of the ancient world, for example, in "The Vatican Library," a parchment depicting the *Lives of Jesus and the Pope* and biographies of the popes by Bartolomeo Platina, in Latin, circa 1474.

Vatican Museums
http://mv.vatican.va/3_EN/pages/MV_Visite.html

The Vatican Museums consists of museums and galleries that originated in the second half of the eighteenth century with the sponsorship of Pope Clement XIV (1769–1774) and Pope Pius VI (1775–1799). Currently five collections are online, and they are organized by rooms within the museums. Within each room visitors can zoom in and explore every object and work of art shown. In addition to the online collections, 60 works and objects from the six collections have been selected for special up-close viewing.

▶ **Gregorian Egyptian Museum**
http://mv.vatican.va/3_EN/pages/x-Pano/MEZ/Visit_MEZ_Main.html

In 1839, Pope Gregory XVI (1831–1846) established the Egyptian Museum. Within the nine rooms are ancient relics found in Egypt as well other pieces such as statues, bas-relief sculptures, and Roman mosaics, some of which came originally from the Vatican, the Museo Capitolino, and the Lateran Profane Museum.

▶ **Gregorian Etruscan Museum**
http://mv.vatican.va/3_EN/pages/x-Pano/MGE/Visit_MGE_Main.html

There are 22 rooms in the Etruscan Museum, which was founded by Pope Gregory XVI (1831–1846) in 1837. The rooms are filled with archaeological treasures such as stone sculptures, jewelry, bronze, silver, glass, ivory, and ceramics.

▶ **Pinacoteca**
http://mv.vatican.va/3_EN/pages/x-Pano/PIN/Visit_PIN_Main.html

The Vatican Pinacoteca (Art Gallery) was created especially for Pope Pius XI (1922–1932) and opened in 1932. Today, the 18-room gallery contains 460 paintings, which are arranged by chronology and school and range in date from the twelfth to the nineteenth centuries.

▶ **Raphael's Rooms**
http://mv.vatican.va/3_EN/pages/x-Pano/SDR/Visit_SDR_Main.html

The Room of Constantine, The Room of Heliodorus, The Room of Segnatura, and The Room of the Fire in the Borgo make up the four rooms know as "Raphael's Rooms" or the Stanze of Raphael. The frescoes were painted by Raphael and his school between 1508 and 1524.

▶ **Sistine Chapel**
http://mv.vatican.va/3_EN/pages/x-Pano/CSN/Visit_CSN_Main.html

The Sistine Chapel, which is named for its founder, Pope Sixtus IV (1471–1484), dates back to the fifteenth century. View the paintings on the walls, including the ceiling, the false drapes (north wall), *The Last Judgement* (altar wall), *The Stories of Moses* (south and entrance walls), *The Stories of Christ* (north and entrance walls), and the portraits of the popes (north, south, and entrance walls) separately and up close.

Vatican Secret Archives
http://asv.vatican.va/home_en.htm

Under orders from Pope Paul V, the registers of the papal bulls and briefs, the books of the Apostolic Camera, and the collections of documents up to the papacy of Pius V were moved to three rooms that make up what is now called the Vatican Secret Archives. Take a virtual tour of the frescos on the walls of the Archives, view the collection of Vatican seals, and access the many archival documents that have been digitized.

Chapter 6

North America

INTRODUCTION

Nnorth America generally refers to the United States, Canada, Mexico, and often Greenland, Saint Pierre and Miquelon, and Bermuda. North America is the northernmost continent of the Americas and the third largest on earth. It lies generally between the Arctic Circle and the Tropic of Cancer. It is almost completely surrounded by bodies of water, including the Pacific Ocean, the Bering Strait, the Arctic Ocean, the Atlantic Ocean, the Caribbean Sea, and the Gulf of Mexico (*Encyclopaedia Britannica Online*, 2010). This area of the world includes some of the most developed countries rich in cultural heritage and libraries and comfortable with today's advanced technology. This combination is responsible for producing a huge number of digital collections and a web presence for libraries of all types (national, government, state, university, regional, and special).

In a recent research article, Shiri (2009) examined 269 North American digital library collections. Shiri reviewed the importance of using a standard for organizing collections so that they can be accessed throughout the world. A knowledge organization system (KOS) is a way of arranging information (its subject classification) to facilitate searching and retrieving materials in digital collections. Like a physical library, items can be searched by subject, author, or title. The *Library of Congress Subject Headings* is the most used tool, followed by thesauri, and then by locally developed taxonomies. It is yet another aspect essential for the organization and management of digital collections by a library. This model is evidenced in the digital collections of the Library of Congress, many Canadian libraries, and now many other libraries. As the number of digital libraries continues to grow in North America and around the world, using one model for organizing and accessing materials is important. However, what is still imperative is that countries have materials and historical documents representative of their cultural heritage to begin with and then the funds, skilled personnel, and technology to digitize the materials and make them available on the web.

Regarding the digital collections of countries of the North American continent, it is important to note that there is some disparity. The greatest number of digital collections comes from the United States, followed by Canada. This chapter lists digital collections across the North American continent by country. When there are few digital collections found for a country, an organization, university, or other source providing digitized materials for the country will be listed so that each country is represented. A major section reviews the collections of the United States, with a focus on the Library of Congress and separate listings for each of the 50 states and the District of Columbia.

Of special interest in this chapter are the Library of Congress's Digital Collections and Programs. One, the American Memory Project, offers a number of digital collections featuring maps, videos, and audio files presented with special capabilities, such as zooming in on a map, and incorporating multimedia elements and virtual tours, for example, of the Lewis and Clark exhibit gallery (Eden, 2005). The American Memory Project created a virtual museum where one can learn about well-known Americans, historical events in American history, and life as an American today. The collections offer a valuable glimpse into historical photographs, editorial cartoons and caricatures, posters, and maps (Novotny, 2005). Another project of the Library of Congress is its Digital Exhibitions. Many of the Library of Congress's past exhibitions have been re-created in digital form and are now on the web. A variety of formats are used to reflect the history, culture, and historical issues and events of the United States and other countries.

Another valuable source of digital collections is the 19 Smithsonian libraries, archives, and museums. Numerous collections in diverse formats from these organizations represent a wealth of resources for research, educational purposes, or to satisfy the curious. The Smithsonian Institution's website provides links to each organization's collections so that one can peruse them as well. One example of an online project is the Smithsonian Photography Initiative, which features a search engine to find photographs for exhibitions, public forums, and educational programs (Gefter, 2008).

An online visit to Canada at the Images Canada website reveals cultural and digital collections of historic value coming from many participating archives, libraries, museums, and universities across Canada. The website's "Image Trails" link provides up to 150 images on a particular topic or theme, such as trains, planes, and the arctic. The "Photo Essays" link provides groups of photos that tell a story, usually written by a photo archivist or historian. For example, "Nittoy-yiss: The Blackfoot Tipi" is a photo essay about the Blackfoot nation of southern Alberta. Anther online digital collection site worthy of mention is the Caribbean Newspaper Digital Library (CNDL). CNDL provides access to digitized versions of Caribbean newspapers, gazettes, and other research materials currently held in archives, libraries, private collections, and the National Library of Jamaica. As with other countries throughout the world, it is expected that more and more digitizing projects will come online for the North American countries that appear to lack a presence at this time.

References

Eden, Brad. 2005. "Innovative Digital Projects in the Humanities." *Library Technology Reports* 41, no. 4 (July/August): 24–44.

Encyclopaedia Britannica Online. 2010. "North America." Encyclopaedia Britannica, Inc. Accessed August 23. http://www.britannica.com/EBchecked/topic/418612/North-America.

Gefter, Philip. 2008. "Type in 'Native American' and Search (Someday) 13 Million Photos." *New York Times*, March 12, 2008: 36. http://0-www.lexisnexis.com.library.dowling.edu/us/lnacademic/auth/checkbrowser.do?rand=0.7680832254355058&cookieState=0&ipcounter=1&bhcp=1.

Novotny, Eric. 2005. "Finding United States Historical Images in Print and Online." *Reference and User Services Quarterly* 45, no. 1: 11–21.

Shiri, Ali. 2009. "Knowledge Organization Systems in North American Digital Library Collections." *Emerald Program: Electronic Library and Information Systems* 43, no. 2: 121–139. http://www.emeraldinsight.com/0033-0337.htm.

CONTINENT

CONTENTdm Collection of Collections
http://collections.contentdm.oclc.org/index.php

CONTENTdm is a product of OCLC (Online Computer Library Center). OCLC is a computer library service and research organization dedicated to the public purpose of furthering access to the world's information. It serves over 72,000 libraries in 171 countries and territories around the world. CONTENTdm lists over 500 collections of numerous topics representing the United States and other countries. On the CONTENTdm Collection of Collections website are a sampling of digital collections created by libraries and cultural heritage organizations using the CONTENTdm software. On the homepage are search and browse features to access the collections. Some records represent individual collections; some connect to entire digital libraries. For each collection there is an image, title, description, and note of topics included in the collection. The titles are links to further collection descriptions, including formats, and links to the collection's host site. A sampling of collections include The History of Medicine; African American Women; American Journeys: Eyewitness Accounts of Early American Exploration and Settlement; Civil War Letters Collection; and European Performance Arts—17th through 19th Centuries (which includes music, noted images of Shakespeare's plays, lesser known works, and images and biographies of some of the better known French theater personalities).

Digital Library of the Caribbean
http://ufdcweb1.uflib.ufl.edu/ufdc/?n=dloc&g=dloc1&m=hhh

This digital library was established in 2004 and is administered by Florida International University in cooperation with the University of Florida and the University of the Virgin Islands. Content includes newspapers, photographs, maps, and historical documents of participating nations from both the Caribbean and the surrounding areas. Content has already been contributed by the national libraries of Aruba, Haiti, and Jamaica, as well as by many universities. Click the "Partner Collections" tab in the upper right corner for a full list and links to the collections of each. The site is translatable into English, Spanish, and French, and an advanced search page allows cross-searching of both the digital library as well as the Caribbean Newspaper Digital Library subset of materials.

▶ ### Caribbean Newspaper Digital Library
http://web1.dloc.com/ufdc/?c=cndl

The Caribbean Newspaper Digital Library is a subcollection of the Digital Library of the Caribbean. It contains digitized full texts of newspapers for which permission has been granted to make available to the public online. The "All Items" tab at the top provides a list of 135 titles, and with each title is a list of individual issues. Some entries, such as *The Bermudian*, have only one issue of one volume (this one from January 1877). Another, *Jamaica Journal*, has issues of many volumes from 1968 to 2007. Navigation and searching capabilities are the same as those of the parent collection, Digital Library of the Caribbean, but with the limited scope of containing just newsprint resources from Caribbean and surrounding nations.

John S. Kiewit Photography Collection
http://www.library.ucsb.edu/speccoll/digital/Kiewit/

This is a collection of over 10,000 images taken by an American photographer of the American West, Central America, and the Pacific. The collection is now housed in the library of the University of California at Santa Barbara and is available for use online. Written permission must be obtained from the Head of Special Collections at the library to publish images in the collection; further details are given on the website. The images are grouped by location or topic and are not accompanied by metadata at this time.

Latin American Pamphlet Digital Collection
http://vc.lib.harvard.edu/vc/deliver/home?_collection=LAP

This collection, housed at the Widener Library at Harvard University, contains thousands of digitized pamphlets from Latin American countries. Most heavily represented are Bolivia, Chile, Cuba, and Mexico. The pamphlets focus mainly on social life and customs, including the evolution of original colonies into the Latin American countries we know today. The collection can be keyword searched or browsed by title, author, or subject. Printing as PDFs requires use of Adobe Acrobat reader and is permissible for individual use or research. Institutional permission is required for any other purpose.

University of Washington Special Collections
http://content.lib.washington.edu/cdm4/lists.php

The University of Washington Libraries website has several dozen digital collections created with the CONTENTdm software. The images were scanned in grayscale and saved JPEGs. Two of the collections are related to western Canada and the western United States, including Alaska. Keyword searching is available, as is browsing by Library of Congress subject headings. Full metadata is available for each item.

▶ **Alaska, Western Canada, and United States Collection**
http://content.lib.washington.edu/alaskawcanadaweb/index.html

This is a collection of nearly 3,000 photographs of the area taken around the time of the gold rush at the turn of the twentieth century.

▶ **Alaska-Yukon-Pacific Exposition Photographs**
http://content.lib.washington.edu/aypweb/index.html

This collection contains over 1,300 photographs of the Exposition held at the University of Washington in 1909.

ANTIGUA AND BARBUDA

Arawwwak: Antigua Historic Community Archives
http://devweb.tc.columbia.edu/php/arawwwak/index.html

This website was created by the Institute of Learning Technologies at Teachers College of Columbia University. It contains print, sound, and video materials regarding the history of the islands, donated by contributors and free for anyone to access and use. The search page has options to limit by topic, date range, or both. Viewers must log in (for tracking purposes only) to download and view content. Logged-in users can also contribute content. The site currently contains 76 items.

BAHAMAS

New York Public Library Digital Gallery
http://digitalgallery.nypl.org/nypldigital/dgkeysearchresult.cfm?keyword=bahamas

A search for "Bahamas" retrieved 86 photos, including many images of persons and places, maps, and a dinner menu for the Hotel Colonial in Nassau, 1901.

World Digital Library
http://www.wdl.org/en/search/gallery?ql=eng&s=bahamas

Two images are classified under "Bahamas" in this collection. Both are maps of the general area created by explorers, one Dutch and one Spanish.

BARBADOS

East Carolina University—Joyner Library Digital Collections
http://digital.lib.ecu.edu/search.aspx?q=Special%20Collections%20Staff%20Pick%
    20Collection&index=collection&cid=staffpick&ff=photographs&pf=Barbados--
    Bridgetown%20(Barbados)

The digital collection of East Carolina University (ECU) contains one photograph showing Victoria Street in Bridgetown, Barbados, dating to 1875. The ECU website provides access to over 25 distinct digital collections; the photos are cross-listed in both the Architecture and the Staff Pick Collections.

BELIZE

World Digital Library
http://www.wdl.org/en/search/gallery?ql=eng&s=belize

Four images are classified under "Belize" in this collection. Two show maps of Central America, one is a photo of a ceramic sculpture jaguar created sometime between the seventh and tenth centuries, and the fourth is an aerial view of buildings in Belize City, circa 1914, taken before the country gained independence and was still called British Honduras.

CANADA

British Columbia Digital Library
http://www.bcdlib.tc.ca/general-collections-canada.html

The British Columbia Digital Library website contains links to individual online projects around the country. Instead of being sorted alphabetically, it is organized with national collections listed first and then sources by province. This site is also useful for its inclusion of both public library and university library websites, which opens up whole new doors to more digital content. The rest of the collections detailed under "Canada" are linked in one or both of the first two listings and serve only as a sample of what is out there for the online researcher of this country.

Canada's Digital Collections
http://epe.lac-bac.gc.ca/100/205/301/ic/cdc/E/Alphabet.asp

This is a digital collection of digital collections. Canada has been one of the most active countries in the world when it comes to creating and archiving online content and collections. The link provided here accesses an alphabetized list of hundreds of links to digital projects created in the 1990s and early 2000s, which are now archived by Library and Archives Canada. Collections range from the Alberta Newspapers Collection to Women Artists of Canada. The scope and breadth of collections available from this website make it a necessary starting gate for anyone doing online research into the cultural history of Canada.

Historic Niagara Digital Collections
http://www.nflibrary.ca/nfplindex/

This collection is hosted by the Niagara Falls Public Library and groups a number of online resources related to Niagara Falls in one place. Four separate database links on the homepage allow users to search for images, newspapers, printed texts, and artwork. The images and art databases provide the most useful online content, because they provide the ability to search by a list of preselected subjects. The content may be used for research or personal use only, with additional permissions obtainable from the library.

Images Canada
http://www.imagescanada.ca/index-e.html

This database is hosted by the National Archives of Canada and pulls together thousands of images from the online collections of many Canadian cultural institutions around the country. Follow the "Partners" link to see a list of the 15 current partner institutions along with a brief description of each institution and its contribution. The "Image Trails" link provides predefined searches to help users narrow in on their desired search topic. Copyright and contact information links are also on the homepage. As with many Canadian websites, the page is translatable from English to French. Items in the collection have considerable metadata attached, and clicking on the search results takes viewers to the image hosted on the partner's website.

Our Roots: Canada's Local Histories Online
http://www.ourroots.ca/

This database contains local histories from around the country that are ideal for young student researchers. The histories are complete full-text scans of resources related to Canadian history. Click the "Search" tab at the top of the page to search by title, author, subject, or province. Click the "About Us" tab to access the list of over 20 partners and contributors from which the source materials come.

Timarit.is
http://www.timarit.is/listing_init.jsp?lang=en&order=country&filteron=&filterval=

The national libraries of the Faroe Islands, Greenland, and Iceland have collaborated to create this database, which includes periodicals from the three countries, as well as Denmark and Canada. A search for "Canada" in the title list retrieved over 20 publications. *See also* TIMARIT.IS *under* EUROPE: CONTINENT.

University of Saskatchewan Archives: Exhibits and Special Projects
http://www.usask.ca/archives/projects.php

The University of Saskatchewan lists its digital collections under the headings of either "Special Projects" or "Virtual Exhibits and Digital Initiatives." Under the second heading, for example, is Wish You Were Here: Saskatchewan Postcard Collections, which contains over 4,500 postcard views of the area.

University of Toronto Digital Collections
http://www.library.utoronto.ca/fisher/digital-collections/index.html

This page provides descriptions of and links to ten digital collections created by the Thomas Fisher Rare Book Library at the university for the stated purpose of expanding access to its print and manuscript collections. All of the collections present images of textual pages and are capable of full-text searching. Some of the more unique collections are briefly described here.

▶ **Agnes Chamberlin Digital Collection**
http://chamberlin.library.utoronto.ca/index.cfm

This collection contains over 300 color paintings (by Agnes Chamberlin) of Canadian flora and mushrooms created during the latter half of the nineteenth century. The contents can be browsed or searched by English and Latin botanical names or by grouping, such as "Paintings of Fungi."

▶ **Anatomia**
http://link.library.utoronto.ca/anatomia/application/index.cfm

This collection has 4,500 digital images of illustrations of human anatomy from over 90 different texts dated from the sixteenth to nineteenth centuries. Links on the homepage provide detailed copyright and contact information.

▶ **The Barren Lands**
http://link.library.utoronto.ca/Tyrrell/

This collection has over 5,000 digital images of texts and photographs from two expeditions in the 1890s to Manitoba, Saskatchewan, and the area now known as

Nunavut. Some text images, as well as the maps showing trail routes, come from the original field notebooks of the explorers.

▶ **Canadian Pamphlets and Broadsides**
http://link.library.utoronto.ca/broadsides/

This collection has over 70,000 page scans of broadsides and pamphlets dated from the sixteenth century to 1930. The content includes items by Canadian authors, about Canada as a subject, and items printed in Canada.

▶ **Canadian Printer and Publisher**
http://link.library.utoronto.ca/cpp/

This collection contains over 8,000 page scans of the first 20 years (1892–1911) of an important Canadian trade periodical.

▶ **The Discovery and Early Development of Insulin**
http://link.library.utoronto.ca/insulin/

This collection pulls together several thousand page images of text, photographs, and ephemera dealing with the science, research, and study of insulin done at the University of Toronto during the first quarter of the twentieth century.

▶ **Wenceslaus Hollar Digital Collection**
http://link.library.utoronto.ca/hollar/

This collection contains over 2,500 prints of the artist Wenceslaus Hollar from the seventeenth century. The subjects of his works are wide ranging, and the collection also contains some of the illustrations from texts containing his original etchings.

COSTA RICA

John S. Kiewit Photography Collection
http://www.library.ucsb.edu/speccoll/digital/Kiewit/Color-CentralAmerica.html

This is a collection of images from various North American locations. The "Central America" link contains images from Costa Rica, El Salvador, and Guatemala. Twenty-two images are from Costa Rica, all dated December 1972. *See also* JOHN S. KIEWIT PHOTOGRAPHY COLLECTION *under* NORTH AMERICA: CONTINENT.

CUBA

Caribbean Newspaper Digital Library
http://web1.dloc.com/ufdc/?c=cndl

The Caribbean Newspaper Digital Library is a subcollection of the Digital Library of the Caribbean and contains digitized texts of four Cuba-related publications: *Republica Cubana*, 82 volumes from 1896 to 1897, published in France; *Republique Cubaine*, one volume from 1896, published in Cuba; *Diario de la marina*, 305 issues from 1959, published in Cuba; and 7 *Dias del Diario de la marina en el exilio*, 19 issues from 1960 and 1961, published in Miami, Florida. *See also* CARIBBEAN NEWSPAPER DIGITAL LIBRARY *under* NORTH AMERICA: CONTINENT.

Castro Speech Data Base
http://www1.lanic.utexas.edu/la/cb/cuba/castro.html

This collection is part of the University of Texas Latin American Network Information Center and contains English translations of many of Fidel Castro's speeches, interviews, and press conferences from 1959 to 1996. The speeches are sorted by year and month and can be browsed accordingly, or an advanced keyword search can cross-search them all. All content is in the public domain. The site does not claim to be complete or exhaustive, and updates and corrections are not always provided; the site suggests users verify a text with an original source if necessary. Dates, places, and some other contextual information may accompany the texts.

Cuban Heritage Collection
http://merrick.library.miami.edu/digitalprojects/chc.php

This website is maintained by the University of Miami Libraries and provides access to over 30 digital collections with content relating to Cuba. Several collections are based on the papers of individual persons, including Alberto Arrendondo (Cuban economist), Lydia Cabrera (Cuban writer), Tomas Estrada Palma (Cuban general and president, 1902–1906), Polita Grau (former Cuban first lady), Jose Lezama Lima (Cuban poet and novelist), Enrique Labrador Ruiz (Cuban journalist and poet), and Gerardo Machado (Cuban general and president, 1925–1933). Others are photograph, postcard, and manuscript collections created by various individuals with some connection to the country as well as organizational papers and records from the Lyceum and Lawn Tennis Club (women's organization) and the Truth About Cuba Committee, Inc. (organization of Cuban exiles in Miami, Florida), which disseminated information from their various points of view. By housing these collections together, the university provides for federated searching of any or all of the collections at one time.

Cuban Poster Collection
http://www.oac.cdlib.org/findaid/ark:/13030/hb2k4008kp/

This collection is made available through the Online Archive of California, a website that pulls together digital materials from participating libraries, museums, special collections, and archives from around the state, including all of the University of California campuses. The Cuban Poster Collection contains images of 346 Cuban posters from 1960 to 2000, made available through a partnership between the University of California at Berkeley and the Jose Marti National Library of Cuba. The collection focuses primarily on Cuban culture and can be browsed or searched, with only basic metadata available for each item (title, creator, and contributing institution). Access is available for research, with permissions for other uses to be obtained from the Bancroft Library at the University of California at Berkeley.

Deena Stryker Photographs, 1963–1964 and Undated
http://library.duke.edu/digitalcollections/stryker/

This collection is housed in the Duke University Libraries and contains over 1,800 digital photographs taken by a journalist (then known as Deena Boyer) during a trip to

Cuba in 1963 and 1964. The content focuses on members of the Castro administration, as well as everyday life in both Havana and some more rural areas. The collection is available for research, with permissions for other uses to be obtained from the university. Each image has a caption along with basic metadata but no additional description. A search for "Castro" yielded 286 items; a search for "Havana" yielded 888 items.

Latin American Pamphlet Digital Collection
http://vc.lib.harvard.edu/vc/deliver/home?_collection=LAP

This collection, housed by the Widener Library at Harvard University, contains thousands of digitized pamphlets from several Latin American countries. A basic search for "Cuba" returned 916 items, with links to the full-page image scans and full bibliographic data. The content is in Spanish. *See also* LATIN AMERICAN PAMPHLET DIGITAL COLLECTION *under* NORTH AMERICA: CONTINENT.

DOMINICA

New York Public Library Digital Gallery
http://digitalgallery.nypl.org/nypldigital/dgkeysearchresult.cfm?keyword= dominica

A search for "Dominica" retrieved 22 photos, including two views of the nation's Boiling Lake, one of the largest hot springs in the world. There are also several images of native peoples.

World Digital Library
http://www.wdl.org/en/search/gallery?ql=eng&s=dominica

Two images are classified under "Dominica" in this collection. One is a survey map of buildings on the Atlantic side of the island, and the other is a military map of Grenada during the Seven Years War, after which Dominica, Grenada, and several other lands were ceded from the French to the British.

DOMINICAN REPUBLIC

New York Public Library Digital Gallery
http://digitalgallery.nypl.org/nypldigital/dgkeysearchresult.cfm?keyword=dominican+
  republic

A search for "Dominican Republic" retrieved 35 photos, many of which are black-and-white views of persons and places. There are two color images; one shows the flag, and the other is a rendering of "fashionable ladies" showing some of the stylish local dress at the time (1920s).

World Digital Library
http://www.wdl.org/en/search/gallery?ql=eng&s=dominican+republic&page=1

Three images are classified under "Dominican Republic" in this collection. One is an artist's rendering of a native woman, and the others are maps of the island.

EL SALVADOR

John S. Kiewit Photography Collection
http://www.library.ucsb.edu/speccoll/digital/Kiewit/Color-CentralAmerica.html

This is a collection of images from various North American locations. The "Central America" link contains images from Costa Rica, El Salvador, and Guatemala. Five images show El Salvador, all dated December 1972. *See also* JOHN S. KIEWIT PHOTOGRAPHY COLLECTION *under* NORTH AMERICA: CONTINENT.

GREENLAND

Timarit.is
http://www.timarit.is/listing_init.jsp?lang=en&order=country&filteron=&filterval=

The national libraries of the Faroe Islands, Greenland, and Iceland have collaborated to create this database, which includes periodicals from the three countries, as well as Denmark and Canada. A search for "Greenland" in the title list retrieved five publications. *See also* TIMARIT.IS *under* EUROPE: CONTINENT.

GRENADA

New York Public Library Digital Gallery
http://digitalgallery.nypl.org/nypldigital/dgkeysearchresult.cfm?keyword=grenada

A search for "Grenada" retrieved 32 images. Views of and from hills, market squares, and streets dominate this group of images.

World Digital Library
http://www.wdl.org/en/search/gallery?ql=eng&s=grenada

Seven images are classified under "Grenada." Some are maps of the vicinity, and others show people engaged in dance and other ceremonies. There is also an Independence Day photo of a parade in 1974.

GUATEMALA

American Philosophical Society
http://www.amphilsoc.org/library/digcoll

The American Philosophical Society was founded in Philadelphia by Benjamin Franklin in the eighteenth century and maintains a museum and library along with a discussion group. Its website contains digital collections with both audio and image content that is accessible to all. Collections can be searched individually, or multiple collections can be selected for a group search. A search for "Guatemala" across all collections returned 17 images, mostly related to the Mayan Indian history of the area. All images have full bibliographic data and are copyrighted by the society. Permission to use must be obtained.

John S. Kiewit Photography Collection
http://www.library.ucsb.edu/speccoll/digital/Kiewit/Color-CentralAmerica.html

This is a collection of images from various North American locations. The "Central America" link contains images from Costa Rica, El Salvador, and Guatemala. Thirty-eight images show Guatemala, all dated December 1972. *See also* JOHN S. KIEWIT PHOTOGRAPHY COLLECTION *under* NORTH AMERICA: CONTINENT.

Oberlin College Digital Collections
http://www.oberlin.edu/library/digital/

This website contains 20 digital collections that can be searched individually or as a group. A search for "Guatemala" across all collections returned 39 images, mostly in color and related to contemporary people and places. All images have full bibliographic data and are available for scholarly research. Permission to use differs depending on the collection from which the images come.

HAITI

Digital Library of the Caribbean
http://ufdcweb1.uflib.ufl.edu/ufdc/?n=dloc&g=dloc1&m=hhh

Click "Partner Collections" to access the Archives Nationale d'Haïti's (National Archives of Haiti) contribution of 385 images. All items can be sorted by title or date, and an advanced search page is available to narrow the content even further. Citation information and a zooming tool are provided for each image. Also listed under "Partner Collections" is the Bibliothèque Nationale d'Haïti (National Library of Haiti), which contributed 12 titles. Individual page scans of these Spanish-language texts are available. *See also* CARIBBEAN NEWSPAPER DIGITAL LIBRARY *under* NORTH AMERICA: CONTINENT.

HONDURAS

New York Public Library Digital Gallery
http://digitalgallery.nypl.org/nypldigital/dgkeysearchresult.cfm?keyword=honduras

A search for "Honduras" retrieved 59 photos, most of which show native peoples engaged in daily activities.

World Digital Library
http://www.wdl.org/en/search/gallery?ql=eng&s=honduras

Five images are classified under "Honduras" in this collection. Some are maps of the area, and one shows three men playing the marimba, a percussion instrument native to the area and similar to a xylophone.

JAMAICA

Caribbean Newspaper Digital Library
http://web1.dloc.com/ufdc/?c=cndl

The Caribbean Newspaper Digital Library is a subcollection of the Digital Library of the Caribbean containing digitized full-text runs of the Jamaican newspapers *Jamaica Journal* and *Jamaica Times*. For *Jamaica Journal*, the site claims many (but not all) issues ranging from volume 1 (1967) to volume 30 (2007). For the *Jamaica Times*, the site claims 19 issues ranging from 1901 to 1905. *See also* CARIBBEAN NEWSPAPER DIGITAL LIBRARY *under* NORTH AMERICA: CONTINENT.

National Library of Jamaica
http://www.nlj.gov.jm/

The National Library of Jamaica provides links to four digital collections. One is to The Slave Trade, with materials in "commemoration of the abolition of the slave trade," and another is to the Digital Library of the Caribbean (*see* CARIBBEAN NEWSPAPER DIGITAL LIBRARY *under* NORTH AMERICA: CONTINENT). The other two collections are described here.

▶ **Jamaica Unshackled: Freedom to Be**
http://www.nlj.gov.jm/index.php?q=digitalcollections/jamaica-unshackled

This collection contains resources ranging from print materials, serials, and documents to visual items such as maps and photographs. However, they all relate to one of three historical events: the 1831 Sam Sharpe Rebellion/Baptist War, the 1865 Morant Bay Rebellion, and the 1938 Labour Riots. Currently, only the 1831 Sam Sharpe Rebellion has content (books, pamphlets, maps, photographs, and prints) that is available online.

▶ **Picture Dis: The National Online Album of Jamaica**
http://www.nlj.gov.jm/index.php?q=digitalcollections/picture-dis

The images in this digital collection were selected as representatives to preserve and promote the history of the country. The homepage contains a ring of links representing the collections of the 14 Jamaican parishes. Between four and eight photos are provided for each parish. The site uses Flickr to host its photos and descriptions.

MEXICO

Digital Collection of Mexican and Argentine Presidential Messages
http://lanic.utexas.edu/larrp/pm/sample2/mexican/index.html

This online collection is part of the Latin Americanist Research Resources Project, an effort to convert microfilmed texts of presidential speeches of Mexican and Argentinean presidents into online documents. Currently it contains over 51,000 scans of Mexican texts, easily navigable and neatly subdivided by leader and time period.

Latin American Pamphlet Digital Collection
http://vc.lib.harvard.edu/vc/deliver/home?_collection=LAP

This collection, housed at the Widener Library at Harvard University, contains thousands of digitized pamphlets from several Latin American countries. A basic search for "Mexico" returned 850 brief records, with links to full-page image scans and detailed bibliographic data. The content is in Spanish. *See also* LATIN AMERICAN PAMPHLET DIGITAL COLLECTION *under* NORTH AMERICA: CONTINENT.

Mexico: Photographs, Manuscripts, and Imprints
http://digitalcollections.smu.edu/all/cul/mex/

This database is part of a larger collection of materials (all of which are not currently available online) of Southern Methodist University in Dallas, Texas. It contains over 550 digitized items representing both images and textual materials mostly related to the Mexican Revolution. Click on "Browse Items" to see the entire collection, or click "Search" to narrow the focus. Each item is accompanied by full metadata. Copyright is retained by the university, and contact information is provided.

A Nation Emerges: 65 Years of Photography in Mexico
http://www.getty.edu/research/conducting_research/digitized_collections/photography_
  mexico/

This digital collection is maintained and made available by the Getty Research Institute, a California-based group dedicated to promoting the arts. It contains images of Mexico circa 1860–1920 and combines the contributions of around 30 different photographers from various nations who spent time in Mexico. Some are focused on the government and prominent persons and others on the landscape and natural settings. A keyword search for "Mexico" returned 603 results, each with an enlargeable image and full metadata.

Oberlin College Digital Collections
http://www.oberlin.edu/library/digital/

This website contains 20 digital collections that can be searched individually or as a group. A search for "Mexico" across all collections returned over 890 images, mostly in color and related to contemporary people and places. All images have full bibliographic data and are available for scholarly research. Permission requirements differ depending on the collection.

NICARAGUA

New York Public Library Digital Gallery
http://digitalgallery.nypl.org/nypldigital/dgkeysearchresult.cfm?keyword=nicaragua

A search for "Nicaragua" retrieved 68 photos, many of which are from a collection of New York World's Fair photos showing Nicaraguan statesmen posing with New York Mayor Fiorello La Guardia, Grover Whalen, and other New York officials. Other images include native peoples and places in Nicaragua.

World Digital Library
http://www.wdl.org/en/search/gallery?ql=eng&s=nicaragua

Nine images are classified under "Nicaragua" in this collection. Most are maps of the area; a few others are candid images of native people dancing, playing dominoes, and riding in a cart along the beach.

PANAMA

Freshwater and Marine Image Bank
http://content.lib.washington.edu/fishweb/index.html

The University of Washington Libraries has a number of digital collections available on its website. One of these, the Freshwater and Marine Image Bank, contains over 21,000 images. The content is grouped by subjects that are listed in the right menu. One of these subjects is the Panama Canal, with 175 images. The images range from maps and views of structures, to images of ships going through, to local fish species. Each image contains basic metadata, and all images in the Image Bank are in the public domain.

Panama and the Canal
http://web1.dloc.com/pcm

This digital library is administered jointly by the University of Florida George A. Smathers Libraries and the Panama Canal Museum and includes resources from the museum and the George A. Smathers Libraries' Latin American Collection, Government Documents Collection, and Map & Imagery Library. The site is translatable into English, Spanish, and French. Currently four specialized collections are planned for the website: Panama Canal Museum, The Leonard Carpenter Panama Canal Collection, Documents of the Panama Canal Commission and Its Predecessor Agencies, and Newspapers from Panama. One subcollection is The Panama and the Canal Oral History Project.

ST. KITTS AND NEVIS

New York Public Library Digital Gallery
http://digitalgallery.nypl.org/nypldigital/dgkeysearchresult.cfm?keyword=st+kitts
http://digitalgallery.nypl.org/nypldigital/dgkeysearchresult.cfm?keyword=nevis

Individual searches for "St. Kitts" and "Nevis" retrieved 17 and 16 images, respectively. They are predominantly views of places and activities. The St. Kitts results include images of a sugar mill and the interior of a sugar boiling house.

ST. LUCIA

New York Public Library Digital Gallery
http://digitalgallery.nypl.org/nypldigital/dgkeysearchresult.cfm?keyword=st.+lucia

A search for "St. Lucia" retrieved eight images. Included is an interesting black-and-white of mangoes and banana plants, circa 1900.

World Digital Library
http://www.wdl.org/en/search/gallery?ql=eng&s=lucia

Two items are classified under "Lucia" in this collection. One is an undated photo from the late twentieth century of a group of local women doing laundry, and the second is a book by Nathaniel Uring titled *A Relation of the Late Intended Settlement of the Islands of St. Lucia and St. Vincent, in America; in Right of the Duke of Montagu, and Orders, in the Year 1722.*

ST. VINCENT AND THE GRENADINES

New York Public Library Digital Gallery
http://digitalgallery.nypl.org/nypldigital/dgkeysearchresult.cfm?keyword=st.+vincent
  +grenadines

A search for "St. Vincent Grenadines" retrieved three images. All are landscape views around Kingston (Kingstown).

TRINIDAD AND TOBAGO

National Library and Information System Authority
http://www2.nalis.gov.tt/Collections/ExhibitionsandPhotoGalleries/tabid/89/Default
  .aspx

This webpage provides links to the collections, which are listed as either "Online Exhibitions" or "Photo Galleries." Currently, there are 14 exhibitions and over 20 photo galleries ranging from "First Peoples" to the "Independence Day Parade 2009." Clicking on each image produces a larger view.

UNITED STATES

Colorado Plateau Digital Archives
http://library.nau.edu/speccoll/index.html

The Colorado Plateau Digital Archives is a special collection of the Cline Library, Northern Arizona University. Click "Colorado Plateau Resources" in the left menu to see a description of the online content, which includes photographs, diaries, letters, oral history interviews, films, and maps about the history of the Colorado Plateau (Arizona, New Mexico, Utah, and Colorado) and of the university. The website can be searched using Boolean operators (AND, OR, NOT) or browsing by collection, creator, year, textual materials, visual materials, maps, sound recordings, moving images, or digital exhibits.

Columbia River Basin Ethnic History Archive
http://www.vancouver.wsu.edu/crbeha/

The Columbia River Basin Ethnic History Archive (CRBEHA) is a collaborative project of Washington State University Vancouver, the Idaho State Historical Society, Oregon Historical Society, Washington State Historical Society, and Washington State University Pullman. The archive contains selections from the ethnic collections of these institutions. Searches can be conducted by ethnic group, keyword, historical society, material type, date, and subject. In addition to the archive, CRBEHA provides tutorials on how to research and interpret library and museum resources, teaching materials, and historical overviews.

The Library of Congress
http://www.loc.gov/index.html

The Library of Congress is the United States' oldest federal cultural institution and the research arm of Congress. It is also the largest library in the world, with millions of books, recordings, photographs, maps, and manuscripts in its collections. Since the conception of digitization and with the collaborative efforts of libraries, museums, and other partners worldwide, it is now possible to view numerous digital collections online offering a wealth of information in multiple formats for general readers, students, and researchers alike. One of its latest developments is the YouTube pilot project that provides historical videos to be viewed on YouTube. Other major projects include Digital Collections and Programs, American Memory Project, Rare Books and Special Collections, Portals to the World, The Virtual Reference Shelf, Digital Exhibits, and Teaching with Primary Resources. The main building is located at 101 Independence Ave., SE, Washington, DC 20540. A selected number of projects are described here.

▶ **American Memory Project**
http://memory.loc.gov/ammem/index.html

The American Memory Project has a number of collections in various formats, such as audio, maps, and video. Browse the collection by topic, time period, place, or format, such as maps and sheet music, or use the "Search All Collections" keyword search box. For example, a search for "Lewis and Clark" retrieved over 200 links, including "First American West," a recounting of the Lewis and Clark expedition written by Lewis and Clark and published in 1814. This link offers a reading of the text and includes digitized images of the actual book. The various options for searching through the American Memory webpages lead to a number of wonderful collections and to one's own discovery of this great nation. Teachers, educators, researchers, librarians, students, and the general public will find many resources to fit their needs. This is a great site for exploration and learning.

▶ **Browse by Topic**
http://www.loc.gov/topics/

The links on this webpage are arranged by topic. Links include "American History," "Arts & Culture," "Government, Politics & Law," "Maps & Geography," "Sports, Recreation & Leisure," "Science, Technology & Business," "Religion & Philosophy," and "News, Journalism & Advertising." Each of these links leads to numerous collections.

▶ **Chronicling America: Historical American Newspapers**
http://chroniclingamerica.loc.gov/

The Chronicling America: Historical American Newspapers website contains American newspapers dating from 1860 to 1922, with further information about other newspapers published from 1690 to the present. This initiative is sponsored by the Library of Congress and the National Digital Newspaper Program. A valuable search option allows one to search newspapers by state and by newspaper title.

▶ Digital Collections and Services
http://www.loc.gov/library/libarch-digital.html

The Library of Congress's Digital Collections and Services offers a gateway to digital photographs, maps, sound recordings, motion pictures, manuscripts, books, and other materials that are either rare or not found elsewhere. The digital collections include American History, Historical Newspapers, International Collections, Performing Arts, Prints and Photographs, Veterans, and Web Site Archiving. Because this is a major resource for the United States, it is worthwhile visiting frequently for new collections as they are added.

▶ Exhibitions
http://www.loc.gov/exhibits

Discover the Library of Congress's current and past online exhibitions. These wonderful and inspiring exhibits provide a wealth of information for all who view them. Following is a list of the exhibits and a brief description of each.

▶ The African American Mosaic: A Library of Congress Resource Guide for the Study of Black History and Culture
http://www.loc.gov/exhibits/african/learnmore.html

This exhibit explores what being black meant in the Western hemisphere over a span of nearly 500 years. Sections include "Colonization," "Abolition," "Migrations," and the "WPA" (the Works Progress Administration in the Franklin Delano Roosevelt era). View digital photographs, books, periodicals, manuscripts, recorded sound, maps (for tracing migration patterns or the distribution of black populations), an antislavery advertisement, and an antislavery almanac. For further study of the subject, the "Learn More About It" link leads to related links such as "Civil Rights," "From Slavery to Civil Rights," "Born in Slavery," and "Voices from the Days of Slavery." "Voices from the Days of Slavery" offers podcasts of original interviews conducted with slaves in the 1930s and 1940s. Click on "Essays" and then "Faces and Voices" to one such podcast featuring an interview with Fountain Hughes, who reflects on his childhood experiences and life as a slave in Charlottesville, Virginia.

▶ African American Odyssey
http://lcweb2.loc.gov/ammem/aaohtml/

This exhibit follows the history of the African American experience and showcases the contributions of black leaders, artists, actors, authors, soldiers, and others who sought to find their place society. Included are the undertakings of abolitionists and the post–Civil War journey as they suffered segregation and discrimination and tried to achieve equality in employment, education, and the political arena. This online black history exhibit includes maps, musical scores, plays, films, recordings, documents, pamphlets, and books. Link to related digital collections, for instance, The Frederick Douglass Papers at the Library of

Congress; Jackie Robinson and Other Baseball Highlights, 1860s–1960s- Born in Slavery: Slave Narratives from the Federal Writers' Project, 1936–1938; From Slavery to Freedom: The African-American Pamphlet Collection, 1822–1909; and Slaves and the Courts, 1740–1860.

▶ **Al Hirschfeld, Beyond Broadway**
http://www.loc.gov/rr/print/swann/hirschfeld/

This exhibit features 25 original drawings given to the Library of Congress in honor of the library's bicentennial. Hirschfeld's work, which began in the 1920s, represents the rising trend of caricature as a form of experimental portraiture. Read his biography and view photographs of his drawings and caricatures of such celebrities as Charlie Chaplin and Liza Minnelli, advertisements, magazine covers, and places he visited, such as Persia, Africa, and Russia.

▶ **American Treasures of the Library of Congress**
http://www.loc.gov/exhibits/treasures/

American Treasures of the Library of Congress is a permanent online exhibition of over 250 rare items reflecting American history and culture. Featured documents include a draft of the original Declaration of Independence, original manuscripts of the Gettysburg Address and the Emancipation Proclamation, and other important historical documents such as Lincoln's statement (letter) on slavery. There are also personal letters, prints, maps, lithographs, and photographs related to Columbus, Lincoln, Jefferson, Mason, and Lafayette.

▶ **Arthur Szyk: Artist for Freedom**
http://www.loc.gov/rr/print/swann/szyk/

This exhibition features the illustrations and cartoons of Arthur Szyk (1894–1951), a leading political artist during World War II. Szyk focused on human rights and civil liberties. Originally from Poland, he trained in Paris and emigrated to the United States in 1940. Some of his works include *The United States of America*, which portrays African and Native Americans, *The New Order*, and *Ink and Blood*. His anti-Axis cartoons appeared in popular magazines such as *Collier's*. The exhibition section "Masterpieces of Illumination" includes beautifully crafted watercolors and ink images of the Declaration of Independence of the United States (1950) and the Bill of Rights (1949).

▶ **Benjamin Franklin: In His Own Words**
http://www.loc.gov/exhibits/treasures/franklin-home.html

This exhibition focuses on Franklin's achievements as a printer, writer, cartoonist, inventor, scientist, and politician. The site contains samples of Franklin's letters, books, manuscripts, and cartoons; his "Join, or Die" woodcut image printed in the *Pennsylvania Gazette* (Philadelphia, May 9, 1754); and notable examples of works he printed, such as *M.T. Cicero's Cato Major, or, His Discourse of Old-Age* (printed in 1744) and one of American's first magazines (1741), *The General Magazine, and Historical Chronicle, for All the British Plantations in America*.

▶ **Blondie Gets Married! Comic Strip Drawings by Chic Young**
http://www.loc.gov/rr/print/swann/blondie/

This exhibition contains 27 of Chic Young's comic strip drawings of *Blondie*, which appeared in 2,000 newspapers. Exhibition panels include "Courtship," "Wedding," and "Work." The strips exhibited were donated by Jeanne Young O'Neil, the daughter of Chic Young.

▶ **Bob Hope and American Variety**
http://www.loc.gov/exhibits/bobhope/

This is a wonderful site for exploring the vaudeville, radio, and television entertainment venues popular during Bob Hope's long career. Photographs, images of show bills, prints, and other formats spotlight a host of celebrities, such as Ed Wynn, James Cagney, and Mae West. View photographs of Bob Hope's visits to the troops around the world during World War II and the Vietnam conflict; portraits of Bob Hope; his personal joke file; and other interesting items including a script, a telegram, and letters written to him.

▶ **Bound for Glory: America in Color**
http://myloc.gov/exhibitions/boundforglory/pages/default.aspx

The *Bound for Glory: America in Color* online exhibit features 70 digital prints made from color transparencies taken between 1939 and 1943. The pictures mark the beginning of color photography and the Kodachrome era. Dramatic scenes and portraits of people from small towns during the Depression are depicted.

▶ **Canadian Counterpoint: Illustrations by Anita Kunz**
http://www.loc.gov/rr/print/swann/kunz/

Canadian artist Anita Kunz and 16 of her artworks are featured in this online exhibit. Kunz is known for her caricatures, including "Ray Charles," "Whoopi," "St. Hillary," and "Serial Killers." Select "Object Checklist" to view these and other examples of her art. Cartoon paintings include such themes as women's issues, health, and political satire.

▶ **Cartoon America**
http://www.loc.gov/exhibits/cartoonamerica/

Editorial cartoonist Art Wood copied the styles and characters of his favorite cartoonists. Over his lifetime he corresponded with many of them and collected their original works. The Library of Congress's Art Wood Collection of Cartoon and Caricature today contains more than 36,000 cartoon drawings. *Cartoon America* features 102 of these innovative artworks created by both Wood and other famous cartoonists. Works include illustrations, comic strips, political illustrations, and caricatures from the nineteenth century's Gilded Age to more recent times, all with accompanying descriptions. View, for example, "Davy Crockett," "Judith Shakespeare," "William Randolph Hearst," and numerous illustrations from such popular newspapers and magazines as *Life, Harper's Weekly*, and the *New York Journal*.

▶ **A Century of Creativity: The MacDowell Colony 1907–2007**
http://www.loc.gov/exhibits/macdowell/

Edward MacDowell and wife Marian founded the MacDowell Colony in New Hampshire in 1907 as a sanctuary for writers, composers, and artists. Famous people such as James Baldwin, Leonard Bernstein, Aaron Copland, and Thornton Wilder honed their creative abilities here and collaborated with other talented people. Read about the history of the colony over the years and view photographs, samples of musical scores, political commentary, and other works of these famous artists.

▶ **Churchill and the Great Republic**
http://www.loc.gov/exhibits/churchill/

This exhibit highlights an important time in the history of the United States and its relationship with Britain during the D-Day allied invasion of Nazi-occupied France during World War II. The life and career of Winston Churchill are portrayed through letters, documents, photographs, prints, books, maps, newspaper clippings, and sound recordings of his speeches. The materials open up a window for all into the personhood of Churchill and his relationship with Roosevelt and the United States. Of interest also are letters exchanged between Churchill and his wife. Follow the links under "Exhibition Sections" to view images of documents, pages from manuscripts, portraits, and photographs representative of his life and the times he lived in.

▶ **Creating the United States**
http://myloc.gov/exhibitions/creatingtheus/Pages/default.aspx

Through scanned images of original documents, letters, newspaper articles, photographs, and illustrations learn how the United States was formed. The exhibit sections, based on the three founding documents of the United States, are "Creating the Declaration of Independence," "Creating the U.S. Constitution," and "Creating the Bill of Rights." Click "Exhibition Items" to view the objects, which include maps, images, and texts. The section "Creating the Constitution Interactive" shows how the document's language was crafted.

▶ **Creative Space: Fifty Years of Robert Blackburn's Printmaking Workshop**
http://www.loc.gov/exhibits/blackburn/

View almost 60 lithographs by Robert Blackburn (1920–2003) and other lithographic artists in this online exhibition about Blackburn's Printmaking Workshop, which he founded in 1948. Blackburn and others he inspired experimented in graphic art, which led to the development of abstract color lithography. Select "Checklist of Objects" to view, for example, Hale Woodruff's (1900–1980) "By Parties Unknown," circa 1935; John Von Wicht's (1888–1970) "Dawn," 1953; and Will Barnet's "Child Alone," 1951.

▶ **The Cultures and History of the Americas: The Jay I. Kislak Collection at the Library of Congress**
http://www.loc.gov/exhibits/kislak/

This online exhibit explores the pre-Columbian cultures of Central America and the Caribbean, encounters between the Europeans and the indigenous peoples, piracy, and trade in the American Atlantic. View images of rare books (with accompanying descriptions) of such titles as *Priest's Handbook* (ca. 1550), Christopher Columbus's *Epistola . . . de Insulis Indie . . . nuper inventis* (Letter Concerning the Islands Recently Discovered in the Indian Sea, 1493), George Washington's *The Virginia Almanack for the Year of Our Lord God 1762*, and Martin Waldseemüller's *Carta Marina Navigatoria Portugallen Navigationes . . .* (Carta Marina: A Portuguese Navigational Sea-Chart of the Known Earth and Oceans, 1516). Click "Interactive Exhibit Objects" and explore the book *The Buccaneers of America*, a three-dimensional digital model that simulates turning the pages of a real book.

► **Declaring Independence: Drafting the Documents**
http://www.loc.gov/exhibits/declara/declara4.html

Declaring Independence features images of unique documents from the collections of the Library of Congress. For example, view "An 1876 print representing the 'Declaration Committee,' chaired by Thomas Jefferson"; "A contemporaneous print representing the destruction of the statue of King George III in New York City following the reading of the Declaration of Independence to the American army, July 9, 1776"; and "Fragment of the earliest known draft of the Declaration of Independence, written by Thomas Jefferson in June 1776." The site offers a history of the Declaration's drafting and a chronology of events.

► **The Dream of Flight**
http://www.loc.gov/exhibits/treasures/wb-home.html

View rare images of etchings, engravings, original photographs, and pages from rare books depicting man's fascination with flight spanning a thousand years, beginning in 1000 BCE in China with the invention of the kite through man's travels into space. Among the images are "Phaeton in Chariot" in Dante Alighieri's *La Commedia* (1491). The author compares "his journey to that of Phaeton, the mortal son of the Greek god Helios, who drove the chariot of the Sun across the sky." Another image is "Elijah in the Flying Chariot" in *Bi0blia* (1702) published by H. Keuer in Dordrecht. The exhibition also honors the Wright brothers' achievements, Charles A. Lindbergh, Frank Whittle (British inventor of the jet), Amelia Earhart, the Boeing 247, Russian space exploration (and Sputnik 1 and Salyut 1), astronauts Neil A. Armstrong and Edwin E. Aldrin (who first walked on the moon), the Columbia shuttle, and the first International Space Station.

► **Earth as Art: A Landsat Perspective**
http://www.loc.gov/exhibits/earthasart/

View infrared images of the Earth taken from the Landsat 7 satellite and meant more for aesthetic purposes than for scientific data. The images were donated to the Library of Congress by the National Aeronautics and Space Administration and the U.S. Geological Survey.

▶ **Enduring Outrage: Editorial Cartoons by Herblock**
http://myloc.gov/exhibitions/enduringoutrage/pages/default.aspx

View a collection of original cartoons created by the Pulitzer Prize–winning political cartoonist Herblock (Herb Block). The exhibition's sections are based on themes in Herblock's works: "Environment," "Ethics," "Extremism," "Get Out the Vote," "Middle East," "Privacy/Security" and "Wars" (World War II, Vietnam, and Bosnia). Image descriptions contain details such as the date and name of the newspaper or other publication and the medium used. Icons are included when appropriate to indicate the format of the drawing or collection of drawings: multiple images, video, audio, or interactive. Another icon indicates inclusion of discovery facts for kids. Click "Ethics" to view, for example, "Quitting time and all's well" (*Washington Post*, October 3, 1976). It depicts Congress failing to censure unethical behavior by members of both houses. An example for a wartime cartoon is "American Doubt about the Vietnam War." It depicts Uncle Sam carrying an M-16 rifle (*Washington Post*, January 28, 1968).

▶ **Exploring the Early Americas**
http://myloc.gov/exhibitions/earlyamericas/Pages/default.aspx

This exhibition highlights selections from the Jay I. Kislak Collection and examines the early encounters between Native Americans and Europeans. The exhibition's main sections are organized chronologically: "Pre-Contact America," "Exploration and Encounters," and "Aftermath of the Encounter." Of special interest is the *Codex Vindobonensis*, a manuscript predating the Spanish conquest of the Mixtec Indians of Oaxaca, Mexico. Another section, "Interactives," offers opportunities to learn directly from artifacts, books, documents, paintings, and maps. Among these items is a wooden box called the "Tortuguero Box," which had been owned by a seventh-century Mayan lord. A video tells the story of the box and its hieroglyphs that describe the dynasty of the ruler. The "Conquest of Mexico Paintings Interactive" examines paintings that tell the story of the conquest of the Aztecs by Spanish conquistador Hernán Cortés in 1521. The interactive includes information about Columbus, Pizarro, and the Incas and the culture, rituals, and ceremonies during this period of history, making it a valuable source of information.

▶ **For European Recovery: The Fiftieth Anniversary of the Marshall Plan**
http://www.loc.gov/exhibits/marshall/

This exhibition honors the fiftieth anniversary of Secretary of State George Marshall's speech that addressed a solution to the difficulties faced by the Europeans after World War II. It became one of the greatest speeches in history. Highlights include the online book *The Marshall Plan and the Future of U.S. European Relations* (click "Learn More About It"). Other items include papers, articles from newspapers and magazines (such as *Kiplinger Magazine* and the *Washington Post*), a poster, and political cartoons drawn in response to the Marshall Plan depicting Communist, Soviet, Dutch, and German viewpoints.

▶ **1492: An Ongoing Voyage**
http://www.loc.gov/exhibits/1492/

Explore the Mediterranean world at the time of Columbus's voyage to the new world. This is a great educational site for children and history buffs. The online exhibit displays illustrations, images, photographs, drawings, manuscripts, maps, and text bearing information on Columbus's expedition. Sections of the online exhibit include "The Mediterranean World," "Christopher Columbus: Man and Myth," "Inventing America," and "Europe Claims America." The site examines the interactions among the Native Americans and the European explorers, conquerors, and first settlers between the years 1492 and 1600. This is also the period when African slaves were taken to America.

▶ **Frank Lloyd Wright: Designs for an American Landscape, 1922–1932**
http://www.loc.gov/exhibits/flw/flw.html

The *Frank Lloyd Wright* exhibition outlines notable architectural projects in the 1920s such as the Gordon Strong Automobile Objective on Sugarloaf Mountain, the Doheny Ranch in California, the San Marcos luxury resort in an Arizona desert, the A.M. Johnson Desert Compound in California, and a summer colony at Lake Tahoe. Interspersed in the text are some photographs and architectural designs.

▶ **From Haven to Home: 350 Years of Jewish Life in America**
http://www.loc.gov/exhibits/haventohome/

Two major themes, haven and home, spotlight the Jewish experience in America through an impressive number of items, including photographs, images of manuscripts and rare books, music, letters, and a map. "Haven" represents the Jewish ideal for freedom. "Home" represents the American Jewish experiences with acculturation dating back to 1654. Click "Timeline" to view an interactive version of "American Jewish History 1492–2004." Other sections of the exhibit include "Haven," "A Century of Immigration," and "Confronting Challenges." Click "Checklist of Objects" to see a list of items in the exhibition. Examples include a photograph of Jewish refugee children aboard the liner *President Harding* waving at the Statue of Liberty; pages from the rare book *Bay Psalm Book* (the Whole Booke of Psalmes Faithfully Translated into English Metre, 1640); the wood carving "Torah Ark Lintel" (Lancaster, Pennsylvania, mid-eighteenth century); and a piano vocal score by Irving Berlin (1888–1989) and Emma Lazarus (1849–1887), "Give Me Your Tired, Your Poor," from *Miss Liberty*, 1949.

▶ **From the Home Front and the Front Lines**
http://www.loc.gov/exhibits/treasures/homefront-home.html

This exhibition is a wonderful tribute to U.S. veterans based on materials from the Veterans History Project. World War I (1914–1918), World War II (1939–1945), the Korean War (1950–1953), the Vietnam War (1965–1975), and the Persian Gulf War (1991) are featured through photographs, diaries, albums, correspondence, maps, flags, military papers, and other items of interest. A sample of the more interesting photographs include "War Weary *USS Clarendon*," 1945; "Troops Preparing to Disembark," November 1945; and "Bunkhouse, Augusta Arsenal Training School," circa 1917. Maps include "The Blue

Ridge Path," May 22, 1945; and "Raids," July 1942. Interesting ephemera include a "Chemical Warfare Agents: Reference and Training Chart," circa 1918; a "War Service Certificate," circa 1918; images from the diary "Viet Nam Log: A Story of the Air War in Viet Nam by Capt. R.E. Pierson"; and civilian items such as a "War Ration Book Four" (issued to Rosalind Sandler), "War Ration Stamps," a "Ration Card" (ca. 1969), and a civilian photo ID card for Clare Marie Johns (June 23,1943).

▶ **The Gettysburg Address**
http://myloc.gov/Exhibitions/gettysburgaddress/Pages/default.aspx

View photographs depicting the battlefield of Gettysburg (July 1863) and its cemetery, Lincoln on a speaking platform, a personal note from Lincoln, and images of the Gettysburg Address from copies given to Lincoln's private secretaries John Nicolay and John Hay. Select "Learn More" for supplemental information on the Emancipation Proclamation and the assassination of Abraham Lincoln, including historical descriptions, timelines, galleries of photos, articles, and other items of interest. For example, related to the assassination are pictures of Lincoln, reward posters, newspaper articles, and images depicting Lincoln's death on that fateful night.

▶ **Herblock!**
http://myloc.gov/Exhibitions/herblock/Pages/default.aspx

Here is another exhibition featuring Pulitzer Prize–winning cartoonist Herb Block and his career. Block's cartoons denounced injustice and inequality and featured communism, the Cold War, the Reagan era, and more. Category links include "The Approaching Perils," "Psychopathic Ward," and "White Is Black, Black Is White, Night Is Day—."

▶ **Herblock's History: Political Cartoons from the Crash to the Millennium**
http://www.loc.gov/rr/print/swann/herblock/

This website presents many more cartoons by Herblock caricaturizing the nation's presidents from Herbert Hoover to Bill Clinton and major issues facing each presidency and its politics. Exhibition sections focus on specific eras. Each cartoon has a title, description of its topic, its medium, and the name and date of the publication it appeared in. This is a great site for students and serious researchers who may be studying and writing about a specific era. For example, the cartoon *Animal Farm* (April 2, 1961) was drawn with ink, graphite, and opaque white over graphite, with the underdrawing on layered paper, and published in the *Washington Post*. In the cartoon Block depicts inequality by suggesting that farm animals get greater representation than humans—referring to the 1964 decision in which Chief Justice Earl Warren of the Supreme Court issued a "one-man, one-vote" ruling designed to correct the imbalance in representation.

▶ **Humor's Edge: Cartoons by Ann Telnaes**
http://www.loc.gov/exhibits/telnaes/

Over 80 editorial cartoons portray the actions of influential public figures and some troublesome issues of the day by the talented Swedish-born American artist Ann Telnaes. Unlike her peers, who were usually associated with a newspaper or magazine, Telnaes worked freelance. Her excellence in drawing, illustrative and editorial effect, and originality helped her to win the Pulitzer Prize for editorial cartooning in 2001. One of her Pulitzer Prize–winning cartoons, *The Choice*, depicts the presidential candidates in the 2000 election campaign. In the cartoon we observe an unshaven American trying to choose which boring cereal to eat, the cereals being Bran (Gore) or Frosted Flake (Bush). "The cartoon is ink brush over blue pencil and graphite underdrawing with opaque white." Each of Telnaes's works includes information on the cartoon and a description of the medium used. Many of her cartoons also portray how other countries view the United States, focusing on foreign affairs issues.

▶ **"I Do Solemnly Swear . . .": Inaugural Materials from the Collections of the Library of Congress**
http://www.loc.gov/exhibits/treasures/inaugural-home.html

This exhibit offers a keen perspective into the history of American presidential inaugurations. Presidents from George Washington to John F. Kennedy are featured. Items include photographs, campaign posters, letters, inaugural speeches, and manuscripts. An example is images of pages from the inaugural address given March 4, 1829, by Andrew Jackson (1767–1845). One can also view the transcript in whole. Other examples are sheet music dated March 4, 1801, titled *Pieces*, and a lithograph of Lincoln, "The 'Wigwam' Grand March" (published in Boston by Oliver Ditson & Co., ca. 1860).

▶ **Illuminating the Word: The St. John's Bible**
http://www.loc.gov/exhibits/stjohnsbible/

St. John's Bible was commissioned by the Benedictine Monastery of St. John's in Collegeville, Minnesota, under the direction of a world-renowned calligrapher, Donald Jackson from England. Jackson is coordinating a project to scribe and illustrate an illuminated Saint John's Bible in the tradition of medieval calligraphy and "craftsmanship combined with the latest capabilities of computer technology and electronic communication." View these beautiful images created to illustrate a bible that is a modern work of art. The bible is illuminated through the use of medieval techniques, such as quills and paints hand-ground from minerals and stones, including 24-karat gold. Several other priceless volumes from the Library's collection of 1,500 printed bibles housed in the Rare Book and Special Collections Division are featured as well, reflecting a wide range of formats, printing techniques, and artistry. An example of an illuminated page from a medieval bible is "The Bible and Holy Scriptures Conteyned in the Olde and Newe Testament" (1560), and "The Life of Paul" is an example of a modern illuminated page.

▶ **In the Beginning Was the Word: The Russian Church and Native Alaskan Cultures**
http://www.loc.gov/exhibits/russian/russch0.html

View photographs of lithographs, manuscripts, and other items from a relatively unknown archive of important documents. This exhibit explores exchanges that took place between the Russian Orthodox Church in Alaska and Native Alaskans between 1794 and about 1915. Examples include a lithograph of Catherine II; the manuscript *Order to the Citizen of Rylsk and Companion of the Northeastern American Company Mr. Shelekhov, from Her Imperial Majesty Catherine II, May 12, 1794*; and a photograph of Eskimos.

▶ **John Bull and Uncle Sam: Four Centuries of British-American Relations**
http://www.loc.gov/exhibits/british/

The *John Bull* (a representative figure for Great Britain depicted in political cartoons) *and Uncle Sam* (representing the United States) exhibit gathers treasures from two great libraries, the British Library and the Library of Congress, spanning the eighteenth to the late twentieth centuries. View cartoons, maps, photographs, sheet music covers, and manuscript pages presented in sections including "Exploration and Settlement," the "American Revolution," "Inventions and Discoveries," and "Popular Culture from Baseball to Rock and Roll." Each section examines an aspect of the relationship between the two countries. Topics, for example, from the Popular Culture era, include sports and famous personalities such as Gershwin, Twiggy, the Beatles, and the Stones.

▶ **Language of the Land: Journeys into Literary America**
http://www.loc.gov/exhibits/land/

The "Object List" provides links to view this unusual and delightful online exhibit. It takes one on a journey through the literature of famous authors, such as Mark Twain's *The Adventures of Huckleberry Finn* and John Steinbeck's *The Grapes of Wrath*, by showing maps, photographs, and excerpts from the works. The book *Language of the Land: The Library of Congress Book of Literary Maps* by Martha Hopkins and Michael Buscher was inspired by this exhibit. Examples of items found online (and in the book) are "A Pictorial Chart of American Literature," Ethel Earle Wylie, compiler, and Ella Wall Van Leer, illustrator (Chicago: McNally, 1932); the photograph "Portland Head Light Maine," John Marshall, photographer (1935); and "A Map of Sinclair Lewis' United States as It Appears in His Novels," George Annand, illustrator (New York: Doubleday, Doran, 1934).

▶ **Library of Congress Bible Collection**
http://myloc.gov/exhibitions/bibles/Pages/default.aspx

Explore the importance of the Giant Bible of Mainz, the Gutenberg Bible, and 16 other bibles from the Library's collections. View images comparing and contrasting aspects of the Mainz Bible and Gutenberg Bible in an interactive display. Learn about the history and characteristics of each of the bibles. Other bibles include The Eliot Indian Bible: First Bible Printed in America, the first bible published in North America; the King James Bible; and the Geneva Bible.

▶ **Life of the People: Realist Prints and Drawings from the Ben and Beatrice Goldstein Collection**
http://www.loc.gov/exhibits/goldstein/

The *Life of the People* exhibit features American prints and drawings that reflected social concerns and political issues shared by women artists, African

Americans, and Mexican muralists. Articles, cartoons, essays, images, lithographs, etchings, and wood engravings are displayed in the sections "Art of the People," "The Radical Impulse," "City Life," "Capital and Labor," "The American Scene," and "Ben Goldstein." One example is the cartoon by Fred Ellis (1885–1965) *54 Hour Week / Low Wages* (ca. 1930s), drawn in crayon, ink, pencil, and opaque white and published in the *Daily Worker.*

▶ **Los Angeles Mapped**
http://www.loc.gov/exhibits/lamapped/

View historical maps of Los Angeles from the Library's Geography and Map Division. Click "Online Exhibition" to view examples such as the "Map of Baja California Shown as an Island," a manuscript map of the Baja Peninsula drawn by Johannes Vingboons for the Dutch West India Company around 1639; a "Map of the City of Los Angeles Showing Railway Systems" printed in 1906; and the "Free Harbor Jubilee poster," a lithograph poster from Los Angeles printed in 1899.

▶ **Louis Braille: His Legacy and Influence**
http://myloc.gov/exhibitions/braille/Pages/default.aspx

Read about the legacy of Louis Braille (1809–1852), who invented the tactile system enabling the blind and visually handicapped people to read and to write. He also devised systems for use with music and mathematics. View a number of images reflecting his legacy and his influence, for instance, photos of Helen Keller, the "Next Generation Perkins Brailler," the "Braille Edition of Scrabble," "Jot a Dot Pocket Brailler," a Braille calendar, and a tactile watch.

▶ **Madison's Treasures**
http://www.loc.gov/exhibits/madison/

This site examines documents related to Madison and his political career, such as the drafting and ratification of the U.S. Constitution, amendments for the Bill of Rights, and documents related to the freedom of religion. Read autobiographical information and correspondence between Madison and George Washington and between Madison and Thomas Jefferson. Included are images of the first edition of *The Federalist*, an important publication on statecraft and political theory written by Madison and Alexander Hamilton with assistance from John Jay.

▶ **Maps in Our Lives**
http://www.loc.gov/exhibits/maps/

View images of maps in the Library's American Congress on Surveying and Mapping Collection. The exhibition includes historical maps, for example, "A Map of General Washington's Farm of Mount Vernon from a Drawing Transmitted by the General" and a "Map of George Washington's Land at Mount Vernon, Fairfax County, Virginia, 1850." Click "Online Exhibitions" to watch the video *Maps in Our Lives.*

▶ **Margaret Mead: Human Nature and the Power of Culture**
http://www.loc.gov/exhibits/mead/

This online exhibit includes manuscripts, notes written about Mead by her grandmother, photographs, a diary, and a self-portrait manuscript of Mead's life and career as an anthropologist. Select "Exhibit Sections" to view items.

▶ **Monstrous Craws & Character Flaws: Masterpieces of Cartoon and Caricature at the Library of Congress**
http://www.loc.gov/rr/print/swann/craws/

This exhibition portrays social and political commentaries created by great graphic artists dating back to the eighteenth century. Each print is accompanied by the name of the artist, date, and medium used to create the work. One example is an ink, white-out, pencil, and tonal film overlay on paper by Garry Trudeau, "I really didn't want you anyway, you stupid mourning cloak," a *Doonesbury* cartoon from 1971.

▶ **Oliphant's Anthem: Pat Oliphant at the Library of Congress**
http://www.loc.gov/exhibits/oliphant/

View over 50 cartoon drawings by Pat Oliphant, a Pulitzer Prize winner in 1966 for editorial cartooning. The works address the political and social issues for over 30 years. Oliphant did caricatures of seven presidents, including Clinton and Lyndon Johnson, as well as major significant historical events such as Watergate, Vietnam, the collapse of communism in Europe, and the Gulf War. In addition to the cartoons are sketchbooks and selected installments from the *Socks Goes to Washington* comic strip.

▶ **A Petal from the Rose: Illustrations by Elizabeth Shippen Green**
http://www.loc.gov/rr/print/swann/petal/about.html

Elizabeth Shippen Green (1871–1954) is one of the remarkable women illustrators working at the turn of the twentieth century. She is distinguished for her originality and the quality of her works. Her illustrations focused on dramatic situations, moods, and domestic life. Elizabeth Shippen Green used charcoals, watercolor, and oil for her illustrations. Read about her life, and view examples of her work, including "Life was made for love and cheer," a watercolor and charcoal on board published in *Harper's Magazine* in September 1904. One photograph shows Elizabeth at her desk.

▶ **Religion and the Founding of the American Republic**
http://www.loc.gov/exhibits/religion/

This online exhibit documents the role religion played in the shaping of early American life and in forming the American republic. The history of how the United States of America was settled and the religious beliefs of the first settlers are recounted through photographs, illustrations, text, and images taken from rare books. The efforts of the founders to define the role of religious faith in public life are revealed in the sections "America as a Religious Refuge: The Seventeenth Century," "Religion in Eighteenth-Century America," "Religion of the American Revolution," "Religion of the Congress of the Confederation,

1774–89," "Religion and the State Governments," "Religion and the Federal Government," and "Religion and the New Republic."

▶ **Revising Himself: Walt Whitman and Leaves of Grass**
http://www.loc.gov/exhibits/treasures/whitman-home.html

View Whitman's personal letters to others, notes on his poems, photos of him and his home, and photographs he took. The images and notes trace the development of Whitman as a poet and author of the famous work *Leaves of Grass* (1855).

▶ **Rivers, Edens, Empires: Lewis & Clark and the Revealing of America**
http://www.loc.gov/exhibits/lewisandclark/

Materials in the exhibition span the mid-eighteenth to mid-nineteenth centuries and illustrate the search, including the expedition of Lewis and Clark, to connect the East and the West. One diary describes the expedition conducted by Franciscan priests Silvestre Veléz de Escalante and Francisco Dominguez and their route through what is now Colorado, Utah, and Arizona, which began at Santa Fe on July 29, 1776. Another item is Sitting Rabbit's 1906–1907 map of the Missouri River from the South Dakota–North Dakota boundary to the mouth of the Yellowstone River. View a virtual tour of the exhibition, drawings, letters by Lewis and Clark, illustrations, pictures of artifacts given to the Indians on their journey, some personal artifacts of Lewis and Clark, and art (wood cuts and engravings) depicting events and encounters with Indians and the wild life experienced on the expedition.

▶ **Roger L. Stevens Presents**
http://www.loc.gov/exhibits/stevens/

Roger Lacey Stevens was a theatrical producer, arts administrator, and real estate entrepreneur in the United States and Britain during the 1950s and 1960s. As an arts administrator, he organized the National Endowment for the Arts and served as its first chairman, and he established the John F. Kennedy Center for the Performing Arts in Washington, DC. His theatrical productions include 100 plays and musicals, including *West Side Story*, *Pippin*, and *A Man for All Seasons*. View photographs of his productions and their playbills.

▶ **Stagestruck! Performing Arts Caricatures at the Library of Congress**
http://www.loc.gov/rr/print/swann/stagestruck/

Performing arts caricatures became fashionable in the early twentieth century. View caricatures of famous celebrities of the stage and screen created by various illustrators and artists that appeared in newspapers and magazines. Celebrities became icons and raised circulation rates for magazines and newspapers as a result of this new and entertaining art form. The exhibition displays works of artists such as Oscar Cesare, John Sloan, Alfred Bendiner, Miguel Covarrubias, Kenneth Chamberlain, and Makoto Wada. Caricatures show Mae West, George Burns, Gracie Allen, and others. Information about each artist is provided, as well as a description of each caricature. For example, "The Wonder Bar," a portrayal of Al Jolson, was done in ink and published in the *New York Times* on March 29, 1931.

▶ Temple of Liberty: Building the Capitol for a New Nation
http://www.loc.gov/exhibits/us.capitol/s0.html

This inclusive exhibition provides a history of the U.S. Capitol building's design and structure. George Washington and Thomas Jefferson wanted it to symbolize the political and social values of the Constitution and express America's new political order. Topical headings lead to illustrations of architectural designs, images of symbols selected in the design, early drawings of floor plans, portraits of historical figures, and photographs of the House and Senate wing. This exhibition is a wonderful source of historical information about America's Capitol building. Although the building was originally completed in 1826, it would experience further expansion in the future.

▶ Thomas Jefferson
http://www.loc.gov/exhibits/jefferson/

Thomas Jefferson, one of America's founding fathers and the third president of the United States, was also an architect, inventor, farmer, slaveholder, book collector, scholar, and diplomat. His great legacy is captured in this exhibition, which displays personal letters, photographs, artifacts, and other documents that portray him as a person and as a political figure in the world. The exhibit includes paintings, such as Pitford Braddick Peticolas's "View of the West Front of Monticello" (1827), a portrait of "Lucy" (1845), and a reproduction of a newspaper, *The Genius of Liberty*, dated July 3, 1798.

▶ Thomas Jefferson's Library
http://myloc.gov/exhibitions/jeffersonslibrary/Pages/default.aspx

The history behind the Library of Congress interestingly is entwined with Thomas Jefferson and his fascination with books. He accumulated thousands of books in his personal collection. When the British burned the Capitol and its Congressional Library in 1814, Jefferson offered to sell his library to Congress to replace the library that was destroyed. Jefferson's book collection is the core of the Library of Congress, currently the world's largest library. The main exhibition sections are "Memory," "Reason," and "Imagination," which Jefferson translated into "History," "Philosophy," and the "Fine Arts." Other sections include "Interactives," showcasing several rare books; and "Related Multimedia," which offers a number of videos such as *A Spiteful Souvenir* and further links for "Students and Teachers" (lesson plans) and a "Virtual Tour."

▶ Voices of Civil Rights
http://www.loc.gov/exhibits/civilrights/

This exhibit documents events during the civil rights movement in the United States through personal stories, oral histories, and photographs taken during the seven-day bus tour that began in Washington, DC, on August 3, 2004. It traveled through 22 states and 39 cities following the 1961 freedom rides to Jackson, Mississippi. View historical photographs, such as "Participants Marching in the Civil Rights March from Selma to Montgomery, Alabama in 1965" by photographer Peter Pettus; "Man Drinking at 'Colored' Water Cooler in the Street Car Terminal Oklahoma City, Oklahoma, July 1939" by photographer

Russell Lee; and "School Integration in Little Rock, Arkansas, 1957" by photographer Bern Keating. Additional photographs include important figures involved in the civil rights movement, including Reverend James Jackson, who joined the Selma-to-Montgomery march two weeks after the original march ended violently on what became known as "Bloody Sunday." View a photo of President Lyndon B. Johnson giving Dr. Martin Luther King one of the pens used in the signing of the Voting Rights Act of 1965. Teachers and students can further explore this unfortunate time in the history of America and on slavery by linking on to "Learn More About It."

▶ **Voices, Votes, Victory: Presidential Campaign Songs**
http://myloc.gov/exhibitions/presidentialsongs/Pages/default.aspx

Sung long ago but not forgotten are the songs and lyrics used in presidential campaigns of the past. View sheet music covering a large variety of topics and national issues used as early as 1844. The exhibition's sections are organized by theme: "Early Rally Songs" (such as "Washington's March"), "Songsters" (such as "Whig Songs, Selected, Sung, and Published by the Choir of the National Clay Club") "Forgotten Candidates" (such as "Tilden and Hendricks Grand March"), and "Issues and Slogans" such as ("Tea Pot Dome"). Select "Links to Family or Past Presidents" for information and photographs, such as "Grover Cleveland's Bride."

▶ **The Water-Babies Illustrations by Jessie Willcox Smith**
http://www.loc.gov/rr/print/swann/waterbabies/

In 1916 Jessie Willcox Smith created beautiful drawings to illustrate the famous Victorian fairy tale *Water Babies* written by Reverend Charles Kingsley (1819–1875) of England. Read about this well-known artist and the wonderful fairy tale. The exhibition contains 14 beautiful drawings.

▶ **West Side Story**
http://www.loc.gov/exhibits/westsidestory/

West Side Story, a successful Broadway musical, opened on September 26, 1957. It dealt with the serious issues of violence, racial prejudice, and gangs. It became famous for its music, script, and dancing and had a great influence on musicals themselves. Read the background history of *West Side Story*, including the contributions of composer Leonard Bernstein, lyricist Stephen Sondheim, director and choreographer Jerome Robbins, and Arthur Laurents, who placed William Shakespeare's Romeo and Juliet story in contemporary Manhattan. The exhibition features production photographs, images of sheet music and set designs, Bernstein's letters, opening night telegrams, choreographic notes, and other memorabilia.

▶ **When They Were Young: A Photographic Retrospective of Childhood**
http://www.loc.gov/exhibits/young/

View experiences of childhood through the photographs of many—across time, diverse cultures, and different economic backgrounds. The photographs capture and celebrate the many qualities of children, their vulnerability, playfulness, spirit, impulsiveness, restlessness, and dignity. The exhibition was created to launch the book *When They Were Young: A Photographic Retrospective of Childhood from the Library of Congress*, published by Kales Press, New York, in 2002. The quotes throughout the exhibit are from an essay in the book written by Pulitzer Prize–winning author Robert Coles. Images in this wonderful exhibit include "Mother and Child—Sunlight" (1906) by Edward J. Steichen; "Asian (?) Baby Holding Spoon or Ladle," a gelatin silver print taken by Frances Benjamin Johnston in 1892; and another gelatin silver print, "Apache Girl with Basket," taken by Carl Werntz in 1902.

▶ **"With an Even Hand": Brown v. Board at Fifty**
http://www.loc.gov/exhibits/brown/

This is a great site for the researcher or student who wants to investigate the history and gain an understanding of racial segregation in the United States. The exhibit commemorated the fiftieth anniversary of the landmark judicial case *Oliver Brown v. Board of Education of Topeka, Kansas,* which concluded that "separate educational facilities are inherently unequal." The exhibition features more than 100 items, including books, documents, photographs (e.g., "Mrs. Rosa Parks Being Fingerprinted in Montgomery, Alabama, 1956"), personal papers, manuscripts, maps, music, newspapers and magazines, films (listing only), political cartoons, and prints. The history of racial segregation is traced from 1849 to 1950, with court cases and related documents, such as *Educational Laws of Virginia; The Personal Narrative of Mrs. Margaret Douglass, a Southern Woman, Who Was Imprisoned for One Month in the Common Jail of Norfolk, under the Laws of Virginia, for the Crime of Teaching Free Colored Children to Read.*

▶ **With Malice Toward None: The Abraham Lincoln Bicentennial Exhibition**
http://myloc.gov/exhibitions/lincoln/Pages/default.aspx

This exhibition commemorates the two-hundredth anniversary of Abraham Lincoln's birth. Explore interactive presentations to learn directly from artifacts, books, documents, paintings, maps, and photographs, and view the video *Watch a President Age.* Exhibition sections include "Rise to National Prominence," "The Presidency," and "'Now He Belongs to the Ages.'"

▶ **Witness and Response: September 11 Acquisitions at the Library of Congress**
http://www.loc.gov/exhibits/911/

Witness and Response exhibits materials such as prints, photographs, drawings, poems, newspapers, and other important documents about this infamous day in U.S. history. Select "American Folklife Center" to watch a video describing the September 11 disaster and to view the poignant drawing "Statue of Liberty—'It's Okay'" by Eddie Hamilton, a third grader at Sequoyah Elementary School, Knoxville, Tennessee. It captures the response of a child to this horrific event. In the 2001 drawing, a crying Statue of Liberty is consoling a tearful bald eagle that is standing on the U.S. flag. Listen to a number of audio recordings from eyewitnesses. Select "Geography and Map Division" to view images of cartographic material and aerial views and maps of Ground Zero of the World Trade Center. Select "Object List" for a listing of newspaper articles. Select "Prints and Photography" to view a gallery of pictures, posters, and documentary photographs of the World Trade Center, the Pentagon in Washington, DC, and the Shanksville, Pennsylvania, crash site. The exhibition is beyond doubt a vital resource that documents a day in U.S. history that will not be forgotten.

▶ **The Wizard of Oz: An American Fairy Tale**
http://www.loc.gov/exhibits/oz/

This wonderful exhibit commemorates the one-hundredth anniversary of the publication of *The Wonderful Wizard of Oz*, an American classic children's fairy tale. Author L. Frank Baum (1856–1919) also wrote several other books set in Oz. The fame of the book has generated theatrical plays, musicals, movies, and television shows. View images of some of Baum's books; illustrations; and photographs of Dorothy, the lion, the scarecrow, and others from the movie set. Also view images of artifacts (games, toys, etc.) produced in response to the popularity of the story and its characters.

▶ **Women Come to the Front: Journalists, Photographers, and Broadcasters During WWII**
http://www.loc.gov/exhibits/wcf/wcf0001.html

The stories of women journalists who secured a place for themselves in the newsroom, on the battlefield, and in the workplace during World War II are told in this exhibit. Read about these courageous and talented women. Featured are Therese Bonney, whose images of homeless children and adults in Europe touched millions of viewers in the United States and abroad; Toni Frissell, who produced thousands of images of nurses, frontline soldiers, WACs, African-American airmen, and orphaned children; Marvin Breckinridge Patterson, the first female staff broadcaster in Europe for CBS; Clare Boothe Luce, a congresswoman, ambassador, playwright, socialite, and author of *Europe in the Spring* (1940) and articles for *Life* magazine; Janet Flanner, columnist for *The New Yorker* magazine; Esther Bubley, who focused on the human dimension of mobilization during the war; Dorothea Lange, responsible for documenting displaced farm families and migrant workers during the Great Depression; and May Craig, who wrote eyewitness accounts of V-bomb raids in London, the Normandy campaign, the liberation of Paris, and other events. Their stories are told through their personal papers, photographs, and magazine and newspaper articles. The site also provides a long list of other women correspondents during World War II.

▶ **The Work of Charles and Ray Eames: A Legacy of Invention**
http://www.loc.gov/exhibits/eames/

Read biographical information on Charles and Ray Eames, a famous couple who helped to form America's culture in the twentieth century. View photographs of Charles and Ray, images of their architecture, such as "Life in a Chinese Kite," published in *Architectural Forum*, September 1950, and many images from various slide presentations they made representing everyday objects in new ways and new relationships to each other.

▶ **Global Gateway: World Culture and Resources**
http://international.loc.gov/intldl/intldlhome.html

The Global Gateway is a collaborative effort among the Library of Congress and countries worldwide to provide a portal to their projects. Five wonderful collections are described here.

▶ **The Atlantic World: America and the Netherlands**
http://international.loc.gov/intldl/awkbhtml/awkbhome.html

The Atlantic World: America and the Netherlands collection present the history of the Dutch presence in America from Henry Hudson's 1609 voyage to the post-World-War-II period. This cooperative effort of the Library of Congress, the National Library of the Netherlands, and Dutch libraries, museums, and archives provides access to digitized books, manuscripts, maps, photographs, and prints. The website is available in both English and Dutch.

▶ **France in America**
http://international.loc.gov/intldl/fiahtml/fiahome.html

France in America is a bilingual, multiformat English–French digital library depicting the story of the French presence in America from the early sixteenth to the late nineteenth centuries. This is a great site for students, scholars, and researchers. The digitized collection contains historical documents, travel narratives, missionary accounts, administrative reports, maps, prints, and drawings covering topics such as exploration, Native American customs, the colonies, rivalries, the Creole culture, evangelism, and slavery.

▶ **Meeting of Frontiers**
http://international.loc.gov/intldl/mtfhtml/mfhome.html

Meeting of Frontiers, a bilingual, multimedia English–Russian digital library, provides a history of American exploration of the West, the parallel exploration and settlement of Siberia and the Russian Far East, the Russian–American frontier in Alaska, and the Pacific Northwest. The over 2,500 hundred items include rare books, manuscripts, photographs, maps, and sound recordings. This is a great site for schoolchildren and for the general public. It is also invaluable for scholars because of the many primary source materials it contains.

▶ **Parallel Histories: Spain, the United States, and the American Frontier**
http://international.loc.gov/intldl/eshtml/eshome.html

Parallel Histories: Spain, the United States, and the American Frontier is a bilingual, multiformat English–Spanish digital library website. Select "Collections" to view books, maps, prints, photographs, manuscripts, and other documents. Select "Themes" or "Site Map" to explore the parallel histories of the United States and Spain from the fifteenth to the early nineteenth centuries.

▶ **The United States and Brazil: Expanding Frontiers, Comparing Cultures**
http://international.loc.gov/intldl/brhtml/brhome.html

The United States and Brazil: Expanding Frontiers, Comparing Cultures collection explores the history of Brazil and the relationship between Brazil and the United States. The time period spans the eighteenth century to the present. View documents, books, maps, prints, photographs, and manuscripts that cover aspects of Brazilian history, such as ethnic diversity, culture and literature, and biodiversity. The website is a collaboration between the Library of Congress and the National Library of Brazil and is available in both English and Portuguese.

▶ **The Rare Book and Special Collections Division**
http://www.loc.gov/rr/rarebook/guide/

The Rare Book and Special Collections Division is the result of Thomas Jefferson's desire to create a library for the new nation. He sold his personal library to Congress in 1815, thus providing the foundation for the new Library of Congress and the heart of the division. Website links include "American History," "American Literature," "Europe," "Book Arts," "The Illustrated Book," and "List of Selected Special Collections." There are digital images for each book, many of which can be viewed in their entirety online page by page.

▶ **Recorded Sound Reference Center—Tony Schwartz Collection**
http://www.loc.gov/rr/record/schwartzcollection.html

Listen to recordings of the people, everyday sounds, and music of New York City captured on audiotape by Tony Schwartz. Schwartz began using audiotape technology in the late 1940s. The sample online recordings date back to the 1960s. Click "Selected Recordings from the Collection" to listen to them. Two examples are *How We Remember* (1970), in which a group of schoolchildren tell the same story in different ways, and *Sounds from New York* (1962), one of many audio Christmas cards offered to New York City radio listeners over the years.

▶ **Teaching with Primary Resources**
http://www.loc.gov/teachers/

This is a superb site for teachers. It provides them primary source materials for the classroom. Select "See All Primary Source Sets" for an alphabetical list of topics. Materials are available in printable PDF format and include background material and tools to guide teachers and students. Other links are "Themed Resources," "Teacher Update," "Lesson Plans," "Presentations and Activities," and "Professional Development." Materials vary in each of the resource collections and may include maps, illustrations, documents, photographs, manuscripts, audio presentations, and videos. Some examples are described here.

▶ **Abraham Lincoln**
http://www.loc.gov/teachers/classroommaterials/primarysourcesets/lincoln/

The Abraham Lincoln resource set contains illustrations, a map, pictures, speeches, Lincoln's correspondence, and an audio.

▶ **Advertising**
http://www.loc.gov/teachers/classroommaterials/themes/advertising/

This set presents a history of advertising and studies the consumer, product development, and print advertisements from historic newspapers, magazines, and posters as well as historic film footage.

▶ **Asian Pacific Americans**
http://www.loc.gov/teachers/classroommaterials/themes/asian-pacific/

This set studies Japanese and Chinese immigration in the nineteenth and twentieth centuries through documents, prints, art exhibitions, and presentations.

▶ **Baseball**
http://www.loc.gov/teachers/classroommaterials/themes/baseball/

Students can study the history of baseball through primary source songs, baseball cards, letters, and speeches. Learn about famous baseball personalities, such as Roger Maris, Ty Cobb, Babe Ruth, and Jackie Robinson.

▶ **Civics and Government**
http://www.loc.gov/teachers/classroommaterials/themes/civics/

Materials include an early draft of the Constitution with its revisions and notations, the Declaration of Independence, and the Emancipation Proclamation. Students can study the presidents and their presidencies, inaugurations, other national leaders, as well as women's suffrage, slavery, and desegregation. There are photographs, documents, interactive online activities for students, and much more.

▶ **Civil Rights**
http://www.loc.gov/teachers/classroommaterials/themes/civil-rights/

Students can study about the fight for voting rights, the racial history of sports and segregation in the schools, the struggle for citizenship, the civil rights movement, and *Brown v. Board of Education*. Items include study maps, baseball cards, and political cartoons as well as pamphlets, legal documents, poetry, music, and personal correspondence and oral histories of the famous and the ordinary.

▶ **The Civil War**
http://www.loc.gov/teachers/classroommaterials/themes/civil-war/

This set presents varied points of view from both the Union and the Confederacy through poetry, music, images, maps, photographs, letters and diaries, oral histories, and other primary documents. Stories from former slaves and firsthand accounts by Civil War women are included.

▶ **Colonial and Early America**
http://www.loc.gov/teachers/classroommaterials/themes/colonial-america/

Maps, images, letters, and other primary documents provide a history of the colonial experience, including the celebration of Thanksgiving. Learn about this period by examining maps, letters, and other primary documents. Read about the European colonization of America from early settlers through George Washington's presidency.

▶ **Elections**
http://www.loc.gov/teachers/classroommaterials/themes/elections/

Study the electoral process, the voting franchise, first ladies, and presidential inaugurations in materials such as political cartoons, photographs, and drafts of inaugural addresses.

▶ **Exploration and Explorers**
http://www.loc.gov/teachers/classroommaterials/themes/exploration/

Study the exploration of the Americas from the time of Amerigo Vespucci and Columbus through the westward expansion. Resources include maps, an animated presentation, photographs, documents, and a virtual tour.

▶ **Flight and Early Aviators**
http://www.loc.gov/teachers/classroommaterials/themes/flight/

Study the scientific evolution of flight and early inventors and aviators, including Bell, the Wright brothers, Lindbergh, and Earhart. View materials and many items, such as thumbnail images, photos, letters, and a PowerPoint presentation.

▶ **Geography and Maps**
http://www.loc.gov/teachers/classroommaterials/themes/geography/

View U.S. history and change over time through maps and related historical materials

▶ **The Great Depression**
http://www.loc.gov/teachers/classroommaterials/themes/great-depression/

Students gain insight into the effects of the Great Depression and World War II on various ethnic groups. View a host of photographs, posters, and prints, and listen to songs such as "Soldier's Joy" and "Sally Goodin" and play-party rhymes like "Skip to My Lou" and "Old Joe Clark."

▶ **Hispanic Americans**
http://www.loc.gov/teachers/classroommaterials/themes/hispanic-americans/

View maps, paintings, drawings, photographs, and inscriptions that recount the contributions and interactions of Hispanic peoples in North America from 1492 to present.

▶ **Holidays**
http://www.loc.gov/teachers/classroommaterials/themes/holidays/

Materials include songs, images, and historical perspectives of holidays as varied as Thanksgiving, Veteran's Day, Labor Day, and Mother's Day. Feasts and parades are among the ways Americans celebrate holidays and special events such as inaugurations. Discover holiday traditions through music, songs, photographs, and letters.

▶ **Immigration**
http://www.loc.gov/teachers/classroommaterials/themes/immigration/

Trace the immigrant experience and study contributions by immigrant Americans through historic film clips and images of Ellis Island, Angel Island, immigrant groups, letters, and manuscripts.

▶ **Labor**
http://www.loc.gov/teachers/classroommaterials/themes/labor/

Study the history of workers, including women, union members, and children, through historic films and photographs. Films show workers and a typical factory during the late 1890s and early 1900s.

▶ **The Lewis and Clark Expedition**
http://www.loc.gov/teachers/classroommaterials/themes/lewis-clark/

Westward expansion and exploration are chronicled in letters, journals, maps, and manuscripts from the Lewis and Clark expedition. Study this great era and Thomas Jefferson's role in expansion. Materials include images, photographs, a virtual tour, documents, maps, and manuscripts.

▶ **Literature and Poetry**
http://www.loc.gov/teachers/classroommaterials/themes/literature/

Historical documents and manuscripts aid in the study of literature and poetry. "Exhibitions and Presentations" includes links to images, manuscripts, maps, sound files, webcasts, online publications, letters, books, cartoons, and a streaming video of poets. Thornton Wilder, James Baldwin, William Blake, Edwin Booth, and Shakespeare are a few of the writers highlighted here.

▶ **Music and Dance**
http://www.loc.gov/teachers/classroommaterials/themes/america-music/

The stories of the nation are told in sound recordings, video recordings, dance manuals, sheet music, and correspondence. View historic sheet music as well as presentations about the role of music in America. Some of the links present the history of the American brass movement, American choral music, and Civil War music.

▶ **Native Americans**
http://www.loc.gov/teachers/classroommaterials/themes/native-americans/

Study Native Americans through essays, photographs, documents, legislation, treaties, and sound recordings through the links "Exhibitions and Presentations," "Primary Source Sets," and "Lesson Plans."

▶ **Nature and the Environment**
http://www.loc.gov/teachers/classroommaterials/themes/nature/

Study nature, the environment, and natural disasters through a host of online resources accessed through the links "Exhibitions and Presentations" and "Curriculum Connections." Materials include essays, images of books with illustrations related to the environment, photographs, art, and the exhibit *Earth as Art: A Landsat Perspective*, which showcases Landsat 7 images of Earth. Use maps to trace the growth and unique features of the national parks. Learn about nature writers and visual artists.

▶ **Political Cartoons**
http://www.loc.gov/teachers/classroommaterials/themes/political-cartoons/

This set provides resources to support instruction about American political cartoons, including expert presentations, exhibitions, bibliographies, and webcasts. One link is "Humor's Edge: Cartoons by Anne Telnaes," showing and explaining some of her Pulitzer Prize–winning cartoons. Other links highlight cartoons as commentary on political events or issues, such as the response to the September 11, 2001, attack. Other cartoons reflect on the Cold War with the Soviet Union as well as the British perspective of the American Revolution. Explore this sampling of digitized eighteenth- and nineteenth-century political and satirical cartoon prints by cartoonist and theme.

▶ **Science and Invention**
http://www.loc.gov/teachers/classroommaterials/themes/science/

Study science, technology, engineering, conservation, inventions, and a number of advancements going back to the 1700s. Alexander Graham Bell, Benjamin Franklin, and other important inventors are included here. It is a wonderful resource for teachers and students. Several collections are listed, and, depending on the collection, the materials offered are images, photographs, notebooks, letters, films, and primary source documents.

▶ **Summertime and Recreation**
http://www.loc.gov/teachers/classroommaterials/themes/summertime/

Study the culture and traditions of Americans with a focus on sports, leisure activities, songs, and dance through images, manuscripts, maps, and sound files. Link to "Baseball: Across a Divided Society" to view song sheets, video clips, images, trading cards, and photographs that chronicle the story of how baseball emerged as an American national activity. Another link, "Popular Culture: From Baseball to Rock and Roll" studies favorite American pastimes that have British roots by featuring items in the *John Bull and Uncle Sam* exhibition, such as the article "My First Football Match" in the British newspaper *The Boy's Own Paper* (London, No. 1, Vol. 1, January 18, 1879).

▶ **Wars and the Home Front**
http://www.loc.gov/teachers/classroommaterials/themes/warpeace/

The experiences of veterans, civilians, and women during the Civil War and World War II are conveyed through oral histories, letters, photos, military campaign maps, historic newspapers, and songs. See film clips of the Spanish-American War, the first war to be captured on film. Listen to recordings from World War I and the 1920 election. Analyze Ansel Adams' photodocumentary of life at Manzanar to deepen one's understanding of Japanese internment. In "Veterans' Stories: The Veterans History Project" find out the personal stories of American war veterans and the civilian workers who supported them through recorded interviews, personal diaries, and photos.

> ### Women's History
> http://www.loc.gov/teachers/classroommaterials/themes/womens-history/
>
> Study the contributions of women to American history and culture as reformers, crusaders, inventors, and first ladies during wartime, the suffrage movement, and the Harlem Renaissance through photographs, webcasts, books, articles, scrapbooks, speeches, comic strips, and other materials.

Veterans History Project
http://www.loc.gov/vets/

The Veterans History Project of the American Folklife Center is a valuable website for anyone interested in learning about war through the eyes of its veterans. Photographs, letters, postcards, personal diaries, and other materials are presented. There are also links to topics such as "Women Serving in Combat: A Panel Discussion," which includes audio and a podcast.

Virtual Reference Shelf
http://www.loc.gov/rr/askalib/virtualref.html

The Virtual Reference Shelf offers links to a wealth of reference sources, such as encyclopedias (e.g., Britannica.com) directories, and dictionaries. Link to selected sites categorized by subject, for example, health, education, law (e.g., FindLaw), gemology, science, business, grant resources, awards or prizes, books, and periodicals. Other links are organized by intended audience, such as "Children, Teachers, and Parents." This is unquestionably an important resource for conducting research.

YouTube Library of Congress
http://www.youtube.com/loc

An exciting development at the Library of Congress is its online video portal on YouTube. View historic films from a long playlist arranged by categories. For example, "Books and Beyond" contains a number of author presentations; "Kluge Center Series" presents lectures; and "America at Work, America at Leisure" and "Theodore Roosevelt: His Life and Times on Film" provide films. The videos on this website open the viewer to rare footage of American history and the fiber of American culture and its heritage.

National Agricultural Library
http://www.nal.usda.gov/

The National Agricultural Library contains one of the world's largest collections of agricultural information. Subject links are listed in the menu on the left and include "Animals and Livestock," "Education and Outreach," "Food and Nutrition," "History, Art, and Biography," "Laws and Regulations," "Marketing and Trade," "Natural Resources and Environment," "Plants and Crops" and "Research and Technology." They link to books, articles, images, photographs, and reports depending on the subject category. Clicking on "In the News" leads to items such as press releases, RSS feeds, the NAL blog, and an archive of webpages and spotlights. Scroll down to the "Agricultural Research Service" link at the bottom of the page to access the department's monthly science magazine *Agricultural Research.*

National Archives and Records Administration (NARA)
http://www.archives.gov

The NARA holds over 10 billion documents and is currently in the process of digitizing many of the historical ones. Click "Online Exhibits" to view "Featured Exhibits," such as *The Deadly Virus: The Influenza Epidemic of 1918* and *The National Archives: Documented Rights,* which contains selected documents, photographs, and original testimonies chronicling the evolution of human and civil rights in the United States. Also available are historical American documents such as the Magna Carta and the Emancipation Proclamation. Other links include "Information for Educators" and "Information for Students."

National Gallery of Art
http://www.nga.gov/collection/index.shtm

The National Gallery of Art offers a wonderful place to visit online to become familiar with famous artists and to view images of their artworks and more. Images show American, British, Dutch, Flemish, French, Italian, European, and Spanish modern, contemporary, and historical paintings. Examples include works by Fra Angelico (e.g., *The Adoration of the Magi,* ca. 1440/1460) and by Fra Filippo Lippi. In addition to "Painting," other links on the homepage include "Sculpture," "Works on Paper," "Photographs," "Decorative Arts," and "Architecture." Searches can by conducted by artist's name, title of the work, or the medium, school, style, or previous owner of the collection. The Gallery also features a series of art, video, and music podcasts and "Streaming Slideshows."

National Library of Education
http://ies.ed.gov/ncee/projects/nat_ed_library.asp

The National Library of Education does not have digital collections per se but is a major source of education information. The library holds more than 800 English-language journals in education and related fields; the complete ERIC (Education Resources Information Center) microfiche collection; archives of official print and electronic documents published by the U.S. Department of Education; and histories and documentation of education legislation passed by Congress. The library serves as a depository under the Federal Depository Library Program and makes documents and reports available online produced by various other federal government agencies. In addition there are links to reports and documents for research, statistics, and evaluation covering early childhood to postsecondary education.

United States National Library of Medicine (NLM) National Institutes of Health—Online Exhibitions and Digital Projects
http://www.nlm.nih.gov/onlineexhibitions.html

The NLM is located on the campus of the National Institutes of Health in Bethesda. It is the largest medical library in the world and a provider of information on research in the areas of biomedicine and health care. The homepage has links to a number of exhibits, or viewers can access full lists by choosing "All Exhibitions by Subject" or "All Exhibitions by Date." Following is a sampling of the exhibits. *See also* UNITED STATES NATIONAL LIBRARY OF MEDICINE (NLM) *under* WORLD INITIATIVES.

▶ **Against the Odds: Making a Difference in Global Health**
http://apps.nlm.nih.gov/againsttheodds/index.cfm

This NLM exhibition looks at the increase in global health taking place around the world. The link "Online Activities and Resources" is for students and teachers to investigate their knowledge of the world's global health. "Downloads" provides audio talks about global health topics by leaders and advocates featured in the exhibition.

▶ **Changing the Face of Medicine**
http://www.nlm.nih.gov/exhibition/changingthefaceofmedicine/index.html

View photographs and information on the lives and achievements of America's women physicians in this NLM exhibit. Engage in online learning about how the human body works through such interactive activities as "Circulation Station," "A Closer Look at Chromosomes," and "Sickle Cell Anemia." Under "Resources" teachers and students will find lesson plans, a reading list, and information on various topics in health.

▶ **Digital Repository: Films and Video**
http://collections.nlm.nih.gov/muradora/browse.action?parentId=nlm%3Ahmdvid
    -coll&type=1

View a number of interesting original training films and videos on public health. Among the titles are *Combat Fatigue Irritability*, *Purification of Water*, *Work of the Public Health Service*, and *Strictly Personal*.

▶ **Dream Anatomy**
http://www.nlm.nih.gov/exhibition/dreamanatomy/index.html

Dream Anatomy is a superb exhibition on the human anatomy drawn from the NLM's extensive historical and rare collections. Illustrations taken from numerous sources (manuscripts, books, prints) from the 1500s to the present portray human anatomy in woodcuts and wood engravings,, copperplate engravings, hand-colored drawings, etchings, lithographs, photographs, and X-ray images. Click "Introduction" and then "History of Anatomy" to view a brief timeline beginning with Greek anatomical treatises from 275 BCE and ending with the 1600s–1900s and the role anatomy played in medical education and research. One person featured in the exhibit is B.S. Albinus, professor of anatomy at Leiden, who published part of a detailed and comprehensive anatomical atlas, *Tabulae Sceleti e Musculorum Corporis Humani* (1747).

▶ **Profiles in Science**
http://profiles.nlm.nih.gov/

This NLM website is a wonderful resource for researchers of twentieth-century public health and biomedicine. Links to specific scientists are organized by "Biomedical Research," "Health & Medicine," and "Fostering Science & Health." Associated with each name are links to biographical information, photographs, documents and manuscripts on their research, diagrams, related slides, and links to their publications. Among the scientists included are Adrian Kantrowitz, the surgeon who performed the first human heart transplant in the United States; and Harold Varmus, who shared in the Noble Prize with J. Michael Bishop in 1989 "for their discovery of the cellular origin of retroviral oncogenes." The C. Everett Koop Papers are available for use by educators and researchers.

▶ **Turning the Pages Online**
http://archive.nlm.nih.gov/proj/ttp/books.htm

This NLM website shows historical books using advanced three-dimensional computer-generated imagery, digital image enhancement, animation, and illumination models. Virtually flip through the pages of such historical books as Hieronymus Brunschwig's *Liber de Arte Distillandi*, printed in Strasbourg in 1512, a manual on chemical, alchemical, and distillation devices and techniques used to manufacture drug therapies; and Johannes de Ketham's *Fasiculo de Medicina*, a "bundle" of six medieval medical treatises, first printed in 1491 in Latin. For each book viewers have the option to "Turn the Pages" or to view individual images by clicking "Gallery of Images."

▶ **Visible Proofs: Forensic Views of the Body**
http://www.nlm.nih.gov/visibleproofs/

Read about the history of forensic medicine and biographies of physicians, surgeons, and others who developed scientific methods to study the body. This science helped to shape the forensic details now used as evidence in court cases for solving crimes. Select "Galleries" and then "Cases" to read interesting case histories or "Biographies" to view photographs and biographical information. "Technologies" explores DNA; "Artifacts" includes images of Bertillon cards (based on a system of measuring humans that helps to identify suspects) and other items; "Multimedia" contains videos, for example, *Autopsy*; and, finally, "Exhibition Images" includes items such as the 1699 book *The Tryal of Spencer Cowper, Esq.* Listen to radio programs involving the use of forensics by selecting "Resources" in the top menu. One example here is from the radio show *All Things Considered*, in which NPR's Eric Niiler reports on identifying the remains of the Columbia space shuttle astronauts.

Alabama

Alabama Department of Archives and History (ADAH) Digital Archives
http://216.226.178.196/

This website contains nine different digital collections that can be searched separately or together. Some contain government publications and statistical registers, while others are photograph and picture collections that began with the digitization of images from the files requested by patrons over the years. There is also a run of issues of the *Alabama Historical Quarterly*, a collection of narratives of ex-slaves, and a personal collection of Frank W. Boykin, a congressman who represented Alabama's First Congressional District for nearly 30 years. Most collections have their own homepage with descriptions; all have brief annotations on the collection's homepage. Click a collection name or "Advanced Search" at the top of the page to search across multiple collections.

AlabamaMosaic
http://www.alabamamosaic.org/collections.php

The AlabamaMosaic website is a one-stop shop for digital content on Alabama's history and culture. Administered by the Network of Alabama Academic Libraries, it allows for cross-searching of many different digital collections from different organizations around the state, primarily universities and public libraries. Because of the collection's specific focus on cultural history, it does not cover all institutions with digital collections, nor does it include all of the content from the institutions that do participate. However, for someone who is researching the history of the state, it is an excellent place to start and an essential resource. The "Browse Collections" link in the top menu bar provides a list of the 18 members currently contributing content. Clicking on a name will provide a sublist of that participant's contributions to the project. Several of the contributors are further described in this chapter as individual entries; others are available only through AlabamaMosaic, not their own websites. One of these unique library contributions is the Scarboro Photo Collection from the Gadsden Public Library, an image collection of over 4,000 photographs taken in the Gadsden area by a local photographer in the late nineteenth and early twentieth centuries. The full physical collection contains over 15,000 images.

Auburn University Library Digital Collections
http://diglib.auburn.edu/browse.html

This group of over 15 digital collections focuses primarily on promoting the institution's history and on providing research content for its students. Historic collections range from meeting minutes, theater scrapbooks, faculty lecture series, and football programs to photograph and postcard collections and community plans of the grounds and surrounding areas. There is also the Caroline Dean Wildflower Collection, containing over 400 images of various species growing in the southeastern United States, primarily in Alabama. Each image contains metadata, including a brief description.

Birmingham Public Library Digital Collections
http://www.bplonline.org/resources/Digital_Project/Collections.asp

This public library website currently contains over 25 digital collections with significant research content specifically about the city of Birmingham. In addition to photographs of old homes and buildings, there are scans of some high school yearbooks and a newspaper clippings database about prominent inventors in the city's history. One database contains scans of issues of the *Birmingham Iron Age*, a newspaper that began shortly after the creation of the city; items in the Women Artists of Birmingham Collection showing the works of some trailblazing female artists from the early twentieth century; and an extensive collection of clippings, photographs, and documents relating to the KKK's Sixteenth Street Baptist Church bombings, which killed four African-American girls in 1963. All collections are annotated, and some have individual homepages with further information. Click the links at the top left to browse the content by type, or click a collection title. Some collection titles link to individual collection pages, and others simply enter the database as a full-content link for that collection.

Jacksonville State University Digital Collections
http://www.jsu.edu/library/collections/

This university's library page has eight digital collections, most of which relate to the university's history, including its school newspaper and prominent persons. In addition, there is a digital collection of a run of issues of the *Jacksonville Republican* from 1837 to 1895, one of the oldest newspapers in the area, and also an Oral History Collection that grew out of a class project, containing hundreds of MP3 files of interviews with people who lived through a "pivotal era of U.S. history." The files are listed by number and person's name; however, all names have a PDF file attached that details who they are and what they speak about. Research in this database will take some digging to find the right person to listen to, but topics covered include the World Wars, segregation, and the Depression.

University of Alabama Digital Collections
http://www.lib.ua.edu/digital/browse

The University of Alabama at Tuscaloosa has a large number of digital collections that can be browsed using an alphabetical index. All collections are annotated, and many have links to guides as well as to the actual content. Click "Digital Collections" in the left menu, and then click "Search" for a tool allowing for federated searching across the collections and tabs allowing for federated searching by type of material. Some collections are small, such as a handful of letters from a particularly prominent person; or the individual page scans of one item only, such as the Civil War era log books of the *CSS Alabama*. Other items listed are digital guides to collections of physical items not represented online. On the whole, there is a wealth of information for researchers investigating the state, but users must have a target topic in mind, as most of the legwork on this site will be done by the user.

University of North Alabama Digital Collections
http://www.una.edu/library/about/collections/digital.html

This institution has three small digital collections, two of which contain images of postcards and historical markers on the campus and in the surrounding areas. The third collection currently contains approximately 60 images and accompanying metadata for the U.S. Nitrate Plant No. 2, the second of two facilities built in northern Alabama in the early twentieth century in response to the country's World War I need for war materials.

Alaska

Alaska's Digital Archive
http://vilda.alaska.edu/

Alaska's Digital Archive is a joint project of the Rasmuson Library (University of Alaska Fairbanks), the Consortium Library (University of Alaska Anchorage), and the Alaska State Library in Juneau. Providing access to over 10,000 items, this website is a portal to materials in libraries, museums, and archives across the state. Access to what is available online is through either individual collections, such as the Alaska State Library Historical Collections or the Alaska State Museums—Sheldon Jackson Museum—Sitka, or through two special pathways that are highlighted here.

▶ **Alaska Native History & Cultures**
http://vilda.alaska.edu/cdm4/pathway.php

Learn all about the history and culture of Alaska through "pathways" such as "Religion and Church Leadership," "Traditional Spiritual Practices," "Ceremonial Life," "Traditional Ways of Learning," and the "Art of the Indigenous People of Alaska." The collection can be browsed by topic, region, or time period, prehistoric through current day. The webpage also includes a link to the "Alaska Native Timeline."

▶ **Movement to Statehood Pathway**
http://vilda.alaska.edu/cdm4/statehood.php

This collection is a compilation of photographs showing the people, events, and places in Alaska from the 1860s through the early years of statehood (1959). The collection can be browsed by topic links, such as "Business and Commerce," "Natural Resources," and "Society and Daily Life"; by region; or by time period, prehistoric through current day.

Alaska's Gold
http://www.eed.state.ak.us/temp_lam_pages/library/goldrush/index.htm

The Alaska's Gold website was made possible by a grant from the National Historical Publications and Records Commission to the Alaska Rich Mining Project Committee. The five topical links are "The Discovery of Gold," "Getting to the Gold Fields," "Gold Mining," "Daily Life," and "Our Legacy." Activities are designed around specific questions related to each of the themes and provide access to historic primary source material from the Alaska Gold Rush (1880–1915.) A Teacher's Guide webpage and a page of links provide supplementary information to each of the teacher's resources packets.

Tundra Times Photograph Project
http://tundratimes.ilisagvik.cc/index.htm

Between 1962 and 1967, the *Tundra Times* was a statewide newspaper written by and for Alaska Natives. Around 5,000 of the over 15,000 black-and-white prints that were acquired by the Ukpeagvik Iñupiat Corporation (UIC) of Barrow and given to the Tuzzy Consortium Library will be made available. Some of the photographs do not contain background information. The collection can be searched by keyword or by preselected topics accessed by clicking on "Photographs" in the left menu.

Arizona

Arizona Archives Online
http://azarchivesonline.org/

Arizona Archives Online is a collaborative project of Arizona State University, Northern Arizona University, and the University of Arizona. The website is still under development. The long-term goal is to make finding aids for all archival collections accessible and searchable from one website. Direct access to each of the individual collections that finding aids have been created for is not available from this website.

Arizona Memory Project
http://azmemory.lib.az.us/index.php

The Arizona Memory Project, which began in 2006, contains items about Arizona's history and culture from contributing libraries, museums, universities, and other archival, historical, and cultural institutions. The project offers access to over 67,000 digitized materials contained in over 90 collections. Browse the site by collection(s), topic, format (image, sound, or text), and time period (pre-1863 to present) or from a select list of popular searches. A few of the collections are highlighted here.

▶ **Arizona Aviation History: The Ruth Reinhold Collection**
http://azmemory.lib.az.us/cdm4/index.php?CISOROOT=/ahfrein

Ruth Reinhold (1902–1985) was one of the first woman aviation pilots in Arizona. This collection contains 150 images dating from the early 1900s through the late 1970s of air pilots such as Ruth Reinhold, Charles Lindbergh, and Amelia Earhart, as well as aircraft, airports, and landing fields.

▶ **Arizona's Saints and Shady Ladies**
http://azmemory.lib.az.us/cdm4/index.php?CISOROOT=/ahfsaints

This small collection of images is dedicated to Arizona women and the many and diverse contributions they made to the growth and civilization of the American West.

▶ **Cochise College Libraries—Cochise County Historical & Archeological Collection**
http://azmemory.lib.az.us/cdm4/index.php?CISOROOT=/cclhadc

This unique collection focuses on the history and culture of southeastern Arizona. It includes photos, oral histories, historical and cultural documents, lectures, PowerPoint slide shows, and videos.

▶ **Sharlot Hall Museum American Indian Image Collection**
http://azmemory.lib.az.us/cdm4/index.php?CISOROOT=/shmamerind

Over 450 images of Native American Indians include the Navajo, Apache, Yavapai, Hualapai, Papago, Hopi, Mohave, Paiute, Yaqui, Havasupai, Pima, and Maricopa tribes, prehistoric cliff dwellings, villages, and rock art.

Historical Photograph Collections at the Arizona State Archives
http://photos.lib.az.us/index.cfm

Over one-fourth of the 130,000 images in the Arizona State Archives have been digitized and made available here, providing a glimpse into the cultural legacy of Arizona through a variety of formats, such as photographs, tintypes, and postcards. The majority of photographs predate 1940, some dating back as far as 1863. The database can be searched by subject, place, photographer, description, date, or photo ID. Many of the photos are also in the Arizona Memory Project, and a link to the project is provided.

Little Cowpuncher: Rural School Newspaper of Southern Arizona
http://cowpuncher.library.arizona.edu/

Little Cowpuncher is a newspaper written and illustrated by the Anglo, Mexican, and Mexican American students of teacher Eulalia Bourne in five southern Arizona K–8 schools between 1932 and 1943. The issues of *Little Cowpuncher* include original and unedited stories and drawings of ranch and school life, and they are reproduced on this site without editing of the original content.

▶ ### School on the Range: The Little Cowpuncher Roundup
http://parentseyes.arizona.edu/LC2/

School on the Range is an oral history project sponsored by the University of Arizona and the Arizona Humanities Council. Click on the ranch schools listed in the left menu to see video interviews with former *Little Cowpunchers*, Eulalia Bourne's video interview, photographs, and a small selection of video transcripts.

Arkansas

Arkansas Digital History Institute
http://adhi.atu.edu/

The Arkansas Digital History Institute accepts and digitizes audio, video, and image items donated by users who want to preserve information about the state's history. All users can register with a valid e-mail address and download copies of the images. The site claims usage is free, provided it is for a noncommercial purpose. Copyright rules and terms of use information are clearly linked on the site. Click on "Search Galleries" in the left menu for a basic search box to browse the collection. A search for "Arkansas" returned 458 results, with each image accompanied by a brief description.

Arkansas History Commission Photographs
http://www.ark-ives.com/photo/

As the official archives of the state, Arkansas History Commission maintains a large amount of information from census records, land records, death lists, historical newspapers, and other collections of note to Arkansas researchers. This website currently contains over 13,000 images. Click "Gallery" to access links in the left menu to the collections (e.g., "1927 Tornado"). Images are scrolled through, each one containing background information. Also note the "Help" link in the left menu, which gives keywords for searching all items in each individual collection.

Butler Center Online Collections
http://www.digital.butlercenter.org/

Maintained by the Central Arkansas Library System, this website offers a handful of online collections with Arkansas-based content drawn from its holdings. The Aftermath Collection is about the 1957 Little Rock Central High desegregation crisis. The AV/AR Audio Video Collection contains oral histories about state history. Other collections feature participation of Arkansas citizens in the Korean War and lesson plans for teaching state history to elementary and secondary school children. Each collection has its own page and description as well as its own method of search. Not all content from each collection is digitized.

University of Arkansas—Digital Collections
http://libinfo.uark.edu/eresources/digitalcollections.asp

This website contains links to 13 digital collections from the University of Arkansas. Among them are a database of images and speeches by J.W. Fulbright, an Arkansas

U.S. Senator for 30 years during the twentieth century; a collection of textual materials and photographs documenting the history of the civil rights struggle in Arkansas; and transcriptions of interview questionnaires documenting the personal histories of African Americans in Arkansas.

University of Arkansas for Medical Sciences Library—Historical Research Center Digital Collections
http://libcontentdm.uams.edu/HRCDigitalCollections.htm

This website contains digital content related either to the history of the institution or to the history of medicine in Arkansas. The entire site can be browsed by collection type or by topic, or an advanced search can be used to search across any and all collections. Collections include campus publications, oral histories, and ephemera; there is also a large photograph database and a "Mystery Photos" link to images with no description or identification. See the list of individual collections by viewing the dropdown list under "Browse by Collection."

California

California State Archives
http://www.sos.ca.gov/archives/collections/1879/

This California State Archives website currently has one digitized collection, the 1878–1879 Constitutional Convention Working Papers. It contains over 1,000 records created during the convention, such as administrative records, minutes, resolutions, committee papers and reports, and public petitions. The working papers can be searched by document type, subject keyword, or phrase. A list of subject topics is provided. The webpage also has links to the 1879 Constitution of the State of California and to the current Constitution of the State of California.

California State University—Sacramento Library Digital Collections
http://digital.lib.csus.edu/

This website offers access to four digital collections.

▶ **The California Underground Railroad**
http://digital.lib.csus.edu/curr/

Through newspaper and journal articles, letters, personal communications, photographs, and other documents, this website, focused exclusively on the history of the California Underground Railroad, brings the experiences of African-American slaves in California and their quest for freedom to life. Browse the collection by resource, or search it by keyword or by specific collection.

▶ **The Honorable Robert T. Matsui Legacy Project: Road to Redress and Reparations**
http://digital.lib.csus.edu/mats/

Through photographs, documents, and video and audio clips, this website acknowledges the career of Congressman Robert T. Matsui (1941–2005), particularly the work he did on the issues of redress and reparations on behalf of the Japanese Americans who were interned during World War II.

▶ **The Japanese American Archival Collection**
http://digital.lib.csus.edu/jaac/

A selection of nearly 1,400 photographs and images of objects (clothing, jewelry, paintings) linked to the imprisonment of Japanese Americans during World War II are featured. Browse the collection by internment camp, time frame, or topic. Search the collection by keyword or by choosing a specific collection.

▶ **Sokiku Nakatani Japanese Teaware Digital Collection**
http://digital.lib.csus.edu/teaware/

Sokiku Nakatani (1903–1990) was both a student and practitioner of Chado (the Way of Tea). The teaware collection contains photographs of over 140 items from Sokiku Nakatani's personal collection and includes such items as baskets, vases, water jars, pottery, scrolls, cloths, and tea utensils.

LearnCalifornia.org
http://www.learncalifornia.org/

This website is a resource for teachers, students, and researchers interested in the history of California. The teacher lesson plans meet California Department of Education standards and are designed for use both "online" (for students who have access to a computer) and "offline" (for those who don't). The lesson plan links include the "1906 San Francisco Earthquake," "Planning a Railroad," "Census/Gold Rush Town," and "California During the Great Depression." The resources come from the California State Archives and other archives, libraries, historical sites and societies, and museums.

Online Archive of California (OAC)
http://oac.cdlib.org

OAC is a portal to primary resources housed throughout California in libraries, archives, historical societies, museums, and the University of California campuses. There are over 170,000 digital images and documents and over 20,000 finding aids. Browse the collections by contributing institution or collection name or by choosing a city and campus on the interactive map. Selected online collections are highlighted here.

▶ **California Indian Baskets**
http://www.oac.cdlib.org/findaid/ark:/13030/kt067nc5q5/

This is a small collection of photographs taken of baskets made by the Panamint Shoshone (Timbisha Shoshone tribe), the Pomo Indians, the Shasta Indians, and the Hupa, Yurok, and Karuk tribes from the 1800s and 1900s . The baskets are part of the UCLA Fowler Museum of Cultural History collection.

▶ **Japanese American Relocation Photograph Collection**
http://www.oac.cdlib.org/findaid/ark:/13030/tf0q2nb0mp/

View over 220 photographs taken by *Los Angeles Examiner* and wire service photographers of the relocation of Japanese Americans in Southern California during World War II and their subsequent life in the internment camps at Manzanar, Santa Anita, Tanforan, and Tule Lake. The collection is part of the Regional History Collection of the Department of Special Collections, University of Southern California (Los Angeles).

▶ **Kern County Local History Photograph Collection**
http://www.oac.cdlib.org/findaid/ark:/13030/kt3n39q3mw/

This collection of 260 photographs illustrates the social and cultural heritage, local sights, people, businesses, and buildings of Bakersfield and other areas of Kern County from the late 1800s through 2001.

▶ **1906 San Francisco Earthquake and Fire Digital Collection**
http://bancroft.berkeley.edu/collections/earthquakeandfire/splash.html

The more than 8,900 images and pages of text here are from the archives and special collections of The Bancroft Library, University of California, Berkeley; the California Historical Society, San Francisco; The California State Library, Sacramento; Stanford University, Stanford; The Huntington Library, San Marino; and The Society of California Pioneers, San Francisco. Search the website by keyword or repository, or browse from lists of subjects and genre topics. Special features include an online exhibit, a panoramic collage of photographs showing the destruction of San Francisco after the earthquake, an interactive map designed to illustrate how areas of the city were affected by the earthquake and the ensuing fire, and a bibliography of resources (books, articles, and unpublished items and dissertations).

Oviatt Library Digital Collections
http://digital-library.csun.edu/

The digitized collections website of the Oviatt Library, California State University at Northridge, currently contains five unique collections and several online exhibits.

▶ **International Guitar Research Archive (IGRA)**
http://library.csun.edu/igra/

The IGRA collection contains over 2,400 phonograph recordings of acoustic guitar performances. Two indexes are provided, the "IGRA Discography," an alphabetical list of album titles, some with notes on associated composers, performers, album tracks, and record companies; and the "Artists' Biographies and Program Notes." Only a handful of the biographies contain an MIDI (Musical Instrument Digital Interface) file of a selected work.

▶ **Latino Cultural Heritage Digital Archives**
http://digital-library.csun.edu/LatArch/

This small archive contains links to 12 collections: Rodolfo Acuña Papers; Antonio and Luz (Mendez) Calvo Family Collection; Comisión Femenil San Fernando Valley; Culture Clash Collection; Frank del Olmo Papers; ILWU, Local 13-Henry Gaitan Papers; Millie Moser Smith Papers; Mothers of East Los Angeles (Madres del Este de Los Angeles) Papers; Julian Nava Collection; Felipe and Blandina (Guerro) Rodriguez Family Papers; and the Supreme Council of the Mexican American Movement Papers. The site also contains a link to the virtual exhibit *20 Years of Culture Clash*.

▶ **Old China Hands Archive**
http://library.csun.edu/OldChinaHands/

This archive was created as a testimony to the many people from around the world who have lived and worked in China. The small online collection of photographs is titled the Faces of Tientsin. Browse the entire collection, or search by keyword.

▶ **San Fernando Valley History Digital Library**
http://digital-library.csun.edu/SFV/

Documents, manuscripts, photographs, and oral histories illustrate the San Fernando Valley from the early 1800s through 1999 accessed from six topical links: "Labor," "Politics," "Industries," "Transportation," "Social Life and Customs," and "Natural Resources." Suggested search terms are provided for each topic. Choose one, copy and paste it into the search box, and click "Go."

▶ **Tseng Family Collection of Chinese Antiquities**
http://library.csun.edu/Collections/SCA/SC/Tseng

Images of a prehistoric axe blade, several bronze bulls with gilding, a bronze kettle, and several ritual vessels, all with gilding, and a glass weight in the shape of a water buffalo were chosen to represent the larger Chinese antiquities collection.

University of Southern California (USC) Digital Library
http://digitallibrary.usc.edu/search/controller/index.htm

The USC Digital Library is a gateway to over 30 collections owned by USC and other libraries and institutions, with special emphasis on Los Angeles, Southern California, the western United States, and the Pacific Rim region. Browse the site by choosing a link in the left menu: "Collections," Featured Content," "Time Periods," or "Places."

Colorado

Colorado College Special Collections
http://www.coloradocollege.edu/library/index.php/specialcollections/

The Tutt Library at Colorado College maintains a Special Collections webpage with some digital materials. Click "Digital Collections" on the right side or scroll to the bottom of the page to access the collections. Content includes the history of the college and biographies and photos of former college presidents; a section about Colorado's geography, including images of landscapes; and a menu collection from various eateries. An international section has images of World War I posters and a collection of famous persons' autographs.

Colorado State Digital Archives
http://www.coloradodigitalarchives.org/Collections.aspx

The Colorado State Digital Archives currently offers four record series online. The Audio collection contains oral interviews with Department of Corrections personnel Edward Grout, Carl Jacobson, Earle Meyer, Wayne Patterson, and John Yurko. The other record series are the Social Security Death Index (SSDI) database, Naturalization Records, and Misc. Historical Records. The latter contains more than 40 subcollections, for example, the 1870 Colorado Census, Burial Records, Civil War Casualty Records, Ditch Claim Statements, Horseshoers, and Prohibition Arrests.

Colorado State University Libraries—Digital Collections
http://digital.library.colostate.edu/cdm4/collections.php

This university website currently has 16 digital collections. Each one is briefly described on the homepage, with a corresponding link. The collections can be browsed individually, or an advanced keyword search can be performed across multiple databases. Collections include Garst Wildlife Photographs, with over 1,300 image slides; Caspar Collins Map Collection, containing hand-drawn maps by Lieutenant Caspar Collins during the mid-1800s; and Rocky Mountain Farmer's Union, featuring photographs commemorating its one-hundredth anniversary.

Denver Public Library: Western History and Genealogy—Digital Collections
http://history.denverlibrary.org/images/index.html

The Denver Public Library has an image collection exceeding 600,000 physical items. While only about 15 percent of these are currently available online, the ones that are allow for research into the history of the people, towns, and transportation methods in the geographic area. An advanced keyword search with a date limiter is the search tool provided to examine this collection. Returned search results have complete metadata descriptions.

University of Colorado Digital Library
https://www.cu.edu/digitallibrary/search_all.html

This University of Colorado website pulls together more than 40 digital collections from both its own collections and collections of contributing partners throughout the United States. The collections are listed in alphabetical order, with the holding institution and access restrictions clearly stated. The collections are also fully described on the homepage. A few of the collections are highlighted here.

▶ **Ben Gray Lumpkin Digital Folk Music Collection**
http://libluna.lib.ad.colorado.edu:8081/insight/sample/SoundModel/index.htm

Traveling throughout the state, Professor Ben Gray Lumpkin (University of Colorado, Boulder English Department) made nearly 2,000 recordings of folk songs sung by people who lived in Colorado during the 20-year span of 1950 to 1970. Search the collection by keyword, title, or performer, or browse the collection by performer or by an A to Z list of song titles. Audio samples of each of the recorded songs are provided, along with a brief biography of the performer.

▶ **Bent–Hyde Papers, 1905–1918**
http://libluna.lib.ad.colorado.edu:8081/BrowserInsight/BrowserInsight?cmd=
    start&cid=32&ig=Bent-Hyde++Papers&gwisp=&iia=0&gwia=3&ir=-1&id=
    -1&d=0&iwas=2&gc=0&isl=0&ss=0

The Bent–Hyde Papers include 14 original maps of Indian and military positions along with letters written between George Bent, a Cheyenne mediator and translator, and George Hyde, a historian of Native Americans.

▶ **Historical Hats and Headdresses**
http://libluna.lib.ad.colorado.edu:8081/BrowserInsight/BrowserInsight?cmd=
    start&cid=UCBOULDERCB1-52-NA&iia=0&gwia=3&un=guest&pw=guest&ig=
    Historic+Hats+and+Headdresses

The Clifford P. Westermeier Portfolio of Illustrations of Historical Hats and Head-dresses collection contains 76 watercolor plates of hats and headdresses from various historic time periods, some as early as Ancient Egypt and as late as the seventeenth century.

Connecticut

Connecticut History Online
http://www.cthistoryonline.org/cdm-cho/index.html

Click "Journeys" on the homepage to access links to over 15,000 primary resources that capture the history of Connecticut. For example, "The Eye of the Storm: A Journey into the Natural Disasters in Connecticut" leads to photo essays recounting the blizzard of 1888, the floods of 1936 and 1955, and the hurricanes of 1938 and 1954. Other noteworthy links are "The Textile Industry in Connecticut," "Connecticut Goes to the Beach," "War on the Homefront," and "Connecticut Towns and Cities: How They Grew." This is a wonderful history resource for teachers and students. The "Classroom" tab on the homepage provides links to curriculums, lesson plans, interactive games, and instructions on how to use primary sources, and the "Search" tab reveals a list of subcollections to help narrow a search.

Connecticut's Heritage Gateway
http://www.ctheritage.org/default.htm

View online exhibits and an encyclopedia of the history of Connecticut. This website also provides an ample directory of the state's history resources for teachers, students, and researchers regarding Connecticut's culture and heritage. The "Records of Our Past" and "Connecticut Photo Album" links yield thousands of historical photographs, records, oral histories, and letters that document the state's rich heritage.

Connecticut State Library Digital Collections
http://cslib.cdmhost.com/index.php

The Connecticut State Library offers digitized aerial photos, images, and text. Select from a list of over 20 topical links, including "Founding Documents of Connecticut," "Native Americans," "Law and Legislation," "Religious History," and "Roads and Bridges."

University of Connecticut Libraries Digital Collections
http://digitalcollections.uconn.edu/imagesearch.html

View digitized documents, photographs, maps, and data that have been described and organized by the University of Connecticut Libraries for researchers, students, and the general public. Collection links are provided in the left menu. Collections include the Map and Geographic Information Center, containing scans of Connecticut maps dated 1676–1930; the Charles Olson's Melville Project, which contains a series of handwritten research notecards by the poet Charles Olson that were water-damaged but subsequently renovated; the Benthic Marine Algal Herbarium of Long Island Sound, showing algae plants indigenous to Connecticut; and The Public Records of the Colony of Connecticut, 1636–1776.

Delaware

Delaware Public Archives—Digital Archives
http://archives.delaware.gov/exhibits/exhibits-toc.shtml

Explore the history of Delaware through nearly 800,000 photographs, historic audio clips, documents, maps (1688 to the twentieth century), and more in this Delaware Public Archives website. For example, read records related to Delaware's involvement in the American Civil War or "Reverend Turner's Collection of genealogical notes and correspondence concerning about three thousand Delmarva Peninsula families." View "John Dickinson's Report from the Annapolis Convention (Sept. 14, 1786)" or Delaware's oldest known document, *A 1653 Financial Account of Swedish Settler Jon Nielson.*

University of Delaware Library Digital Collections
http://fletcher.lib.udel.edu/

The Library Digital Collections webpage on the University of Delaware website contains links to over ten digital collections. Browse the entire website, or browse each collection separately. Some of the more prominent collections are highlighted here.

▶ **American Civil War Digital Collections: Rosenthal Lithographic Prints of Civil War Encampments**
http://fletcher.lib.udel.edu/collections/rlp/index.htm

This collection contains color lithographs printed between 1861 and 1865 by Rosenthal's Lith. of Philadelphia.

▶ **Delaware Postcard Collection**
http://fletcher.lib.udel.edu/collections/dpc/index.htm

This collection of over 2,000 postcards showcases predominantly Delaware buildings, monuments, and historic structures, beaches and boardwalks, and social life from the late nineteenth to mid-twentieth centuries. Some of the postcards contain personal messages, cancelled stamps, and postmarks, and views of these postcard backs are accessible. Browse the entire collection or limit the search geographically or by subject.

▶ **Historic Maps of Delaware & the Mid-Atlantic Region**
http://fletcher.lib.udel.edu/collections/hmc/index.htm

Over 300 maps can be browsed by of a wide range of types, including antiquarian, bird's-eye view, cadastral, nautical charts, and railroad. Other sheet maps show Delaware, Maryland, New Jersey, Pennsylvania, New York, Virginia, West Virginia, and Washington, DC, and four state atlases. Search the entire collection by subject, creator, type, or date (1666–2000).

Florida

Central Florida Memory
http://www.cfmemory.org/

This digital collection is a collaborative project among seven partner institutions in the Central Florida area. It was created to be an all-access online resource for digitally documenting the history of the region and currently contains over 12,000 items of content totaling over 80,000 individual images. Content ranges from textual materials such as diaries and letters, to visual content such as maps, photographs, and postcards, to government and genealogical data including funeral records and city directories. A fairly advanced search tool is available to cull the data, allowing for limiting by format, theme, decade, place, and contributing institution. To get to this tool, click the center image on the screen when the blue "Collection" arrow on the left is highlighted, or hover the cursor over "Collection" in the top green menu bar and choose from the list of options provided. A "Partners" link at the bottom of each page provides the names of and links to the partner institutions.

Florida Atlantic University—Collections @ Digital Library
http://www.library.fau.edu/depts/digital_library/collections.htm

Florida Atlantic University has several unique collections available on its Digital Library website. The "Judaica Sound Archives" link yields musical selections from Jewish performers that have been digitized. Currently over 8,000 songs from more than 800 albums are available. The selections can be browsed in several ways, including by album title, song title, and genre. One-click icons initiate the play, and each item has a "Send a Note" link for user comments to be sent in. Also, the "Mutanabbi Street Starts Here" link provides images of dozens of hand-printed broadsides that were created to raise money for the Mutanabbi Street Coalition. This organization came into being after the March 2007 deadly bombing on Mutanabbi Street in Baghdad, Iraq. Scroll down on the page to see the individual collections.

Florida Folklife from the WPA Collections, 1937–1942
http://memory.loc.gov/ammem/collections/florida/

The Works Progress Administration (WPA) was created by Franklin D. Roosevelt during the 1930s to help employ people during the Great Depression. Moved to state control in 1939, the Florida organization produced significant written and audio content that is now available online. This archive contains both written and audio content accumulated by WPA workers, whose mission was to document folktales, histories, music, and other information about various ethnic communities around the state. The materials are available through the American Memory Project of the Library of Congress. The collection can be browsed by subject, performer, or place or by format using the links in the left menu under "Browse Collection By." There are approximately 375 audio and 100 manuscript items.

Florida International University Digital Collections Center
http://digitalcollections.fiu.edu/

The Florida International University's Digital Collections Center contains links to about ten digital collections. Many are collaborative projects with other institutions, such as the Florida Heritage Collection, which digitizes and preserves items of relevance to the state's history; and the Everglades Digital Library, which contains content from several organizations regarding the environment of South Florida. The Miami Metropolitan Archive combines digitized documents from the university and various local agencies relating to the history of the Miami area. The Wolfsonian Collection is an image database of Dutch artifacts and documents. Click on any of the collection names in the left menu to access the collection.

Florida Memory Project
http://www.floridamemory.com/

This website is maintained by the State Library and Archives of Florida. It highlights resources for historical research that address key moments in the state's history, and the content is pulled from the collections of the State Archives. Some collections are summarized here.

▶ **Florida Photographic Collection**
http://www.floridamemory.com/PhotographicCollection/

This collection contains over 160,000 images from the State Archives. It includes still photos as well as films and video clips. A basic search tool is provided to browse the items, and some items have full metadata descriptions. Some creative search strategies may be required for users to find what's really valuable to them. A basic search on "Key West" returned over 7,000 results. A search on "Key West Hurricane" returned nearly 350 items.

▶ **Highlights of Florida History**
http://www.floridamemory.com/FloridaHighlights/

This website is a list of links to about 50 documents deemed to be core to the state's history and pulled together in one place for ease of use. There is no need to search; the items are listed chronologically and users need simply scroll down the list to browse the collection. When clicked on, images are shown enlarged with accompanying descriptions detailing their significance.

▶ **Other Collections**
http://www.floridamemory.com/Collections/

On this webpage is access to ten additional collections with narrower focuses. Included, for example, are a database of transcriptions and digital images of Florida's early state constitutions, scans of World War I service cards from service members, a database of Confederate pension records, and various collections of prominent families' papers.

Florida Southern College—McKay Archives Center Digital Collections
http://archives.flsouthern.edu/cdm4/about.php

Currently four collections are available on this website of Florida Southern College. One is an ongoing project to scan the issues of the student newspaper *The Southern* from 1908 to the present. Another is a growing photograph collection of black-and-white and color images relating to the *Child of the Sun* buildings designed by Frank Lloyd Wright in the 1940s and 1950s, which stand on the college's campus in Lakeland, Florida. Click the collection titles to access their content.

Florida Writer's Project Digital Collection
http://voyager.ju.edu/ju-images/cdcorse/about.html

This digital collection is maintained by Jacksonville University. The Federal Writer's Project was a government-funded program supporting writers during the Great Depression. The digitized documents in this collection represent written works of authors under the Florida Federal Writer's Project and were donated to the university by Dr.

Carita Doggett Corse, the Director of the Florida Project from 1935 to 1942. All items are page scans of original typed texts. They are organized by a sequential numbering system, and the list of documents must be browsed on the webpage. Click the linked name of Dr. Corse to access the list.

Heritage Museum of Northwest Florida Digital Collection
http://www.heritage-museum.org/wp/?page_id=118

This museum is dedicated to preserving the history of the northwest area of the state and maintains a digital collection page on its website. The Vintage Gulf Coast Postcard Collection is featured on the homepage, and other collections are listed under "Archives" in the right menu. These include images of boats being built, fishermen's tools, and photographs of a traveling museum with a replica of the Vietnam Veterans Memorial Wall.

Legacy Florida Digital Collections
http://dig.tblc.org/dig/index2.html?collectionid=Any

This website contains mostly electronic records contributed by Tampa Bay Library Consortium member libraries. The "Browse Collections" link in the left menu provides a list of all collections, which can be clicked and browsed individually. Only about 10 percent of the online record mentions contain actual online content, but there may be some diamonds in the rough for users who would like electronic access to digital collections from mostly public libraries in the Tampa area. The site is a little hard to navigate, but an advanced search can pull content from multiple collections, and a small camera icon is placed next to any search results that actually have an image file attached. This allows for easily identifiable digital content.

PALMM: Publication of Archival Library & Museum Materials
http://palmm.fcla.edu/

The PALMM initiative combines the efforts of the State University Libraries of Florida to make digital collections available for research, benefitting both the users at the participating institutions and also the public at large. All PALMM collections must be tied, in whole or in part, to a participating academic university. The homepage currently lists over 30 collections, many of which are described in other areas of this chapter under their home institutions. Because the PALMM project requires adherence to certain standards when collections are contributed, the site allows for federated searching of all collections at once. Metadata of individual items contain home institution of the original physical item and the collection to which each item belongs. The site is clearly intended to maintain a strict research focus and quality standard. To see the content, click the "View Collection" link after each collection description, or choose one of the federated search options in the right menu, either "Photographs & Images" or "Books & Text."

PRISM: Political & Rights Issues & Social Movements
http://palmm.fcla.edu/prism/

This website is a collaboration between Florida Atlantic University and the University of Central Florida. Containing over 700 items, these scanned images of textual items cover social, economic, and religious topics from around the world dating from the mid-nineteenth to the late twentieth centuries. Individual items have full metadata and are viewed in PDF format.

Reclaiming the Everglades: South Florida's Natural History, 1884–1934
http://international.loc.gov/ammem/collections/everglades/index.html

This website gathers content from 16 collections about the Florida Everglades and makes part or all of these collections available in one location. Content is from or closely related to the Everglades Digital Library described in the Florida International University entry in this section. Click the "About This Collection" link in the left menu to get more information about the content formats and the contributing institutions. Other links in the left menu allow for browsing the collection by title, author, and subject. Each entry has an image file with accompanying descriptive metadata.

University of Florida Digital Collections
http://ufdcweb1.uflib.ufl.edu/ufdc/

This University of Florida website boasts over 100 digital collections. The website also states that all users, both local and remote, have free access to all content. The site has basic and advanced search tools that work across all collections. Individual collections feature the arts, humanities, social sciences, natural sciences, maps, collections about the people and history of Florida, collections with world themes, and the history of the University of Florida. Click "Florida Photograph Collections" to view a number of collections or "Florida Newspaper Digital Library" to see recent and historic newspaper issues from publications around the state.

University of Miami Libraries Digital Initiatives
http://merrick.library.miami.edu/

This website contains 35 different collections, which are roughly grouped into categories and listed down the center of the page. Included are the University of Miami Archives, which is one photographic collection split into ten categories; Digital Initiatives Collections; and the Swingle Plant Digital Archive, containing images of over 250 plant species from around the world. The extensive Cuban Heritage Collection contains more than 25 separate digital collections ranging from oral histories and photographs to donations of individual and corporate sets of papers. The "Special Collections" link provides 17 other collections to browse. Searching can be a little tricky; there is a prominent "Browse All Collections" link in the left menu that provides a long alphabetical list of every resource. The "Search" link in the top menu takes users to the standard CONTENTdm advanced search page.

University of South Florida Libraries, Special & Digital Collections—CORAL
http://guides.lib.usf.edu/digital-collections#

This university's digital collections page is one of the easiest to use. It has a tab format, and clicking the "Collections by Subject" tab at the top allows for browsing the dozens of digital collections available for use by the general public. One can also search "Collections by Title." Collections include a number of state history and genealogy resources, photograph collections, and oral history collections. One of the more unique sections is the "Holocaust & Genocide Studies Center," which includes a small but growing collection of digitized interviews with both holocaust survivors and concentration camp liberators.

Georgia

Georgia State University Library—Special Collections and Archives
http://www.library.gsu.edu/spcoll/

This Special Collections and Archives homepage has links to seven thematic collections. Individual collections are listed on the right side and need to be investigated separately. Some of the available content from all collections has been migrated to the OCLC CONTENTdm platform, where it can all be viewed and cross-searched at once (by going to the Digital Collections website at http://dlib.gsu.edu/index.php). Other information can still be found only through this Special Collections and Archives webpage.

Georgia Tech Digital Collections
http://www.library.gatech.edu/archives/digital_collections.html

This website provides access to over a dozen digital collections, most of them dealing with the history of or products created by the institution itself, including the building and renovations of the campus, the institution's electronic publications, school yearbooks and newspapers, and texts of the institution's presidential speeches. One particularly interesting item is the digital representation of the rare book *A Photographic Atlas of Selected Regions of the Milky Way* by E.E. Barnard (1927). The software allows users to view images from the atlas based on the area of the sky entered numerically by the user.

Georgia's Virtual Vault
http://content.sos.state.ga.us/

This website is part of an ongoing project to digitize and make available valuable resources in the Georgia State Archives. Some were scanned in and entered systematically, such as series of county and local maps. Others were added when a patron requested a copy of a specific item, such as a digital copy of a rare photograph or document to be used in an exhibit. By including materials each time they are requested for some other purpose, the Vault continues to grow and make the State Archives content available for users electronically. Collection links are listed alphabetically in the left menu on the homepage. Some interesting collections include Confederate Enlistment Oaths and Discharges, which contains handwritten documents; and Leo Frank Clemency Application, containing documents and letters pertaining to the clemency of Leo Frank, a citizen who was convicted of murder, given clemency, and afterward lynched by others anyway.

Historically Black College and University Library Alliance
http://contentdm.auctr.edu/index.php

This digital collection highlights the history and contributions to American culture of many of the historically black colleges and universities by making much of the contents of their archives and special collections available online. Basic and advanced search tools on the homepage allow for searching across all collections, with an alternative link on the homepage to "View Collections by Participating Institution" (a list of the 20 institutions and a description of what can be found in each collection). The collection in total is not very large (only a few hundred items combined) but contains unique materials from each institution chosen to represent its history. Basic metadata is available for each item. Note the "Browse" and "Advanced Search" links at the very top of the page.

University of Georgia Libraries
http://www.libs.uga.edu/

The University of Georgia Libraries provides access to a number of digital collections, some of which were created from its own rare materials. Other collections are accessible through this website but are part of a larger initiative called GALILEO, which was created to provide institutions across the state with access to educational materials. Some of the more prominent collections are highlighted here.

▶ ### Civil Rights Digital Library
http://crdl.usg.edu/?Welcome

This digital collection makes a wide-ranging collection of educational resources on the civil rights movement available to all learners. Basic and advanced search tools are available to sift through the content, but the real impressive navigating tool is the browse menu on the left. Materials in the collection are sorted alphabetically by person's name or topic, by individual years from 1954 to 1968, by place through an interactive map, or by type of media, which include sound, text, and visual resources. Educational resources such as teaching tools and lesson plans are also available.

▶ ### Digital Library of Georgia
http://dlg.galileo.usg.edu/?Welcome&Welcome

This digital library is an excellent, well-organized collaborative project designed to bring together historical and cultural resources from around the state in a virtual forum. The site currently contains over 100 individual virtual collections shared by various statewide public, private, and governmental institutions. The browse tools in the left menu allow users to easily narrow down the search by choosing a topic, location (county), time period, contributing institution, and media type. A different list allows an A–Z browse of all collections at once. Once the desired collection is found, the basic and advanced search tools can search across the collection. Media types include text, sound, and visual materials.

▶ ### Hargrett Rare Book and Manuscript Library
http://www-test.libs.uga.edu/hargrett/digital/index.html

Some of the rare materials in this library have been converted into digitally available content. This link provides access to over 20 specific digital collections, including historic maps and broadsides, as well as two separate collections about Sherman's Civil War march through Georgia: one in the form of historic photographs and the other a diary kept by a Union soldier.

Hawaii

The Annexation of Hawaii: A Collection of Documents
http://libweb.hawaii.edu/digicoll/annexation/annexation.html

The modest Hawaiian Collection at the University of Hawai'i at Mānoa Library contains materials pertaining to the annexation of Hawaii. Topical links include "Blount Report [Affairs in Hawaii]," "Congressional Debates on Hawaii Organic Act," "Anti-Annexation Petition [Palapala hoopii kue hoohuiaina]," and "Anti-Annexation Protest Documents." "People and Places Connected with the Annexation" is a link to photographs from the Hawaii State Archives.

Hawaii State Archives Digital Collections
http://archives1.dags.hawaii.gov/gsdl/cgi-bin/library

The Hawaii State Archives provides access to a plethora of materials among which can be found marriages, divorces, wills, citizenship records, vital statistics for the years 1826 to 1929, judicial records, sales of governmental lands, lists of passengers traveling to and from Hawaii between 1843 and 1900, and records of World War I military service. Not all documents are in English.

Kalok–Honokohau National Historical Park: A Collection of Family Traditions Describing—Customs, Practices and Beliefs of the Families and Lands of Kaloko and Honokohau, North Kona, Island of Hawai'i
http://www.nps.gov/archive/kaho/home/oralhistory/index.htm

This website is a document in PDF format providing the results of a U.S. National Park Service study of the Kaloko-Honokohau region. It includes oral history interviews conducted by Kepā Maly between 1996 and 2001 along with excerpts from several 1962 interviews with native residents of the Kaloko-Honokōhau area. In addition to the oral histories, three articles written between 1875 and 1924 provide firsthand descriptions of the culture and history of nineteenth-century Kaloko, Honokōhau, and Kekaha areas. The articles, originally appearing in Hawaiian-language newspapers, were translated by Kepā Maly.

Political Caricatures of the Hawaiian Kingdom, ca. 1875–1905
http://library.kcc.hawaii.edu/~soma/cartoons/index.html#lorelei

This website contains political caricatures and cartoons printed before and during the annexation of Hawaii. The majority of the prints originally appeared in two American magazines, *Puck* and *Judge*.

Ulukua: The Hawaiian Electronic Library
http://ulukau.org/index.php?l=en

Ulukau was founded by Hale Kuamo'o to bring resources together for the purpose of teaching and using the Hawaiian language. The books in this library can be read in both Hawaiian and English, and searches can be conducted in both languages. The library contains both fiction and nonfiction works. Special features include a Hawaiian bible, an English/Hawaiian dictionary, Hawaiian curriculum materials, and genealogy indexes.

Idaho

Benedicte Wrensted: An Idaho Photographer in Focus
http://www.nmnh.si.edu/anthro/wrensted/

Photographer Benedicte Wrensted (1859–1949) specialized in taking pictures of Indians from southeastern Idaho reservations between 1895 and 1912. Along with her photographs of Indians, there are also photographs of her family, her studio, and the town of Pocatello where her studio was located. Click "Proceed to the Main Menu" at the bottom of the page to access the site's main links. Links include "How Images Are Influenced," "Reading Historical Photographs," and the "Continuation of the [Benedicte Wrensted] Studio." A selected bibliography of resources about Miss Wrensted and a small glossary are also available.

Idaho Digital Resources
http://idahodocs.cdmhost.com/

This repository website was created by The Idaho Commission for Libraries as a central location for state publications. Currently it is a portal to more than ten digital collections, a few of which are highlighted here.

▶ **Boise Public Library Ethnic History Archive**
http://idahodocs.cdmhost.com/cdm4/browse.php?CISOROOT=%2Fp4012coll2

The collection contains over 200 newspaper clippings, some as early as the mid-1800s, featuring Basque, Chinese, Hispanic, and Japanese people who lived in Idaho.

▶ **Edward Stevenson Collection**
http://idahodocs.cdmhost.com/cdm4/browse.php?CISOROOT=%2Fp2003coll2

This is a collection of costume sketches done by Edward Stevenson, the head the costume department for RKO Pictures and DesiLu. Among the 1,115 images (mostly color) are sketches from films such as *I Remember Mama* and *The Magnificent Ambersons* and of actresses such as Barbara Stanwyck, Lucille Ball, and Carol Channing.

▶ **Fred Nordgaard Barbershop Quartet Scrapbooks**
http://idahodocs.cdmhost.com/cdm4/browse.php?CISOROOT=%2Fp4012coll4

This is a small collection of photographs, newspaper clippings, and advertisements featuring barbershop quartets.

Kate and Sue McBeth: Missionary Teachers to the Nez Percé
http://www.lib.uidaho.edu/mcbeth/welcome.htm

The McBeth sisters were missionary teachers to the Nez Percé tribe in the late 1800s and often engaged in disputes with federal agents, the Nez Percé, and each other. The website examines the interactions among these three groups and the key people involved through letters, diaries, and journal entries. The site also provides additional background materials in the form of text treaties, commission and agency reports, historic maps, and photographs. Kate McBeth collected Nez Percé legends for her book *The Nez Percé Since Lewis and Clark* (ca. 1890), and four of these legends were specially chosen to be illustrated by Keith TwoHatchet and are viewable by clicking on "Images" from the left menu.

Oroitzapenak Memories: Basque Oral History Project
http://www.basquemuseum.com/oralhistory/

Over 150 recorded interviews with Basque people are available. The interview summary for each person can be read in its entirety. Availability of select audio snippets and personal photos varies from person to person. The interviews are archived at the Basque Museum & Cultural Center in Boise, Idaho, or in the Basque Studies Library at the University of Nevada, Reno.

University of Idaho Library Special Collections and Archives
http://www.lib.uidaho.edu/special-collections/

The collections are an eclectic mix of personal papers, the papers of government officials, archives of various businesses, photographs, books, blueprints, maps, oral history interviews, and much more. Browse by keyword or by specific collections. Several of the digital collections are highlighted here.

▶ **Historical Photograph Collections**
http://www.lib.uidaho.edu/special-collections/pgfindingaids.html

This collection of historic photographs focuses on the university and the state of Idaho. The Barnard-Stockbridge Collection, which is as subset of this collection, contains an extensive photographic record of Wallace, Idaho, and the Coeur d'Alene mining district between 1894 and 1956.

▶ **Idaho Waters Digital Library**
http://contentdm.lib.uidaho.edu/iwdl/

Water issues involving key Idaho river basins are the focal point of this collection of scientific and technical reports.

▶ **International Jazz Collections**
http://www.ijc.uidaho.edu/

The International Jazz Collections features the papers and photographs of legendary Lionel Hampton along with other jazz notables such as Leonard Feather, Lee Morse, Joe Williams, Dizzy Gillespie, Conte Candoli, and Al Grey.

Illinois

Digital Illinois
http://www.digitalillinois.org/

View digital collections (images, photographs, texts, and audio files) from libraries, historical societies, museums, and other cultural institutions. The "Collections" link provides a list of the collections. A sampling of collections includes Abraham Lincoln—Full Text Books and Documents; Algonquin and Lake in the Hills Local History; Chicago Post Cards; Ethnic Heritage Museum; and American Library Association Archives Digital Collections. Search the collections by keyword or phrase, across all collections or by specific collections. Direct links to the individual collections are accessible from the right menu bar.

Illinois Historical Digitization Projects
http://dig.lib.niu.edu/

This is one of the most interesting collections reflecting Illinois history. It is a wonderful source of primary materials for students, teachers, and researchers. Four of the 15 topical links include "Illinois During the Gilded Age, 1866–1896," "Illinois During the Civil War, 1861–1865," "Lincoln/Net: Abraham Lincoln Historical Digitization Project," and "Prairie Fire: The Illinois Country, 1673–1818." Some collections have additional features, such as lesson plans and a teachers' link to audio and video files that can be downloaded to play in the classroom. Historical themes, narratives, sound (music of the era), maps, photographs, and more richly enhance the collections. One of the unique collections, "Prairie Fire," is described here.

▶ **Prairie Fire**
http://dig.lib.niu.edu/prairiefire/index.html

This collection of photographs, maps, text, and interpretive history videos presents the history of Illinois beginning with the French settlements in 1673 to its statehood in 1818. Search the entire collection or the "Text" page by keyword or phrase. "Images" allows users to limit their searches by a number of criteria, including title, date, category, and historical theme.

Wilmette Public Library—Digital Exhibits
http://www.wilmettelibrary.info/localhistory/exhibits/children.php

The Wilmette Public Library Local History Collection provides access to several digital exhibits, including oral histories and personal letters. Two of the exhibits are *Children of Wilmette and World War I, 1917–1919*, a collection of photographs and newspaper clippings of the children's efforts to support the war effort; and *Letters from the Gold Fields to Wilmette*, photos and letters written during the Gold Rush era.

Indiana

Digital Media Repository
http://libx.bsu.edu/

The Digital Media Repository of Ball State University provides a wide range of primary source materials, including photographs, oral histories, scrapbooks, artworks, video recordings, and maps. Users can search the more than 80 collections using the advanced search option, browsing an A–Z list of collection titles, or searching by subject, location, format, or contributors. The collection of Eleanor Roosevelt's speeches (listed as Roosevelt, Eleanor Speech Collections) includes an audio recording and accompanying transcript of her speech to a convocation in Muncie, Indiana, on May 6, 1959. Another collection title is the Vietnam War Era Veterans Histories.

Indiana Memory
http://www.in.gov/memories/collections.html

View digital collections pertaining to the cultural heritage and history of Indiana. Descriptions of the subject and the format of the individual collections are provided by the host institutions, which are libraries, historical societies, museums, and archives. The

Indiana Memory website can be navigated by topical links such as "Agriculture" and "Daily Life," by keyword, or by clicking on one of the individual collection links.

Iowa

Iowa Heritage Digital Collections
http://iowaheritage.org/

The Iowa Heritage Digital Collections website provides access to over 40 collections representing Iowa's history and culture. Collections include The Editorial Cartoons of J.N. "Ding" Darling from the Cowles Library Collection at Drake University (a collection of editorial cartoons by Pulitzer Prize winner Jay Norwood Darling) and the Historic Des Moines Collection from Drake University (featuring early twentieth-century photographs of homes and public places).

The University of Iowa Libraries—Iowa Digital Library
http://digital.lib.uiowa.edu/

About 300,000 digital images were created from the holdings of the University of Iowa Libraries and collaborating partners. Browse through individual collections accessed by topical links in the left menu, such as "Music" and "Business and Industry," or by more general links, such as "Decades" and "Contributing Departments."

Kansas

Kansas State Historical Society
http://www.kshs.org/research/collections/documents/online/index.htm

This is a great website for educators and researchers alike. Collections accessible online include the Western Trails Project, which incorporates two online exhibits, *Railroad Immigration* and *Advent of the Automobile*, photographs, and print materials; Territorial Kansas Online, a compilation of personal correspondence, diaries, photos, and maps created to bring to life the settling of Kansas between 1854 and 1861; and War Letters, which includes letters written by Kansas soldiers during various wars from the "Bleeding Kansas" struggle through the Gulf War, plus photographs.

Territorial Kansas Online 1854–1861
http://www.territorialkansasonline.org/~imlskto/cgi-bin/index.php?SCREEN=topics&
    showfull=1

This website offers great links to Kansas history, including the six-year struggle called "Bleeding Kansas" and the expansion of the slavery debate involving abolitionist John Brown and others through text, documents, letters, images, photographs, and maps. Topical links include "Territorial Politics and Government," "Border Warfare," "Immigration and Early Settlement," "Personalities," and "National Debate about Kansas." The "Territorial Kansas Timeline" lists major events from 1854 to 1861, and "Annals of Kansas" provides excerpts pertaining to the years 1854–1861 from D.W. Wilder's *Annals of Kansas, 1541–1885* (published in 1886). The "Historic Sites" link provides information on sites maintained by the Kansas State Historical Center. Lesson plans are included, along with a bibliography, making this site a gem for teaching Kansas history.

Kentucky

Digital Library of Appalachia
http://www.aca-dla.org/index.php

This digital library is a collaborative effort of several institutions from various states in the Appalachian area. The content is drawn from the special collections of some of these institutions and housed on the website of the Appalachian College Association, based in Berea, Kentucky. The Association was created to combine efforts in furthering scholarly research and study of the southern and central Appalachian region. Although the Association has 34 member institutions, only 13 have contributed digital content. Content contributed by individual institutions can be browsed by using the "Browse by Library" limiting tool in the left menu of the homepage. Some contributors have provided thousands of items, others much less. An advanced search can be conducted across any and all collections at once or browsed by such topics as education, music, and religion. Content includes images, texts, personal correspondence, books, music, and oral histories with the objective of bringing forward primary source materials for serious researchers. Click "About the DLA" to access detailed copyright and permissions information.

Kentuckiana Digital Library
http://kdl.kyvl.org/

This digital library is a gateway to content (more than 550,000 image scans) held by many different institutions statewide that has a subject focus on the state and a strong research purpose. Appropriate content is identified and contributed from participating institutions, which are the members of the Kentucky Virtual Library. The Kentuckiana website is a statewide resource, with the technology and infrastructure managed and maintained by the University of Kentucky. Although a basic search box is available to keyword search across all collections at once, content can also be accessed through links based on resource format (e.g., "Images," "Maps," "Newspapers," and "Oral Histories") and their individual search tools. Amount of content varies widely for different formats. "Books" currently contains 1,104 titles, each with full-text page scans. "Journals" has only three journal titles, each with various full-text issues. "Newspapers" has over 60 titles, some with long runs and others with only one issue. Clearly, the size, breadth, and variety of this website make it a must for users researching the state of Kentucky.

Kentucky Historical Society Digital Collections
http://205.204.134.47:2005/

The Kentucky Historical Society has a great deal of material documenting the state's past and makes a significant portion of its physical holdings available online. More than 30 collections can be accessed by links based on format. For example, "Oral History" provides a brief description of how the collections came about, and an "Individual Collection Descriptions" link provides separate descriptions for each one. Clicking on the individual collection titles provides a browse list of all content for that collection. Some subjects in the oral history collections are the civil rights movement, Holocaust survivors in Kentucky, and the history of the tobacco industry in the state. Other collections contain personal correspondence; maps showing ownership boundaries, political boundaries, and transportation routes; photographs; rare imprints; and engravings and lithographs. An "Advanced Search" tab at the top of every page allows for keyword searching across all collections.

University of Louisville Digital Collections
http://digital.library.louisville.edu/cdm4/collections.php

This institution has created digital content from its own materials and archives. An "About" link in the top menu details both the origin of the content and the technology used to process and preserve the new digital materials. "Collections" lists and briefly describes all the collections. "Browse" allows for easy access to all items in any one collection; there are also dedicated searches for a few obvious subjects such as Kentucky and Louisville. It also offers the option to browse the collections by subject; choose a subject in the dropdown menu to generate a list of suggested collections to browse. Advanced keyword searching allows for cross-searching any and all collections at the same time, and all items retrieved have accompanying metadata. The collection subjects vary widely, but some of the more interesting ones include Macauley's Theatre Collection, containing studio portraits of actors and actresses in the Louisville area during the nineteenth and twentieth centuries; and Stereographic Views of Louisville and Beyond, containing hundreds of views also from the nineteenth and twentieth centuries.

Louisiana

LOUISiana Digital Library
http://louisdl.louislibraries.org/

This digital library is a collaborative project of more than 20 institutions around the state, including museums, public libraries, state agencies, and academic institutions (e.g., Louisiana State University, Tulane, New Orleans University, and Loyola University of New Orleans). Much of what is available digitally throughout the state is included in this one library. For example, Loyola University provides both on its own website and through the LOUISiana Digital Library electronic scans of its school paper, *The Maroon*, from 1972 to 1973; a pamphlet collection about all things New Orleans; and a late nineteenth-century Jesuit scrapbook of a New Orleans mission (click on "Institution" in the left menu and then on the institution's name). The LOUISiana Digital Library currently contains over 144,000 items in a variety of formats, including textual, visual, and audio. The "Collection Name" link in the left menu provides an alphabetical list of over 100 collections; clicking individual collection names allows for exclusive searching of just that collection. The "Search All Collections" link in the top menu allows users to pick and choose any and all collections to search at one time. Other limiting options include searching by format, geographic location, and time period.

Louisiana Map Collection
http://www.nutrias.org/~nopl/maps/maps.htm

This website contains selected maps in the New Orleans Public Library's Louisiana Map Collection. Nineteen digital maps represent only a portion of what is physically available at the library, and they are shown with a minimum of accompanying information. Some of the maps are clearly identified as being available in the LOUISiana Digital Library as well, while other content is available only on this website. The maps focus primarily on New Orleans.

Louisiana State Documents Digital Archive
http://louisdl.louislibraries.org/cdm4/index_p267101coll4.php?CISOROOT=/p267101coll4

This archive is a storehouse of electronic documents issued by various state agencies. Not all government publications are issued in electronic format, so not all are included in this collection. Click "Browse" in the top menu bar to access over 4,600 documents. "Advanced Search" can help users narrow their focus.

Maine

Maine Memory Network
http://www.mainememory.net/

The Maine Memory Network provides access to numerous historical collections created by museums, historical societies, libraries, and other institutions. Major sections are "Online Exhibits" (such as *Art of the People: Folk Art in Maine* and *Blueberries to Potatoes: Farming in Maine*), the "Maine Community Heritage Project" (links to community websites to view individual digitized collections), "Schools" (a major resource for teachers, including the "Finding Katahdin: An Online Exploration of Maine History" link to over 50 lesson plans and primary sources related to the textbook *Finding Katahdin* published in 2002). "Maine History Online" explores Maine's history. A sampling of content is described here.

▶ **Amazing! Maine Stories**
http://www.mainememory.net/sitebuilder/site/155/page/414/display?use_mmn=1

Amazing! Maine Stories is an online exhibit. Read interesting stories of inventors, showmen, a railway agent, and others dating back to 1759. Three slide shows help illustrate the stories with photos and other images. One story is about Henry Thurston Clark and his trunk, circa 1872. Henry, "a baggage agent of the European and North American Railway, was determined to prove that checked baggage could be sent quickly and efficiently from one side of the country to the other. So he packed a small hand trunk with a canteen of Atlantic Ocean water, a bottle of Halifax brandy, a railroad timetable, letters, and newspapers, and sent it on its way." To find out what happened, you will have to go to the site for the rest of the story.

▶ **Maine History Online**
http://www.mainememory.net/mho/

Maine History Online provides key topics and events related to Maine history through a series of background essays organized by time period, theme, and critical approach.

Maine State Archives
http://www.maine.gov/sos/arc/exhibits/index.html

View selections of photographs, documents, maps, newspapers, and more on the Maine State Archives website. For example, view Maine's first State of the State address by Governor William King in June 1820 along with King's photograph, or read a letter signed by Daniel Webster to the Governor of Maine dated 1843 about the final settlement of the northeast boundary dispute between the United States and Great Britain. Exhibits accessible from this page include *Septentrionalis*, featuring maps of North America in the Baxter Map Collection that date back to 1636; *Workaday World of Maine*, photographs depicting daily life; and *The 20th Maine's Battle Flag*, based on the flag used by Joshua Chamberlain and the 20th Maine Regiment on Little Round Top at the Battle of Gettysburg.

Windows on Maine
http://windowsonmaine.library.umaine.edu/

View artifacts or online streaming video clips featuring both primary and secondary resources on this educational website. The "Subject Category" dropdown menu lists over 35 topics to search by, including "Basket Making," "Climatic Change," "Shipping/Shipbuilding," "United States History," and "Native Americans." Click "Map/Timeline" to access resources by selecting a specific location on the interactive state map or a time period from the timeline.

Maryland

Albin O. Kuhn Library & Gallery Digital Collections
http://contentdm.ad.umbc.edu/index.php

This digital collections website is maintained by the University of Maryland, Baltimore County. It provides access to 12 collections, most of which are composed of content from the institution's own holdings. A simple search tool can be used to search one collection or all at once; and an advanced search tool is also available to search multiple collections at once. Alternatively, click "Browse" in the top menu bar, and then choose a collection from the dropdown menu. Some individual collections have no descriptions, and access to the collection of university theses and dissertations is restricted to local users. Most content is presented through thumbnail images that when clicked yield larger images accompanied by full descriptive and technical metadata, although there are some textual materials as well.

Archives of Maryland Online
http://www.archivesofmaryland.net/html/index.html

This website is the digital arm of the Maryland State Archives. While most documents and records at the Archives are physical items only, many municipal records, laws, directories, and other items have been digitized and made available electronically. The site is well organized, with a list of various types of records available in the left menu. In addition to legislative and fiscal records, there are also military records, land records, and the State Constitution.

Enoch Pratt Free Library
http://www.prattlibrary.org/digital/index.aspx

This public library website provides access to 21 collections. These include Film in Maryland, containing movie programs and advertising flyers; Great Baltimore Fire of 1904, with a map showing the location of each image presented; Prominent Marylanders; Seventeenth and Eighteenth Century European Maps; and War Posters Collection, with original propaganda pieces from World Wars I and II. Click the collection titles to browse their content.

Maryland Digital Cultural Heritage
http://www.mdch.org/collections.aspx

This website is a collaborative project among a number of institutions around the state. It is centered at the Enoch Pratt Free Library in Baltimore and contains text and image collections contributed by the partner institutions. The more than 35 collections focus mainly on Maryland's cultural history. Collections are listed alphabetically, with a brief description and a notation of the contributing institution and the date contributed. Click on the collection titles to view more detailed descriptions and to browse the collections. A simple search tool at the top of all pages allows for searching all collections at once. Some highlights include a photograph collection of Baltimore streetcars and a collection of the personal papers of Edgar Allan Poe.

Maryland Memory Projects
http://www.mdhs.org/library/mmphome.html

This website contains the digital collection of the Maryland Historical Society. Click the "Photograph Collections" link on the lower part of the page to find the actual digital images available. A keyword search tool returns results from both the finding aids and the actual images. To see only the available images, choose "Collections Cross-Section" under "Browse the Photograph Collections." "Subject Index" yields an alphabetical list of subjects through which users can browse the images. Subjects range from maps, railroads, and portraits to Civil War, World War I and II images, and, of course, all things Baltimore. Images have titles only, with no accompanying metadata. The "A Statement about Copyright" link on the homepage provides thorough information about use, citing materials, and obtaining permissions.

Maryland State Law Library
http://mdlaw.ptfs.com/awweb/html/portal/index.html

The State Law Library, based in Annapolis, makes some of its historical legal materials available online for both legal professionals and the public to use. The content is organized into three sections: "Rules Committee Materials," "Task Force Reports," and "Judicial Conference Proceedings." Each section has an "About" link, explaining what types of documents are contained in it and what they are for. Each section can be keyword searched individually, and the annual Conference Proceedings can be limited by year. Rules Committee Materials and Conference Proceedings can be browsed by year (dating back to 1947) and Task Force Reports by subject. For legal researchers, these documents shed light on what the legal machinery of the state has focused on for the past half-century.

University of Maryland Digital Collections
http://www.lib.umd.edu/digital/

This institution has a number of digital collections, with content drawn primarily from its own holdings. Some content is available for all website viewers to see, such as images of twentieth-century America in the National Trust Library Historic Postcard Collection. Other collections, like The Jim Henson Works, including video footage of *Muppet Show* and *Fraggle Rock* episodes, are restricted to viewing from specific locations on campus. The homepage offers multiple search options, including searching by keyword, browsing by individual collection, or browsing by 18 predetermined categories across multiple collections. The results pages can be somewhat unusual, with check-box limiters on the left and dropdown sorting features on the upper right, but the tools are powerful enough to help experienced users find what they need.

Western Maryland's Historical Library
http://www.whilbr.org/

This website brings together a number of digital collections that highlight the histories of Maryland's three westernmost counties: Garrett, Alleghany, and Washington. The site's content comes from libraries, historical societies, and individuals within these three counties. The website's structure is extremely user-friendly, with both simple and advanced search tools in the upper right of the page. Searches can be limited to one collection at a time, or all can be searched at once. Collections are grouped into one of six categories. There is one each for the three counties, within which are materials related to that county. The other categories are the Civil War in Maryland, including content related to local veterans, local conflicts, payroll records, etc.; genealogical records, containing tax, jury, and business directories, among others; and photographs and prints, containing image collections. To see a list of collection titles or to limit a search to one collection, use the dropdown menu in the lower left section of the page under "Collections, Gateways, and Tools."

Massachusetts

Boston College Digital Collections
http://www.bc.edu/libraries/collections/collinfo/digitalcollections.html

Boston College Libraries presents a number of digital collections, for example, the Thomas P. O'Neill, Jr. Photographs collection. A few of the collections can be accessed only by Boston College students. Those listed here are quite unique and are available to all.

▶ **Becker Collection**
http://dcollections.bc.edu/R/?func=collections-result&collection_id=1131

View over 600 drawings by Joseph Becker and others that illustrate nineteenth-century American life. The drawings focus largely on the Civil War, but other topics include the Pacific railroad construction, the trans-Atlantic cable, and the Great Fire in Chicago. A companion website (available at http://idesweb.bc.edu/becker/) includes biographies of the artists and a slide presentation of the drawings.

▶ **Boston Gas Company Photographs**
http://dcollections.bc.edu/R/?func=search&local_base=gen01-bcd01-gs

View a wonderful collection of 4,500 photographs (1880s to 1970s) documenting the laying of gas pipes underground and building construction. Most photographs were taken between 1885 and 1910 and offer a fascinating look at early life in Boston.

▶ **Brooker Collection**
http://dcollections.bc.edu/R/?func=collections-result&collection_id=1742

This collection contains nearly 2,500 American legal and land use documents dated between 1716 and 1930. Documents include a property deed from 1738, an 1802 letter concerning a guardianship appointment of children, and an indentured servant contract from 1797. A companion website (at http://www.bc.edu/schools/law/library/about/rarebook/exhibitions/broker.html) provides a more detailed explanation of the documents.

▶ **Liturgy and Life Artifacts Series**
http://dcollections.bc.edu/R/?func=search&local_base=gen01-bcd01-lt

View nearly 1,200 liturgy-related artifacts dating between 1925 and 1975, such as vestments, statuary, rosary beads, medals, chalices, crucifixes, sick call sets, prayer cards, relics, and original paintings. This collection provides a rich documentation of both the public and private devotional lives of American Catholics prior to the Second Vatican Council reforms.

▶ **Sacred Heart Review**
http://dcollections.bc.edu/R/?func=collections-result&collection_id=1764

Read issues of the *Sacred Heart Review*, a Catholic newspaper published between 1888 and 1918. The publication includes local (such as about the Archdiocese of Boston), national, and international news items.

Digital Commonwealth
http://www.digitalcommonwealth.org/

Digital Commonwealth is a wonderful resource for Massachusetts history. One can select from a number of links to view the collections, such as "Subjects," which include history, architecture, and parades; "Archives"; "Creators"; "Sources"; and "Types" (such as text, photographs, audios, and newspaper clippings). "Building Poultry House for Essex County Egg Laying Contest, 1915," "Churches—Appleton Street," and "In the Rag Room, Holyoke, Mass." (a group of women at work sorting rags at a paper-making company) are three examples of photographs in the archives.

Northeast Massachusetts Digital Library
http://www.nmrls.org/nmdl/

The Northeast Massachusetts Digital Library is a portal to various digital library collections located within the Northeast Massachusetts Regional Library System.

Michigan

Grand Valley State University Libraries—Special Collections and University Archives
http://gvsu.cdmhost.com/gvpages/gvhome.php

View a selection of photographs, letters, diaries, interviews, and publications from the holdings of the Libraries' Special Collections and University Archives. Collections offer full-text search, browse, zoom and pan, and side-by-side comparison of documents and transcriptions. Select "View the Collections" for a listing. Several collections of interest are noted here.

▶ **Civil War & Slavery Collection**
http://gvsu.cdmhost.com/gvpages/civilwarslavery.php

View the diaries of a surgeon, an artillery officer, and a fruit farmer; correspondence between government officials and a Whig political appointee; slavery documents; and other Civil War correspondence. Select "Browse All Items in the Collection" for a full listing, or use the search bar to locate a specific collection.

▶ **D.J. Angus Photographs**
http://gvsu.cdmhost.com/gvpages/djangus.php

View photographs taken by D.J. Angus as he traveled the United States and Mexico from the late 1920s to the 1940s. View over 900 photographs of "manmade and natural phenomenon centered on engineering projects, such as dams, bridges, cliff dwellings, quarries, and mines." Select "Browse Items by State" and then a specific state for items, or select "Browse All Items in This Collection" for a full listing of photographs.

▶ **Decorated Publishers Bindings**
http://gvsu.cdmhost.com/gvpages/publishers.php

View over 160 images of commercial book covers designed from the early 1870s up to 1930 that exhibit a variety of graphic illustrations and designs. Select "Browse All Items in This Collection" for a full listing of book covers along with a description of each.

▶ **Fore-Edge Paintings**
http://gvsu.cdmhost.com/gvpages/paintings.php

View miniature watercolors, a genre of painting that began in the 1500s and is still done today. The painting's fanned edges on a book disappear when the book is closed. Select "Browse All Items in This Collection" for a listing of paintings with images and a description.

▶ **Incunabula & 16th Century Printing**
http://gvsu.cdmhost.com/gvpages/incunabula.php

View examples of incunabula (books that were printed before 1501), including Saint Jerome's *Epistolae* (1497) with woodcuts. Select "Browse All Items in This Collection" to view over 50 books with images and descriptions provided. Select "View a List of Complete Collection" for a PDF file listing items by country.

▶ **Mathias J. Alten**
http://gvsu.cdmhost.com/gvpages/mjalten.php

View the paintings and personal papers of one of Michigan's most significant painters, Mathias J. Alten (1871–1938), as well as a diary by his daughter Camelia. Select "Browse All Items in This Collection" for a listing of items along with descriptions.

▶ **Veterans History Project**
http://gvsu.cdmhost.com/gvpages/veterans.php

Listen to oral histories given by those who served in various military branches from World War I through the Iraq War. Photographs of the veterans are included. Histories are searchable by selecting "Browse by War or Conflict" or "Browse by Branch of Service."

M Library—Digital Collections
http://quod.lib.umich.edu/lib/colllist/

This University of Michigan website hosts dozens of digital collections, including many on the local history of the state and the area of Ann Arbor surrounding the institution. Click the title of the collection to enter each one. Selected collections are described here.

▶ **Anarchism Pamphlets in the Labadie Collection**
http://quod.lib.umich.edu/l/labadie/

The Labadie Collection contains anarchist materials and social protest literature. Over 600 pamphlets (which is just a small portion of the collection) can be viewed here.

▶ **Ann Arbor Postcards**
http://quod.lib.umich.edu/cgi/i/image/image-idx?c=moaapcic

This collection includes over 250 postcards of buildings and sites in the Ann Arbor area. The images are available for public use, can be enlarged for easier viewing, and are accompanied by full metadata.

▶ **Civil War Collection**
http://quod.lib.umich.edu/c/civilwar1/

This collection, donated by friends of the Western Michigan University Libraries, contains diaries and textual translations of persons from Michigan who participated in the Civil War. The translations are searchable by word and phrase, or the whole collection can be browsed by name, title, and about a dozen broad subject headings.

▶ **Diversity in the Desert: Daily Life in Greek & Roman Egypt**
http://www.lib.umich.edu/diversity-desert/welcome.html

This online exhibit re-creates the lives of people in ancient Egypt after the Alexander the Great (332 BCE–641 CE) conquest when Egypt became a Hellenistic (Greek) kingdom. View documents written on papyrus and other materials that form part of the Papyrus Collection of the University of Michigan. Select "Browse All Images" to view images of papyri and other examples of writings along with descriptions.

▶ **Enchanting Ruin: Tintern Abbey and Romantic Tourism in Wales**
http://www.lib.umich.edu/enchanting-ruin-tintern-abbey-romantic-tourism-wales/

This collection of images and manuscripts tells the story of Tintern Abbey. It commemorates the well-known poem by William Wordsworth, "Lines, Written a Few Miles Above Tintern Abbey." The imaginary impressions of this Romantic site have been used in poetry and other writing. Image viewing is easy, with seven zoomable views of the item to choose from.

▶ **Michigan County Histories and Atlases**
http://quod.lib.umich.edu/m/micounty/

This collection contains over 400 digitized titles that can be browsed by title, author, and subject. Selected from various library holdings for their historical and genealogical value, these volumes have been digitized and made freely available to the public through the collaboration of 16 different institutions and libraries. Click on the embedded word "more" in the middle of the page text to see the list of participating institutions. Then use the search tools at the bottom of the page to explore the collection.

▶ **Transportation History Collection: Railroads**
http://quod.lib.umich.edu/r/railroad/

Select "Browse the Collection" to see railroad company annual reports and issues of *Locomotive World*, a monthly magazine beginning with volume 1, number 12 (April 1909). Type "Locomotive World" in the search box to limit to its articles.

Michigan eLibrary—MeL Michigana
http://mel.org/SPT—BrowseResourcesMichigana.php?ParentId=687

The MeL Michigana website provides access to a number of digital collection projects housed in libraries throughout the state representing Michigan's history and culture. These include public, university, and special libraries and a historical society. Some of the collections are described here.

▶ **Archives of Michigan Image Collection**
http://seekingmichigan.org/

Stories, documents, maps, photographs, and artifacts documenting Michigan's rich heritage are organized into four links. "Seek" contains more than 15 individual collections; "Discover" contains records of the state's early historical beginnings; "Look" is the place to read stories of personal interest about the state; and "Teach" provides content resources for K–12 teachers.

▶ **Civil War Diaries**
http://quod.lib.umich.edu/c/civilwar1/

This website contains letters and diaries from the mid-1860s related to the Civil War. View individual diary pages, or read full transcriptions. There are various ways to search the collection. "Browse the Collection" leads to options to search by name, topic, or author/title. The site alerts searchers when some diaries are lengthy and may take long to download.

▶ **Early Detroit Images from the Burton Historical Collection**
http://quod.lib.umich.edu/cgi/i/image/image-idx?sort=title;rgn1=ic_all;med=1;
    c=dpa1ic;back=back1267034810;size=20;q1=dpa1ic;start=1;type=boolean;
    view=thumbfull

View pre-1922 photographs of Detroit illustrating its social and cultural history and documenting its historical events. The more than 12,000 images are from the Detroit Public Library's Burton Historical Collection and include glass negatives, lanternslides, cased images, albumen prints, and stereograph cards. Select "Images with Records" to view images with a description.

▶ **Grand Valley State University Digital Collections**
http://gvsu.edu/library/digitalcollections/index.cfm?id=9A1B72EB-C65F-8B84-3D36F11A7644CB45

View photographs, paintings, book covers, diaries, letters, audio and video interviews, and publications covering topics from the Civil War to Michigan philanthropists. Click on "View the List of Collections" for a full list of titles, such as the Civil War & Slavery Collection and the Veterans History Project. Each collection is briefly described. Click a linked collection title and then "Browse All Items in This Collection" to reveal its contents.

▶ **John Todd Photography Collection**
http://heritage.portagelibrary.info/cdm4/Arowse.php

The John Todd Photographic Collection comes from the Portage District Library. Photographs feature local sights, people, and buildings from southwest Michigan from 1940 to 1981. Over 1,000 images are listed by title and subject and include a description. A dropdown box lists individual collection titles to select from.

▶ **Keweenaw Digital Archives—Michigan's Copper Country in Photographs**
http://digarch.lib.mtu.edu/

View photographs of the Keweenaw Peninsula, where more than 1 billion pounds of copper were produced during the mineral rushes (1844–1985). Select "Subject Browse" for an alphabetical list of subjects. For example, the subject of disasters includes photos of copper mine disasters.

▶ **Making of Ann Arbor**
http://moaa.aadl.org/moaa

The Making of Ann Arbor is captured in photographs of its historical buildings, postcards, and maps from 1824 to 1974. The materials belong to the Ann Arbor District Library, the Bentley Historical Library, and the University of Michigan.

▶ **Making of Modern Michigan: Digitizing Michigan's Hidden Past**
http://mmm.lib.msu.edu/

Fifty-two Michigan libraries worked collaboratively to record Michigan's heritage. View photographs, genealogical materials, family papers, and oral histories. Select "Browse Collections" and then "By Subject" to view a substantial list of topics.

▶ **Michigan County Histories and Atlases**
http://quod.lib.umich.edu/m/micounty/

The Michigan County Histories and Atlases Digitization Project offers a number of online books about the histories of Michigan counties, for example, *An Account of Flint and Genesee County from Their Organization*, by William V. Smith (editor). This collection contains over 400 digitized titles published before 1923 and almost 200 histories from 1866 to 1926. To search the collection, select "Browse Michigan County Histories and Atlases."

▶ **Polar Bear Expedition Digital Collections**

http://polarbears.si.umich.edu/index.pl?node_id=272&lastnode_id=1163

A U.S. military operation called the "American Intervention in Northern Russia, 1918–1919" (nicknamed the "Polar Bear Expedition") took place at the end of World War I. Many of the veterans were from Michigan. Study the scrapbooks, diaries, chronologies, eulogies, newspaper clippings, maps, audio clips, cartoons, essays, and photographs of those who served the war effort. The site can be searched by subject, geographic location, organization, and media type.

▶ **Selected Library of Congress Resources for Michigan**

http://www.loc.gov/teachers/classroommaterials/presentationsandactivities
/presentations/states/michigan/index.html

This Library of Congress website highlights selected images and audio files pertaining to Michigan. It is a good starting place for primary sources. Examples include Irving Berlin's music sheet *I Want to Go Back to Michigan; Down on the Farm* (1914) and a poster showing a panoramic view of the launch of the ship *Lady Janet*.

▶ **Upper Peninsula Digitization Center**

http://updigit.uproc.lib.mi.us/index.php

View photographs, newspaper clippings, and documents from the late nineteenth and twentieth centuries about the Upper Peninsula area. Materials on the history of Michigan transportation are contributions from Michigan libraries. Select "Click for a List of Projects & Participants" to view the full list of projects, or select "Browse Projects" to view individual items in the collection. A dropdown box at the top of the page lists titles of items in the collection to select from. Depending on the individual collection, items include artifacts, postcards, photographs, scrapbooks, newspaper articles, images, oral histories, and interviews with an audio version and a PDF file transcript of the interview.

▶ **Virtual Motor City**

http://dlxs.lib.wayne.edu/v/vmc/topics.php

The collection can be accessed by 11 topical links, for example, "Auto Industry." Each topic is subdivided into the three broad categories of general, people, and places. Photo viewing is easy, with five zoomable views of the item to choose from. Great figures such as Martin Luther King and Henry Ford are among those featured.

▶ **Virtual Motor City Detroit News Newsreels**

http://www.lib.wayne.edu/resources/digital/vmc_newsreels/

This is one of the premier photojournalistic resources freely available from a national-level newspaper. View live digitized newsreels from the 1920s *Detroit News* newsreels.

▶ **War of 1812 Digitization Project: Footsteps to the Battlefield**

http://monroe.lib.mi.us/war_of_1812/main.htm

Access digitized books, photos, slides, postcards, letters, and original artwork pertaining to the War of 1812. Links include "Galleries," "Battle of the River Raisin,"

"The Durocher Letters," "The John McCalla Letters," "The Battle of Lake Erie—A Discourse," "An Authentic History of the Late War Between the United States and Great Britain," and "The Memoirs of the Campaign of the Northwestern Army of The United States."

Seeking Michigan
http://seekingmichigan.org/about

This site is a collaborative effort to provide cultural heritage materials from the Library of Michigan and the Archives of Michigan of interest to educators that can be used for teaching purposes. It is a growing digital collection of unique historical information, including source documents, maps, films, images, oral histories, and artifacts. Each collection is accessible through its own "Seek," "Discover," "Look," and "Teach" links. Several collections are highlighted here.

▶ **Civil War Manuscripts**
http://seekingmichigan.org/discover-collection?collection=p129401coll15

The Civil War Manuscripts collection consists of "letters and diaries from Michigan soldiers who served during the Civil War period (1861–1865)."

▶ **Civil War Photographs**
http://seekingmichigan.org/discover-collection?collection=p4006coll3

View over 1,000 photographs from the Archives of Michigan of Michigan soldiers who served during the Civil War. There are also images of sheet music and broadsides dating from the mid-1800s.

▶ **Civil War Service Records**
http://seekingmichigan.org/discover-collection?collection=p4006coll15

Muster rolls, letters, and lists of dead are a small sample of the over 1,400 items in this collection.

▶ **Death Records, 1897–1920**
http://seekingmichigan.org/discover-collection?collection=p129401coll7

Nearly 1 million death certificates are contained in the Library of Michigan's collection. "Information includes the decedent's birth date and place, parents' names and birthplace, cemetery name, and location."

▶ **Early Photography**
http://seekingmichigan.org/discover-collection?collection=p4006coll4

This is a unique collection of more than 200 nineteenth-century daguerreotypes, ambrotypes, and tintypes of soldiers, men, women, and children. Examples include "Woolsey Dare in his Civil War Uniform," "Chief Okemos," and "City of Lansing."

▶ **Maps**
http://seekingmichigan.org/discover-collection?collection=p129401coll3

View a sampling of online maps from the Archives of Michigan. This small collection includes survey, county, and railroad maps dated between 1841 and 1900.

▶ **Music of Michigan**
http://seekingmichigan.org/discover-collection?collection=p4006coll5

View over 400 pieces of sheet music. Select "View Collection" for a list of song titles, such as "Kalamazoo," an original ragtime cake-walk by Edward Desenberg, or "Ain't We Got Fun," lyrics by Gus Kahn and Raymond B. Egan and music by Richard A. Whiting.

▶ **Oral Histories**
http://seekingmichigan.org/discover-collection?collection=p4006coll17

Listen to interviews with Michigan citizens who share their memories of the past, adding another dimension to the written historical record. Select "View Collection" for a list of interviews. Many contain a photograph of the person interviewed.

▶ **Works Progress Administration (WPA) Property Inventories**
http://seekingmichigan.org/discover-collection?collection=p129401coll0

The WPA collected data about lands and buildings throughout the Michigan countryside between 1936 and 1942. Online documents contain information about the land, structures, and surrounding area in Hillsdale, Isabella, Jackson, and Oakland counties. Select "View Collection" for a list of documents.

Virtual Archives and Exhibitions of the Charles H. Wright Museum of African American History
http://chwmaah-archive.com/

From the right menu choose "Image Database" to view the online collections. One features Tutankhamen, with images of adornment, jewelry, ceremonial art, and paintings. The Doll Collection displays dolls of various makers portraying children of African descent. The Artifact Collection contains images of artifacts, art, and black memorabilia from Africa, Haiti, Japan, and the United States. Two other exhibitions, which are accessible from the side menu by selecting "Virtual Exhibitions," are described here.

▶ **Women of a New Tribe**
http://chwmaah-archive.com/?page_id=103

Visit a virtual exhibition giving tribute to black women and their contributions from all walks of life through oral histories, images, and biographies.

▶ **Wonderful Things from the Pharaoh's Tomb**
http://chwmaah-archive.com/?page_id=99

This exhibition explores Tutankhamen's African heritage through artifact images that are displayed in five groupings: ancient Egypt, archaeological discoveries, his private life as pharaoh, his public life, and his royal burial.

Minnesota

Ironworld Discovery Center—Iron Range Women's History Project
http://www.ironrangeresearchcenter.org/RC5/ironworld_women.htm

Click "Women at Work" to view photographs of the activities of women on Minnesota's Iron Range in the early twentieth century from a collection of the Iron Range Research Center.

Minnesota Digital Library—Minnesota Reflections
http://reflections.mndigital.org/cdm4/about.php

Minnesota Reflections provides links to 45,000 images and documents shared by more than 98 cultural heritage organizations across the state. It is a rich resource for Minnesota teachers, students, and researchers. For example, there are maps and photographs from the Soudan Underground Mine State Park and oral histories from Northeast Minnesota Historical Center. The homepage lists the contributors alphabetically with descriptions and links to their materials. Visitors can also search across all collections by keyword. For example, a search for "Indians" retrieved 275 items, including a photograph of American Indians in ceremonial clothing circa 1890. Selected collections are highlighted here.

▶ **Luther Seminary Archives**
http://reflections.mndigital.org/cdm4/browse.php?CISOROOT=%2Flsm

The Luther Seminary Archives, St. Paul, includes material from all of its predecessor schools. The project documents church, academic, and ethnic culture among Minnesota's Scandinavian people through papers, photographs, audio and video materials, oral histories, and objects.

▶ **Winona County Historical Society**
http://reflections.mndigital.org/cdm4/browse.php?CISOROOT=%2Fwch

The mission of the Winona County Historical Society is to document the human history of Winona County. The Historical Society maintains a very active educational programming schedule and features many special events and publications.

▶ **Winona State University**
http://reflections.mndigital.org/cdm4/browse.php?CISOROOT=%2Fwinona

Winona State University holds the distinction of being not only the "the oldest 'normal school' west of the Mississippi River" but also the "birthplace of the National Education Association." The library archives contain images of campus activities, student life, and class photographs.

University of Minnesota Libraries—Digital Collections
http://digital.lib.umn.edu/dcu-home.phtml

The Digital Library Services of the University of Minnesota has made accessible research and scholarly materials online through collection links. Materials come from various departments, labs, and centers of the university and are shared through an institutional depository. Collections from the university's Electronic Text Research Center can also be viewed by clicking its link in the right menu under "Other Digital Resources." Several collections are highlighted here.

▶ **Early Modern French Women Writers**
http://etrc.lib.umn.edu/frenwom.htm

This is a great resource for faculty and students studying important women writers of the fifteenth through seventeenth centuries of early modern France. View biographies and images of, for example, Christine de Pizan, Diane de Poitiers, Louise Labé, Madeleine de Scudéry, Marguerite de Navarre, Marie de Gournay, and

Pernette du Guillet. The site also includes texts by Marie-Catherine d'Aulnoy, Anne-Marie-Louise Montpensier, and 11 other women writers from this period.

▶ **Early 19th Century Russian Readership & Culture Collection**
http://etrc.lib.umn.edu/rusread.htm

Read excerpts from fiction, journals, memoirs, and travel accounts of early nineteenth-century Russians. Links lead to biographies of important people, a dictionary, thumbnail images of "personalia," scenes of bookstores, maps, and "The Table of Ranks," which is a system of advancement applied to those who work for the government. Some of the larger images can be accessed only by University of Minnesota faculty and students.

▶ **Undergraduate Victorian Studies Online Teaching Anthology**
http://etrc.lib.umn.edu/uvsota/index.htm

The Victorian Studies Anthology project is a digital archive of primary source materials. Choose from a list of over 25 short biographies, including Marie Corelli, Herbert Cowell, Charles Darwin, and Charles Dickens. Click "The Victorian Web" to access a comprehensive resource on Victorian history, literature, social life, and customs, including book reviews, periodicals, Victorian texts, and much more.

▶ **Women's Travel Writing, 1830–1930**
http://etrc.lib.umn.edu/womtrav.htm

The focus of this website is travel literature by women recounting trips to and from Africa, Latin America, and the United States during the period 1830–1930. Resources include biographies, maps, photographs, and portraits of five of the women travelers.

Mississippi

Mississippi Department of Archives and History (MDAH)—Mississippi Archives
http://www.mdah.state.ms.us/arrec/digital_archives/

MDAH is located in the state capital of Jackson, Mississippi; however, this website makes much content available electronically for the online researcher, with links to more than 15 collections relating to the history of the state, most of which are photograph collections. Topics include the Mississippi River Flood of 1927, the devastation caused by Hurricane Camille in 1969, the Mississippi State Penitentiary, and some notable persons in the state's history. There is also a collection of Jefferson Davis Estate Papers and an ABC book for the antislavery abolitionist. Each collection has a full description and is searched separately. To access government publications click "Government Archives," embedded in the text near the top of the page.

Mississippi Digital Library
http://www.msdiglib.org/index.php

The Mississippi Digital Library was originally a partnership project among several academic institutions around the state, including the Mississippi Department of Archives and History. Its goal is to highlight and make available its cultural materials online, and it now accepts contributions from other museums and cultural institutions as well. In addition to links to the University of Mississippi, Mississippi State University, and University of Southern Mississippi, which are described separately later in this section, the Mississippi Digital Library also contains links to smaller collections from other participating institutions. These include Delta State University, Jackson State University, Mississippi Gulf Coast Community College, and Tougaloo College. To see the participating institutions, click "Browse the Collections" in the left menu; then click "Browse by Institution" to access the materials.

Mississippi State University Digital Collections
http://library.msstate.edu/digitalcollections

This website has links to seven different digital collections. There is a collection for all things Ulysses S. Grant, including his papers as well as political cartoons and sheet music. The Congressional and Political Research Center Collection contains digitized correspondence and other documents of several Mississippi senators and representatives. Other collections are part of the CHARM project (Consortium for the History of Agricultural and Rural Mississippi) and contain photographs, farm journals, and images of antique tools and farm equipment. Two other collections are a photographic history of the institution and an online database of events that have taken place at the institution over the years. Each collection has a full description, is searched separately, and can be browsed by collection-specific criteria.

University of Mississippi Digital Collections
http://clio.lib.olemiss.edu/digital.php

The digital collections available on this website are primarily from within the archives and special collections of the university. An advanced search tool allows for cross-searching of all collections at one time. The website's two main sections are described here.

▶ **Accounting Collections**
   http://clio.lib.olemiss.edu/accounting/index.php

   This section is under construction. Documents currently online detail the history of U.S. accounting and auditing standards, as well as examples of documentation.

▶ **Archives and Special Collections: Digital Collections**
   http://clio.lib.olemiss.edu/archives/

   This section has 13 different collections, providing materials in a variety of formats. Highlighted in these collections are political cartoons and broadsides, a photographic history of the advent of music known as the blues, a sheet music archive, historical documents of the university, and images and letters of alumni and others who served in the Civil War. There are also some publications of the Mississippi Woman Suffrage Association.

University of Southern Mississippi Digital Collections
http://digilib.usm.edu/cdm4/browse_coll.php

This website has links to 14 digital collections, with content taken primarily from the library's own collections. Several databases have digitized content from an extensive library of children's books and materials. Other collections include political cartoons and historic maps, manuscripts, photographs, and oral histories relating to the Civil War, the civil rights movement, the history of Mississippi, and the university. A small collection of images show selected items in the institution's permanent art collection, and the link "Civil Rights in Mississippi Digital Archive" provides access to over 1,500 items with full metadata and descriptions.

Missouri

Missouri Digital Heritage
http://www.sos.mo.gov/mdh/collections.asp

The Missouri Digital Heritage is a portal to Missouri's heritage and history resources located throughout the state in archives, museums, and libraries. The resources are organized into 18 general topics, with links such as "Agriculture," "Art, Architecture, Literature, Music, and Theater," "Family and Faith," "Photographs and Images," and "Sports and Recreation." Search by individual collection under each topic, or click "All Collections" for a combined A–Z list. A sampling of the individual collections is highlighted here.

▶ **American Regionalism: Visions from the Heartland**
http://maa.missouri.edu/exhibitions/americanregionalism/index.html

View images of paintings, prints, and drawings by a group of artists (including John Curry, Grant Wood, and Thomas Hart Benton) whose subject was daily life from the 1920s to the 1950s in the heartland of the Midwest. Click "Enter" and then "Menu" to access this collection of images and biographical information.

▶ **Buck Clayton Collection**
http://digital.library.umsystem.edu/cgi/i/image/image-idx?c=claytonic;page=index
  ;sid=d9ad73639b7f0875857537a65cf1737b;g=vm

Wilbur "Buck" Clayton was a jazz arranger, composer, trumpeter, and band leader from 1928 to 1991. This collection of over 1,500 photographs provides a glimpse into Clayton's life and career through photos of his family and musical performances.

▶ **Carrie Watkins Cookbook**
http://campus.jewell.edu/academics/curry/library/digital/cwatkins/index.html

Caroline Emma "Carrie" Watkins began collecting recipes sometime around 1868–1869. This website provides access to the over 275 recipes that were found in an old ledger in a trunk. In addition to ingredient lists and cleaning solutions that she used during her lifetime, the site includes instructions and measurements for cooking historic recipes, photographs of the Watkins home and summer kitchen, and the test results of a selection of recipes that have been tried at the Watkins Woolen Mill Historic Site Living History Farm Program (North Lawson, MO). Some of the recipes were handwritten, while others were clipped from newspapers.

▶ **Civil War Letters of Lewis Riley**
http://whmc.umsystem.edu/invent/0326.html

The Riley Papers consist of letters written between 1862 and 1863 by Lewis Riley, a 6th Missouri Union cavalryman, to his wife, Anna Little Riley. In these letters he describes battles and scrimmages, particularly those at Vicksburg (MS), Memphis (TN), and Little Rock (AK), and the state of morale in his unit at that time. The entire collection is housed at the Western Historical Manuscript Collection-Columbia.

▶ **Hezzie Goes to War: World War I through the Eyes of a Mid-Missourian**
http://anthromuseum.missouri.edu/pattrickwwi/default.shtm

Acquire an understanding of what it was like to be a soldier during World War I through the letters and postcards John Hezekiah ("Hezzie") Pattrick wrote and the photographs he sent to his parents. Read a biography of Hezzie, who was born on December 24, 1888, and view other images, such as his "American Expeditionary Forces Identity Card."

▶ **Ticket to the Past: The First 25 Years of the Missouri State Fair**
http://www.sos.mo.gov/archives/exhibits/StateFair/

Life was an economic hardship for Missouri farmers around the turn of the twentieth century, and many left their farms to find work closer to the cities. To ease their minds about all the modern farming technology being developed, such as gasoline-powered tractors, the state's legislators held the first Missouri State Fair in 1901. This online exhibit consists of a selection of advertisements, premium lists, posters, and photos of attractions such as "Ruth Law's Flying Circus" (1921), the "Koalhou Hawaiian Singers" (1922), and "Jimmy Costa in his Fiat" (1921). Also included is a link to an interactive lesson for elementary teachers.

University of Missouri Digital Library
http://digital.library.umsystem.edu/

Since 2001, the University of Missouri Digital Library has been digitizing and providing access to items on behalf of the University of Missouri Libraries. This website contains 30 text collections and 36 image collections and provides links to other online collections within the state, including the Missouri Historic Newspapers repository. All the collections can be browsed or keyword searched. A few of the collections are highlighted here.

▶ **4th of July Speeches**
http://digital.library.umsystem.edu/cgi/t/text/text-idx?page=home;c=jul

The collection contains published pamphlets of Fourth of July addresses made between 1791 and 1925. The focal points of the speeches are varied and include the Revolutionary and Civil Wars, westward expansion, politics, and the fiftieth and one-hundredth anniversaries of the Declaration of Independence.

▶ **Joplin 1902 Picture Booklet**
http://digital.library.umsystem.edu/cgi/i/image/image-idx?page=index;c=jplpb02ic

This booklet contains 125 photographs that show the city of Joplin circa 1902. Images include private residences, businesses and industries, schools, and churches.

▶ **Lloyd L. Gaines**
http://digital.library.umsystem.edu/cgi/t/text/text-idx?page=home;c=gnp

The correspondence, photographs, and other primary and secondary materials in this collection are related to the 1938 court case *State of Missouri ex rel Lloyd L. Gaines v. Canada*. Lloyd Gaines disappeared in 1939 shortly after winning his Supreme Court civil rights case against the University of Missouri School of Law.

Montana

Maureen and Mike Mansfield Library Digital Collections
http://www.lib.umt.edu/digital

This website of the Maureen and Mike Mansfield Library (University of Montana) provides access to a handful of special collections and digitized books. Several are featured here.

▶ **Archives & Special Collections Regional and Historic Maps**
http://www.lib.umt.edu/asc/historicmaps

This collection of over 120 maps focuses on the northwestern section of Montana, particularly Missoula and nearby towns, in the late nineteenth and early twentieth centuries.

▶ **The Char-Koosta News**
http://skclibrary.skc.edu/?q=node/8

Serving as "an attempt to increase communication between the tribal members on and off the reservation as well as among other United States Indian Tribes and whites," the *Char-Koosta News* has, except for a ten-year hiatus from December 1961 through May 1971, continuously published a weekly issue since 1956. The newspaper is published by the Confederated Salish and Kootenai tribes of the Flathead Indian Reservation.

▶ **Harold Wave Whicker Collection**
http://www.lib.umt.edu/asc-whicker

This small collection contains books, manuscripts, and personal missives by such authors as Robert Browning, Henry Wadsworth Longfellow, and Samuel Taylor Coleridge. The collection also contains a preliminary version of Elizabeth Barrett Browning's poem "Human Life's Mysteries." Browse the entire collection, or search by author name.

▶ **Leeson's History of Montana 1735–1885**
http://www.lib.umt.edu/node/336

First published 125 years ago, Leeson's *History of Montana* is a wealth of information about the history of Montana from 1735 to 1885. This website contains a scanned version of the book. Chapter titles include "Exploration and Occupation," "Gold and Silver Mining," "The Secret Tribunal of Montana," and "Navigation of the Missouri and Yellowstone." The book also contains many individual memories and over 500 illustrations.

▶ **Progressive Men of the State of Montana**
http://forms.lib.umt.edu/gsdl/cgi-bin/

This website contains a scanned version of *Progressive Men of the State of Montana*. Originally published over a century ago, this book contains over 2,500 biographies of prominent people in Montana history between the 1850s and 1900. The book can be searched through dropdown menus from the links "Name," "County," "City," "Occupation," and "Illustration" across the top of the page. The "Search" link does not search the text of biographies, just the words in all indexes.

▶ **The Walter Bone Shirt Ledger**
http://www.lib.umt.edu/digital/walterboneshirt

This website features the drawings of Walter Bone Shirt, a Brule Lakota, in the 1890s.

Montana Memory Project
http://cdm15018.contentdm.oclc.org/

The Montana Memory Project is a collaborative effort among educational institutions, museums, archives, libraries, and other cultural institutions around the state to provide online access to materials pertaining to Montana's cultural heritage and government. New content is continually being added, including digitized newspapers, historic documents, diaries, oral histories, audio and video clips, and visual renderings. The database can be browsed or searched by keyword across one or more of the 39 collections.

Montana State University Libraries Digital Collections
http://www.lib.montana.edu/digital/

In addition to providing access to theses and dissertations, Montana State University Libraries has three other special collections.

▶ **Indian Peoples of the Northern Great Plains**
http://www.lib.montana.edu/digital/nadb/

The images in this unique database come from three Montana State University campus library collections (Bozeman, Billings, and Havre), the Museum of the Rockies, and Little Big Horn College. In addition to photographs are ledger drawings, serigraphs, and paintings. Six search links in the left menu are "Subject," "Date," "Biographical," "Location," "Tribal," and "Artist/Photographer." Four collection links are "Barstow Ledger Drawing Collection," "Blackfeet Indian Tipis/Design and Legend," "Tipi Serigraph Prints by Jessie Wilber," and "1874–1875 Treaty."

▶ **James Willard Schultz Photographs Collection 10**
http://arc.lib.montana.edu/schultz-0010/

James Willard Schultz (1859–1947) was a noted Montanan author. The Schultz Collection contains photographs of his family, Native Americans, Glacier and Waterton Lakes National Parks, and scenic views of Montana, Wyoming, and Arizona. The collection also contains works by photographers H.T. Cowling and T.J. Hileman of Kalispell. This collection of more than 500 images can be browsed by keyword, title, date, or item number.

▶ **Thomas Brook Photographs Collection 771**
http://arc.lib.montana.edu/brook-0771/

Thomas Brown Brook (1890–1966) Photograph Collection 771 contains over 1,000 nature and scenic photographs of southwest Montana, with a special focus on Madison and Beaverhead Counties. The collection can be browsed by keyword, title, genre, and date.

Nebraska

Nebraska State Historical Society—Collections Treasures
http://www.nebraskahistory.org/museum/collect/treasures.htm

View a number of images of selected artifacts owned by but not currently on display at the Nebraska State Historical Society. Artifacts include World War II posters; a batik map of Nebraska; a turtle bone necklace that belonged to Young Spotted Tail, a son of the Brulé Lakota Chief Spotted Tail; inaugural ball gowns worn by several governors' wives; illustrations and sketches of John Falter, who was elected to the Illustrator's Hall of Fame in 1976; and an 1815 Indian commission signed by William Clark of the Lewis and Clark Expedition.

Nebraska Treasures from the Library/Archives
http://www.nebraskahistory.org/lib-arch/research/treasures/index.htm

View photographs, maps, manuscripts, books, and other materials documenting Nebraska's history collected over the past hundred years by the Nebraska State Historical Society. The unique collections include historical materials about Nebraska's Indians, territory, and life during the late 1800s. The collections are good for primary source material. A few are mentioned here.

▶ **Exaggeration Postcards**
http://www.nebraskahistory.org/lib-arch/research/treasures/exaggeration_
postcards.htm

These "exaggeration" postcards from 1910 to the 1950s were used to humorously promote agriculture and wildlife in Nebraska. View images of huge vegetables and a giant grasshopper, among others.

▶ **John Gregory Bourke Photographs of Native Americans**
http://www.nebraskahistory.org/lib-arch/research/treasures/bourke_photos.htm

View original photographs of Indians taken by John Gregory Bourke, a second lieutenant with the Third U.S. Cavalry. Bourke served during the Indian wars (1871–1883) but became sympathetic and later fought for Indian rights.

▶ **Native American Baseball Teams Photographs**
http://www.nebraskahistory.org/lib-arch/research/treasures/native_baseball.htm

View several photographs of Native American baseball teams.

▶ **Nebraska Territory Map, about 1854**
http://www.nebraskahistory.org/lib-arch/research/treasures/nebraska_territory_
map.htm

View this historical map of the Nebraska Territory, which was organized and opened for settlers with the Kansas/Nebraska Act in 1854.

▶ **Susan Bordeaux Bettelyoun Autobiography**
http://www.nebraskahistory.org/lib-arch/research/treasures/cheyenne_outbreak
.htm

Read pages from the autobiography of Susan Bordeaux Bettelyoun (born in 1857 to fur trader James Bordeaux and Huntkalutawin, a Brulé Lakota woman) that describe the Cheyenne Outbreak from Fort Robinson, Nebraska, in 1879.

▶ **Wild Bill Hickok Court Documents**
http://www.nebraskahistory.org/lib-arch/research/treasures/wild_bill_hickok.htm

Read the original court papers documenting the Hickok/McCanles dispute over a land purchase that ended with Hickok killing McCanles in 1861.

Nebraska Western Trails
http://www.nlc.state.ne.us/westerntrails/

View artifacts, maps, photographs, documents, postcards, and paintings from the Western Trails Project. This website is a primary source for Nebraska history from the holdings of museums and libraries across the state. The "Photo Galleries" link offers photographs depicting early transportation, including stagecoaches, horses, and mules; and photographs of Chimney Rock, a National Historic Site. One exhibit features the Lincoln Highway, the nation's first transcontinental highway. The site also includes lesson plans for teachers.

Nevada

Buckaroos in Paradise: Ranching Culture in Northern Nevada, 1945–1982
http://memory.loc.gov/ammem/collections/buckaroos/

View over 40 motion pictures produced from 1945 to 1965 and more than 25 sound recordings telling the story of the buckaroos and what work and life were like on the Ninety-Six Ranch. The documentation was gathered primarily for the Paradise Valley Folklife Project (1878–1982) of the Folklife Center of the Library of Congress. The website also contains over 200 photographs dating from 1870 to 1958 and historical and cultural information portraying ranching in northern Nevada.

Discover Nevada History
http://nsla.nevadaculture.org/index.php?option=com_content&view=article&id=660
&Itemid=441

This website of the State Library and Archives division of the Nevada Department of Cultural Affairs offers a wealth of historical information about Nevada. Many links lead to historical records of the territory and to over 100,000 images of Nevada people and places that provide visual information that complements the documentation. Explore the links to find gems such as "Nevada Riches: The Land and People of the Silver State," a multimedia presentation.

Oroitzapenak Memories: Voices from Basque America
http://basque.unr.edu/oralhistory/

A series of interviews was recorded with Basque people living in the western United States as an oral history research project called "Oroitzapenak Memories." This website shares the language and experiences of the Basque people through a collaborative project between the University of Nevada, Reno, and the Basque Museum and Cultural Center in Boise, Idaho. Select from a list of interviews and go back in time to hear what life was like for the Basque people. A few of the interviews are in the Basque language. For example, the link "Richard Gabica" offers three recorded interviews, *Early Experience with Sheepherding and Camp Tending*, *Transition from Sheep to Cattle Ranching*, and *Narration about Family's Fox Farm*. All three recordings are in English. Richard talks about his family history, the lifestyle of Basque sheepherders, and the sheep industry during the Great Depression, and pictures show his wedding and the Reynolds Creek Ranch in Idaho. Also view a sampling of 41 colorful and interesting posters advertising Basque festivals, clothing, and customs.

Three Historic Nevada Cities: Carson City, Reno, and Virginia City—A National Register of Historic Places Travel Itinerary
http://www.nps.gov/history/nr/travel/nevada/welcome.htm

Read all about the history of Carson City, Reno, and Virginia City. Select "Click Here to Proceed to Introduction" to view texts, photographs, images, and embedded links to important sites and maps.

University Digital Conservancy
http://contentdm.library.unr.edu/

Eighteen online collections in the Digital Conservancy (maintained by the University of Nevada at Reno) contain images and text relating to the history of Nevada. Collection links include "Sheep Industry of Northern Nevada," which contains over 500 photographs to accompany the *Sheepherders of Northern Nevada* online exhibit; "Sagebrush Vernacular," comprising photographs of barns, ranch bunkhouses, and other buildings found in the Nevada countryside; and "Arborglyphs on Peavine," showing photographs of arborglyphs on aspen trees on Peavine Mountain in Reno.

University of Nevada Las Vegas (UNLV) Digital Collections
http://digital.library.unlv.edu/

UNLV hosts a number of digital collections containing maps, images, documents, oral histories, and audio and video clips. Select "List of Collections" or "View Items by Format" or enter a term in the search bar. Collection links include "Nevada Test Site Oral History Project" (2008), which documents the era of Cold War nuclear testing at the Nevada Test Site through nearly 200 full-text searchable transcripts and audio clips; "Showgirls" (2007), composed of colorful illustrations of costumes, texts, photographs of famous Las Vegas shows, and the story of Jean Devlyn, a producer and choreographer of Las Vegas shows in the 1950s; "Early Las Vegas" (2003), containing six galleries of historical photographs; "Howard Hughes"; and "Menus: The Art of Dining."

New Hampshire

University of New Hampshire Library Digital Collections
http://www.library.unh.edu/diglib/

These collections contain materials from state libraries and government agencies and include documents, maps, and images. Selected links include "Historic USGS Maps of New England and New York," containing 1,500 maps from the 1890s to the 1850s; *Northern Junket*, a magazine containing riddles, recipes, and tunes for square and folk dances; "Atlas to Accompany the Report on Geology of New Hampshire, 1878," with views of the roads and places that were settled in the 1870s; "The Boy Made of Meat," a poem by W.D. Snodgrass; "New Hampshire History Bookshelf," containing the State and Provincial Papers of New Hampshire (going back to the 1600s); and *Augustus Ayling's Revised Register of the Soldiers and Sailors of New Hampshire in the War of the Rebellion, 1861–1866* (published in Concord, NH, in 1895), containing personal information on soldiers, unit histories, and historical information on New Hampshire's involvement in the Civil War.

New Jersey

New Jersey Department of State—Imaged Collections
http://www.njarchives.org/links/imgcollections.html#military

This website contains over 4,600 images, photographs, and manuscripts. Select "Searchable Databases" in the left menu to access marriage records from 1665 to 1799, death records from 1878 to 1886, and several other unique sets of records. Select "Imaged Collections" to access hundreds of photographs of soldiers, historic structures and parks, New Jersey institutions, military service records, and slave records.

New Jersey Digital Highway (NJDH)
http://njdigitalhighway.org/index.php

The NJDH offers a number of ways to search the collections provided by New Jersey libraries, organizations, foundations, and other organizations. Click "Advanced Search" to view an alphabetical list of institutions and from there limit a search by the type of resource (text, image, audio, video, or all). Links in the top menu, "Librarians & Curators," "Educators," and "Students," provide results by audience. Materials included throughout are biographies, oral histories, photographs, letters, scrapbooks, interviews, postcards, written histories, and paintings, to name a few. This is a great site for research. Sample collections are mentioned here.

▶ **Grover Cleveland Birthplace Historical Site**
http://njdigitalhighway.org/search/results.php?searchtype=simple&query=&field=object&booltype=OR&query2=&field2=object&format=& timeperiod=&orderby=relevance&maxnum=10&collection[0]= rucore00000002020

Grover Cleveland (twenty-second and twenty-fourth president of the United States) was born in New Jersey in 1837. This collection contains important papers, letters, some photographs, and telegrams from Roosevelt and other important figures upon Cleveland's death.

▶ **Jersey City Free Public Library**
http://njdigitalhighway.org/search/results.php?searchtype=simple&query=&field=
    object&booltype=OR&query2=&field2=object&format=& timeperiod=
    &orderby=relevance&maxnum=10&collection[0]= rucore00000001042&
    collection[1]=JCDC

This website presents materials involving the first European immigrants to New Jersey. It was the Dutch who established what now is Jersey City. One very interesting item in this website is an electronic version of the book *The History of the Reformed Church at Peapack, N.J. with Biographical Sketches*, written in 1881. There are similar church histories available as well. Other materials are property deeds, photographs, and documents, for example, the genealogies of founding families.

New Mexico

New Mexico Office of the State Historian
http://www.newmexicohistory.org/

This website is meant to be much more than a digital collection. Its narrative focuses on the history of the state, and it contains many interactive areas to explore and enjoy. The ultimate goal is to be a resource for educational purposes. To search the digital content, click "Resources" in the bottom menu bar, and choose "Advanced Search" to see the search page. A basic keyword search box is available, along with a dropdown menu to choose the type of resource desired. Textual, audio, video, and image content is accessible directly from the site.

New Mexico's Digital Collections
http://econtent.unm.edu/

This website is hosted by the University of New Mexico and has content from both the university as well as several other statewide institutions, including the Institute of American Indian Arts and the Silver City Museum. The focus is primarily on the history and culture of New Mexico, with some specific materials on land and water issues. The homepage has a list of contributing partners, and scrolling across each name under "View by Repository" provides links to the separate collections contributed. Scrolling over "View by Subject" provides broad category links to help new users get started. Over 40 collections can be browsed one at a time, or an advanced search tool can be used to search multiple databases. Content has full metadata and descriptions.

New York

Digital Metro New York
http://cdm128401.cdmhost.com/index.php

This website is a collaborative effort to support digitization projects of collections held by METRO member libraries in New York City and Westchester County. A list of specific collection titles and institutions is found by selecting "Browse" and then clicking on the dropdown box or by selecting "Advanced Search." Materials include World War II scrapbooks, three volumes of an eighteenth-century Prague bible (the Torah,

Nevi'im [Prophets], and Ketuvim [Hagiographa]) from Yeshiva University, and many other texts, photographs, and illustrations.

Hamilton College Library Digital Collections
http://elib.hamilton.edu/hc/hc-main.php?id=col_home

Hamilton College (Clinton, New York) hosts unique collections for researchers, teachers, and anyone else interested in the history of the area. Collections include images and manuscript materials related to Rev. Samuel Kirkland (1741–1808), founder of Hamilton College (click "College Archives" to access); photographs, images, and documents pertaining to the history of the Shakers (click "Communal Societies"); Civil War documents, letters, diaries, and photographs especially as they relate to the 117th New York Volunteer Infantry Regiment mustered in on August 8, 1862, in Oneida County (click "Civil War"); and video recordings of interviews with jazz musicians, arrangers, writers, and critics (click "Jazz Archive").

Hudson River Valley Heritage
http://www.hrvh.org/

Discover the history of the New York Hudson River Valley through photographs, documents, maps, audio and video clips, and other materials. This is a great resource for teachers and history buffs. The homepage contains a slide presentation and links to a featured exhibit and a featured collection. Click "Explore HRVH" to use dropdown boxes to search by topic, county, or format. For example, click "Audio/Video" in the format dropdown box to access *Backyard Breweries*, a sound recording on how wine was made, or the *Alfred Terwilliger Oral History Interview*. Additional search options include browsing by collection, contributing organization, corporate name, personal name, location, or collection across New York State. For example, the exhibition *The Missing Chapter: Untold Stories of the African American Presence in the Mid-Hudson Valley*, which includes lesson plans and support documents, images, newspaper clippings, and history of slavery in the Hudson River Valley, was found by browsing the collections and exhibitions section. This site is a wonderful resource on the heritage of New York State.

Long Island Memories
http://www.longislandmemories.org/

Long Island Memories is the website of the Long Island Resources Council, a collaborative digitization effort of libraries, museums, and archives to capture and make accessible visual and oral records of Long Island's history and culture. A number of formats (text, graphics, postcards, audio and video clips, and photographs) are represented. Enter a term in the search box, or select one of the links based on collection type, such as historical documents, genealogies, newspapers, and audio and video materials. Because this website is part of an ongoing project, some of the pages are under construction. However, the "New York State Archives Digital Project" link provides access to a number of established collections, such as New York State Canal System, Factory Investigating Commission, and Governors of New York.

New York Heritage Digital Collections
http://www.newyorkheritage.org/

Explore hundreds of wonderful digital collections maintained by a number of New York colleges, historical societies, archives, libraries, and museums. The homepage contains a slide presentation of photographs representing the rich history and heritage of New York State. The link "Browse by Collections" reveals a long list of institutions that have contributed material. "Other Digital Resources" leads to further collections under the categories of institutional repositories, historical newspapers, teaching resources, and digitization standards and best practices. Explore this site for the numerous individual collections too many to mention here.

New York Public Library Digital Gallery
http://digitalgallery.nypl.org/nypldigital/explore/dgexplore.cfm?topic=all

The New York Public Library maintains a number of digitized collections reflecting the culture and history of America as well as other countries. Visit the site for a full list. Several examples are mentioned here.

▶ **Africana & Black History**
   http://digitalgallery.nypl.org/nypldigital/explore/dgexplore.cfm?topic=all&col_id=147

   Learn about African-American experiences through more than 11,000 images of historical documents and rare photographs, dating back to the sixteenth century.

▶ **After Columbus: Four-Hundred Years of Native American Portraiture**
   http://digitalgallery.nypl.org/nypldigital/explore/dgexplore.cfm?topic=all&col_id=182

   Learn about the history and culture of Native Americans. View almost 400 prints and drawings by Simon van de Passe, George Catlin, Karl Bodmer, and other artists dating from 1627 to the 1830s.

▶ **"America's National Game": The Albert G. Spalding Collection of Early Baseball Photographs**
   http://digitalgallery.nypl.org/nypldigital/explore/dgexplore.cfm?topic=all&col_id=198

   View this wonderful collection of over 500 photographs, prints, drawings, caricatures, and illustrations related to baseball and other sports gathered by the early baseball player and sporting-goods tycoon A.G. Spalding. The collection includes studio portraits of players and teams of the day, rare images, photographs, and original drawings from the mid-1800s to about 1914.

▶ **Ellis Island Photographs from the Collection of William Williams, Commissioner of Immigration, 1902–1913**
   http://digitalgallery.nypl.org/nypldigital/explore/dgexplore.cfm?topic=all&col_id=165

   View almost 100 photographs relating to Ellis Island and immigration into the United States in the early twentieth century. Select "Collection Contents" and then "Photographs of Ellis Island" or "William Williams Papers" to access the content. Each image has accompanying information.

▶ **Lewis Wickes Hine: Documentary Photographs, 1905–1938**
http://digitalgallery.nypl.org/nypldigital/explore/dgexplore.cfm?topic=all&col_id=175

View over 500 silver gelatin photographic prints depicting American social conditions and labor, immigration at Ellis Island, and construction of the Empire State Building. Each image has detailed information.

▶ **Photographic Views of New York City, 1870s–1970s**
http://digitalgallery.nypl.org/nypldigital/explore/dgexplore.cfm?topic=all&col_id=219

This collection contains almost 35,000 photographs of New York City from the 1870s to the 1970s. Select "Collection Contents" and then "Photographic Views of New York City, 1870s to 1970s" or "Photographic Views of New York City, 1870s to 1970s, from the Collections of the New York Public Library" to access the photographs. Each subcollection can be limited by borough and street by selecting "Source Titles."

▶ **Picturing America, 1497–1899: Prints, Maps, and Drawings Bearing on the New World Discoveries and on the Development of the Territory That Is Now the United States**
http://digitalgallery.nypl.org/nypldigital/explore/dgexplore.cfm?topic=all&col_id=190

View over 2,000 original drawings, prints, and maps featuring American towns and cities, events, places, and battles in American history from 1497 to 1899 taken from Gloria Gilda Deák's book. Select "See All Images" to view items with descriptions. In the search bar next to "Search Collection" type in "New York" to limit to over 1,000 items related to New York.

New York State Archives—Where History Goes on Record
http://www.archives.nysed.gov/a/digital/images/browse.shtml

View digital copies of photographs, documents, and videos by selecting one of the topical links. For example, "Business and Labor" lists the collection Document Showcase—Industrialization and Child Labor, 1880–1937, featuring resources related to child labor. "Environment and Landscape" leads to the Environmental History Collection, containing photographs, maps, and other materials. "Legal" includes Women's Rights in Early New York (1643–1848), a collection of documents comparing women's rights under Dutch, English, and American governments. "Military" includes the collection Harlem Hellfighters, containing images of military records of World War I New York National Guard regiments. "Transportation" includes the New York State Canal System (1827–1925) collection of images of maps, drawings, and other records. "Politics" contains the Governors of New York (1873–1982) collection, with photos and documents related to Grover Cleveland, John A. Dix, Theodore Roosevelt, Franklin D. Roosevelt, Herbert H. Lehman, Thomas E. Dewey, W. Averell Harriman, Nelson A. Rockefeller, and others. "People, Groups, Cultures" leads to the Native American Collection, a collection of documents, artifacts, photographs, and publications documenting the history of native peoples in New York State. Explore the links on this site for many other collections as well. There are also keyword search boxes to sort by documents or images.

Syracuse University Digital Library
http://digilib.syr.edu/

This website provides access to a number of digital collections, each offering a variety of formats and materials. Three of those deemed excellent are mentioned here.

▶ **The Erie Railroad Glass Plate Negative Collection**
http://library.syr.edu/find/scrc/collections/diglib/erie.php

Over 700 images show railroad stations and other railroad structures along the Erie's tracks during the early twentieth century.

▶ **Gerrit Smith Broadside and Pamphlet Collections**
http://library.syr.edu/find/scrc/collections/diglib/gerritsmith.php

Smith, a philanthropist and social reformer, authored circulars, speeches, sermons, and tracts on such topics as abolition, suffrage, temperance, transportation, and the postal system. To view the texts, click "Browse the Collection." Next click on a title from the list, and then click "Access the Item" to view it.

▶ **Medieval Manuscripts**
http://libwww.syr.edu/digital/collections/m/MedievalManuscripts/mainpage/

Ten medieval manuscripts from the thirteenth through the sixteenth centuries are featured. They include an apocalyptic text, glossed papal decrees or edicts of Pope Innocent IV and Pope Gregory IX, a section of the Old Testament (consisting of a fragment of the Books of Tobit and Esther), and a complete Book of Judith. Also view the six Books of Hours.

Talking History
http://www.talkinghistory.org/

Listen to an exceptional collection of audios of speeches, debates, oral histories, and documentaries produced by the University at Albany, State University of New York. The dropdown box "The Radio Archive" allows selection of audio recordings by date. All recordings are extensively described. Examples include *From the Archives: John Steinbeck Interview* (Feb. 11, 1952; currently listed on the homepage) and *Thurgood Marshall as a Litigator in Brown v. Board of Education, 1954* (accessed by selecting "Jan–June 2009"). This website offers a rare and interesting insight into the history surrounding the events discussed.

Throughout the Ages
http://www.archives.nysed.gov/projects/throughout/about.shtml

Throughout the Ages is an online digital resource from the New York State Archives to encourage pre-K to grade 6 teachers to use historical records as learning tools. Click on the link "Social Studies Instructional Strategies and Resources Pre-Kindergarten Through Grade 6" to access extensive materials about curriculum strategies and resources to meet learning standards and detailed information about state assessment tests. Select "Document Index" on the homepage to access Visual Learning Projects arranged by theme, each containing further links to hundreds of images, historical photographs, letters, maps, and paintings. Read historical background information, focus questions, activities, and additional resources.

U.S. Labor and Industrial History World Wide Web Audio Archive
http://www.albany.edu/history/LaborAudio/index.html

This site features audio recordings from several archives but mainly from the University at Albany History Department. View the listing on the webpage and select the links to plenary session speeches or to recordings by important figures such as William Jennings Bryan (1896), William Howard Taft (1906), Woodrow Wilson (1912), Theodore Roosevelt (1912), Tom Mooney (1939), and Fiorello LaGuardia (1945) as they address issues related to labor in the United States. Other recordings include, for example, a two-hour radio interview exploring the career of Sam Darcy (an immigrant from the Ukraine in 1908) in the CPUSA (Communist Party of the USA). He led the largest protest of unemployed workers, was active in organizing longshoremen and farm workers, and was an important figure behind the San Francisco general strike in 1934. The audio recordings give a rare glimpse into this important era in the history of U.S. labor.

North Carolina

Duke Digital Collections
http://library.duke.edu/digitalcollections/index.html

The homepage contains an A–Z list of more than 30 digital collections, each with a brief description of its content. Some of these have content combined in the same database and thus are searchable at the same time; others need to be viewed individually. The collections can also be browsed by subject matter. Subjects include eight photograph collections, African-American history collections, and the history of Duke University and Durham, North Carolina. Also of note are collections of television and print advertisements, a collection of almost 1,400 papyri from ancient Egypt, an American sheet music collection, and a collection of drafts and revisions of Walt Whitman's poetry and prose.

East Carolina University—Joyner Library Digital Collections
http://digital.lib.ecu.edu/collections.aspx

This webpage provides access to more than 25 digital collections. Basic and advanced search tools in the upper right of the homepage allow users to search across all collections at the same time and to limit by format. The materials in the collections come primarily from the holdings and archives of the East Carolina University Library and include an oral history collection of alumni stories, a postcard collection of eastern North Carolina, items reflecting the military and naval history of the area, and other assorted maps and historical information.

Eastern North Carolina Digital Library
http://digital.lib.ecu.edu/historyfiction/

This digital library was created to make available educational materials relating to the history of eastern North Carolina. According to the homepage, the content currently includes full texts of both fiction and nonfiction materials and images of artifacts, maps, and other educational materials. The content can be browsed from the homepage by several criteria, including format, location, title, author, and subject. Only a basic search tool is available, but search results are returned sorted by format for easier browsing. Text viewing is easy, with zoomable views of the item itself available as well as just the text alone.

North Carolina Census Data: 1960–1980
http://statelibrary.ncdcr.gov/dimp/digital/census/index.html

With data supplied by the North Carolina State Data Center, the State Library of North Carolina created this online database to provide access to public state census information. The database contains hundreds of full-text searchable census profiles from the 1960s, 1970s, and 1980s. There are nearly 1,000 individual documents in the collection, and the homepage breaks down the data by demographic categories, including population and housing, income, age, relationship, gender, and occupation. The site also includes a link to the State Data Center's current page, where more recent information can be found.

North Carolina State Archives Digital Collections
http://ncecho.contentdm.oclc.org/cdm4/about.php

The links on this page provide a wealth of data and history about the state. Three large digitization initiatives are featured on the website.

▶ **Black Mountain College Publications**
http://www.archives.ncdcr.gov/bmc_web_page/bmc4.htm (photo gallery)

Black Mountain College was a short-lived institution in Asheville, North Carolina, founded in 1933 and closed in 1957. The school was widely considered experimental and was focused primarily on teaching the arts. The State Archives has a repository of publications and records of the institution and has made a portion of this collection available online.

▶ **North Carolina Family Records Online**
http://statelibrary.ncdcr.gov/dimp/digital/ncfamilyrecords/

This online resource provides birth, marriage, and death information recorded in both newspapers and bibles during the eighteenth, nineteenth, and twentieth centuries. The collection can be searched by keyword, topic, or date. It can also be browsed by location or family name, or the entire content of over 700 items can be browsed at one time using the "Browse Collection" link at the top of the homepage. A link at the bottom of the page allows users to track recent additions to the collection.

▶ **North Carolina Newspaper Digitization Project**
http://www.archives.ncdcr.gov/newspaper/index.html

This collection contains digitized runs of more than 20 news publications from six cities. The more than 4,000 entries can be browsed from a link on the homepage. A "Newspapers Included" link in the top menu bar provides the complete list of publications. Only a basic search tool is available ("Search Collection" in the top menu bar), but the results can be limited by both year and publication name.

North Carolina State University—Special Collections Research Center
http://www.lib.ncsu.edu/specialcollections/digital/title.html

This website of the North Carolina State University Libraries contains an alphabetical list of links to 19 digital collections, each with descriptive annotations. The collections contain thousands of images of photographs and textual materials housed in the university's archives. The collections can be searched by both title and subject, and each can be browsed individually or included in a search performed across all databases. Topics include architecture and buildings around North Carolina, agriculture, and local flora and fauna. The University Archive Photograph Collection is included as well.

Transforming the Tar Heel State: The Legacy of Public Libraries in North Carolina
http://statelibrary.ncdcr.gov/dimp/digital/publiclibraries/

This collection of over 800 items includes scanned versions of materials (predominantly photographs with other ephemera such as postcards, pamphlets, advertisements, etc., sprinkled in) from the Public Library History Files of the State Library of North Carolina. The collection can be searched by date, format, library system, county, or keyword across all fields. The "Project Partners" link details which library systems contributed materials. Images contain full metadata where available.

University of North Carolina—Digital Collections
http://www.lib.unc.edu/digitalprojects.html

This UNC University Libraries digital collections website contains over 60 digital collections. Some contain materials just from the university; others are the result of collaborations among faculty, museums, cultural institutions, and other partner libraries. Collection topics vary from the general (history of North Carolina, Civil War, etc.) to the specific (e.g., an image collection of medieval medical illustrations). Some links lead to other web resources and exhibits, and others go to specific digital content. Click "Search This Site" at the bottom of the homepage to search in one or across all 22 collections that have actual digital content. Some of these are highlighted here.

▶ **Hugh Morton Collection of Photographs and Films**
http://www.lib.unc.edu/dc/morton/

This collection is part of the North Carolina Collection Photographic Archives housed at the Louis Round Wilson Special Collections Library of the University of North Carolina at Chapel Hill. Its subject is the life and times of Hugh MacRae Morton, a prominent politician, businessman, and photographer in North Carolina in the twentieth century. While the entire physical collection contains over 500,000 items, several hundred still photographs were selected for this digital collection and made available for research purposes.

▶ **The MacKinney Collection of Medieval Medical Illustrations**
http://www.lib.unc.edu/dc/mackinney/

This collection includes over 1,000 images from color slides of texts with medical illustrations dating from the sixth to the sixteenth centuries. The images contain full metadata and brief descriptions and can be browsed by a number of criteria, including date, medical subject, and the title of the text including the image.

▶ **Southern Oral History Program**
http://www.lib.unc.edu/dc/sohp/

The Southern Oral History Program has gathered more than 4,000 interviews of prominent southerners to digitally document their contributions to society. Some interviews and related transcripts have been digitized and are available online. These can be browsed by name, occupation, ethnicity, and the subject grouping for which they were chosen to be included (politics, notable North Carolinian, southern women, etc.). Use the dropdown menu under "Browse By" to limit the results this way.

University of North Carolina–Wilmington Digital Collections
http://digitalcollections.uncw.edu/

This website contains 14 collections, primarily focusing on art, digitized by the university's Randall Library. Basic and advanced tools are available to search a single collection only or across all at the same time. "More about our '*collections*'" (below "Our Collections" on the left) lists each collection with a brief annotation of its content. Content includes artworks from public places around the city of Wilmington, newsletter and exhibition catalogs from local museums, student works and other items from the university's collections, and a digital database of text and images relating to military chaplains.

North Dakota

North Dakota State University—Libraries Digital Collections
http://library.ndsu.edu/digital/

The digital collections available here emphasize North Dakota and life on the Northern Plains. Select from the links in the left menu. For example, "Dakota Lithographs and Engravings" contains historical photographs from the Fargo Public Library Collection. "H.L. Bolley Photograph Collection" includes 80 lanternslides taken in 1903 by Professor Bolley as well as the article "Flax Culture," published in the *North Dakota Agricultural College Experiment Station Bulletin* No. 71 (October 1906: 137–214). Collections can be browsed or searched individually or in combination.

State Historical Society of North Dakota—Archives—Digital Resources— Frontier Scout
http://history.nd.gov/archives/frontierscout.html

Frontier Scout was the first newspaper published in northern Dakota Territory. Four issues were published at Fort Union. The newspaper continued publication a year later at Fort Rice. The North Dakota State Historical Society has scanned all known issues and made them available online, beginning with volume 1, number 2, issued at Fort Union on July 7, 1864.

Ohio

Alliance Memory
http://www.alliancememory.org/index.php

Alliance Memory is an interesting website for those who appreciate the history of Ohio. It is divided into individual collections. The Alliance Places Collection contains more than 1,000 photographs of historic buildings, communities, and parks. The Alliance People Collection includes photographs of sports teams, military units, schools, and portraits of Underground Railroad conductors Jonathan and Sarah Haines. The Taylor-craft Collection contains photographs of airplanes manufactured in Alliance, Ohio, from 1935 to 1946. The Voices of Alliance Collection contains oral history sound recordings, video recordings, photographs, and transcripts. Worthy of note is a letter written by William H. Morgan regarding the Olive Poisoning Tragedy of 1919, when seven Alliance residents, including Col. Charles C. Weybrecht, died from botulism poisoning. The site has a search bar, and each image is accompanied by a description.

The Cleveland Digital Library—Virtual Cleveland History
http://www.clevelandmemory.org/SpecColl/cdl/

The Virtual Cleveland History website contains images, maps, postcards, photographs, magazine articles, newspapers, and other items relating to the history of greater Cleveland and the Western Reserve region of northeastern Ohio. This site, originally developed in 1997, is gradually being repositioned to better serve the way local history materials are now being presented by the Cleveland Memory Project and the Ohio's Heritage Northeast collaboration. The resources can be searched by subject, or one can follow links to the homepages of more archives, history departments, historical societies, and other organizations that may not necessarily offer digital collections online. Click "Cleveland Cartography" for maps.

The Cleveland Memory Project—Postcards of Cleveland
http://www.clevelandmemory.org/postcards/index.html

View this wonderful collection of nearly 8,000 postcards depicting many facets of Cleveland, its churches, sights, markets, rivers, cityscapes, aerial views, and other points of interest. Walter Leedy began the collection, and items date back to 1898. Search by keyword or by selecting a subject from a dropdown menu, or browse all at once. Click "Video Tribute to Walter Leedy" to learn more about the collector.

Ohio Memory
http://www.ohiomemory.org/

More than 75,000 primary sources from over 300 archives, historical societies, libraries, and museums recording the history of Ohio can be viewed here. Browse by subject, such as astronauts, to look at photographs of John Glenn, Scott Carpenter, and the Gemini 8 spacecraft. Browse by place within Ohio (and outside Ohio) to read texts from local publications, such as the *Ohio Jewish Chronicle*. Visitors can also browse by contributor, for example, the State Library of Ohio or the Wadsworth Public Library. Searches can be restricted by format, as well, such as manuscripts, photographs, video, newspapers, and archaeological objects. The homepage also contains links to two featured collections. One is the Oral History Collection. From this collection visitors can also access the World War II Oral History Collection and listen to and view over 50 accounts from Ohio residents during the war. Short videos of interviews are accompanied by transcripts in PDF format. One example is a video of women talking about their experiences during the prewar depression.

Ohio's Heritage Northeast
http://www.ohiosheritagenortheast.org/

Ohio's Heritage Northeast is an archive of images, sound recordings, videos, texts, and photographs from several Ohio public libraries, universities, and colleges. Select "Summit Memory" and click on "Browse Collection" to access some of the newest collections added. For example, read the *Wingfoot Clan—Aircraft Edition* (1941–1945) or *Wingfoot Clan—Akron Edition* (1939–1946) newsletters published by the Goodyear Company in Akron for their employees. They contain information about scientific and manufacturing advances as well as the social news of the day. Click "Online Map Room" to view historical maps of Akron and Summit County; "Barberton Churches Collection" to view postcards and photographs of Ohio's churches; and "Civil War Collection" for documents relating to Summit County residents.

Oklahoma

Oklahoma Crossroads: Documents and Images
http://www.crossroads.odl.state.ok.us/

This site consists of selected digital collections from the Oklahoma Department of Libraries. Select the "By Collection" search box and choose from a list of collections, such as 100 Years of Oklahoma Governors, Oklahoma Authors, Oklahoma Postcards, and Cultural Crossroads. Each collection is organized by topic and contains items in a number of formats. For example, Cultural Crossroads includes *Indians of Oklahoma*, an online book of text and images about the Indian tribes of Oklahoma. It also contains a number of radio programs to listen to. Each item has an accompanying description. The Tulsa Race Riot Documents collection contains documents generated by various government agencies regarding the Tulsa Race Riot of 1921.

Oklahoma Heritage Online (OHO)
http://www.okheritage.org/

The OHO website is a project of the Oklahoma Department of Libraries and the Oklahoma Museums Association and offers digital collections documenting the history and culture of Oklahoma. Materials are digital copies of original photographs, documents, and artifacts contributed by a number of Oklahoma cultural institutions. Click "Exhibits" on the homepage and then the "Exhibits" link in the menu at the top of the page. The "Heritage Spotlight" option features the Bray Collection, which contains materials such as U.S. World War II financial records, wartime promotional materials, and other ephemera. The "Virtual Journeys" leads to selected online exhibitions. One of the exhibitions is highlighted here.

▶ ### Newcomers to a Newland
http://www.okheritage.org/check.asp?id=top2-2-10

Listen to five-minute radio programs about Oklahoma history. The programs were produced as part of the Oklahoma Image Project to increase public awareness about Oklahoma's diverse legacy. These interesting and educational short audios include such titles as *The Buffalo–Indian*, about the demise of the buffalo; *Father Urban de Hasque–Belgian*, about a Catholic priest; and *Orphan Train*, about the trains that brought over 100,000 abandoned children from various east coast cities to Oklahoma from 1855 to 1904 through the efforts of Charles Loring Brace. Other radio programs associated with Oklahoma history include *Francisco Valdez Zamudio–Mexican, Bill Pickett–Black, Edward Everett Dale, Roberta Lawson–Delaware Indian, Samuel Worcester–English, Wild Mary Sudik–Gas Well, Joseph Danne–German, Alex Posey–Creek Indian, Boley–Black Town,* and *Joe Abraham–Lebanese.*

Oklahoma State University Electronic Publishing Center
http://digital.library.okstate.edu/

Oklahoma State University created a digital library of information about the university and the state of Oklahoma. A sampling of the collections includes Oklahoma Today, which presents over 50 years of issues of the state magazine *Oklahoma Today*; and From Warrior to Saint, featuring the letters and photos of David Pendleton Oakerhater to tell the story of Making Medicine, a Cheyenne warrior who became the first Oklahoman to be added to the Episcopal Church's calendar of saints.

Rosie the Riveters
http://www.rose.edu/EOCRHC/Rosie-Index.htm

The Rosie the Riveters website is a collection of interviews with women who worked in the defense factories during an important period of time and need in the United States. Women filled the gap in the workforce while men served in World War II. Some photographs accompany the interviews conducted as part of an oral history project of Rose State College.

University of Oklahoma Libraries—Western History Collections
http://libraries.ou.edu/locations/?id=22

The University of Oklahoma makes available its collections related to the history of the American West, particularly the trans-Mississippi West and Native American cultures. Links on the homepage include "Photographic Archives Division," which focuses on Native Americans, Oklahoma land openings and subsequent settlement, outlaws and lawmen, the cattle trade, and other themes during 1870–1940; "Transportation Manuscripts," which cover the 1860s to 1980s; "Doris Duke Collection"; "Indian Pioneer Papers"; "Native American Manuscripts"; and "Our Sooner Heritage." Two online exhibits feature items in the W.S. Campbell Collection and in the B.M. Bower Collection, including texts, photographs, illustrations, and drawings.

Oregon

Baker County Oregon Library—Directory of Online Digital Archive Collections
http://www.bakerlib.org/webphoto/links.htm

This is a portal to online collections from archives, museums, and other institutions that feature Oregon or the Northwest. A photo gallery in the left menu can be browsed by topical links, including "Baker City," "Small Towns & Ghost Towns," "Mines & Mining," "Transportation & Forest Industry," "People, Schools, Organizations & Churches," and "Scenic, Agriculture, Military, Fire Dept., Sports, & Music." The photo gallery is also searchable by keyword or phrase.

Lewis & Clark College—Digital Collections
http://digitalcollections.lclark.edu/

Lewis & Clark College's Digital Collection is a mixture of photographs, drawings, maps, broadsides, documents, and other items. There are 16 collections, several of which are highlighted here.

▶ **Karl Bodmer American Indian Images**
http://digitalcollections.lclark.edu/cdm4/browse.php?CISOROOT=%2Fbodmer

Karl Bodmer was a Swiss painter of the American West. Between 1832 and 1934 he accompanied Prince Maximilian zu Wied-Neuwied, a German explorer, ethnologist, and naturalist on his Missouri River expedition for the express purpose of documenting the different American Indians they encountered along the way. This collection contains hand-colored engravings derived from Bodmer watercolors found in Lewis and Clark's journals.

▶ **Poetry Broadsides**
http://digitalcollections.lclark.edu/cdm4/browse.php?CISOROOT=/broadsides

The broadsides contain poems by William Stafford, Robert Bly, Charles Simic, and Primus St. John.

▶ **Wood Family Collection**
http://digitalcollections.lclark.edu/cdm4/browse.php?CISOROOT=/erskinewood

From the family of Charles Erskine Scott Wood, a prominent attorney and author (*Heavenly Discourse*, 1927), this collection of over 300 images includes family photographs and original C.E.S. Wood watercolors and sketches.

Oregon Digital: Unique Digital Collections from OSU and UO Libraries
http://digitalcollections.library.oregonstate.edu/

Diverse collections of the Oregon State University (OSU) and University of Oregon (UO) libraries comprise Oregon Digital. Collections include the Braceros in Oregon Photograph Collection, the Pacific Northwest Stream Survey, Rising Flood Waters: 1964 Corvallis, and Linus Pauling and the Race for DNA. The OSU Archives contains more than 275,000 images in over 240 photographic collections. The Oregon Multicultural Archives Digital Collection includes images related to the social life and customs of minority groups living in Oregon. View the collection in one of three ways: select from the A–Z title list of collections, search by keyword, or watch a slide show of selected images and documents from the various collections.

The Oregon History Project
http://www.ohs.org/education/oregonhistory/index.cfm

The Oregon History Project website offers narratives, educational resources, biographies, and an interactive timeline to aid in learning about Oregon's history. Search the collection by keyword or by choosing from preselected lists of format type, subject theme, time period, and regional area. Especially interesting is the "Historic Viewers" link to a small selection of "interactive and layered electronic images."

Oregon Institute of Technology Digital Collections
http://www.oit.edu/libraries/collections/digital

The Oregon Institute of Technology provides access to three digital collections. The Klamath Waters Digital Library contains materials associated with Klamath watershed water issues from the 1800s to the present. The Crater Lake Digital Research Collection is a joint project between the Oregon Institute of Technology Library and Crater Lake National Park, and the Geo-Heat Digital Library contains materials about geothermal energy.

Oregon State Archives—Web Exhibits and Projects
http://arcweb.sos.state.or.us/banners/exhibits.htm

The web exhibits and projects are a mix of documents, images, and photographs. Selected exhibit titles include *Crafting the Oregon Constitution: Framework for a New State*, *Life on the Home Front: Oregon Responds to World War II*, *Sold in Oregon: Historical Oregon Trademarks*, *Historical Travel Photographs*, and *Historical Travel Photographs.*

Salem Public Library—Oregon Historic Photograph Collections
http://photos.salemhistory.net/

The Oregon Historic Photograph Collections website contains thousands of photographs. The Ben Maxwell Collection contains photographs taken by Mr. Maxwell, a well-known Salem photographer and historian. The Statesman Journal Collection photographs come from the files of the *Statesman Journal* newspaper and are principally about the Salem area in the late 1930s through the 1980s. The Oregon State Archives Collection consists of photographs predominantly agricultural in nature. The Marion County Historical Society Collection is a selection of photographs of the Salem and Marion County area spanning from the 1880s through the 1950s. The Special Collections contains photographs from numerous sources. Browse through the collections, or search by keyword across one or more collections.

Southern Oregon Digital Archives
http://soda.sou.edu/index.html

Southern Oregon University's Hannon Library, through a grant from the Institute of Museum and Library Services, created two collections that combined contain over 1,500 documents. The Bioregion Collection features the plants and animals in the Klamath-Siskiyou bioregion in southern Oregon. The First Nations Collection is about Native American tribes in southwestern Oregon and northern California, including the Coos, Hupa, Karuk, Klamath, Modoc, Takelma, Shasta, Siuslaw, Cow Creek Band of Umpqua, Yahooskin, and Yurok. This collection will be expanded to include material on tribes from the Siskiyou-Cascade-Klamath bioregion. A third collection was subsequently added to the website, the Southern Oregon History Collection. This is a diverse compilation of resources about Southern Oregon, many of which highlight Coos, Curry, Douglas, Jackson, and Josephine Counties. Each collection can be accessed through its own "Author List" or "Title List" or searched by keyword, author, subject, year, or title.

Pennsylvania

Access Pennsylvania
http://www.accesspadigital.org/

Access Pennsylvania is a repository of digital collections from colleges and libraries across the state. The participating institutions are listed alphabetically. Click an institution's name to read a description of the materials it provides and links to access them. For example, Pennsylvania Highlands Community College offers photographs of the devastation caused by the Johnstown Flood of 1889. The State Library of Pennsylvania provides materials about Ben Franklin, Abraham Lincoln, and the Civil War, as well as some Pennsylvania historical newspapers. Collections include documents, maps, pamphlets, books, and other materials depending on the collection. Check out each one for its wonderful digital collections.

DEILA: The Dickinson Electronic Initiative in the Liberal Arts
http://deila.dickinson.edu/

DEILA provides access to digital scholarly projects developed at Dickinson College. Select "Projects" for links to the James Buchanan Resource Center's materials (books, articles, cartoons, and other resources) about and by Buchanan, the fifteenth president of the United States. Select "Patagonia Mosaic" in English or Spanish and learn about the "historic experience of the community of Comodoro Rivadavia and its influence nationally and internationally." Select "Virtual Museum" to view photographs of the migrations, lives, and history of these people. Select "Three Mile Island" for information about the emergency incident at the nuclear power plant. "Their Own Words" links to a digital collection of books, pamphlets, letters, and diaries (eighteenth to twentieth centuries) reflecting the history of the United States, including colonial politics, U.S. politics, foreign relations, biographies, slavery and abolition, the Civil War, and the temperance movement. This is a good site for educators and researchers.

ExplorePAhistory.com
http://explorepahistory.com/

This site offers a number of features to explore the history of Pennsylvania. Read about the Gettysburg Campaign, and view photos of Robert E. Lee, Abraham Lincoln, and scenes from the battle. The "Stories from PA History" section offers individual stories, each accompanied by history, photos, images, and historical markers and some also with audio and video clips and maps. Selected story links include "The Indians of Pennsylvania," "The Vision of William Penn," "Set Apart: Religious Communities in Pennsylvania," "The French and Indian War in Pennsylvania," "The American Revolution, 1765–1783," "Underground Railroad," "Crossing the Alleghenies," "Abraham Lincoln and the Politics of the Civil War," "The Gettysburg Campaign," "Pennsylvania Politics, 1865–1930," "Making Steel," "Fine Arts" (gallery of famous artworks), "Pennsylvania Sports," and "Pennsylvania and the Great Depression." The "Visit PA Regions" section features historical sites of interest. "Teach PA History" contains lesson plans for teachers complete with information on academic standards and grade level (elementary, middle, and high school). Materials here include documents, maps, videos, interactives, photographs, and supplementary materials.

Historic Pittsburgh
http://digital.library.pitt.edu/pittsburgh/

This website contains a comprehensive collection of resources supporting research of the western Pennsylvania area. Browse collections categorized by images, text, maps, census records, videos, and chronology for over 300 years. The image collections include over 22,000 images from the archives of local cultural heritage institutions.

Pennsylvania State Archives
http://www.digitalarchives.state.pa.us/

The Archives Records Information Access System (ARIAS) provides access to archival records created by the Pennsylvania State Government. For example, there are digitized records pertaining to veterans of several wars, a Pennsylvania National Guard Veteran's Card File, and Militia Officers' Index Cards for various years.

Rhode Island

American Centuries—Online Collections
http://www.americancenturies.mass.edu/collection/index.html

View over 2,000 artifacts, maps, photographs, documents, and books about Native Americans in and around Rhode Island through the early twentieth century. Items are from the Memorial Hall Museum and represent New England's history. Links include "Civil War Newspaper Index," "People, Places, and Events," and "Highlights of the Digital Collection." Subsections of the "Highlights" include "Art," "Children," "Documents," "Entertainment," "Military," "Religion," "Rituals," and "Work." For information specifically on Rhode Island, type "Rhode Island" in the search box on the homepage.

The National Museum of American Illustration
http://www.americanillustration.org/

View illustrations by many noted artists, such as N.C. Wyeth, Normal Rockwell, Jessie Willcox Smith, and Maxfield Parrish. This virtual exhibit features beautiful pictures and artworks from the "Golden Age of American Illustration" and provides a historical overview of this distinctive society and era. Each selection includes a biography of the artist, photographs, and a sampling of their works.

Reed Digital Collection—Indian Converts Collection
http://cdm.reed.edu/cdm4/indianconverts/index.php

This website offers a rare view into the lives of four generations of Native American Indians, the Wampanoag Indians of Martha's Vineyard and the New England area. Information and images come from the 1727 book *Indian Coverts*, although it is not available to read online. Rather, the website offers study guides containing images of gravestones, artifacts, documents, illustrations, and maps related to the Wampanoags and white settlers. Click the "Study Guide" tab at the top of the homepage and follow the topical links, such as "Children and Education," "Death," "Household," "Island Christianity," "Reading Gravestones," and "Social Hierarchies" to learn about the Wampanoag Indians. Use the "Browse" tab to limit to "Time Periods" (1500s to the twenty-first century), "Geographic Regions," "Ethnic Group," "Religious Affiliation," and "Cemeteries." There are also links to Algonquian texts. This is a great site for educators and students.

South Carolina

Clemson University Libraries Digital Library Initiative
http://digital.lib.clemson.edu/

As part of Clemson University's goal of making available digital content highlighting the institution and surrounding area of upstate South Carolina, Clemson University Libraries currently hosts seven digital collections on its website. The largest four are the photograph collection of James F. Byrnes, noted politician and Supreme Court Justice; a photograph collection of life in Greenville, South Carolina; a postcard collection of scenes from around the state; and an image collection of the covers of the university's football game programs. The total number of items from all collections is currently under 1,000. Click "Collection Descriptions" in the left menu to read more about the collections, or click "Browse All Collections" in the left menu or "Advanced Search" at the top to search through the content.

South Carolina Digital Library
http://www.scmemory.org/index.php

This digital library is a collaborative effort among educational institutions, museums, archives, libraries, and other cultural institutions around the state to provide online access to as much of the state's cultural history as possible to web users. A blog-like news bulletin on the homepage called "Newest Collections" announces new additions, while standard browse and search capabilities are available to dig through the current content. The best place to start is to click on the "Browse" link at the top. More than 100 current collections can be sorted by person (for notable persons in the state's history), county or region, time period, contributing institution, or media type. The "Browse All South Carolina Collections" link provides an alphabetical list of all collections, and the "Browse Newest Collections" link displays the most recently added collections. Each collection has a link to view all items within, or view the collection homepage to learn more about it. The advanced search tool allows users to do a federated search by selecting or deselecting as many of the individual collections as desired.

University of South Carolina Digital Collections
http://www.sc.edu/library/digital/daccollections.php

The homepage lists more than 60 digital collections in alphabetical order, with descriptions and links to access them. Sorting links at the top of the page allow the list to be streamlined by type of resource (maps, rare books, photos and images, etc., under "Categories"). Search tools vary from collection to collection. Interesting materials include digitized sheet music and the full text of an 1874 anti-marriage speech by Victoria Woodhull, the first woman ever to run for president of the United States.

University of South Carolina School of Law Digital Collection
http://law.sc.edu/digital_collection/

The University of South Carolina School of Law has its own digital collection, which includes images of artwork depicting key persons in the history of South Carolina's legal profession. Sortable both alphabetically and chronologically, the list includes persons as far back as Nicholas Trott (1663–1740), who was Attorney General of Bermuda before becoming Chief Justice of South Carolina by 1703. The most recent image is of James Hodges, former governor of South Carolina (1998–2002).

South Dakota

Digital Library of South Dakota
http://dlsd.sdln.net/index.php

Begin by selecting one of the institutions listed. Each offers a number of interesting collections that in total provide a unique look into the history of South Dakota. For example, one of the collections, The Karl Mundt Archives at Dakota State University, contains a variety of resources about the congressman, such as artifacts, documents, media, photographs, and books. A Civil War diary, provided by the University of South Dakota, was written by a young soldier in 1861–1863 describing his service. Browse each of the collections individually or by institution, or search by keyword across all the collections.

Tennessee

Calvin M. McClung Historical Collection
http://cmdc.knoxlib.org/

This digital library made available by the Knox County Public Library contains a number of photograph collections related primarily to the history of the eastern portion of the state. Click "Browse" in the top menu bar, and then choose an individual collection from the dropdown menu to access all items in that collection. Use the "Advanced Search" link to search across multiple collections. While the collections mostly contain photographs, some full-page scans of textual materials are also included. For example, many of the approximately 300 items from the Women's Suffrage collection are documents. Search results lists can be refined by date, subject, and creator. Individual search results contain detailed descriptions and full metadata.

Nashville Public Library
http://digital.library.nashville.org/portal/

This library website has a digital collections page with access to over 1,600 image, audio, and video files primarily related to the history of the region. Clicking on the rotating images will only provide information on the random image selected. Click "Local History & Info" to view the full collection. Six categories are listed on the main page. Click a category title to browse that set of materials, or use the basic search box to search across all categories. Searches can be limited by material format. For further help, click "Tips on Searching Digital Collections" under "Research Guides & Bibliographies." Individual results can be viewed in small and large scale, with detailed descriptions and full accompanying metadata.

Tennessee Virtual Archive
http://teva.contentdm.oclc.org/

This archive is a project of the Tennessee State Library and Archives to digitize and make available online items from the physical collections. As stated in the "About" link, online content is only a selection of what is available in the physical collections. Click "Collection List" in the top menu to view a list of all available collections, with links to both the collection content and a PDF file of the finding aid to the physical collection if available. There are currently more than 25 collections, many of which focus on the Civil War era and the state's history in general. There are textual and image collections and even a music collection, the Kenneth D. Rose Sheet Music Collection, with music relating to various subjects. Each collection title links to an in-depth description of it. A keyword search box enables searching across all collections, or all items in one collection can be viewed by choosing a collection title from a dropdown list.

University of Tennessee
http://www.lib.utk.edu/digitalcollections/

The University of Tennessee has over 20 digital collections on its library website. Click the "Digital Collections A–Z" link to access an alphabetical list. Then click on a title to read a brief description of it and to use its search feature. Many items are about the university itself, such as catalogs and yearbooks. There are also several donated photograph collections and a fascinating herbarium collection with images and details of many plants native to the state, organized by their taxonomical classifications. This site also links to the Volunteer Voices collection described next.

Volunteer Voices
http://volunteervoices.org/

Volunteer Voices is a statewide initiative to gather resources documenting Tennessee's history and culture and to make them available to both teachers and students as well as the general public. Basic and advanced searching tools can be used, or the collection can be browsed by predetermined topic (25 of them), era (10 time periods), or county or contributing institution (both in alphabetical lists). These options can be found under "Browse the Collection" in the left menu. A basic search for "Tennessee" returned over 4,000 results from all collections combined. Also note the top menu bar on the homepage. Scroll over the individual tabs (e.g., "For Educators") for links to additional Internet sites to explore.

Texas

Austin Treasures: Jane McCallum and the Suffrage Movement
http://www.cityofaustin.org/library/ahc/suffrage/

The Austin Suffrage Association was first begun in 1908 and was followed four years later by the San Antonio Club. Through correspondence, diaries, photographs, reports, flyers, and other resources, the Jane Y. McCallum Papers not only sheds light on McCallum's personal and professional life but also traces the history of the suffrage movement in Texas.

Online Exhibits—Texas State Library and Archives Commission
http://www.tsl.state.tx.us/exhibits/

Learn about Texas and its history through various formats such as photographs, drawings, documents, and letters incorporated into the online exhibits produced by the Texas Library and Archives Commission. The exhibits are listed in newest to oldest order and include such titles as *Hard Road to Texas: Texas Annexation, 1836–1845*, about the nine-year struggle and the culmination that almost did not come about; *The McArdle Notebooks*, featuring the notes, photographs, maps, and personal recollections that Henry McArdle used as the basis for two of his best-known paintings, *Dawn at the Alamo* and *The Battle of San Jacinto*; *Texas Treasures*, a rotating exhibit spotlighting the best of the Texas State Library and Archives; and *Civilian Conservation Corps Plans and Drawings*, a selection from a collection of 3,900 drawings, which are also accessible through The Commons on Flickr project.

Portal to Texas History
http://texashistory.unt.edu/

This website is a gateway to the digital collections of museums, archives, historical societies, and libraries throughout Texas. Over 70 unique collections include numerous resources about the prehistory of Texas through the twentieth century. A few of the collections found here include Agricultural Design: Creating Fashion from Fruit, Vegetables, and Flowers, containing photographs from Weslaco's annual "Birthday Party" fashion shows in which the clothing is made from local produce and flora and modeled by local residents; the Clyde Barrow Gang Collection, with photographs of Bonnie Parker and Clyde Barrow as well as "mug shots, fingerprint cards, wanted notices, and images of their bullet-ridden car"; and the Ruth Scantlin Roach Salmon (1896–1986) Collection, which features photographs of the world champion rodeo performer. Browse through individual collections by clicking on "More Collections" in the "Featured Collection" box. Collections can also be viewed using "Search within the Portal to Texas History," which allows searches to be limited by material type and format.

Tejano Voices
http://libraries.uta.edu/tejanovoices/

Between 1992 and 1999, Dr. José Angel Gutiérrez, a professor of political science at the University of Texas at Arlington, interviewed 77 Mexican American leaders with an eye toward their personal stories of struggle against racial discrimination. Listen to the oral interviews (which require an Apple QuickTime plug-in) or read the transcripts. Search the collection from an A to Z list of the interviewees' names or from an interactive regional map.

Texas A&M Digital Library Digital Collections
http://digital.library.tamu.edu/digital-collections

The Texas Digital Library and the Texas A&M Digital Library have combined their online resources to support and advance scholarly research, teaching, and learning. Historic collections range from football programs (1906–1921) to campus, athletics, student life, faculty members, visiting dignitaries, university and student activities, and other key events. The 300,000 historic images, which are part of the Cushing Memorial

Library and Archives, Texas A&M's photostream collection on Flickr, reflect campus life from 1876 to the 1980s. A few of the collections are highlighted here.

▶ **Geologic Atlas**
http://repository.tamu.edu/handle/1969.1/2490

The *Geologic Atlas of the United States* consists of over 200 folios published by the U.S. Geological Survey between 1894 and 1945. Features of each folio include topographical and geological maps and descriptions of the geology of the area. This website can be browsed by issue date, author, title, and subject or by choosing a folio number from the integrated Yahoo map. A search for "Texas" retrieved ten results.

▶ **Images of a Rural Past**
http://www.flickr.com/photos/cushinglibrary/collections/72157617092580769/

Rediscover rural Texas through this extensive collection of mostly black-and-white photos, the majority of which were taken over a 40-year period from the 1930s to the late 1970s. Previously owned by the Agricultural Communications Office of the Texas Agricultural Extension Service, the nearly 7,000 photographs are in categorized collections such as Poultry Science; Boys and Girls 4-H; Home Industries and Agricultural Planning; Foods, Clothing, and Home Management; and Agricultural Pest Control.

Utah

"Always Lend a Helping Hand": Sevier County Remembers the Great Depression
http://newdeal.feri.org/sevier/interviews/index.htm

This website was developed by honors English students at Richland High School (Utah) as part of the Sevier County Oral History project. Listen to 24 oral histories from residents who lived during the Great Depression in rural areas and on the farms as they recount hard times and small-town life. In addition to "Interviews," from the dropdown menu at the top of the page, choose "Essays" to read two essays by teacher Judy Busk and the students' reflections and advice or "Photos" to view a small selection of the photographs used in the project.

Brigham Young University—Harold B. Lee Library Digital Collections
http://www.lib.byu.edu/digital/#1

Brigham Young University offers a host of digital collections not only about the heritage of Utah but also extending out into the world in a wide variety of formats. Search by subject category, by type of format, or by title name. The Provo Historical Images collection contains over 800 photographs of Provo, Utah, from the 1870s through the 1990s. Letters of Philip II, King of Spain, consists of 176 letters (in Spanish and with an English translation) to Don Diego de Orellana de Chaves, Royal Governor of Spain's northern coast (during the naval war against England and France between 1592 and 1597). Two other great collections include Overland Trails—Trails of Hope: Overland Diaries and Letters, showcasing the writings of early pioneers (1846–1869); and German Maps, a set of topographic maps of pre–World War II Germany.

UMFA: Utah Museum of Fine Arts
http://www.umfa.utah.edu/pageview.aspx?id=25861

The Utah Museum of Fine Arts website provides links to both exhibitions and collections online. Click "Exhibitions" and then "Virtual Exhibitions" to view, for example, *Influences of the Silk Road*, *Patrick Nagatani's Nuclear Enchantment*, and *Splendid Heritage: Perspectives on American Indian Art*. From "Collections" select "Collections Database" and then browse by artist, object type, medium, origin, century, collection, and exhibition or use the search box to search by keyword or name of artist.

University of Utah—J. Willard Marriott Library Digital Collections
http://content.lib.utah.edu/cdm4/digitalcollections.php

The J. Willard Marriott Library offers over 100 digital collections online containing audio recordings, maps, photographs, books, and other materials. Selected collections include Arabic Papyrus, Parchment & Paper Collection, one of the largest collections of Arabic documents with over 770 on papyrus and over 1,300 on paper; Western Soundscape Archive, which features animal and other nature sounds of the West; and Utah Digital Newspapers (18 newspaper titles from the late nineteenth century through 1922), including the *Salt Lake Telegram* (1924–1952) and the *Davis County Clipper* (1967–1971). Browse through the collections or search by keyword through one or more collections.

Utah State Archives and Records Service—Digital Archives
http://www.archives.state.ut.us/digital/index.html

The Digital Archives holds many documents, images, and information related to Utah's Board of Pardons (copies of pardoning documents), Division of Animal Industry (brand books, 1849–1930), Vital Records and Statistics, Lieutenant Governor, Legislature House, and the Governors of Utah Digital Collection (containing governors' papers). A number of additional links lead to similar materials of interest to state historians, occasionally including some images with the texts.

Utah State History
http://history.utah.gov/index.html

Discover the history of Utah from the pages of the Utah State History website. Read about Utah's latest listings on the National Register of Historic Places with photographs, or view an online slide presentation, *Agriculture of Utah*, with great historical photographs of life on the farms. Use the tabs at the top of the homepage to access the links to the materials. For example, click "Learn and Research" to access the links "Explore Utah History" or "Photos" for online photo collections.

Vermont

Digital Collections at Middlebury College
http://middarchive.middlebury.edu/

Middlebury College provides a host of digital collections. Select from a list of individual collections by name by clicking on "Browse" and using the dropdown menu, or simply view over 750 items with a brief description of each. "Advanced Search" allows searching by keyword or phrase across one or more of the collections. Materials include digitized images of rare books and manuscripts (e.g., a letter from Daniel Webster) and video and audio recordings of lectures.

Landscape Change Program
http://www.uvm.edu/landscape/menu.php

The Landscape Change Program at the University of Vermont is a virtual collection of hundreds of images that document 200 years of Vermont's growth. All images are online and free to the public. The almost 40,000 images were created between 1690 and 2010. Select "Search" to access several search options, including an interactive map and a basic search box. Select "Learn" to link to "Educational Resources" (lesson plans, Vermont history, etc.) and "Using Photos" for information on how to use the photos and photo sets.

Vermont Historical Society
http://www.vermonthistory.org/

Among the wealth of resources available on this website are five online exhibits that chronicle various topics in Vermont's history. Select "Museum" and then "Online Exhibitions" to view *Vermont Historical Society*, an online tour; *Rugg Collection*, featuring Harold Rugg's photo galleries; *Faces of Vermont*, showcasing important families or individuals; *Baseball in Vermont*; and *Before the Golden Dome*, about Vermont's State House.

Vermont in the Civil War
http://www.vermontcivilwar.org/index.php

The goal of the organization Vermont in the Civil War is to document those who served in the War of Rebellion by amassing official rosters, published books, diaries, letters, journals, and unpublished diaries. Included is a transcription of George G. Benedict's book *Vermont in the Civil War* and genealogical resources. The "Menu Options" dropdown list provides topical links for searching, such as "Units," "Battles," "Books," "Cemetery," "Collections," and "Medal of Honor." The site is a mix of history, photographs (including gravesites), and articles.

Virginia

Colonial Williamsburg Digital Library
http://research.history.org/DigitalLibrary.cfm

This website, maintained by the Colonial Williamsburg Foundation, contains four sections built from the content of the organization's historical documents. The Manuscripts section contains groups of documents relating to a number of different people in the seventeenth and eighteenth centuries. Research Report Series contains historic maps of the town. The other sections contain digital scans of the colonists' *Virginia Gazette* publication from the eighteenth century (can be browsed by date and index) and of estate inventories from Williamsburg and Yorktown.

George Mason University Libraries Digitized Collections
http://sca.gmu.edu/digitize.html

This website contains 19 collections, the content of which are all drawn from the institution's holdings. Several collections relate to the institution's history, including facilities planning, anniversary celebrations, and sports history. Other collections include maps donated by the C. Harrison Mann family, papers of Virginia state politicians, Richard Nixon 1972 campaign photographs, a database of digitized theater posters, and a database of illustrations published in *Harper's Weekly* during the Civil War, originally drawn by newsmen sent on location by the publisher. Each collection has a separate description and homepage and is searched separately.

School Desegregation in Norfolk, Virginia
http://www.lib.odu.edu/special/schooldesegregation/

This website is maintained by Old Dominion University Libraries, and its content comes from the university's collections. The focus is the *Brown v. Board of Education* ruling in 1954 and its resulting backlash in the Norfolk, Virginia, area, affecting the status of more than 10,000 school children, the largest displacement of any school district in the state. The "About the Project" link in the top menu bar contains detailed information about the technology used as well as copyright guidelines. Most of the items are images of textual materials (several hundred items grouped into about ten different collections), with a handful of oral history interviews available as well.

University of Virginia Digital Collections
http://www.lib.virginia.edu/digital/collections/

The University of Virginia's digital collections are organized into three categories: texts, images, and finding aids. Simple and advanced search options are available within each category and across all categories. To see descriptions of individual collections, click either "Text" or "Images" in the top menu bar. Then scroll down to the "Featured Collections" area for the descriptions. Note that, currently, five of the eight text collections and three of the eight image collections are restricted to the university community and not available to external online users. Of the collections available for public use, image collections relating to architecture and Indian paintings are notable, as are text collections about the westward expeditions of Lewis and Clark.

Virginia Commonwealth University Libraries Digital Collections
http://dig.library.vcu.edu/

This website currently contains more than 15 digital collections. Each one has an icon, short description, and link on the homepage. Or click "Advanced Search" at the top of the homepage for an alphabetical list of all databases. Searches can be conducted in single collections or across multiple collections. Some collections are as small as one item, for example, Confederate Military Hospitals in Richmond; others include oral histories of prominent university persons; and another includes interviews (with audio and video) of prominent members of Virginia's civil rights movement.

Virginia Historical Society—Digital Collections
http://www.vahistorical.org/research/digitalcollections.htm

This historical society created a number of digital collections based on its holdings. Some are online exhibitions, some are finding aids for physical collections, and a number of them contain significant amounts of digitized materials. The website's organization is user friendly. The more than 25 collections are listed on the homepage, and each has a "Browse Collection" link. Browsing is easy, as each item has a description and a thumbnail image. The "Search Collection" link at the top of the homepage allows for limiting to just items with actual online images. There is some overlap in search results, as some items appear in more than one themed collection (i.e., a photograph collection and a Civil War collection). The photograph collections seem to be the largest ones.

Virginia Memory
http://www.virginiamemory.com/collections/

This webpage contains the online collections of the Library of Virginia, which is the state archives. It is one of the best-organized and well-sorted state archives websites. Materials are accessed by the links "Collections A to Z," "Collections by Topic," "What's New?," "Featured Collection," "Virginia Newspapers," "Online Photo Collections," and "Archival Web Collections." The archived collections contain websites related to a particular Virginia theme. For example, the Tragedy at Virginia Tech collection includes websites created by both the state government and the institution to preserve the audios and images that were posted on those sites at the time of the school shooting in April 2007. All collections can be viewed on one page via the "Collections A to Z" link, where all are described and some have additional homepage links. Collections are searched separately. Notable is that RSS feeds are available from this website, including notifications when new collections are added to the Virginia Memory page.

Virginia Tech ImageBase
http://imagebase.lib.vt.edu/

The Virginia Tech University Libraries' Digital Library and Library website includes a number of online finding aids and some in-process digitization of materials. The largest currently available digital resource at the site is the image database called ImageBase. The "Browse" link in the left menu shows the categories into which images have been sorted; images are grouped into a tree format using "folios" and "sub-folios" to narrow the focus. Topics range from history, to architecture, to the Civil War, and some historical images relate to the university. Images have some brief metadata, and copyright is maintained by the Digital Library and Archives at Virginia Tech.

Washington

Central Washington University Brooks Library Digital Collections
http://digital.lib.cwu.edu/cgi-bin/library?a=p&p=home

The Brooks Library of Central Washington University offers 12 unique digital collections. In addition to ones that focus on the university itself, others include six photographic collections, a digital collection of illuminated manuscripts, music newsletters from 1959 to 1997, and materials highlighting the 1977 Washington State Women's Conference.

Eastern Washington University Digital Collections
http://econtent.library.ewu.edu/

The digital collections here contain scanned images of numerous photographs held in private collections as well as in the Archives and Special Collections of the Libraries of

Eastern Washington University. The photos highlight the history of the university, Cheney, nearby Inland Northwest communities, and the Pacific Northwest. The collection can be accessed by browsing, searching by keyword, or selecting one of the 13 individual collections.

Seattle Public Library: Special Collections
http://www.spl.org/default.asp?pageID=collection_specialcollections

The Seattle Public Library has three online digital collections.

▶ **The Alaska-Yukon-Pacific Exposition Digital Collection**
  http://cdm15015.contentdm.oclc.org/cdm4/index_p200301coll1.php?
    CISOROOT=/p200301coll1

  This collection was created in celebration of the one-hundredth anniversary of Seattle's first world's fair, called the "Alaska-Yukon-Pacific Exposition." Artifacts from the Museum of History and Industry as well as other resources make up the collection.

▶ **The Northwest Art Collection**
  http://cdm15015.contentdm.oclc.org/cdm4/index_p15015coll5.php?
    CISOROOT=/p15015coll5

  For over 100 years the Seattle Public Library has been collecting the artworks of Northwestern artists such as Mark Tobey, Kenneth Callahan, Helmi Juvonen, Robert Cranston Lee, and Guy Anderson. This website features the works of 39 artists through selections of their prints, drawings, and paintings. It can be browsed or searched by artist, object, or decade.

▶ **The Seattle Historical Photograph Collection**
  http://cdm15015.contentdm.oclc.org/cdm4/index_p15015coll4.php?
    CISOROOT=/p15015coll4

  This collection contains a selection of over 1,000 photographs that were taken by some of Seattle's earliest photographers. Included among the images are those showing Seattle before and after the Great Fire of 1889, Seattle's waterfront, and a selection of Seattle buildings such as churches, libraries, hospitals, and schools. Browse the collection in one of three ways: by photographer, from a preselected list of keywords, or by decade.

University of Puget Sound Digital Collections
http://www.pugetsound.edu/academics/academic-resources/collins-memorial-library/
  digitalcollections

The University of Puget Sound's six digital collections are an outgrowth of faculty projects and research and are a compilation of images, audios, and videos.

▶ **The Abby Williams Hill Collection**
  http://www.pugetsound.edu/academics/academic-resources/collins-memorial
    -library/explore-the-library/university-archives/abby-williams-hill/

  Abby Williams Hill (1861–1943) was a painter and activist, and this collection is a repository for her paintings and collected works.

▶ **Oregon Missions Collection**
http://digitalcollections.pugetsound.edu/cdm5/Arowse.php?CISOROOT=/omml

The Oregon Missions Collection is a small collection of correspondence among missionaries living in the Oregon Territory, which encompassed Oregon, Washington, Idaho, and portions of Wyoming and Montana, as well as other papers and letters dated from the 1820s to the 1850s.

▶ **Slater Museum of Natural History: Bird Wing Collection**
http://www.pugetsound.edu/academics/academic-resources/slater-museum/
　　Aiodiversity-resources/Airds/wing-image-collection/

Wing images for nearly 70 bird species are available for viewing in this database. Many of the original images have been rephotographed onto a standard background and feature "preening," "straightening feathers," and "cleaning wings."

▶ **Western Washington Flora**
http://digitalcollections.ups.edu/cdm5/Arowse.php?CISOROOT=/
　　WesternWashingtonFlora

This collection contains 168 color photographs of flora found in western Washington.

Washington State Archives—Digital Archive
http://www.digitalarchives.wa.gov/default.aspx

The Digital Archives is a portal to nearly 20 online collections with a combined total number of over 28,000,000 records. Search the collection by choosing an option in the search box: "People Search," "Keyword Search," or "Detailed Search." Searches can be limited by also choosing a record series term for birth, marriage, death, census, military, cemetery directories, naturalization, land, or other records. The "Detailed Search" option also allows limiting by county and title.

Washington State Historical Society—Featured Collections
http://research.washingtonhistory.org/collections/default.aspx

This eclectic group of resources illustrates the history of both the state and its people through such objects as tools, clothing, machines, furniture, toys, household items, American Indian relics, photographs, and manuscripts. Several of the 19 collections are highlighted here.

▶ **American Indian Photographs**
http://research.washingtonhistory.org/collections/indian.aspx

The 68 photographs in this collection were taken between the mid-nineteenth century and the late twentieth century and depict the lifestyles of regional Indian tribes, including the Lummi, Makah, Nez Perce, Skokomish, Tulalip, Wanapum, and Yakama. For example, images show canoe carving, basket weaving, and potlatches. Some of the portraits include Chief Seattle, Chief Joseph, Chief Leschi, and Chief Lawyer.

▶ **Basket Collection**
http://research.washingtonhistory.org/collections/Aasket.aspx

This small collection contains images of baskets, the majority of which were crafted by American Indians, but some were made or used by early European settlers.

▶ **Isaac Stevens Railroad Expedition Lithographs**
http://research.washingtonhistory.org/collections/stevens.aspx

This is a collection of illustrations from Isaac I. Stevens's 1853 *United States Pacific Railroad Survey*. The lithographs were created by artists John Mix Stanley and Gustavus Sohon. Isaac Stevens was Washington's first territorial governor (1853–1857).

▶ **Lewis & Clark Expedition, Roger Cooke Paintings**
http://research.washingtonhistory.org/collections/lcexpedition.aspx

Roger Cooke's 98 drawings were made for the express purpose of appearing on the wayside markers placed along the Washington State portion of the Lewis & Clark Trail in celebration of the expedition's bicentennial.

Washington State University (WSU) Libraries Digital Collections
http://content.wsulibs.wsu.edu/

WSU Libraries' extensive digital collection has six main sections: "Photographs," "Maps," "Media & Documents," "Regional & WSU History," "Native American History," and "New Collections." Search by keyword or phrase, browse all collections, or select from a predefined list of search terms to view the collections.

Washington Women's History Consortium
http://www.washingtonwomenshistory.org/themes/collections/default.aspx

The Women's History Consortium's website is a portal to collections germane to the study of women's history. Items are added by the partner organizations, which are a mix of universities, public libraries, historical societies, museums, and special groups. The website is searchable from the menu on the right, by browsing through the direct links to the individual collections, by institution, or by themed links (e.g., "Women's Suffrage," "Clubs and Organizations," "Elected Women," "Expanding Participation," and "Women's Rights in the 20th Century").

Washington, DC

Collections Search Center, Smithsonian Institution
http://collections.si.edu/search/

The Smithsonian Institution has launched a new Collections Search Center, which currently contains more than 5 million searchable records. Resources such as images, videos, sound files, and electronic journals come from the Smithsonian's 19 libraries, archives, and museums. The collections can be searched by category (type, topic, taxonomy, place, name, culture, language, and datasource) or by the tag cloud of popular terms. Click "About" on the top menu of the homepage to browse by links organized by collection type, for example, "Museum Collections," "Archives Collections," "Research Databases," and "Libraries Databases."

West Virginia

Marshall University Libraries—Special Collections—Digital Collections
http://www.marshall.edu/library/speccoll/digitalcoll.asp

The Digital Collections website of Marshall University Libraries contains a handful of special collections that are accessible online. In addition to an obituaries index and some collections of family papers is the section "Do You Know My Name?" This is a database of unidentified images (mostly portraits), and viewers are asked to help identify the people and places. Images are added monthly and must be browsed through one at a time. There is also a stunning virtual tour of 400 glass pieces in a physical collection donated to the university (click the "Wilbur E. Myers Glass Collection" link).

West Virginia Archives and History
http://www.wvculture.org/history/archivesindex.aspx

This website contains a bevy of information typical of a state archives website, including genealogical records and government information. To access the collections, click "West Virginia Memory Project" in the link list near the bottom of the homepage. A sampling of collections includes one relating to John Brown, a Veterans Memorial database with records of native citizens who participated in foreign wars, and a photograph collection (click "Photos") of over 100,000 images illustrating many aspects of the state's history. Each database is searched separately, with dropdown boxes on the search pages to help users limit results.

West Virginia University Libraries Digital Collections
http://www.libraries.wvu.edu/digitalcollections/collections/

This institution's website contains over 20 collections, several of which are grouped and can be accessed on the West Virginia History and Regional Collection webpage (described separately). Other collections include historical items about the institution and materials from the institution's Rare Books Collection. Items from the Rare Books Collection include a set of engravings called "Boydell's Graphic Illustrations of the Dramatic Works of Shakespeare"; illustrations from the first edition of Dickens's *David Copperfield*; and over 1,000 illustrations from the Mark Twain Collection. Each collection is viewed separately. Click "List All" in the left menu for a comprehensive list, or click "Browse All" to see more detailed information on each collection one at a time. Advance through the descriptions using the left and right arrow icons on the page.

▶ ## West Virginia History and Regional Collection
http://www.libraries.wvu.edu/wvconline/digitalcollections.html

This collection is listed along with West Virginia University's other digital collections, but it is accessed from a separate page. It contains historical materials held by the university. The content is organized into four sections. Three of the sections are "Roy Bird Cook Collection: 31st Virginia Regiment," which contains thousands of image scans of primary sources related to the 31st Virginia Regiment of the Confederate Army; "Patrick Ward Gainer: Child Ballads of West Virginia," which contains sound recordings of British folksongs; and "Drawings of David Hunter Strother," containing more than 600 drawings of this state resident in the 1850s, who was a contributing artist to *Harper's Monthly*. The fourth section contains photographs, currently more than 6,000 of the over 200,000 photographs in the overall physical collections. Images in this section can be browsed or searched by keyword, and they are accompanied by descriptive metadata.

Wisconsin

The State of Wisconsin Collection
http://digicoll.library.wisc.edu/WI/

Learn about the state of Wisconsin and its history through various formats, such as books, photographs, maps, manuscripts, and sound recordings. Under "Materials in the Collection" is a lengthy list of topical links, such as "Great Lakes Maritime History Project," "Historic Fort Atkinson," "A History of Agriculture in Wisconsin," "The Home Front: Manitowoc County in World War II," "The Ku Klux Klan in Northwestern Wisconsin, circa 1915–1950," "Wisconsin Goes to War: Our Civil War Experience," "Wisconsin Local Histories," and the "Wisconsin Pioneer Experience," to name a few.

University of Wisconsin Digital Collections
http://uwdc.library.wisc.edu/index.shtml

The materials on this website are organized by subject, for example, art, ecology, literature, history, music, natural resources, science, social sciences, the State of Wisconsin, and the University of Wisconsin. Click "Collections" on the homepage to access an alphabetical list of digital collections, with short descriptions and links to each. Resources include text-based materials (e.g., books, journal series, and manuscript collections), photographic images, slides, maps, prints, posters, audio, and video.

Wisconsin Electronic Reader
http://www.library.wisc.edu/etext/WIReader/Contents.html

This website offers transcribed stories, essays, letters, and poems that are illustrated and that focus on Wisconsin history from 1835 to 1949. View the timeline identifying a specific title for each period. The earliest manuscript is a journal, *A Canoe Voyage up the Minnay Sotor*, kept by George William Featherstonhaugh in 1835 (and published in 1847). Other manuscripts include the letters of Increase Allen Lapham (1843) in *A Winter's Journey from Milwaukee to Green Bay; Sketches of Wisconsin Pioneer Women* by Florence Dexheimer (1924); and *Wisconsin Authors and Their Works* by Charles Rounds (1918). There is also a gallery of images of people and places and of the University of Wisconsin-Madison.

Wisconsin Heritage Online
http://wisconsinheritage.org/providers.html

The institutions, museums, and libraries that provide content are listed alphabetically on the homepage, and clicking on the institution's name provides access to its digitized collections. For example, click "Marquette University" and then "Checklist of Digital Collections" to access Alfred Hamy's Jesuit Portrait Gallery (Jesuit saints' images and a history). Visit each place and view their individual collections.

Wyoming

University of Wyoming Digital Collections
http://uwlib5.uwyo.edu/blogs/digital_collections/

The University of Wyoming offers a wonderful look into the history of Wyoming and the West through a number of specialized digital collections in various formats. There is some overlap in materials between the collections found in the Wyoming Memory and the American Heritage Center collections. View them both so that nothing is missed.

▶ **American Heritage Center (AHC)—Online Collections**
http://ahc.uwyo.edu/onlinecollections/default.htm

Established in 1945, the AHC has collected nearly 90,000 cubic feet of historical documents and artifacts, including letters, photographs, brochures, and other memorabilia related to the West and Wyoming. Many of these archival materials can be viewed online through the links "Virtual Exhibits," "Digital Collections," and "Audio-Visual Collection" in the left menu. "Digital Collections" provides a long list of individual collections, such as the Charles J. Belden Photographs, containing photos from the 1920s and 1930s depicting life on the ranch, Yellowstone National Park, raising antelope, and other subjects taken by Belden. Exhibitions in the "Virtual Exhibit" include *Jack Oakie Room: QTVR Movie*, *J.K. Moore: Documenting the Wind River Indian Reservation* (photographs), and *Thomas Kennet-Were: Nine Months in the United States*, featuring watercolors by this English artist who traveled through the United States in 1868 and 1869. "Audio-Visual Collections" include motion pictures and audios such as *President John F. Kennedy at the University of Wyoming*, *Buster Keaton in "The Playhouse,"* and *West of Hot Dog Motion Picture* (a 1924 motion picture featuring Stan Laurel, who, on his way to collect an inheritance in the small town of Hot Dog, gets robbed by highwaymen).

▶ **Wyoming Memory**
http://www.wyomingmemory.org/

This is a digital archive of Wyoming's history, containing manuscripts, books, photographs, government documents, newspapers, maps, audio, video, and other resources. Click "Featured Digital Collections" to search by topics ranging from arts and leisure, business and industry, government and politics, history and geography, to science and nature, with audiovisual collections and resources for teachers. A few of the collections found here are Greater Yellowstone Sights and Sounds (click "Science & Nature"), containing images of plant and animal life and the Yellowstone National Park environment; Western Heritage Collection (click "History & Geography"), including images, letters, and documents related to the development of the West; and Guns of Record (click "Business & Industry"), featuring images, letters, and drawings related to the early use of firearms in the West.

Wyoming Newspaper Digital Project
http://www.wyonewspapers.org/

This project makes all newspapers printed in Wyoming between 1849 and 1922 accessible in an electronic format for all users. The full-text pages currently include over 700,000 individual page scans. The contents can be browsed in a directory format by city, county, date, or individual publication title. Choose "Browse by City" or "Browse by County" in the left menu to begin exploring. Once an individual issue is located, the text is viewed using a PDF reader. The "About the Project" link on the right provides more information, including that funding was obtained from the State Legislature. Seven partner institutions (e.g., the State Archives, State Library, State Historical Society, and the University of Wyoming) are listed. On the search help page, contact e-mail and mailing addresses for the Wyoming State Library are provided.

Wyoming State Library Digital Collections
http://will.state.wy.us/exhibits/

The state library has links to online PDF documents that are mostly governmental in nature but may be of use to researchers interested in the state's history and laws. Links include "Wyoming Governor Executive Orders" (sorted by date), "Wyoming Planning Publications" (sorted by county and city), "Wyoming State Publications" (sorted by branch of government and subsorted by department), and "Wyoming-Related Federal Publications" (sorted by branch of government and subsorted by department). There are also links to the Wyoming Newspaper Project and the Wyoming Memory Project, both described more fully earlier in this section.

Chapter 7

Oceania

INTRODUCTION

Oceania is the smallest continent in the world. It includes Australia, New Zealand, Papua New Guinea, and the islands of the South Pacific Ocean that make up Micronesia. Oceania is often called Australia Oceania.

For many countries to become active participants in making digital collections available, collaboration is necessary. Major organizations, such as the International Federation of Library Associations and Institutions (IFLA), are working together to support the development, preservation, and digitization of collections around the world. IFLA offers a forum for sharing ideas, projects, and the latest developments in libraries around the globe. The topics of IFLA's latest conference clearly demonstrate how critical a role IFLA is playing in building a worldwide community for developing access to the collections that contribute to society (IFLA, 2010). Sessions 53 and 76 of the IFLA conference included Oceania, although the information shared during the sessions is not posted on IFLA's website. Ellen Tise (2010: 109), IFLA's president, points out a glaring problem:

> [T]he rapid development of technology has, paradoxically, contributed significantly to improving access and expediting growth and development. However, the paradox lies in the fact that as much as technology has the magnetic capacity of bringing the world's information together and breaking geographic boundaries, it has created the converse effect of creating new boundaries and exacerbating information poverty.

That is, "[t]echnology has created . . . the information gap for example between developed and developing countries" (Tise, 2010: 109). Tise's message resonates with librarians and those involved in developing access to the world's collections and poses a challenge for each nation.

Sharing the cultural heritages of continents, including Oceania, is being achieved by various collaborative ventures. The following is a brief description of The National Library of Australia and Australia's state libraries' collaborative efforts. Both national and state libraries are working together to develop the nation's research information infrastructure in order to provide long-term access for present and future digitizing projects. The National Library is a partner of Project ARROW (Australian Research Repositories Online to the World), which is focused on preserving the repository's metadata for use in open-source software. One example of the digital content being developed is the project "Australian Newspapers Beta—Historic Australian Newspapers 1803–1950," offering access to newspapers covering a period of 150 years from the early nineteenth century (Cathro, 2006). A similar paper project developed by the National Library of New Zealand, "Papers Past," provides access to more than one million pages of digitized New Zealand newspapers and periodicals covering the years 1839 to 1932 (ResourceShelf, 2009). It is part of the New Zealand Digital Content Strategy (NDHA).

Of interest to researchers, educators, and the general public is PANDORA, another collaborative project among the National Library of Australia and Australian libraries and cultural organizations. PANDORA is Australia's online archive of images, video files, sound recordings, and publications. Similar projects are underway through collaborative efforts with the Australian National University. It is through these types of collaborative ventures that it is possible for countries like Australia, New Zealand, and the smaller countries and areas of Oceania to plan similar projects and thus preserve their own individual cultural heritages.

With the rapid growth of such projects on the Internet, one must keep a constant vigil of each continent's and country's national libraries, museums, organizations, and universities' websites to learn when the latest collections become available online. For example, the National Library of Australia and the Australian Public Libraries (APL) are creating a Google-like search engine to access over 1.5 million digital images and 35 million printed items through the Information Australian portal (Wade, 2007).

This chapter reviews websites for the continent of Oceania and for the individual countries of Australia, Fiji, Micronesia (Guam, Kiribati, Marshall Islands, Nauru, and Palau), New Zealand, Papua New Guinea, Samoa and Western Samoa, Solomon Islands, Tonga, Tuvalu, and Vanuatu.

References

Cathro, Warwick. 2006. "The Role of a National Library in Supporting Research Information Infrastructure." *IFLA Journal* 32, no. 4: 333–339. http://archive.ifla.org/IV/ifla72/papers/155-Cathro-en.pdf.

IFLA. 2010. "Full Programme." World Library and Information Congress: 76th IFLA General Conference and Assembly, Gothenburg, Sweden, August 10–15. http://www.ifla.org/en/conferences-programme-print/216.

ResourceShelf. 2009. "New Zealand: Papers Past Adds More Digitized Newspapers." ResourceShelf. Posted July 2. http://www.resourceshelf.com/2009/07/02/new-zealand-papers-past-adds-more-digitised-newspapers/.

Tise, Ellen R. 2010. The President's Page. *IFLA Journal* 36, no. 2: 109–110. http://www.ifla.org/files/hq/publications/ifla-journal/ifla-journal-36-2_2010.pdf.

Wade, Martyn. 2007. "New Customers through New Partnerships—Experience in Scotland and Elsewhere." *IFLA Journal* 33, no. 1: 16–22. http://archive.ifla.org/IV/ifla72/papers/117-Wade-en.pdf.

CONTINENT

Island Jurisdictions Index
http://macmeekin.com/Library/Jurisds/aaaindex.htm

This index of documents is part of the larger website Island Law, which is maintained by Dan MacMeekin, a Washington, DC, lawyer. While at first glance this site looks like a regular online resource for each island/territory/country listed, further examination of the individual pages reveals that the site also links to online documents regarding treaties and agreements related to the history of that island, and in some cases governmental structure and legal documents are also included. It should be noted that many of the online documents linked to by this resource are actually hosted on other sites. For example, the American Samoa page links to a guide to previous court decisions, the Administrative Code (Regulations) and rules of court, and content provided by the American Samoa Bar Association. The index is sorted alphabetically and leads to separate webpages for each locale.

Pacific Islands Legal Information Institute
http://www.paclii.org/

This site is maintained by the School of Law of the University of the South Pacific. It is an online collection of legal documents related to many of the Pacific Islands. Researchers can choose the island of interest from the left menu on the homepage to access links available legal information and documents for that locale. The site appears to be kept reasonably current.

PARADISEC (Pacific and Regional Archive for Digital Sources in Endangered Cultures)
http://www.paradisec.org.au/home.html

This site contains a digital archive of over 2,000 hours of audio and video files capturing the cultural histories of endangered ethnic groups in the Pacific region. Access to the content is somewhat restricted; researchers must submit an access form along with a list of materials they wish to explore. Fees may also be charged for files provided on CDs or DVDs. However, the goal of the archive is to preserve and make available for research the cultural histories of the indigenous peoples of the Pacific region. Users engaged in this research should be able to navigate these permissions without too much difficulty. The initiative is jointly funded by the Universities of Sydney, Melbourne, and New England (New South Wales), the Australian National University, the Australian Research Council, and Grangenet, Australia's Academic and Research Network.

AUSTRALIA

Australasian Digital Theses Program
http://adt.caul.edu.au/

This database is a collaborative effort among a number of higher learning institutions to make all PhD dissertations and Masters theses (and their equivalents) available for research purposes. The content is open to all international users and is sorted by institution, which are listed on the homepage.

Australian National University
http://anulib.anu.edu.au/subjects/ap/digilib/about_digilib.html

The Library of the Australian National University has digitized a handful of texts from its collection, which could be of interest to those researching the Pacific Islands area and the South Seas. The texts are accessed from the link provided.

Australian War Memorial
http://www.awm.gov.au/database/collection.asp

The Australian War Memorial is located in Canberra, Australia, and is dedicated to preserving knowledge of and materials related to Australia's involvement in armed conflicts around the world. Its website contains a collection of unique digital content. In addition to art and photograph collections, there are also digital images of Australian army war diaries from World War I, World War II, the Korean War, and other Southeast Asian conflicts. The search tool will search across all collections, but it can also be limited by individual conflict.

National Archives of Australia
http://naa.gov.au/collection/recordsearch/index.aspx

The National Archives has over 18 million images available for the public to view. However, the digital collection is only a small portion of everything the archives holds. Click the "Scope" link in the left menu for a detailed description of the site's content, including "the full range of Australian Government activities since Federation in 1901, and . . . significant 19th-century records dealing with activities that were transferred from the colonies to the Commonwealth." In addition, there are also the records of prominent persons and the correspondence and decisions of the Australian High Court. Click "Research" in the left menu for a very helpful step-by-step guide explaining how the archives are organized and how to best search them to suit a user's needs.

National Library of Australia
http://www.nla.gov.au/digicoll/

The National Library of Australia has digitized a large portion of its materials as part of an initiative to preserve Australia's culture online. The content is divided by format, and online guides and help pages assist researchers in poring through the vast collection. Individual format collections can be accessed at the following links.

▶ **Audio Recordings**
http://www.nla.gov.au/digicoll/audio.html

The Oral History and Folklore Collection contains more than 40,000 hours of audio files. They include stories, speeches, music, and other sounds of historical note.

▶ **Manuscripts**
http://www.nla.gov.au/digicoll/manuscripts.html

This site provides access to over 8,000 digitized manuscripts, including the papers of Australia's first prime minister, Sir Edmund Barton, and the journal of the HMS *Endeavour* kept by Captain James Cook.

▶ **Maps**
http://www.nla.gov.au/digicoll/maps.html

Over 10,000 map images are accessible, from maps of explorers, to town property maps, to atlases of the stars. The entire list can be browsed, or a search tool can be used to narrow by title, author, subject, and additional fields.

▶ **Pictures**
http://www.nla.gov.au/digicoll/pictures.html

The library contains an extensive Pictures Collection, and digital images of over 120,000 works in the collection are accessible on this website. Images include both actual artworks as well as photographs.

▶ **Printed Works**
http://www.nla.gov.au/digicoll/books_and_serials.html

This site contains over 3,500 online books and serials, including both prominent works as well as some rare items of interest. Government publications and some ephemera like posters and pamphlets are grouped into this category.

▶ **Sheet Music**
http://www.nla.gov.au/digicoll/music.html

Over 12,000 pieces of sheet music from the nineteenth and twentieth centuries are digitized.

Pacific Manuscripts Bureau (PAMBU)
http://rspas.anu.edu.au/pambu/photo.html

This site is the result of a project to copy and preserve materials documenting the history and heritage of the Pacific Islands. Its materials are copied and/or scanned from original items held by the project's participating member libraries. The project itself is based at the Australian National University. Some content is available free to online researchers, including a photograph collection, which is still under construction but already contains several photos from the Islands, most notably Papua New Guinea.

Picture Australia
http://www.pictureaustralia.org/

This site is essentially an Internet tool to do a federated search across the image collections of many participating institutions. Artwork, photographs, maps, and manuscripts are included in the content, as well as audio and video clips when available. Search results pull thumbnail images from different collections together into one list, and clicking on a selected thumbnail will link the user to the website containing that image, where permission to use it can be granted by the participating institution. This is an excellent place to start for researchers who want to maximize the effectiveness of their online searching. To see the list of currently participating institutions, click "To Contribute" in the top menu bar, and then "Participants" in the left menu.

South Seas
http://southseas.nla.gov.au/

This is an online collection of documents relating to European voyages to the Pacific Islands in the eighteenth century. The main area of interest is the first voyage of James

Cook's ship *Endeavor* from 1768 to 1771, which can be accessed by clicking on "Cook Journal" in the top menu bar. The full text of the journals of Cook, along with fellow explorers Joseph Banks and Sydney Parkinson, are available to be viewed and compared and contrasted, showing how various events on the voyage were interpreted differently by the three men. The site is also expected to eventually contain even more maps, atlases, and historical accounts of indigenous peoples, making it a comprehensive resource of the time period.

State Library of Queensland Virtual Exhibitions
http://www.slq.qld.gov.au/whats-on/exhibit/online/

The library has an exhibitions page with more than 20 online postings. The subjects vary from photographs of Queensland's history, to children's books and works, to historic maps dating back to the earliest sightings of Australia by European explorers.

University of Adelaide
http://www.adelaide.edu.au/library/special/digital/

This website provides links to the digital collections of the University, which contain mostly manuscripts and texts. Among the collections are notes and manuscripts of various explorers and even a letter written by former president George Washington to William Vans Murray, a European diplomat who was helping to calm tense relations between the United States and France in 1798.

FIJI

Fiji's Treasured Culture
http://museumvictoria.com.au/fiji/index.aspx

This site is an online collaboration between the Fiji Museum and Australia's Museum Victoria. Images and photographs from both museums are blended with descriptive information to shed some light on various cultural and historical artifacts from the island nation. The content can be browsed by subject areas listed on the homepage, or the entire site can be searched by keyword.

George Handy Bates—Samoan Papers
http://fletcher.lib.udel.edu/collections/bsp/index.htm

This photographic collection is mostly from islands in the Pacific Ocean. The content can be browsed by place or by subject from the homepage. Clicking on "Browse by Place" and then "Fiji" retrieved a list of five images. *See also* GEORGE HANDY BATES— SAMOAN PAPERS *under* SAMOA.

Island Jurisdictions Index
http://macmeekin.com/Library/Jurisds/Fiji.htm

This index of documents is part of the larger website Island Law, which is maintained by Dan MacMeekin, a Washington, DC, lawyer. The site has separate pages for each location listed that provide access to online documents. The Fiji page contains links to an online version of the Fiji Islands Law, as well as fishing and fishery regulations. Links to other Internet resources are included as well. *See also* ISLAND JURISDICTIONS INDEX *under* OCEANIA: CONTINENT.

MICRONESIA

The Margo Duggan Collection
http://digicoll.manoa.hawaii.edu/duggan/

This collection, housed at the University of Hawai'i at Manoa, is a set of over 2,000 photographs taken by Margo Duggan, a Marine Corps veteran from World War II who also served subsequently in the United States Trust Territories Administration as a civilian employee. The photographs are from 1949 to 1954, making them a window to the struggle of most Micronesians as they recovered from the war. The collection can be browsed or searched by keyword.

Trust Territory of the Pacific Islands
http://digicoll.manoa.hawaii.edu/ttphotos/

The physical photo archive contains over 50,000 photographs and 2,000 slides accumulated during the time when America had some administrative control over Micronesia (1947–1988). It has been partially digitized and is maintained by the University of Hawai'i at Manoa. The collection itself is a blending of two separate large sets of images. One group was taken by American government personnel and the other created from illustrations of early historic works about Micronesia. The photos can be viewed in groups by reel, or a search box can help narrow down the results by matching search terms with the brief photo descriptions. There are currently over 16,500 images in the database.

Guam

Island Jurisdictions Index
http://macmeekin.com/Library/Jurisds/Guam.htm

This index of documents is part of the larger website Island Law, which is maintained by Dan MacMeekin, a Washington, DC, lawyer. The site has separate pages for each location listed that provide access to online documents. The Guam page contains links to the nation's Code, some Supreme Court decisions from 1996 to the present, and other legal information about the island. Links to other Internet resources are included as well. *See also* ISLAND JURISDICTIONS INDEX *under* OCEANIA: CONTINENT.

The Margo Duggan Collection
http://digicoll.manoa.hawaii.edu/duggan/

A search for "Guam" yielded 168 slides. *See also* THE MARGO DUGGAN COLLECTION *under* MICRONESIA.

Kiribati

Island Jurisdictions Index
http://macmeekin.com/Library/Jurisds/Kiribati.htm

This index of documents is part of the larger website Island Law, which is maintained by Dan MacMeekin, a Washington, DC, lawyer. The site has separate pages for each location listed that provide access to online documents. The Kiribati page contains links to the nation's constitution, as well as other laws and statutes. Links to other Internet resources are included as well. *See also* ISLAND JURISDICTIONS INDEX *under* OCEANIA: CONTINENT.

Marshall Islands

Island Jurisdictions Index
http://macmeekin.com/Library/Jurisds/Marshall%20Islands.htm

This index of documents is part of the larger website Island Law, which is maintained by Dan MacMeekin, a Washington, DC, lawyer. The site has separate pages for each location listed that provide access to online documents. The Marshall Islands page contains links to the nation's constitution, to several agreements into which the Marshall Islands have entered with other nations, to other laws and statutes, and to other Internet resources. *See also* ISLAND JURISDICTIONS INDEX *under* OCEANIA: CONTINENT.

The Margo Duggan Collection
http://digicoll.manoa.hawaii.edu/duggan/

A search for "Marshall Islands" yielded 55 slides. *See also* THE MARGO DUGGAN COLLECTION *under* MICRONESIA.

Nauru

Island Jurisdictions Index
http://macmeekin.com/Library/Jurisds/Nauru.htm

This index of documents is part of the larger website Island Law, which is maintained by Dan MacMeekin, a Washington, DC, lawyer. The site has separate pages for each location listed that provide access to online documents. The Nauru page contains links to the nation's constitution, as well as other laws and statutes. Links to other Internet resources are included as well. *See also* ISLAND JURISDICTIONS INDEX *under* OCEANIA: CONTINENT.

Palau

Island Jurisdictions Index
http://macmeekin.com/Library/Jurisds/Palau.htm

This index of documents is part of the larger website Island Law, which is maintained by Dan MacMeekin, a Washington, DC, lawyer. The site has separate pages for each location listed that provide access to online documents. The Palau page contains links to the nation's constitution and to the Compact of Free Association agreement with the United States. Other documents include domestic fishing laws. Links to other Internet resources are included as well. *See also* ISLAND JURISDICTIONS INDEX *under* OCEANIA: CONTINENT.

The Margo Duggan Collection
http://digicoll.manoa.hawaii.edu/duggan/

A search for "Palau" yielded 152 slides. *See also* THE MARGO DUGGAN COLLECTION *under* MICRONESIA.

NEW ZEALAND

George Handy Bates–Samoan Papers
http://cdm.lib.udel.edu/cdm4/results.php?CISOOP1=exact&CISOFIELD1=covera&
   CISOBOX1=Auckland%20%20N.Z.%20&CISOROOT=%2Fbsp

This photographic collection includes images mostly from islands in the Pacific Ocean. The site can be browsed by place or by topic. This link goes directly to a handful of photographs from Auckland, New Zealand. *See also* GEORGE HANDY BATES—SAMOAN PAPERS *under* SAMOA.

National Library of New Zealand
www.natlib.govt.nz/collections/digital-collections

The National Library of New Zealand contains its own research library, the Alexander Turnbull Library. This library provides access to a group of digital collections focusing on the country's history. The content of these collections varies in format from print items to images to life histories of significant people. The collection descriptions can all be translated into English and Māori, the language of the native peoples of New Zealand of the same name. Many of the collections are highlighted here.

▶ **Discover**
   http://discover.natlib.govt.nz/

   The Discover digital collection provides access to New Zealand art, music, and science content, with a strong emphasis on New Zealand's Māori and Pākehā heritage. The primary goal of the collection is to support school curriculums and is composed of contemporary and historical photographs, paintings, posters, video and music clips, as well as essays and bibliographies. QuickTime or Windows Media Player is required to view videos and listen to recordings. This collection of more than 2,000 items can be browsed by subject (music or visual arts) or full-text searched.

▶ **International Children's Digital Library (ICDL)**
   http://www.childrenslibrary.org/

   The ICDL is an online collection of over 1,500 children's books from many different countries and in many languages. New Zealand was among the few countries to have books included in the ICDL when it was launched in November 2002. The collection can be full-text searched and currently offers approximately 200 books selected by librarians from New Zealand.

▶ **Kilbirnie-Lyall Bay Community Centre Oral History Project**
   http://kilbirnie.natlib.govt.nz/

   This oral history project website contains interviews with seven long-term residents of two Wellington suburbs, Kilbirnie and Lyall Bay. Both audio and video images are available for each interview, which focus mainly on the life and times of Wellington area residents throughout the twentieth century.

▶ **Matapihi**
http://www.matapihi.org.nz/

Matapihi, meaning "window" in Māori, is an online database that allows users to search digital collections held by New Zealand cultural institutions. In addition to scans of printed text and sound and video files, it also contains artwork and photographs of museum objects. The focus is on the people, places, and things found in New Zealand or created by New Zealanders. The collection can be full-text searched by word or phrase or can be browsed by subject through galleries called "showcases."

▶ **Papers Past**
http://paperspast.natlib.govt.nz/cgi-bin/paperspast

Papers Past is a digital collection of New Zealand newspapers and periodicals. It currently contains 61 titles published between 1839 and 1945, and it continues to grow. It is useful for genealogical research, because it contains information regarding births, deaths, and marriages. It also contains regional newspapers as well, and the scans include original advertising. The publications can be full-text searched or browsed by date, region, or title.

▶ **Ranfurly Collection**
http://ranfurly.natlib.govt.nz/content/index.html

As stated on this website, the Ranfurly Collection is an online collection of the private papers and other works of Lord Ranfurly, Governor of New Zealand from 1897 to 1904. The collection has three main sections: paintings and drawings (two sketchbooks and seven watercolor paintings), papers (2,970 pages of letters, account books, diaries, and scrapbooks), and photographs (four albums containing 450 photographs plus 24 separate family photographs). Each section can be browsed separately, or the entire collection can be searched by keyword.

▶ **Rangiātea**
http://rangiatea.natlib.govt.nz/

Rangiātea was the oldest Anglican Māori Church in New Zealand until it was tragically destroyed by fire in 1995. It was recently rebuilt. This website celebrates the unique history of Rangiātea and is based on an exhibition held at the National Library Gallery in 1997, *Rangiātea, Ko Ahau Te Huarahi, Te Pono, Me Te Ora* (Rangiātea, I am the way, the truth, and the life). The site is largely still under construction but already contains several images and accompanying text.

▶ **Te Ao Hou (The New World)**
http://teaohou.natlib.govt.nz/journals/teaohou/index.html

Te Ao Hou is a magazine that focused on the daily lives of the Māori people. It was published from 1952 to 1976, with articles written in both English and Māori. The collection can be browsed by issue number, contributing author, or subject. Page images from all 76 issues can be printed, as well as color images of the covers. Each issue has a linked table of contents navigating to the desired content.

▶ **Timeframes**
http://find.natlib.govt.nz/primo_library/libweb/action/search.do?dscnt=0&vid=
TF&dstmp=1284514278215&fromLogin=true

The Timeframes database is a diverse group of digital content from various collections at the National Library of New Zealand's Alexander Turnbull Library. It predominantly contains photographs, drawings, paintings, maps, manuscripts, cartoons, and other ephemera. Timeframes is perpetually adding content and is fully searchable. The content is free for research or education use, and high-quality reproductions can be purchased through the website.

New Zealand Electronic Text Centre
http://www.nzetc.org/

This site contains a very large database of full-text materials related to New Zealand and the Pacific Islands. The content can be browsed by author, title, or subject, and extensive searching can be done. There is also a Projects link in the right menu that navigates to a page with links to the various projects, including texts on the ancient history of the Māori, New Zealand history, journal runs, and collections of personal letters. Online access to the entire archive is free. The site is hosted by Victoria University of Wellington.

Transactions and Proceedings of the Royal Society of New Zealand
rsnz.natlib.govt.nz/

The Royal Society of New Zealand (formerly the New Zealand Institute) was originally created to collect and publish the research findings of various organizations, including the Auckland Institute, Wellington Philosophical Society, and the Otago Institute. This digital collection includes the full text of all 88 volumes. The full text is searchable, and images can be browsed and printed.

University of Auckland Digital Library
http://www.library.auckland.ac.nz/digitalcollections/

The University of Auckland maintains a number of digital collections, several of which are listed here. The link provided connects to a list of these collections, with a tool for searching across all digital content at one time.

▶ **Anthropology Photographic Archive**
http://magic.lbr.auckland.ac.nz/anthpd/

This collection at the University of Auckland contains over 5,000 images from the university's Department of Anthropology. In addition to New Zealand, Samoa, Tonga, and Papua New Guinea are featured in the content. A significant amount of descriptive information is attached to each entry.

▶ **Architecture Archive Images**
http://magic.lbr.auckland.ac.nz/dbtw-wpd/gummer/basic.htm

This is a small collection of architectural plans and photographs maintained by the university with heavy emphasis in the Auckland area since the nineteenth century. An advanced search page allows for easy narrowing of results.

▶ **Early New Zealand Books**
http://www.enzb.auckland.ac.nz/

This site contains the full texts, complete with images, of more than 200 nineteenth-century New Zealand books. The entire list can be browsed by date of publication, or the full text can be searched by keyword.

▶ **Journal of the Polynesian Society**
http://www.jps.auckland.ac.nz/

This website contains scans of the full text of the *Journal* back to the inception of the Society in 1892. The Society focused on researching the cultures of the Māori and other Pacific Island peoples. The content of the journal is sorted by volume and issue, and contains both articles written by experts in the field and indigenous texts that have been translated into English.

▶ **New Zealand Electronic Poetry Centre**
http://www.nzepc.auckland.ac.nz/

This is an initiative by the University of Auckland to put online an archive of poetry from New Zealand and other Pacific Islands. The poetry is posted in coordination with the authors and publishers, along with commentaries, criticism, interviews, and essays, making the site a more complete resource.

University of Canterbury Photograph Collection
http://library.canterbury.ac.nz/mb/mbphoto.shtml

The University of Canterbury in Christchurch, New Zealand, has a library collection of over 20,000 photographs. Much of this has been digitized and been made available online for research purposes. The topics vary widely, but there are sufficient searching and limiting capabilities to help researchers determine if there is any content useful to them.

PAPUA NEW GUINEA

Anthropology Photographic Archive
http://magic.lbr.auckland.ac.nz/anthpd/

This collection at the University of Auckland contains over 5,000 images from the university's Department of Anthropology. Papua New Guinea is among several countries featured in the database. A basic search for "Papua New Guinea" returned over 2,400 images, with a significant amount of descriptive information attached to each entry.

Island Jurisdictions Index
http://macmeekin.com/Library/Jurisds/Papua%20New%20Guinea.htm

This index of documents is part of the larger website Island Law, which is maintained by Dan MacMeekin, a Washington, DC, lawyer. The site has separate pages for each location listed that provide access to online documents. The Papua New Guinea page contains links to the nation's constitution, laws, and the Fisheries Management Act of 1988. Links to other Internet resources are included as well. *See also* ISLAND JURISDICTIONS INDEX *under* OCEANIA: CONTINENT.

Pacific Manuscripts Bureau (PAMBU)
http://rspas.anu.edu.au/pambu/photo.html

This site is the result of a project based at the Australian National University to copy and preserve materials documenting the history and heritage of the Pacific Islands. Content includes several photos from various islands, most notably Papua New Guinea. *See also* PACIFIC MANUSCRIPTS BUREAU (PAMBU) *under* AUSTRALIA.

SAMOA AND WESTERN SAMOA

American Samoa Digital Library—Environmental Literature of the Samoan Archipelago
http://www.nps.gov/npsa/naturescience/digitallibr.htm

The personnel at the National Park of American Samoa have compiled a bibliography of documents called the Environmental Literature of the Samoan Archipelago and posted PDF versions on the park's website. The bibliography can be viewed alphabetically by author or by subject.

Anthropology Photographic Archive
http://magic.lbr.auckland.ac.nz/anthpd/

This collection at the University of Auckland contains over 5,000 images from the university's Department of Anthropology. Western Samoa is among several countries featured in the database. A search for "Western Samoa" returned 135 images, with a significant amount of descriptive information attached to each entry.

George Handy Bates—Samoan Papers
http://fletcher.lib.udel.edu/collections/bsp/index.htm

This is a special collection of materials housed at the University of Delaware. It was given by George Handy Bates, who served as a special investigator into Samoan affairs during the 1880s. Over 140 photographs in this collection are digitized and can be browsed by place or by topic from the homepage. Clicking on "Browse by Place" and then "Samoa" retrieved a list of 67 images.

Island Jurisdictions Index
http://macmeekin.com/Library/Jurisds/Samoa.htm

This index of documents is part of the larger website Island Law, which is maintained by Dan MacMeekin, a Washington, DC, lawyer. The site has separate pages for each location listed that provide access to online documents. The Samoa page contains PDF documents of the Constitution of the Independent State of Western Samoa as well as a collection of Samoan Law. Links to other Internet resources are included as well. *See also* ISLAND JURISDICTIONS INDEX *under* OCEANIA: CONTINENT.

SOLOMON ISLANDS

Island Jurisdictions Index
http://macmeekin.com/Library/Jurisds/Solomon%20Islands.htm

This index of documents is part of the larger website Island Law, which is maintained by Dan MacMeekin, a Washington, DC, lawyer. The site has separate pages for each location listed that provide access to online documents. The Solomon Islands page contains the nation's constitution, laws, fisheries legislation, and the Townsville Peace Agreement of 2000, which settled an internal conflict among citizens. Links to other Internet resources are included as well. *See also* ISLAND JURISDICTIONS INDEX *under* OCEANIA: CONTINENT.

TONGA

Anthropology Photographic Archive
http://magic.lbr.auckland.ac.nz/anthpd/

This collection at the University of Auckland contains over 5,000 images from the university's Department of Anthropology. Tonga is among several countries featured in the database. A search for "Tonga" returned 192 images, with a significant amount of descriptive information attached to each entry.

George Handy Bates—Samoan Papers
http://fletcher.lib.udel.edu/collections/bsp/index.htm

This photographic collection is mostly from islands in the Pacific Ocean. The content can be browsed by place or by topic from the homepage. Clicking on "Browse by Place" and then "Tonga" retrieved a list of 27 images. There are also links for three other specific Tongan locations. *See also* GEORGE HANDY BATES—SAMOAN PAPERS *under* SAMOA.

Island Jurisdictions Index
http://macmeekin.com/Library/Jurisds/Tonga.htm

This index of documents is part of the larger website Island Law, which is maintained by Dan MacMeekin, a Washington, DC, lawyer. The site has separate pages for each location listed that provide access to online documents. The Tonga page contains the nation's constitution, as well as other laws and statutes. There are also PDF documents regarding the country's local fishing regulations, as well as fishery conservation and management protocols. Links to other Internet resources are included as well. *See also* ISLAND JURISDICTIONS INDEX *under* OCEANIA: CONTINENT.

TUVALU

Island Jurisdictions Index
http://macmeekin.com/Library/Jurisds/Tuvalu.htm

This index of documents is part of the larger website Island Law, which is maintained by Dan MacMeekin, a Washington, DC, lawyer. The site has separate pages for each location listed that provide access to online documents. The Tuvalu page contains the nation's constitution, as well as other laws and statutes. Links to other Internet resources are included as well. *See also* ISLAND JURISDICTIONS INDEX *under* OCEANIA: CONTINENT.

VANUATU

Island Jurisdictions Index
http://macmeekin.com/Library/Jurisds/Vanuatu.htm

This index of documents is part of the larger website Island Law, which is maintained by Dan MacMeekin, a Washington, DC, lawyer. The site has separate pages for each location listed that provide access to online documents. The Vanuatu page contains the nation's constitution, as well as other laws and statutes. Links to other Internet resources are included as well. *See also* ISLAND JURISDICTIONS INDEX *under* OCEANIA: CONTINENT.

Chapter 8

South America

INTRODUCTION

South America is the fourth largest continent of the world and encompasses 12 countries: Argentina, Bolivia, Brazil, Chile, Colombia, Ecuador, Guyana, Paraguay, Peru, Suriname, Uruguay, and Venezuela. South America is well-known for having the largest tropical rain forest in the world, the massive Amazon River, and the Andes Mountains that stretch the length of the continent.

The continent is rich in cultural history and has much to share with the world. However, like many developing countries throughout the world, South America is in need of an adequate library infrastructure and the finances to preserve and develop its archival materials and establish its digitized collections. For these reasons cooperative agreements with organizations, such as UNESCO, become very important. A world initiative to preserve and provide access to geographic sites of importance in South America is the UNESCO Memory of the World Program (Vannini, 2004). UNESCO established an International Consultative Committee in collaboration with IFLA (International Federation of Library Associations and Institutions) and ICA (Institutions and the International Council on Archives) to create a Memory of the World Register, which began adding items in 1997.

Some South American countries participate in the World Heritage program, another UNESCO initiative begun in 1972. On the companion website, important sites are listed under their respective countries, with links to a description of the site, a gallery of pictures, an interactive map, and often a video. Two examples are the sites Galapagos Islands in Ecuador (UNESCO World Heritage Centre, 2010a) and Machu Picchu in Peru (UNESCO World Heritage Centre, 2010b).

This chapter lists libraries, organizations, and institutions that provide access to specialized digital collections containing materials on South America, including documents, periodicals, photographs, books, speeches, video clips, and maps. Presented first are major digital collections to provide an overview of the continent. Individual countries' websites with digital collections on various topics or with specialized formats follow. When relevant, digital collections residing outside South America are included. The researcher should also keep abreast of new developments as they occur. The IFLA World Library and Information Congress held annually includes sessions for Latin America and the Caribbean. The sites most likely to provide future digital collections are the individual national libraries, such as the National Library of Argentina, the National Library of Brazil, and the National Library of Peru. The landscape of digitization of South America's collections is ever changing. The collaborative efforts among South

American libraries, organizations, and governments offer a promising future for educating its own peoples and the world of its history and culture.

References

UNESCO World Heritage Centre. 2010a. "Galápagos Islands." United Nations Educational, Scientific and Cultural Organization. Updated August 24. http://whc.unesco.org/en/list/1.

UNESCO World Heritage Centre. 2010b. "Historic Sanctuary of Machu Picchu in Peru." United Nations Educational, Scientific and Cultural Organization. Updated August 24. http://whc.unesco.org/en/list/274.

Vannini, Margarita. 2004. "The Memory of the World Program in Latin America and the Caribbean." *IFLA Journal* 30, no. 4: 293–301.

CONTINENT

Biblioteca Virtual Miguel de Cervantes
http://www.cervantesvirtual.com/

This Spanish language–only website is an extensive digital library of Hispanic cultural and literature materials. It is maintained by Fundacion Biblioteca Virtual Miguel de Cervantes (Foundation Virtual Library Miguel de Cervantes), which allows free access to all materials. A navigation menu on the right provides searching and browsing of the content, which is organized by format, including video, audio, and text. A separate navigation menu on the left provides links to other collections, including the unusual Biblioteca de Signos (Library of Signs), which contains visual content for the hearing impaired.

CLACSO—Latin American and Caribbean Social Science Virtual Library
http://www.biblioteca.clacso.edu.ar/ingles

CLACSO is a nongovernmental international institution that promotes the social sciences disciplines. The virtual library site provides open access to thousands of Spanish- and Portuguese-language publications from Latin America and the Caribbean. Clicking on "Reading Room" provides a search box for full-text searching of the entire content. There is also the option to select individual countries from a list, each of which has a dropdown box of periodicals available from that country. This resource is an excellent place for open-access searching of selected periodicals from specific countries.

Digital Collection of Mexican and Argentine Presidential Messages
http://lanic.utexas.edu/larrp/pm/sample2/#Navigating

This online collection is part of the Latin Americanist Research Resources Project to convert microfilmed texts of presidential speeches of Mexican and Argentinean presidents into online documents. There are currently over 50,000 images of Mexican and over 23,000 scans of Argentinean texts, easily navigable and neatly divided by country first, then subdivided by leader and time period.

Latin American Pamphlet Digital Collection
http://vc.lib.harvard.edu/vc/deliver/home?_collection=LAP

This collection, housed by the Widener Library at Harvard University, contains thousands of digitized pamphlets from Latin American countries. According to the homepage, "Chile, Cuba, Bolivia and Mexico are the countries most heavily represented in this collection." The content focuses mainly on social life and customs, including the evolution of original colonies into the Latin American countries we know today. Many pamphlets are aimed at influencing public opinion about certain social issues. The collection can be keyword searched or browsed by title, author, or subject.

Latino/Latina Voices Digital Collection
http://digital.lib.usu.edu/latino.php

This digital audio collection was created by the Archives and Special Collections Department of Utah State University and contains nearly 50 interviews of Latino and Latina persons who now live in Utah but are originally from various Latin American countries. The interviews focus mainly on social life and customs, with specific attention paid to individual stories of relocation to the United States. Interviews are in English or Spanish, with some in both, and all have accompanying written transcripts. The audio files are downloadable MP3 files. Home countries represented include Argentina, Bolivia, Brazil, Chile, El Salvador, Guatemala, Mexico, Paraguay, Peru, and Venezuela, along with Puerto Rico.

Paul R. Cheesman Photographs
http://www.lib.byu.edu/dlib/Cheesman/

Here is a collection of over 500 photographs from Central and South America that have been digitized by Brigham Young University. The photographs come from a physical collection of materials donated to the University by Dr. Cheesman's wife after he collected them over several decades when he was a military chaplain and researcher of ancient civilizations. The photographs show landscapes, artifacts, and structures from archaeological sites in Central and South America, predominantly Mexico, Central America, and Peru.

South America and Antarctica
http://www.timvp.com/february2009.html

This is a webpage in the personal website called TimVP.com, maintained by an individual who spent four weeks in South America and Antarctica. There are separate links to pages for each country showing images from that country as well as an occasional video clip.

ARGENTINA

Biblioteca Nacional de la Republica Argentina
http://www.cervantesvirtual.com/portal/BNA/index.shtml

This is the main page of the National Library of Argentina and contains links to several pieces of digital content. "Documentos Historicos" links to some digitized documents online, and "Biblioteca de Imagenes" has links to video clips of interviews with some notable authors, including Julio Cortazar, a famous Argentinean author of novels and short stories. The site is in Spanish only.

Cinevivo
http://www.cinevivo.com.ar/home/?tpl=home

This website is a place for individuals to post independent films in Spanish or with Spanish subtitles. They are grouped by category, including fiction, documentary, experimental, and animated. They tend toward being short in length (under 30 minutes) and are free and easily viewable with a web browser. The site also has a news area and a published newsletter with current information, including upcoming film festivals.

Digital Collection of Mexican and Argentine Presidential Messages
http://lanic.utexas.edu/larrp/pm/sample2/argentin/index.html

This collection currently contains over 23,000 scans of Argentinean texts, easily navigable and neatly subdivided by leader and time period. *See also* DIGITAL COLLECTION OF MEXICAN AND ARGENTINE PRESIDENTIAL MESSAGES *under* SOUTH AMERICA: CONTINENT.

Tiflolibros
http://www.tiflolibros.com.ar/contenido/English.htm

This digital collection is an online database of books for the blind. The link provided is to the English version of the site; it is also available in Spanish, Italian, and German. Created in 1999, the site now contains over 20,000 volumes, predominantly Spanish-language materials. Access to the collection requires a computer with a voice reader or the ability to download MP3 files of recorded voices. Users must register and are asked to provide proof of disability to join. The cost is free, but a small donation is suggested.

XUL: Signo Viejo y Nuevo
http://escholarship.bc.edu/xul/

This webpage offers PDF files of the entire content of an Argentine poetry journal called *Xul: Signo Viejo y Nuevo*, published periodically from 1980 to1997. Near the top of the page is more information about the XUL project and a link to a companion website. Scroll down the page for links to PDFs of individual issues. This page is part of a larger resource of scholarly information called the eScholarship@BC Repository, maintained on the website of Boston College. Click the "Home" or "About" links in the left margin to learn more about the larger focus of this project.

BOLIVIA

Bolivia! A Virtual Photo Album
http://www.robsdemo.com/bolivia/index.html

This is the personal website of an individual who lived in Bolivia as a foreign-exchange student. It contains stunning photos interspersed with some remembrances by the author. Scroll over and click on the bubbles on the right side to access the photographs and descriptions.

Latin American Pamphlet Digital Collection
http://vc.lib.harvard.edu/vc/deliver/home?_collection=LAP

This website is maintained by Harvard's Widener Library. A search for "Bolivia" retrieved over 980 digitized pamphlets. There are individual page scans of the entire works with content in Spanish. *See also* LATIN AMERICAN PAMPHLET DIGITAL COLLECTION *under* SOUTH AMERICA: CONTINENT.

Urban Dreams/Sueños Urbanos
http://www.scu.edu/archives/exhibits/suenos_urbanos/exhibit.cfm

This small collection of photographs is an online exhibit of Santa Clara University. It includes select photos of locations and peoples in Bolivia, both rural and urban. Permission to use the photographs must be obtained from the university.

BRAZIL

Biblioteca Digital de Obras Raras e Especiais
http://www.obrasraras.usp.br/

This digital collection contains content of items considered rare works, based on age, historical value, and lack of newer editions. It is maintained by the Universidade de São Paulo (the University of São Paulo). The site is in Portuguese, and the search tool allows for both simple and advanced searching. One search tool date limiter indicates that the content goes as far back as the fifteenth century.

Brazilian Government Document Digitization Project
http://www.nd.edu/~kic/brazil/brazil1.htm

This project was undertaken as part of the Latin American Microfilm Project from the Center for Research Libraries, with funding from the Andrew W. Mellon Foundation. It is a digital repository of documents issued by various departments of Brazil's government between 1821 and 1993. The link provided is to the English version of the website; it can also be viewed in Portuguese. The site offers a wealth of primary source information, with the content broken into four categories: "Provincial Presidential Reports (1830–1889)" includes annual reports issued by the leaders of each province; "Presidential Messages (1889–1993)" includes the texts of the annual messages of the president starting in 1889 when Brazil became a republic; "Almanak Administrativo, Mercantil e Industrial do Rio de Janeiro (1844–1889)" includes annual reports regarding the Brazilian Royal Court, with other information such as listings of officials, legislation, and census data; and "Ministerial Reports (1821–1960)" includes annual reports, where available, from each official ministry.

Rede Da Memoria Virtual Brasileira (Brazilian Network of Virtual Memory)
http://bndigital.bn.br/projetos/redememoria/galeria.html

This collection is housed on the website of the National Digital Library of Brazil, whose goal is to create a combined digital collection of cultural history gathered from different repositories around the country. There are currently over 40 separate contributed collections available, most with little accompanying metadata. Click on the "Parceiros" (Partners) link in the top menu bar for a list of the contributing institutions.

The United States and Brazil: Expanding Frontiers, Comparing Cultures
http://international.loc.gov/intldl/brhtml/brhome.html

This project is a collaborative effort between the Library of Congress and the National Library of Brazil. It focuses on the history and culture of Brazil, as well as its relations with the United States in the recent past. The website is in both English and Portuguese. Click "Collections" in the top menu bar to search the content, which is separated by format into categories: books, manuscripts, maps, and photographs, with full bibliographic records for all items. Another tool allows searching across all collections at once.

CHILE

Cinemateca Virtual de Chile
http://www.cinechileno.org/

This collection of approximately 150 videos illustrates Chilean heritage. It was created by Arcoiris TV and the National Council of Culture and the Arts and consists of popular movies and television shows from Chile. Access is free.

CIREN Biblioteca Digital—Centro de Informacion de Recursos Naturales (Information Center of Natural Resources)
http://bibliotecadigital.ciren.cl/gsdlexterna/cgi-bin/library.exe?l=es&l=en

This website provides free access to collections of digitized materials relating to the identification and usage of natural resources in Chile. The link provided is to the English-language site; the original site is in Spanish. The content includes both maps and textual information, and many of the documents are posted by the General Water Direction, "an organization dependent on the Chilean Ministry of Public Works." The collections are listed and described on the lower left of the homepage, and a search tool is at the top of the page. On the lower right are some FAQs and a link for librarian assistance.

Latin American Pamphlet Digital Collection
http://vc.lib.harvard.edu/vc/deliver/home?_collection=LAP

This website is maintained by Harvard's Widener Library. A search for "Chile" retrieved over 1,000 results. The pamphlets are in Spanish and are individual page scans of the entire documents. The topics relate primarily to political and social issues. *See also* LATIN AMERICAN PAMPHLET DIGITAL COLLECTION *under* SOUTH AMERICA: CONTINENT.

Museo Chileno de Arte Precolombino—Archivo Audiovisual (Audiovisual Archive of the Chilean Museum of Pre-Colombian Art)
http://www2.precolombino.cl/es/audiovisual/index.php

This archive contains short documentaries and video clips related to Pre-Colombian culture. All were created by the museum staff.

COLOMBIA

CLACSO—Latin American and Caribbean Social Science Virtual Library
http://www.biblioteca.clacso.edu.ar/ingles

This virtual library site provides open access to thousands of Spanish- and Portuguese-language publications. There are more than two dozen periodicals from Colombia in this database. They are all in Spanish and range in subject from history and society to social studies, economics, humanities, politics, and other cultural topics. *See also* CLACSO—LATIN AMERICAN AND CARIBBEAN SOCIAL SCIENCE VIRTUAL LIBRARY *under* SOUTH AMERICA: CONTINENT.

World Digital Library
http://www.wdl.org/en/search/gallery?ql=eng&a=-8000&b=2009&c=CO&r=
   LatinAmericaCaribbean

Four images in this database are classified under "Colombia." Three of the images are of rivers that pass through the area: the Dagua, Orinoco, and Amazon. All items in this database contain descriptive and bibliographic information.

ECUADOR

CLACSO—Latin American and Caribbean Social Science Virtual Library
http://www.biblioteca.clacso.edu.ar/ingles

This virtual library site provides open access to thousands of Spanish- and Portuguese-language publications. The database currently contains 12 periodicals from Ecuador, including *Entre Voces*, a Spanish-language debate and discussion forum on significant issues. PDF documents of selected issues are available and can be searched. *See also* CLACSO—LATIN AMERICAN AND CARIBBEAN SOCIAL SCIENCE VIRTUAL LIBRARY *under* SOUTH AMERICA: CONTINENT.

New York Public Library Digital Gallery
http://digitalgallery.nypl.org/nypldigital/dgkeysearchresult.cfm?keyword= ecuador

There are 32 images classified under "Ecuador" in this collection, including several pictures of Sixto Duran Billen (Ecuador's Duputy Commissioner General) at the New York World's Fair (1939–1940). A number of photos show indigenous peoples, as well as Ecuadorians in cultural clothing.

World Digital Library
http://www.wdl.org/en/search/gallery?ql=eng&a=-8000&b=2009&c=EC&r=
   LatinAmericaCaribbean

Five images are classified under "Ecuador" in this collection. Three show persons engaged in celebratory activities: an Easter parade in the capital city of Quito, a procession in Otovalo of people walking to mass, and a fiesta in a smaller village. One of the other images is a survey chart of the Galapagos Islands.

GUYANA

Guyana Lands and Surveys Commission
http://www.lands.gov.gy/index.html

The Guyana Lands and Surveys Commission produces professional maps of Guyana. Despite its for-profit status, an extensive collection of Guyana maps are accessible for free in PDF format in its online catalog. Scroll over "Products & Services"—"Map Products"—"Digital Map Products" to get to the "Products and Services Catalogue." Maps can also be freely downloaded for noncommercial purposes.

PARAGUAY

Latino/Latina Voices Digital Collection
http://digital.lib.usu.edu/latino.php

This digital audio collection was created at Utah State University and contains nearly 50 interviews of Latino and Latina persons who now live in Utah but are originally from various Latin American countries. A keyword search for "Paraguay" returned three items, one of which is an audio interview of a native Paraguayan who immigrated to the United States when she was a teenager. She tells of her experiences growing up in Paraguay and why she came to the United States. The interview is in Spanish and is 37 minutes long. *See also* LATINO/LATINA VOICES DIGITAL COLLECTION *under* SOUTH AMERICA: CONTINENT.

PERU

Biblioteca Nacional del Peru—Tesoros Bibliograficos
http://bvirtual.bnp.gob.pe/bnpvirtual/pag_web/tesoros_bib.htm#17

The website of the National Library of Peru is entirely in Spanish and contains a small collection of digital content, including both print and visual content. The link provided is to a list of available works sorted by format and all on one page.

Institute of Museum and Library Services—Digital Flora of Ucayali, Peru
http://digir.fiu.edu/jgg.html

This collection is a vast database of flora identified in the Ucayali region of Peru. According to the website, only 17 countries on the planet account for the home of over 70 percent of the biodiversity on the planet. The sites claims the Republic of Peru is one of the most diverse and boasts 3,500 specimens of plant-life collected and cataloged since October 1997. Each entry contains a date and the collector's name, along with a full taxonomic classification of the item. Many specimens have accompanying JPEG images of the flower.

Paul R. Cheesman Photographs
http://www.lib.byu.edu/dlib/Cheesman/

This collection of photographs from Central and South America was donated to and digitized by Brigham Young University. Search for "Peru" in the title box to see photographs of a bath speculated to have been a baptismal font. Click into one of the images, then scroll down in the metadata to "Subject" or "Geographical Place Names" and click "Peru." This links to 46 other images that have been tagged with subjects which are either locations or excavation sites within the country. *See also* PAUL R. CHEESMAN PHOTOGRAPHS *under* SOUTH AMERICA: CONTINENT.

SURINAME

Birds in Suriname, South America
http://www1.nhl.nl/~ribot/english/index.htm

This website is a very extensive resource regarding species of birds found in Suriname. It contains hundreds of images of bird species, and many of the photos link to other information, including maps marking locations where the species was spotted, MP3 files of specific birds' sounds, and other descriptive information.

Viewing Suriname: A Collaborative Collection
http://hitchcock.itc.virginia.edu/Suriname/

This website is a collaborative project between the University of Virginia and Conservation International, an organization dedicated to preserving natural history around the world. The content is broken down into two groups: images and maps. The image collection is browsable using a left navigation bar that brings up thumbnail photos of buildings and other historic spots in addition to natural landscapes. The map collection consists mainly of aerial-view drawings of both terrain and land plots in the cities and towns.

URUGUAY

CLACSO—Latin American and Caribbean Social Science Virtual Library
http://www.biblioteca.clacso.edu.ar/ingles

This virtual library site provides open access to thousands of Spanish- and Portuguese-language publications. The database contains five periodicals from Uruguay, including sets of books and documents (and theses) from the Departments of Economics and Sociology at the University of the Republic. *See also* CLACSO—LATIN AMERICAN AND CARIBBEAN SOCIAL SCIENCE VIRTUAL LIBRARY *under* SOUTH AMERICA: CONTINENT.

Montevideo, Uruguay
http://www.timvp.com/montevideo.html

This is a webpage in the personal website called TimVP.com, maintained by an individual who spent four weeks in South America and Antarctica. There are separate links to pages for each country. The link provided goes to the page for Uruguay, which contains a map of the country; photographs of Montevideo, mostly buildings and other public spaces in the capital city; and an 11-minute video.

VENEZUELA

CLACSO—Latin American and Caribbean Social Science Virtual Library
http://www.biblioteca.clacso.edu.ar/ingles

This virtual library site provides open access to thousands of Spanish- and Portuguese-language publications. It contains five periodicals from Venezuela, including *Revista Venezolana de Economía* (*Venezuelan Magazine of the Economy*) and *Revista Venezolana de Estudios de la Mujer* (*Venezuelan Magazine of Women's Studies*). *See also* CLACSO—LATIN AMERICAN AND CARIBBEAN SOCIAL SCIENCE VIRTUAL LIBRARY *under* SOUTH AMERICA: CONTINENT.

Latino/Latina Voices Digital Collection
http://digital.lib.usu.edu/latino.php

This digital audio collection was created at Utah State University and contains nearly 50 interviews of Latino and Latina persons who now live in Utah but are originally from various Latin American countries. A keyword search for "Venezuela" returned five results, three of which are audio interviews of native Venezuelans. Collectively, they talk about growing up in the country, their families, education, jobs, and cultural interests as they relate to their former homeland. The interviews range in length from 46 to 87 minutes. *See also* LATINO/LATINA VOICES DIGITAL COLLECTION *under* SOUTH AMERICA: CONTINENT.

Index of Reference Resources Described

4th of July Speeches, 246
16th–Early 20th Century Maps of Africa, 20
100 años de imigração japonesa no Brasil, 94
1492: An Ongoing Voyage, 184
1906 San Francisco Earthquake and Fire Digital Collection, 212

A

Abby Williams Hill Collection, The, 278
Aberdeen Art Gallery & Museums, 155
Abraham Lincoln, 196
Access Pennsylvania, 267
Accessorize!, 139
Accounting Collections, 244
Aceh Books, 84
Act of Union Virtual Library, 131
Advertising, 197
Affischer (Posters), 149
Afghanistan Digital Library, 67
Afghanistan: Images from the Harrison Forman Collection, 67
Afghanistan Old Photos, 67
Africa Focus: Sights and Sounds of a Continent, 18
African Activist Archive, 18
African American Mosaic: A Library of Congress Resource Guide for the Study of Black History and Culture, The, 178
African American Odyssey, 178
African Book Bank Online—Abbol, 19
African Digital Library, 19
African National Congress—South Africa's National Liberation Movement, 42
African Orthodox Church, 43
African Studies Center, 19
Africana & Black History, 255
After Columbus: Four-Hundred Years of Native American Portraiture, 255
Against the Odds: Making a Difference in Global Health, 203
Agnes Chamberlin Digital Collection, 167

Agriculture Museum, The, 25
AGSL Digital Photo Archive—Asia and Middle East, 85
Ainu Komonjo (18th & 19th Century Records)—Ohnuki Collection, 62
Al Hirschfeld, Beyond Broadway, 179
Alabama Department of Archives and History (ADAH) Digital Archives, 204
AlabamaMosaic, 205
Alaska, Western Canada, and United States Collection, 164
Alaska Native History & Cultures, 207
Alaska's Digital Archive, 206
Alaska's Gold, 207
Alaska–Yukon–Pacific Exposition Digital Collection, The, 278
Alaska–Yukon–Pacific Exposition Photographs, 164
Albin O. Kuhn Library & Gallery Digital Collections, 231
Alfred Wegener Institute, 52
Alliance Memory, 261
Aluka, 19, 21, 38, 39
Aluka—Namibia Poster Collection, 40
Aluka—Zimbabwe Serials, 47
"Always Lend a Helping Hand": Sevier County Remembers the Great Depression, 273
Amazing! Maine Stories, 230
American Centuries—Online Collections, 268
American Civil War Digital Collections: Rosenthal Lithographic Prints of Civil War Encampments, 216
American Colony in Jerusalem, The, 86
American Geographical Society Library Photo Archive, 66
American Heritage Center (AHC)—Online Collections, 283
American Indian Photographs, 279
American Institute of Indian Studies (AIIS), 81

American Memory Project, 177
American Museum Congo Expedition 1909–1915, 25
American Philosophical Society, 171
American Regionalism: Visions from the Heartland, 245
American Samoa Digital Library—Environmental Literature of the Samoan Archipelago, 297
American Treasures of the Library of Congress, 179
"America's National Game": The Albert G. Spalding Collection of Early Baseball Photographs, 255
Anarchism Pamphlets in the Labadie Collection, 236
Anatomia, 167
Ancient Greek and Latin Inscriptions from Upper Macedonia, Aegean Thrace and Achaia, 128
Ancient Manuscripts: From the Desert Libraries of Timbuktu, 19
Ancient Maps of Jerusalem, 87
Ancient Mathematics, 133
Andrée Expeditionen, 148
Ann Arbor Postcards, 236
Annexation of Hawaii: A Collection of Documents, The, 223
Antarctic Heritage Trust—New Zealand, United Kingdom, 51
Antarctica Time Line: 1519–1959, An, 51
Anthropology Photographic Archive, 295
Antique Maps of Iceland, 130
Arawwwak: Antigua Historic Community Archives, 165
Archaeological and Numismatic, 177
Archaeological Museum, Split, 120
Architecture Archive Images, 295
Archives, 157
Archives and Special Collections: Digital Collections, 244
Archives & Special Collections Regional and Historic Maps, 247
Archives of Maryland Online, 231
Archives of Michigan Image Collection, 237
Arizona Archives Online, 207
Arizona Aviation History: The Ruth Reinhold Collection, 208
Arizona Memory Project, 208
Arizona's Saints and Shady Ladies, 208
Arkansas Digital History Institute, 209
Arkansas History Commission Photographs, 209
Arkitekturmuseet, 148

Armenian Historical Sources of the 5–15th Centuries, 68
Arnold Arboretum of Harvard University, 60
Art Libraries Society of North America (ARLIS/NA), 1
Arthur Szyk: Artist for Freedom, 179
Asia at Work: A Collection of Digital Images, 65
Asian & Pacific Studies—Historical Photographs, 60
Asian Historical Architecture, 60
Asian Pacific Americans, 197
Astrup Fearnley Museum of Modern Art, 140
Atlantic World: America and the Netherlands, The, 195
Atlas: Database of Exhibits, 125
Auburn University Library Digital Collections, 205
Audio Recordings, 288
Austin Treasures: Jane McCallum and the Suffrage Movement, 271
Australasian Digital Theses Program, 287
Australian Antarctic Division, 52
Australian National University, 288
Australian War Memorial, 288
Austrian National Library (Osterreichische Nationalbibliothek)—Austrian Newspapers Online, 117
Austrian National Library—Picture Archive, 118
Azad-Hye (Middle East Armenian Portal), 68
Azerbaijan National Library, 69

B

Bahrain House of Photography, 69
Baker County Oregon Library—Directory of Online Digital Archive Collections, 264
Barren Lands, The, 167
Baseball, 197
Basket Collection, 279
Bauduin Collection: Photographic Albums of Japan Around the End of the Shogunate Period, 92
Beautiful and Diverse, Senegal, Through the Eyes of a Retiree, 41
Becker Collection, 233
Belgian-American Research Collection, 119
Ben Gray Lumpkin Digital Folk Music Collection, 214
Benedicte Wrensted: An Idaho Photographer in Focus, 224

Benin—Kings and Rituals: Court Arts from Nigeria, 21

Benjamin Franklin: In His Own Words, 179

Bent–Hyde Papers, 1905–1918, 214

BibliOdyssey—Armenian Manuscript, 68

Biblioteca de Catalunya, 146

Biblioteca Digital de Obras Raras e Especiais, 305

Biblioteca Nacional de Espaòa (National Library of Spain), 146

Biblioteca Nacional de la Republica Argentina, 303

Biblioteca Nacional de Portugal, 142

Biblioteca Nacional del Peru—Tesoros Bibliograficos, 308

Biblioteca Nationala a României, 142

Biblioteca Virtual Miguel de Cervantes, 302

Bibliotheca Alexandrina, 26

Bibliotheca Alexandrina—Eternal Egypt, 26

Bibliotheca Alexandrina—The Digital Assets Repository (DAR), 26

Bibliotheca Alexandrina—The Supercourse, 27

Bibliotheque de la Sorbonne (Universite de Paris), 123

Bibliothèque nationale de Luxembourg—Luxemburgensia Online, 136

Birds in Suriname, South America, 309

Birmingham Public Library Digital Collections, 205

Black Europeans, 153

Black Mountain College Publications, 259

Block Prints of the Chinese Revolution, 73

Bob Hope and American Variety, 180

Bogd Khaan Winter Palace Museum, The, 77

Bohdan Medwidsky Ukrainian Folklore Archives, The, 152

Boise Public Library Ethnic History Archive, 224

Bolivia! A Virtual Photo Album, 304

Bond Photograph Library, 82

Boreal Wilderness Institute, 52

Boston College Digital Collections, 233

Boston Gas Company Photographs, 233

Botswana Historical Documents, 22

Botswana Serials, 22

Bound for Glory: America in Color, 180

Brazilian Government Document Digitization Project, 305

Brigham Young University—Harold B. Lee Library Digital Collections, 274

British Columbia Digital Library, 166

British Library, The, 153

British Museum, The, 28

Brooker Collection, 234

Browse by Topic, 177

Buck Clayton Collection, 245

Buckaroos in Paradise: Ranching Culture in Northern Nevada, 1945–1982, 250

Butler Center Online Collections, 209

Byrd Polar Research Center Archival Program, 53

C

California Indian Baskets, 211

California State Archives, 210

California State University—Sacramento Library Digital Collections, 210

California Underground Railroad, The, 210

Calisphere—California Cultures: Asian Americans, 60

Calvin M. McClung Historical Collection, 270

Campbell Collections, 43

Canada's Digital Collections, 166

Canadian Counterpoint: Illustrations by Anita Kunz, 180

Canadian Pamphlets and Broadsides, 168

Canadian Printer and Publisher, 168

Caribbean Newspaper Digital Library, 163, 168, 173

Carrie Watkins Cookbook, 245

Cartoon America, 180

Cartoons: British Cartoon Archive, 74

Cartoons of Thomas Nast: Reconstruction, Chinese Immigration, Native Americans, Gilded Era, 74

Castro Speech Data Base, 169

Catalogue of Early Japanese and Chinese Medical Books, 92

Center for South Asian Studies, 61

Central Florida Memory, 216

Central Intelligence Agency—World Factbook, 61, 69, 70, 109

Central Washington University Brooks Library Digital Collections, 277

Centre Pompidou—La Collection du Musee National d'Art Moderne, 124

Century of Creativity: The MacDowell Colony 1907–2007, A, 181

Changing the Face of Medicine, 203

Char-Koosta News, The, 247

Charles Darwin University—East Timor Special Collection, 81

China Christian Colleges and Universities Image Database, 74

China in the 1930s Collection/Tianjin Collection, The, 62

Chinese in California, 1850–1925, The, 74

Chinese Paper Gods, 75

Chinese Public Health Posters, 74

Choijin Lama Temple Museum, The, 78

Chronicling America: Historical American Newspapers, 177

Churchill and the Great Republic, 181

Cimento Academy, 133

Cinecitta Luce, 132

Cinemateca Virtual de Chile, 306

Cinevivo, 304

CIREN Biblioteca Digital—Centro de Informacion de Recursos Naturales (Information Center of Natural Resources), 306

Cities, 66

Civics and Government, 197

Civil Rights, 197

Civil Rights Digital Library, 222

Civil War, The, 197

Civil War & Slavery Collection, 235

Civil War Collection, 236

Civil War Diaries, 237

Civil War Letters of Lewis Riley, 245

Civil War Manuscripts, 240

Civil War Photographs, 240

Civil War Service Records, 240

CLACSO—Latin American and Caribbean Social Science Virtual Library, 302, 307, 309, 310

Clark, The, 2

Clemson University Libraries Digital Library Initiative, 269

Cleveland Digital Library—Virtual Cleveland History, The, 262

Cleveland Memory Project—Postcards of Cleveland, The, 262

Coalition for Networked Information (CNI), 2

Cochise College Libraries—Cochise County Historical & Archeological Collection, 208

Codex Gigas, 149

Collection of Drawings of Architecture and Decoration of the Eighteenth Century, 146

Collection of Francoise Pommaret (Photos), 71

Collections Search Center, Smithsonian Institution, 280

Colonial and Early America, 197

Colonial Williamsburg Digital Library, 276

Colorado College Special Collections, 213

Colorado Plateau Digital Archives, 176

Colorado State Digital Archives, 213

Colorado State University Libraries—Digital Collections, 214

Columbia River Basin Ethnic History Archive, 176

Community Video Education Trust, 43

Connecticut History Online, 215

Connecticut State Library Digital Collections, 215

Connecticut's Heritage Gateway, 215

Contemporary Metalwork, 156

CONTENTdm Collection of Collections, 163

Cornell Modern Indonesia Collection, 84

Cornucopia, 154

Council of Historical Memory of the Liberation Struggle of EOKA 1955–1959 (SIMAE), 80

Creating French Culture: Treasures from the Bibliothèque Nationale de France, 124

Creating the United States, 181

Creative Space: Fifty Years of Robert Blackburn's Printmaking Workshop, 181

Croatian Academy of Sciences and Arts—Glyptotheque Sculpture Museum, 120

Croatian Cultural Heritage, 120

Cuban Heritage Collection, 169

Cuban Poster Collection, 169

Cultural & Museum Centre, Karonga, 37

Cultures and History of the Americas: The Jay I. Kislak Collection at the Library of Congress, The, 181

Cypriot Museum, The, 80

Cyprus Folk Art Museum, The, 80

Cyprus Museum Digital Collections, The, 81

D

D.J. Angus Photographs, 235

Danish National Digital Sheet Music Archive, The, 121

David Allan—Dresses Mostly from Nature, 156

David and Fela Shapell Family Digitization Project—Ketubbot Collection, The, 87

Death Records, 1897–1920, 240

Declaring Independence: Drafting the Documents, 182

Decorated Publishers Bindings, 235

Decorative Arts Collection, 143

Deena Stryker Photographs, 1963–1964 and Undated, 169

DEILA: The Dickinson Electronic Initiative in the Liberal Arts, 267

Delaware Postcard Collection, 216

Delaware Public Archives—Digital Archives, 216

Denggi, 99

Denver Public Library: Western History and Genealogy—Digital Collections, 214

Det Kongelige Bibliotek (Royal Library of Denmark)—Nationalbibliotek og Kobenhavns Universitetsbibliotek (Copenhagen University Library), 121

Devil's Island Paintings, 124

DIGAR (Digital Archives of the National Library of Estonia)—Eesti Rahvusraamatukogu, 122

Digital Collection of Mexican and Argentine Presidential Messages, 173

Digital Collections and Services, 178

Digital Collections at Middlebury College, 274

Digital Commonwealth, 235

Digital Himalaya Project, 102

Digital Illinois, 225

Digital Innovation South Africa, 43

Digital Katei Collection, 96

Digital Library Federation (DLF), 2

Digital Library of Appalachia, 228

Digital Library of Georgia, 222

Digital Library of South Dakota, 270

Digital Library of the Caribbean, 163, 172

Digital Library of the Royal Netherlands Academy of Arts and Sciences, 138

Digital Media Repository, 226

Digital Metro New York, 253

Digital National Library of Serbia, 145

Digital Repository: Cholera Online, 12

Digital Repository: Films and Video, 203

Digital Shizen Shin'eido, 96

Digital Silk Road in Photographs, 90

Digital Somali Library, The, 42

Digital South Asia Library, 61, 82

Digitaliserad dagspress (Digitized Newspapers), 149

Digitized Manuscripts, 88

Discover, 293

Discover Nevada History, 251

Discovery and Early Development of Insulin, The, 168

Diversity in the Desert: Daily Life in Greek & Roman Egypt, 236

Don Quixote Iconography Digital Archive, 2

Drawings and Prints Collection, 143

Drawings by Frederic Christophe de Houdetot [1797–1835], 125

Dream Anatomy, 203

Dream of Flight, The, 182

Drepung Monastery, 79

Dresden: Treasures from the Saxon State Library, 126

Duke Digital Collections, 258

E

Early Detroit Images from the Burton Historical Collection, 237

Early Hebrew Newspapers, 88

Early Modern French Women Writers, 242

Early Netherlandish Paintings in the Rijksmuseum, Amsterdam. Volume I—Artists Born before 1500, 139

Early New Zealand Books, 296

Early 19th Century Russian Readership & Culture Collection, 243

Early Photography, 240

Early Postcards of India and Ceylon, 103

Earth as Art: A Landsat Perspective, 182

East and Southeast Asian Sources, 61

East and Southeast Asian Studies—Taiwan, 108

East Asian Collection, 62, 75

East Asian Collection—Holmes Welch Collection, The, 75

East Carolina University—Joyner Library Digital Collections, 165, 258

Eastern North Carolina Digital Library, 258

Eastern Washington University Digital Collections, 277

Economic Branch Library Muto Collection, 92

Edvard Munch: Prints—The Complete Graphic Works, 140

Edward Stevenson Collection, 224

E-fimeris: National Library of Greece Digital Newspapers Collection, 128

Egypt State Information Service, 28

Egypt State Information Service—Egyptian Obelisks, 29

Egypt State Information Service—Egypt's Monuments, 29

Egypt State Information Service—The Life of Ancient Egyptians, 29

Egypt State Information Service—The Pyramids, 29

Egypt State Information Service—Your Gateway to Egypt, 29

Egypt State Information Service—Your Gateway to Egypt—History, 29

Egyptian Geological Museum, 29
Egyptian National Agricultural Library (ENAL), 30
Egyptian National Agricultural Library—Online Books, 30
Egyptian National Library and Archives, 30
Ehon: The Artist and the Book in Japan, 91
Einstein Archives Online, 88
Elections, 198
Electronic Resources from The Royal Library, 121
Ellis Island Photographs from the Collection of William Williams, Commissioner of Immigration, 1902–1913, 255
Empire That Was Russia: The Prokudin-Gorskii Photographic Record Recreated, The, 104
Enchanting Ruin: Tintern Abbey and Romantic Tourism in Wales, 236
Enduring Outrage: Editorial Cartoons by Herblock, 183
Enoch Pratt Free Library, 231
Ephemera, 123
Erie Railroad Glass Plate Negative Collection, The, 257
Eternal Egypt—Giza, 27
Eternal Egypt—Islamic Ceramic Museum, 28
Eternal Egypt—Sites & Museums, 27
Eternal Egypt—The Coptic Museum, 27
Eternal Egypt—The Graeco-Roman Museum, 28
Eternal Egypt—The Luxor Temple, 28
Ethiopian Manuscript Imaging Project (EMIP) Collection of Ethiopian Manuscripts, 33
Ethnographic Video for Instruction & Analysis (EVIA) Digital Archive, 33
European Art Gallery, The, 143
European Film Gateway (EFG), 3
European Library, The, 115
Europeana: Think Culture, 86
Exaggeration Postcards, 249
Exhibitions, 157, 178
Exploration and Explorers, 198
Explore 1000 Major Exhibits, 139
ExplorePAhistory.com, 267
Exploring the Early Americas, 183

F

Fauna and Flora in Illustrations—Natural History of the Edo Era, 93
Fenian Brotherhood Collection, 131
Fiji's Treasured Culture, 290

Flight and Early Aviators, 198
Floating World of Ukiyo-e: Shadows, Dreams, and Substance, The, 91
Florida Atlantic University—Collections @ Digital Library, 217
Florida Folklife from the WPA Collections, 1937–1942, 217
Florida International University Digital Collections Center, 217
Florida Memory Project, 218
Florida Photographic Collection, 218
Florida Southern College—McKay Archives Center Digital Collections, 218
Florida Writer's Project Digital Collection, 218
For European Recovery: The Fiftieth Anniversary of the Marshall Plan, 183
Forced Migration Online (FMO), 20, 21, 46, 62
Fore-Edge Paintings, 236
France in America, 124
Frank Lloyd Wright: Designs for an American Landscape, 1922–1932, 184
Fred Nordgaard Barbershop Quartet Scrapbooks, 224
Freshwater and Marine Image Bank, 175
Friends United Meeting: Kenya, 36
From Haven to Home: 350 Years of Jewish Life in America, 184
From the Home Front and the Front Lines, 184
Full Text Image Database of Translations of Western Books in the Dawn of Modern Japan, 92
Fundación Eugenio Granell, 147
Fundación Gala-Salvador Dalí, 147
Fundación Picasso, 147

G

Galapagos Islands Image Database, 92
Gallica—Bibliothèque Numerique, 137
Gandan Monastery, 78
GandhiServe Online Image Archive, 83
Genthe Collection, 38
Geography and Maps, 198
Geologic Atlas, 273
George Handy Bates—Samoan Papers, 290
George Mason University Libraries Digitized Collections, 276
George Morgenstierne, 140
Georgia State University Library—Special Collections and Archives, 221
Georgia Tech Digital Collections, 221

Georgia's Virtual Vault, 221
German Emblem Books, 126
German History in Documents and Images, 127
Germany Under Reconstruction, 127
Gerrit Smith Broadside and Pamphlet Collections, 257
Gertrude Bell Archive, 63, 109
Getty Research Institute (GRI), The, 3
Gettysburg Address, The, 185
Gibran Museum, 98
Gifts and Blessings: The Textile Arts of Madagascar, 36
Global Gateway: World Culture and Resources, 195
Global Music Archive—Digital Collection of East African Recordings, 46
Glover Atlas—Fishes of Southern and Western Japan, 93
Goodspeed Manuscript Collection, 69
Göteborgs Konstmuseum, 148
Göttinger Digitalisierungszentrum (GDZ), 127
Grand Valley State University Digital Collections, 238
Grand Valley State University Libraries— Special Collections and University Archives, 235
Great Depression, The, 198
Greek Cartography: The Documents, 128
Greek Painters after the Fall of Constantinople, 129
Gregorian Egyptian Museum, 158
Grover Cleveland Birthplace Historical Site, 252
Gutenberg Digital, 4
Gutenberg-e, 4,
Guyana Lands and Surveys Commission, 308

H
Hacivat and Karagöz, 110
Haldore Hanson's China Collection (1937–1938), 75
Hamilton College Library Digital Collections, 254
Hargrett Rare Book and Manuscript Library, 223
Harold Wave Whicker Collection, 247
Hawaii State Archives Digital Collections, 223
Heavenly Craft: The Woodcut in Early Printed Books, A, 116
Hedda Morrison Photographs of China, 1933–1946, The, 75
Henry VIII: Man and Monarch, 153

Hensley Photo Library, 83
Heraldic Database of Greece, 129
Herblock!, 185
Herblock's History: Political Cartoons from the Crash to the Millennium, 185
Heritage Museum of Northwest Florida Digital Collection, 219
Hezzie Goes to War: World War I through the Eyes of a Mid-Missourian, 246
High-Definition Image Database of Old Photographs of Japan, 93
Highlights of Florida History, 218
Hispanic Americans, 198
Historic Camel Photos—Camels in Asia, 110
Historic Cities, 88
Historic Maps of Delaware & the Mid-Atlantic Region, 216
Historic Niagara Digital Collections, 166
Historic Pittsburgh, 268
Historical Anatomies on the Web, 12
Historical Hats and Headdresses, 214
Historical Newspaper Library, 123
Historical Photograph Collections, 225
Historical Photograph Collections at the Arizona State Archives, 208
Historical Photographs of China, 75
Historical Texts, 154
Historically Black College and University Library Alliance, 221
History of Science and Scholarship in the Netherlands, 138
Holidays, 199
Holy Land Maps from the Eran Laor Cartographic Collection, 88
Hong Kong University Libraries Digital Initiatives, 77
Honorable Robert T. Matsui Legacy Project: Road to Redress and Reparations, The, 210
Hudson River Valley Heritage, 254
Hugh Morton Collection of Photographs and Films, 260
"Human Origins: What Does It Mean to Be Human?," 11
Humor's Edge: Cartoons by Ann Telnaes, 185
Hungarian Digital Archive of Pictures, 129
Hungarian Digital Image Library, 130
HyperHistory, 4

I
"I Do Solemnly Swear . . .": Inaugural Materials from the Collections of the Library of Congress, 186

Ice Station POLarstern (ISPOL)—6
  November 2004–19 January 2005, 53
Icelandic Online Dictionary and Reading, 131
Idaho Digital Resources, 224
Idaho Waters Digital Library, 225
Illinois Historical Digitization Projects, 226
Illuminating the Word: The St. John's Bible,
  186
Images Canada, 166
Images of a Rural Past, 273
Imaging Everest, 102
Immigration, 199
In the Beginning Was the Word: The
  Russian Church and Native Alaskan
  Cultures, 186
Incunabula & 16th Century Printing, 235
Incunabula—Dawn of Western Printing, 94
Indian Peoples of the Northern Great Plains,
  248
Indian Raj British Indian Photography,
  1845–1947, 83
Indiana Memory, 226
Indonesia Independent—Photographs
  1947–1953, 84
Industrial Establishments and Workshops in
  the Aegean, 129
Institute and Museum of the History of
  Science, 132
Institute for Iranian Contemporary Historical
  Studies, 84
Instituto Nacional de Estudos e Pesquisa, 35
International Children's Digital Library
  (ICDL), 293
International Federation of Library
  Associations and Institutions (IFLA), 4
International Guitar Research Archive
  (IGRA), 212
International Islamic Digital Library, 100
International Jazz Collections, 225
International Mission Photography Archive, 19
International Poster Collection, The, 119
Internet Archive, The, 5
Internet Culturale, 134
Iowa Heritage Digital Collections, 227
ipl2—Internet Public Library (IPL)
  Newspapers and Magazines, 5
Ironworld Discovery Center—Iron Range
  Women's History Project, 241
Isaac Stevens Railroad Expedition
  Lithographs, 280
Isaacman Interviews (Mozambique), 39
Islamic Manuscripts from Mali, 37
Islamic Medical Manuscripts, 12
Island Jurisdictions Index, 287

Israel & Palestinian Territories, 103
Israel Museum, 86
Israeli Internet Sites Archive, 89
Ivan Meštrovic Museums, 120

J
Jacksonville State University Digital
  Collections, 206
Jamaica Unshackled: Freedom to Be, 173
James Koetting Ghana Field Recordings
  Collection, The, 34
James Willard Schultz Photographs
  Collection 10, 248
Jamtli, 149
Japanese American Archival Collection, The,
  211
Japanese American Relocation Photograph
  Collection, 211
Japanese and Chinese Prints and Drawings
  Donated by Gillett G. Griffin, 91
Japanese Calendar, The, 94
Japanese Ex-libris Stamps, 94
Japanese Old Photographs in
  Bakumatsu-Meiji Period, 93
JARDA: Japanese American Relocation
  Digital Archives, 91
Jersey City Free Public Library, 253
Jerusalem Virtual Library, 87
Jewish National and University Library, 87
JNUL Digitized Book Repository, 89
John Bull and Uncle Sam: Four Centuries of
  British-American Relations, 187
John Gregory Bourke Photographs of Native
  Americans, 249
John S. Kiewit Photography Collection, 164,
  168, 171–172
John Todd Photography Collection, 238
Joplin 1902 Picture Booklet, 246
Joseph Berry Keenan Digital Collection, 91
Joseph Berry Keenan Papers, 91
Joseph Berry Keenan Visual Materials
  Collection, 92
Journal of the Polynesian Society, 296
Journals, 123

K
Kalok–Honokohau National Historical Park:
  A Collection of Family Traditions
  Describing—Customs, Practices and
  Beliefs of the Families and Lands of
  Kaloko and Honokohau, North
  Kona, Island of Hawai'i, 223

Kansas State Historical Society, 227
Karl Bodmer American Indian Images, 265
Kartor (Maps), 149
Kate and Sue McBeth: Missionary Teachers
    to the Nez Percé, 225
Keagle Photograph Library, 83
Kentuckiana Digital Library, 228
Kentucky Historical Society Digital
    Collections, 229
Kern County Local History Photograph
    Collection, 212
Keweenaw Digital Archives—Michigan's
    Copper Country in Photographs, 238
Kilbirnie-Lyall Bay Community Centre Oral
    History Project, 293
Korea, 102
Kouriun, 81
Kungliga Biblioteket (National Library of
    Sweden), 149

L

La Fayette: Database of American Art, 125
Labor, 199
Landscape Change Program, 275
Language of the Land: Journeys into Literary
    America, 187
Länsmuseet Gävleborg, 187
Lapidarium, 143
Latin American Pamphlet Digital Collection,
    164
Latino Cultural Heritage Digital Archives, 212
Latino/Latina Voices Digital Collection, 303
Latvia in the 16th–18th Century Maps, 135
Latvian Song Celebration Festival
    (1864–1940), 135
Latvians.com, 135
Lazarus Foundation Galdiano, 147
LearnCalifornia.org, 211
Leeson's History of Montana 1735–1885, 247
Legacy Florida Digital Collections, 210
Letter from the South Pole, 140
Letters of Philip II, King of Spain,
    1592–1597, 147
Levensberichten & Herdenkingen, 138
Lewis & Clark College—Digital Collections,
    265
Lewis & Clark Expedition, Roger Cooke
    Paintings, 280
Lewis and Clark Expedition, The, 199
Lewis Wickes Hine: Documentary
    Photographs, 1905–1938, 256
Liber Liber, 134
Libraries of Asia Pacific Directory, 63

Library & Information Technology
    Association (LITA), 5
Library of Congress, The, 6, 177
Library of Congress Bible Collection, 187
Library of Congress—Global Gateway:
    World Culture and Resources, 6
Library of Congress—Portals to the World, 6
Library of Galileo Galilei, The, 133
Libyan Art Galleries, 36
Liechtenstein Museum, 135
Lin Hsin Hsin Art Museum, 107
Lincei Academy, 133
Linnés nätverk (Linnaeus' Network), 149
Literature and Poetry, 199
Little Cowpuncher: Rural School Newspaper
    of Southern Arizona, 208
Little Journeys to the Great War, 76
Liturgy and Life Artifacts Series, 234
Lloyd L. Gaines, 247
Llyfrgell Genedlaethol Cymru—Digital
    Mirror, 157
Long Island Memories, 254
Los Angeles Mapped, 188
Louis Braille: His Legacy and Influence, 188
LOUISiana Digital Library, 229
Louisiana Map Collection, 229
Louisiana State Documents Digital Archive,
    230
Louvain Posters: German-Occupied Belgium
    during the First World War, 119
Louvre—Databases, The, 125
Lunstrum Interviews (Mozambique), 39
Luther Seminary Archives, 242

M

Macau: A Selection of Cartographic Images,
    77
MacKinney Collection of Medieval Medical
    Illustrations, The, 260
Madison's Treasures, 188
Magna Carta, 154
Mahzor Nuremberg, 89
Maine History Online, 230
Maine Memory Network, 230
Maine State Archives, 230
Making of Ann Arbor, 238
Making of Modern Michigan: Digitizing
    Michigan's Hidden Past, 238
Manéga—Musée de la Bendrologie, 22
Manuscripts, 157, 288
Manuskrip Malayu Pusaka Gemilang, 63
Map of Nepal, 102
Maps, 157, 240, 289

Maps in Our Lives, 188

Maps of Antarctica—Described by R.V. Tooley and Illustrated, 51

Margaret Mead: Human Nature and the Power of Culture, 189

Margarita S. Studemeister Digital Collections in International Conflict Management, The, 6, 63

Margo Duggan Collection, The, 291–292

Maritime History, 156

Maryland Digital Cultural Heritage, 232

Maryland Memory Projects, 232

Maryland State Law Library, 232

Masterpieces, The, 139

Matapihi, 294

Mathias J. Alten, 235

Maureen and Mike Mansfield Library Digital Collections, 247

Medieval Manuscripts, 257

Medieval Manuscripts of Syracuse University Library, 116

Meeting of Frontiers, 195

Meiji and Taisho Eras in Photographs, The, 94

Melvin C. Shaffer World War II Photographs, 117

Memorial and Museum—Auschwitz-Birkenau, 141

Meru Nyingpa Monastery, 79

Mexico: Photographs, Manuscripts, and Imprints, 174

Michigan County Histories and Atlases, 237, 238

Michigan eLibrary—MeL Michigana, 237

Middle Eastern Studies, 103–104, 107–108, 111

Military Education Research Library Network (MERLN), 64

Minnesota Digital Library—Minnesota Reflections, 242

Mississippi Department of Archives and History (MDAH)—Mississippi Archives, 243

Mississippi Digital Library, 243

Mississippi State University Digital Collections, 244

Missouri Digital Heritage, 245

Modern Greek Visual Prosopography, 129

Modern Japan in Archives, 94

Modern Medicine Historical Materials, 93

Moderna Museet, 150

Monasteries in Ulaanbaatar, 78

Monastic Archives: Documents from Mount Athos and Patmos, 129

Mongolia Natural History Museum—Pictures, 78

Mongolian Military Museum, 78

Monstrous Craws & Character Flaws: Masterpieces of Cartoon and Caricature at the Library of Congress, 189

Montana Memory Project, 248

Montana State University Libraries Digital Collections, 248

Montevideo, Uruguay, 309

Movement to Statehood Pathway, 207

Movie Posters, 110

Mozambique Liberation Documents, 39

Mozambique Revolution, 39

Munich Digitisation Centre (Munchener DigitalisierungsZentrum Digitale Bibliothek), 128

Murals of Northern Ireland, 155

Musée National Cirta de Constantine, 21

Museo Chileno de Arte Precolombino—Archivo Audiovisual (Audiovisual Archive of the Chilean Museum of Pre-Colombian Art), 306

Museo Nacional del Prado (Prado Museum), 148

Museu de Prehistòria de València, 148

Museum Computer Network (MCN), 7

Museum Gustavianum, 150

Museum Kulenovic Collection, 150

Museum of Applied Art, The, 145

Museum of the History of Cypriot Coinage, 81

Museum of the Macedonian Struggle, 136

Museum of the Mazovian Countryside, 141

Museums and Collections in Romania, 142

Music and Dance, 199

Music of Michigan, 241

Muzeul National de'Arta al Romaniei (National Museum of Art of Romania), 143

Myanmar.com—Arts & Literature, 101

MyLib, 63

N

Nag Hammadi Library, 30

Nagasaki University Digital Collection, 92

Name Changes of Settlements in Greece, 129

Napoleonica.org, 125

Napoleon's Letters to Bigot de Preameneu [1800–1815], 125

Narodni muzej Crne Gore (National Museum of Montenegro), 138

NASA Goddard Space Flight Center—Global Observatory—Image of the Day, 53

NASA—Our Earth as Art, 7
Nashville Public Library, 270
Nation Emerges: 65 Years of Photography in Mexico, A, 174
National Agricultural Library, 201
National and University Library (Narodna in Univerzitetna Knjiznica), 145
National Archives and Records Administration (NARA), 202
National Archives of Egypt (NAE), 31
National Archives of Zambia, 46
National Audiovisual Archive of Hungary (NAVA), 130
National Diet Library (NDL), 193
National Gallery of Art, 202
National Geographic, 7
National Information Standards Organization (NISO), 7
National Library and Information System Authority, 176
National Library of Australia, 53–54, 288
National Library of Australia—Bangladesh Envoy Hossain Ali Presents Letters of Credence in Canberra, 1972, 70
National Library of Australia Digital Collection, 82
National Library of Australia—Stanford's "Treaty Map" of South Eastern Europe and Armenia, 69
National Library of Education, 202
National Library of Finland Digital Collections, 123
National Library of Iran, 85
National Library of Ireland, 132
National Library of Jamaica, 173
National Library of Latvia—Digital Library, 135
National Library of Malaysia (Perpustakaan Negara Malaysia)—List of Digital Initiative Websites, 99
National Library of New Zealand, 54, 293
National Library of Norway, 140
National Library of Russia, The, 105
National Library of Scotland, 156
National Library of Singapore—Singapore Pages, 107
National Library of the Netherlands (Koninklijke Bibliotheek), 139
National Library of Tunisia, 46
National Library of Turkey—Milli Kütüphane, 110
National Library Websites, 8
National Museum, The, 99
National Museum in Poznan, 141
National Museum in Warsaw, 141

National Museum of American Illustration, The, 268
National Museum of Bhutan, 71
National Museum of Contemporary History, The, 146
National Museum of Mongolian History, Ulaanbaatar, The, 78
National Oceanic and Atmospheric Administration (NOAA) Photo Library, 8
National Science Foundation—Digital Libraries—Access to Human Knowledge, 9
Nationalmuseum, 150
Native American Baseball Teams Photographs, 249
Native Americans, 199
Nature and the Environment, 199
Nebraska State Historical Society—Collections Treasures, 249
Nebraska Territory Map, about 1854, 249
Nebraska Treasures from the Library/Archives, 249
Nebraska Western Trails, 250
New Jersey Department of State—Imaged Collections, 252
New Mexico Office of the State Historian, 253
New Mexico's Digital Collections, 253
New York Heritage Digital Collections, 255
New York Public Library Digital Gallery
    Africa, 21, 23–25, 32–36, 38, 40–42, 44–45
    Asia, 70, 85–86, 96
    Europe, 117–119, 136–137, 144
    North America, 165, 170–172, 174–176, 255
    South America, 307
    World Initiatives, 9
New York Public Library Digital Gallery—Middle East in Prints and Photographs, 103
New York State Archives—Where History Goes on Record, 256
New Zealand Electronic Poetry Centre, 296
New Zealand Electronic Text Centre, 295
Newcomers to a Newland, 263
Newton's Secrets, 89
Nicolas Sursock Museum, 99
Nippon in the World, 94
North Carolina Census Data: 1960–1980, 259
North Carolina Family Records Online, 259
North Carolina Newspaper Digitization Project, 259
North Carolina State Archives Digital Collections, 259
North Carolina State University—Special Collections Research Center, 260

North Dakota State University—Libraries Digital Collections, 261
Northeast Massachusetts Digital Library, 234
Northwest Art Collection, The, 278
NOVA—Warnings from the Ice, 54
Nubia Museum, 31

O

Oberlin College Digital Collections, 172
Oceania (Malaysia, Australasia, Polynesia), 100
Ogai Collection and His Notes Database, 96
Ohio Memory, 262
Ohio's Heritage Northeast, 263
Oklahoma Crossroads: Documents and Images, 263
Oklahoma Heritage Online (OHO), 263
Oklahoma State University Electronic Publishing Center, 264
Old China Hands Archive, 76, 212–213
Oliphant's Anthem: Pat Oliphant at the Library of Congress, 189
On the Cutting Edge: Contemporary Japanese Prints, 95
Online Archive of California (OAC), 211
Online Books Page, The, 9
Online Burma/Myanmar Library, 101
Online Computer Library Center (OCLC), 9
Online Exhibits—Texas State Library and Archives Commission, 272
Online Treasury of Talmudic Manuscripts, 89
Open Video Project, The, 10
Opium in Asia, 65
Oral Histories, 241
Oregon Digital: Unique Digital Collections from OSU and UO Libraries, 265
Oregon History Project, The, 265
Oregon Institute of Technology Digital Collections, 265
Oregon Missions Collection, 279
Oregon State Archives—Web Exhibits and Projects, 266
Oriental Art, 143
Oriental Art: Images of the East, 106
Oroitzapenak Memories: Basque Oral History Project, 255
Oroitzapenak Memories: Voices from Basque America, 251
Other Collections, 218
Our Roots: Canada's Local Histories Online, 167
Oviatt Library Digital Collections, 212

P

Pacific Islands Legal Information Institute, 287
Pacific Manuscripts Bureau (PAMBU), 289
Paintings, 110
Pakistan: Historic Karachi, 103
PALMM: Publication of Archival Library & Museum Materials, 219
Panama and the Canal, 175
Pandektis—Digital Thesaurus of Primary Sources for Greek History and Culture, 128–129
Papers Past, 128
PARADISEC (Pacific and Regional Archive for Digital Sources in Endangered Cultures), 287
Parallel Histories: Spain, the United States, and the American Frontier, 195
Paul R. Cheesman Photographs, 303, 308
Penvenne Interviews (Mozambique), 39
Perpustakaan Nasional Republik Indonesia (National Library of the Republic of Indonesia), 84
Perry-Castañeda Library Map Collection—Thailand Maps, 109
Petal from the Rose: Illustrations by Elizabeth Shippen Green, A, 189
Photographic Views of New York City, 1870s–1970s, 256
Photography, 157
Picture Australia, 289
Picture Book Gallery, The, 95
Picture Dis: The National Online Album of Jamaica, 173
Pictures, 157, 289
Picturing America, 1497–1899: Prints, Maps, and Drawings Bearing on the New World Discoveries and on the Development of the Territory That Is Now the United States, 256
Picturing Golda Meir, 90
Pinacoteca, 159
Poetry Broadsides, 265
Points of View, 154
Polar Bear Expedition Digital Collections, 239
Political Caricatures of the Hawaiian Kingdom, ca. 1875–1905, 223
Political Cartoons, 200
Portal to Asian Internet Resources, 64
Portal to Texas History, 272
Portrait Collection, 156

Portraits of Modern Japanese Historical Figures, 95
Portuguese Culture, 142
Posters from the Melville J. Herskovits Library of African Studies, 43
Prairie Fire, 226
Preserving and Creating Access to Unique Afghan Records, 67
Printed Material, 157
Printed Working Documents of the Conseil d'Etat [1800–1814], 126
Printed Works, 289
PRISM: Political & Rights Issues & Social Movements, 219
Proceedings of the Royal Netherlands Academy of Arts and Sciences, 138
Profiles in Science, 203
Progressive Men of the State of Montana, 248
Promise of America, 140
Pysanky—Easter Eggs, 153

Q

Quixotes Collection, 146

R

Råå Museum, 151
Ranfurly Collection, 294
Rangiātea, 294
Raphael's Rooms, 159
Rare Book and Special Collections Division, The, 196
Rare Books of the National Diet Library, 95
Rare Books of the National Diet Library—The 60th Anniversary, 95
Reclaiming the Everglades: South Florida's Natural History, 1884–1934, 220
Recorded Sound Reference Center—Tony Schwartz Collection, 196
Red Book of Estonian Publications, 1535–1850, 122
Rede Da Memoria Virtual Brasileira (Brazilian Network of Virtual Memory), 305
Reed Digital Collection—Indian Converts Collection, 268
Reflections: Russian Photographs, 1992–2002, 105
Religion and the Founding of the American Republic, 189
Resor genom tiderna (Travel through the Ages), 149
Revelations from the Russian Archives, 105

Revising Himself: Walt Whitman and Leaves of Grass, 190
Revolutionary Association of the Women of Afghanistan (RAWA), 68
Rijksmuseum Amsterdam, 139
Rivers, Edens, Empires: Lewis & Clark and the Revealing of America, 190
Robert Henry Chandless Photographs of China, 1898–1908, 76
Roger L. Stevens Presents, 190
Rolf Bergendorff's Radio Museum, 151
Roman de la Rose Digital Library, 126
Romanian Medieval Art, 144
Romanian Modern Art, 144
Rome Reborn: The Vatican Library and Renaissance Culture, 158
Rosie the Riveters, 264
Roskilde University Digital Archive (RUDAR), 121
Royal Geographical Society, 54
Russian Archives Online, 105
Russian History Digital Library, 106
Russian History Online: The Khrushchev Years, 106
Rwanda's National HIV/AIDS Digital Library, 41

S

Sacred, 154
Sacred Heart Review, 234
Sagnanet—Icelandic Medieval Literature, 131
Saint-Louis: Religious Pluralism in the Heart of Senegal, 41
Salem Public Library—Oregon Historic Photograph Collections, 266
Sammlungen, 151
San Fernando Valley History Digital Library, 213
Scholars Resource, 10
School Desegregation in Norfolk, Virginia, 276
School on the Range: The Little Cowpuncher Roundup, 209
Science and Industry Collections, 156
Science and Invention, 200
Scientific Committee on Antarctic Research (SCAR), 54
Scientific Iconography, 133
Scientific Knowledge, 133
Scott Polar Research Institute—Picture Library, 51
Scott Polar Research Institute—Polar Museum, 52

Scrolls from the Dead Sea: The Ancient Library of Qumran and Modern Scholarship, 97
Seattle Historical Photograph Collection, The, 278
Seattle Public Library: Special Collections, 278
Second Nuremberg Haggada, The, 90
Seeking Michigan, 240
Sejarah Melayu—A History of the Malay Peninsula, 100
Selected Library of Congress Resources for Michigan, 239
Selected Mongolian Laws and Regulations, 1917–1940, 78
Sera Monastery, 80
Serge Diaghilev and His World: A Centennial Celebration of Diaghilev's Ballets Russes, 1909–1929, 106
SGCool—Singapore Collections Online, 107
Share the Perspective of Genius: Leonardo's Study for the Adoration of the Magi, 134
Sharlot Hall Museum American Indian Image Collection, 208
Sheet Music, 289
Sidney D. Gamble Photographs, 76–77
Sigmund Freud: Conflict and Culture, 118
Sistine Chapel, 159
Slater Museum of Natural History: Bird Wing Collection, 279
Slavery and Manumission Manuscripts of Timbuktu, 37
Slovak National Gallery, 145
Small Electronic Exhibitions: "Kaleidoscope of Books," 95
Smithsonian: Exhibitions, 11
Society of American Archivists, 11
Sokiku Nakatani Japanese Teaware Digital Collection, 96
Sound and Video, 158
South Africa.info—Gallery—Nelson Mandela, 44
South Africa.info—Gallery—The Rock Art of South Africa, 44
South America and Antarctica, 303
South Asian Studies, 64
South Carolina Digital Library, 269
South Seas, 289
Southeast Asia Digital Library, 64, 72–73, 101
Southeast Asian Studies, 101
Southern Oral History Program, 261
Southern Oregon Digital Archives, 266
Spårvägsmuseet, 151

Stagestruck! Performing Arts Caricatures at the Library of Congress, 190
Stanzino Matematiche, 133
State Historical Museum, Moscow, 107
State Historical Society of North Dakota—Archives—Digital Resources—Frontier Scout, 261
State Library of Queensland Virtual Exhibitions, 290
State of Wisconsin Collection, The, 282
State Regional Archives—Litomerice, 121
Stefan Landsberger's Chinese Propaganda Poster Pages, 76
Suecia antiqua . . ., 150
Sukuma Museum, The, 45
Summertime and Recreation, 200
Susan Bordeaux Bettelyoun Autobiography, 250
Swaziland Digital Archives, 45
Swiss National Library NL—Swiss Poster History, 152
Sydney Cyprus Survey Project: Digital Archive, The, 81
Syracuse University Digital Library, 257

T
Taking Liberties, 154
Talking History, 257
Te Ao Hou (The New World), 294
Teaching with Primary Resources, 196
Tejano Voices, 272
Temple of Liberty: Building the Capitol for a New Nation, 191
Tennessee Virtual Archive, 271
Territorial Kansas Online 1854–1861, 227
Texas A&M Digital Library Digital Collections, 272
Theban Mapping Project, 32
This Month's Object, 140
Thomas Brook Photographs Collection, 771, 249
Thomas Jefferson, 191
Thomas Jefferson's Library, 191
Three Historic Nevada Cities: Carson City, Reno, and Virginia City—A National Register of Historic Places Travel Itinerary, 251
Throughout the Ages, 257
Tibet, 66
Tibet Album: British Photography in Central Tibet, 1920–1950, 79
Tibetan and Himalayan Library (THL), The, 79

Ticket to the Past: The First 25 Years of the Missouri State Fair, 246

Tiflolibros, 304

Timarit.is
  Europe, 116, 121–122, 131
  North America, 167, 171

Timeframes, 295

Timemachine, 151

Tiny Traces, 141

Topaz Japanese-American Relocation Center Digital Collection, 96

Tour Egypt, 32

Transactions and Proceedings of the Royal Society of New Zealand, 295

Transcript of Bauduin's Lectures, 93

Transforming the Tar Heel State: The Legacy of Public Libraries in North Carolina, 260

Transportation Around the World: 1911–1993, 66

Transportation History Collection: Railroads, 237

Travel Literature on Southeast Europe and the Eastern Mediterranean 15th–19th Centuries, 129

Trust Territory of the Pacific Islands, 291

Tseng Family Collection of Chinese Antiquities, 76, 213

Tundra Times Photograph Project, 207

Turn the Pages, 154

Turning the Pages Online, 204

U

U.S. Labor and Industrial History World Wide Web Audio Archive, 258

UIC Sierra Leone (University of Illinois at Chicago), 42

Ukrainian Commercial Recording, 152

Ukrainian Folklore Sound Recordings, 152

Ukrainian Wedding Exhibit, 153

Ulukua: The Hawaiian Electronic Library, 223

UMFA: Utah Museum of Fine Arts, 274

Undergraduate Victorian Studies Online Teaching Anthology, 243

UNESCO—Underwater Cultural Heritage in Asia-Pacific Waters, 64

UNESCO World Heritage, 11, 70, 79

United States and Brazil: Expanding Frontiers, Comparing Cultures, The, 196, 306

United States Antarctic Program—Antarctic Photo Library, 54

United States Antarctic Resource Center (USARC), 54

United States National Library of Medicine (NLM) National Institutes of Health—Online Exhibitions and Digital Projects, 12, 202

University Digital Conservancy, 251

University of Adelaide, 290

University of Alabama Digital Collections, 206

University of Arkansas—Digital Collections, 209

University of Arkansas for Medical Sciences Library—Historical Research Center Digital Collections, 210

University of Auckland Digital Library, 295

University of Canterbury Photograph Collection, 296

University of Colorado Digital Library, 214

University of Connecticut Libraries Digital Collections, 215

University of Delaware Library Digital Collections, 216

University of Florida Digital Collections, 220

University of Georgia Libraries, 222

University of Hawai'i at Manoa Libraries, 73

University of Hawai'i at Manoa Libraries—Asia at Work Collection, 84, 98, 101, 108, 109

University of Hawai'i at Manoa Libraries—Asia Collection, 65

University of Idaho Library Special Collections and Archives, 225

University of Iowa Libraries—Iowa Digital Library, The, 227

University of Louisville Digital Collections, 229

University of Maryland Digital Collections, 232

University of Miami Libraries Digital Initiatives, 220

University of Miami Libraries—East and Southeast Asian Studies, 72

University of Minnesota Libraries—Digital Collections, 242

University of Mississippi Digital Collections, 244

University of Missouri Digital Library, 246

University of Nevada Las Vegas (UNLV) Digital Collections, 251

University of New Hampshire Library Digital Collections, 252

University of North Alabama Digital Collections, 206

University of North Carolina—Digital Collections, 260

University of North Carolina–Wilmington Digital Collections, 261

University of Oklahoma Libraries—Western History Collections, 264

University of Pretoria, South Africa—Africana Books Collection, 44

University of Pretoria, South Africa—Van Warmelo Collection, 44

University of Pretoria, South Africa—Woodhouse Rock Art Collection, 44

University of Puget Sound Digital Collections, 278

University of Saskatchewan Archives: Exhibits and Special Projects, 167

University of South Carolina Digital Collections, 269

University of South Carolina School of Law Digital Collection, 269

University of South Florida Libraries, Special & Digital Collections—CORAL, 220

University of Southern California (USC) Digital Library, 20, 24, 25, 36, 213

University of Southern Mississippi Digital Collections, 244

University of Southern Mississippi Libraries Digital Collection, 73

University of Tartu Library, 122

University of Tennessee, 271

University of Tokyo Library System, The, 96

University of Toronto Digital Collections, 167

University of Utah—J. Willard Marriott Library Digital Collections, 274

University of Virginia Digital Collections, 276

University of Washington—History: Asia, 65

University of Washington—International Collections Database, 65

University of Washington Libraries, 98

University of Washington Special Collections, 164

University of Wisconsin Digital Collection—Philippines Image Collection, 104

University of Wisconsin Digital Collections
    Africa, 22-23, 38, 40-41, 45
    Asia, 71-73
    Europe, 117
    North America, 282
    World Initiatives, 13

University of Wisconsin-Milwaukee—Digital Collections, 66, 71, 73, 97

University of Wyoming Digital Collections, 282

Upper Peninsula Digitization Center, 239

Urban Dreams/Sueños Urbanos, 305

Utah State Archives and Records Service—Digital Archives, 274

Utah State History, 274

V

Vatican Museums, 158

Vatican Secret Archives, 159

Vera and Arturo Schwarz Collection of Dada and Surrealist Art, The, 86

Vermont Historical Society, 275

Vermont in the Civil War, 275

Veterans History Project, 201, 236

Vets with a Vision, 111

Victoria and Albert Museum, 155

Videos, 106

Viet Nam Cultural Profile, 112

Viewing Suriname: A Collaborative Collection, 309

Virginia Commonwealth University Libraries Digital Collections, 276

Virginia Historical Society—Digital Collections, 276

Virginia Memory, 277

Virginia Tech ImageBase, 277

Virtual Antarctica, 55

Virtual Archives and Exhibitions of the Charles H. Wright Museum of African American History, 241

Virtual Exhibition of the Old Photographs, 93

Virtual Motor City, 239

Virtual Motor City Detroit News Newsreels, 239

Virtual Museum of the Ethnographical Monuments in the Romanian Open Air Museums, 144

Virtual Reference Shelf, 201

Virtuelle Transfer, 152

Visible Proofs: Forensic Views of the Body, 204

Visual Resources Association (VRA), 13

Voices, Votes, Victory: Presidential Campaign Songs, 192

Voices of Civil Rights, 191

Volunteer Voices, 271

W

Walter Bone Shirt Ledger, The, 248

War of 1812 Digitization Project: Footsteps to the Battlefield, 239

Wars and the Home Front, 200

Washington State Archives—Digital Archive, 279

Washington State Historical
    Society—Featured Collections, 279
Washington State University (WSU)
    Libraries Digital Collections, 280
Washington Women's History Consortium,
    280
Water-Babies Illustrations by Jessie Willcox
    Smith, The, 192
Web Gallery of Art, The, 13
Web Sirih Pinang (Betel Leaf and Betel
    Nut): Simbol Budaya Melayu (The
    Symbol of Malay Heritage), 100
Webcollection, 152
Welcome to the Land of Smiles—Thailand,
    109
Wellcome Library—Collections, 13
Welsh Biography, 158
Wenceslaus Hollar Digital Collection, 168
West Africa Online Digital Library, 20
West Side Story, 192
West Virginia Archives and History, 281
West Virginia History and Regional
    Collection, 281
West Virginia University Libraries Digital
    Collections, 281
Western Maryland's Historical Library, 233
Western Washington Flora, 279
"What a Piece of Work Is a Man"—Reading
    the Body in Medieval Manuscripts, 14
When They Were Young: A Photographic
    Retrospective of Childhood, 192
Whole Works of Sir James Ware concerning
    Ireland, 132
Wilanów Poster Museum, 142
Wild Bill Hickok Court Documents, 250
William Hervie Dobson Collection, The, 62,
    77
Wilmette Public Library—Digital Exhibits,
    226
Windows on Maine, 231
Winona County Historical Society, 242
Winona State University, 242
Wisconsin Electronic Reader, 282
Wisconsin Heritage Online, 282
"With an Even Hand": Brown v. Board at
    Fifty, 193
With Malice Toward None: The Abraham
    Lincoln Bicentennial Exhibition, 193
Witness and Response: September 11
    Acquisitions at the Library of
    Congress, 193

Wizard of Oz: An American Fairy Tale, The,
    194
Women Come to the Front: Journalists,
    Photographers, and Broadcasters
    During WWII, 194
Women of a New Tribe, 241
Women's History, 201
Women's Travel Writing, 1830–1930, 243
Wonderful Things from the Pharaoh's Tomb,
    241
Wood Family Collection, 265
Work of Charles and Ray Eames: A Legacy
    of Invention, The, 194
Works Progress Administration (WPA)
    Property Inventories, 241
World Civilizations Image Repository
    (WCIR), 14
World Digital Library
    Africa, 22–25, 32–33, 35, 38, 41–42, 46
    Asia, 67, 71–72, 82, 85–86, 97–98, 108,
        111–112
    Europe, 117–119, 136–137, 144
    North America, 165, 170–172, 175–176
    South America, 307
    World Initiatives, 14
World Digital Library—Sixth Map of Asia, 97
World Heritage Sites in Malaysia, 100
World Heritage Sites in Nepal, 102
World Monuments Fund, 14
World Treasures of the Library of Congress:
    Beginnings, 15
World War II Provenance Research Online,
    87
Wyoming Memory, 283
Wyoming Newspaper Digital Project, 283
Wyoming State Library Digital Collections,
    284

X
XUL: Signo Viejo y Nuevo, 304

Y
YouTube Library of Congress, 201

Z
Zanabazar Museum of Mongolian Fine Arts,
    79

Index of Names, Subjects, and Titles

9/11. *See* September 11th
1800 Act of Union, 131
1906 San Francisco Earthquake, 211

A

A Is for Atom (1953) (video), 10
Accademia dei Lincei (Italy), 133
Account of Flint and Genesee County from Their Organization, An, 238
Adventures of Huckleberry Finn, The, 187
Afghanistan
    images, 60, 66
    main entry, 67–68
    multiformat resources, 4, 12, 59, 63–65
Africa: Containing a Description of the Manners and Customs . . . , 34
African Orthodox Church, 43
Ain't We Got Fun, 241
Alabama, 191, 193, 204–206
Alabama Historical Quarterly, 204
Alaska
    Alaska–Yukon–Pacific Exposition, 164, 278
    and Russia, 104, 186–187, 195
    images, 164
    main entry, 206–207
    multiformat resources, 195
Albinus, B.S. (Bernhard Siegfried), 12, 203
Aldrin, Edwin E., 182
Alexander the Great, 103
Alice's Adventures Under Ground, 114
Alighieri, Dante, 182
All Things Considered, 204
Allan, David, 156
Allen, Gracie, 190
Alten, Mathias J., 235
Amazon River, 307
American Archivist, 11
American Civil War (1861–1865)
    diaries, 235–237, 240
    images, 216
    letters, 163, 245

    log books, 206
    multiformat resources, 178, 197, 200, 216, 222, 232, 244, 254, 260, 267, 275, 277
    music, 199
    photographs, 240
    records, 213, 216, 240, 252, 263
    speeches, 246
American Frontier, 104, 195
"American Intervention in Northern Russia, 1918–1919," 239
American Presidential Inaugurations, 186
American Revolution (1775–1883), 187, 189, 200, 247, 267
American West, 208
Amundsen, Roald, 53, 54, 140
Ancient civilizations, 303
Ancient manuscripts, 19
Anderson, Guy, 278
Andersen, Hans Christian, 121
Andorra, 117, 137, 144
Andrée, S.A. (Salomon August), 148
Angus, D.J., 235
Animal Farm, 185
Ann Arbor, Michigan, 236, 238
Annals of Kansas, 1541–1885, 227
Antarctic Sun, The, 54
Antarctica, 7–8, 49–55, 303
Apache (tribe), 208
Apartheid, 17, 18, 42–43
Appalachia, 228
Archaeological sites, 62, 303
Archdiocese of Boston, 124
Archer, John, 153
Architectural Forum, 194
Archival Outlook, 11
Ariadne, 7
Arizona
    architecture, 184
    diary, 190
    images, 248
    main entry, 207–209
    multiformat resources, 176

Arkansas, 192, 209–210
Armstrong, Neil A., 182
Arrendondo, Alberto, 169
Asia
    images, 7, 13–14, 288
    main entry, 57–112
    multiformat resources, 11, 140, 197
    text, 4
Atomic bomb, 92, 106
Au sud de l'Afrique, 35
Auckland, New Zealand, 293, 295
Augsburg Art Cabinet, 150
Auschwitz-Birkenau Concentration and
        Extermination Camp (Poland), 141
Australasian Antarctic Expedition
        (1911–1914), 53
Australia
    images, 7, 70
    main entry, 287–290
    multiformat resources, 286
    resources, 52
Australian Antarctica Magazine, The, 52
Australian High Court, 288
"Australian Newspapers Beta—Historic
        Australian Newspapers 1803–1950,"
        286
Australian War Memorial, 288
Austrian National Library, 114
Aviation, 208
Aztecs, 183

B

Bagerhat, Bangladesh, 71
Bahrain, 69–70
Baja Peninsula, 188
Bakersfield, California, 212
Baldwin, James, 181, 199
Balkan Peninsula, 117
Ball, Lucille, 224
Ballets Russes, 106
Baltic Sea, 135
Bamiyan (Afghanistan), 67, 90
Bamiyan Valley (Afghanistan), 12,
Bangladesh, 64–65, 70–71
Banks, Joseph, 290
Barnard, E.E. (Edward Emerson), 221
Barnet, Will, 181
Barrow, Clyde, 272
Barton, Sir Edmund, 288
Bašagić, Safvet beg, 119
Baseball
    images, 249, 255, 275
    multiformat resources, 179, 187, 197, 200

Basque, 224–225, 251
Bates, George Handy, 290, 297
Battle of Plassey (1757), 71
Battle of San Jacinto, The, 272
Bauduin, Dr. A.F. (Toon), 92
Bauduin, Dr. A.J. (Albert), 92
Baum, L. Frank (1856–1919), 194
Bavaria (Germany), 113
Bavarian State Library, 113
Bay Psalm Book, 184
Bçrzkalns, Valentîns, 135
Beatles, The, 187
Becker, Joseph, 233
Beijing, 75
Belden, Charles J., 283
Belize City, 165
Bell, Gertrude, 62, 109
Bendiner, Alfred, 190
Benedict, George G., 275
Bent, George, 214
Benton, Thomas Hart, 245
Berengario da Carpi, Jacopo, 12
Berlin, Irving (1888–1989), 184, 239
Bermudian, The, 164
Bernstein, Leonard, 181, 192
Betel leaf, 100
Betel nut, 100
Bhotan and the Story of the Dooar War
        (1866), 71
Bhutan, 60, 64, 71–72
Bibles
    Bible of Mainz, 187
    Eliot Indian Bible, The, 187
    English Bible Containing the Old
            Testament and the New, The, 15
    Geneva Bible, 187
    Gutenberg Bible, 4, 153, 187
    King James Bible, 87, 187
    St. John's Bible, 186
Bibliotheca Alexandrina, 17, 26–27
Bill of Rights, The, 179, 181, 188
Billen, Sixto Duran, 307
Birds, 93, 309
Birmingham, Alabama, 205
Birmingham Iron Age, 205
Bishop, J. Michael, 204
Blackburn, Robert, (1920–2003), 181
Blind and visually handicapped, 188, 304
Block, Herb. *See* Herblock
Blondie, 180
Bloody Sunday, 192
Bly, Robert, 265
Bodmer, Karl, 255, 265
Boeing 247, 182

Bogd Khaan Winter Palace Museum, 77
Boiling Lake, Dominica, 170
Boleyn, Ann, 158
Bolivia, 164, 301, 303–305
Bonney, Therese, 194
Borchgrevink, Carsten, 51
Borneo, 4, 72, 100,
Bosnia-Herzegovina, 115, 119, 183
Boston, Massachusetts, 233, 234
Bourne, Eulalia, 208–209
Bouvet de Lozier, Jean-Baptiste Charles, 51
Boxer Rebellion (1900), 76–77
Boyer, Deena. *See* Stryker, Deena
Boykin, Frank W., Congressman, 204
Braille, Louis (1809–1852), 188
Brazil, 196, 301, 303, 305–306
Brazilian Royal Court, 305
Bridgetower, George Polgreen, 153
Britain
    and Ireland, 131
    and United States, 181, 187, 190, 231, 240
    multiformat resources, 154
British Antarctic Expedition (1907–1909), 53–54
British Honduras, 165
British, Australian and New Zealand
        Antarctic Research Expedition, 52
Brown, John, 227, 281
*Brown v. Board of Education of Topeka,
        Kansas,* 193
Brunei Darussalam, 61, 64, 72
Brunschwig, Hieronymus, 204
Bubley, Esther, 194
Buccaneers of America, The, 182
Bucharest (Romania), 143
Buddha, 64, 76, 78, 101–102
Buddhists
    images, 66, 70, 73, 75, 78
    monasteries, 12, 80
    multiformat resources, 79, 90–91
Bunjee (video), 10
Burma. *See* Myanmar
Burns, George, 190
Buscher, Michael, 187
Busk, Judy, 273
By Parties Unknown, 181
Byrd, Richard Evelyn, Jr., 51, 53
Byrnes, James F., 269

C
Cabrera, Lydia, 169
Cagney, James, 180
California
    architecture, 184
    main entry, 210–213
    map, 188
    multiformat resources, 60, 74
    Native American tribes, 266
California Department of Education, 211
California Underground Railroad, 210
Callahan, Kenneth, 278
Cambodia
    images, 60,
    main entry, 73
    multiformat resources, 4, 60, 61, 64–65,
        112
Canada
    images, 164
    main entry, 166–168
    multiformat resources, 162, 247
    periodicals, 117, 122
Candoli, Conte, 225
Canoe Voyage up the Minnay Sotor, A, 282
Cape Adare, 49, 51
Cape Evans, 49, 51
Cape Royds, 49, 51
Cape Verde, 18, 23
Caribbean, 8, 163, 181, 301–302
Caricatures, 162, 179, 189–190, 223, 255
Carroll, Lewis, 114
*Carta Marina Navigatoria Portugallen
        Navigationes . . . ,* 182
Cartoonists, 179–180, 183, 185, 200
Cartoons
    China, 74
    editorial, 73, 183, 185, 227
    immigration, 74
    political, 73, 179, 186–187, 189, 200, 223
    social issues, 189
Castro, Fidel, 169–170
Cathar Writings, 31
Cato Major, 179
Central America, 7, 164–165, 181, 303
Central Europe, 12, 126
Cesare, Oscar, 190
Cesi, Federico, 133
Cetinje (Montenegro), 138
Chado (the Way of Tea), 96, 211
Chamberlain, Joshua, 231
Chamberlain, Kenneth, 190
Chamberlin, Agnes, 167
Chandless, Robert Henry, 76
Channing, Carol, 224
Chapin, James P., 25
Charles, Geoff, 157
Charles, Ray, 180
Chaves, Diego de Orellana de, 147, 273
Cheesman, Paul R., 303, 308

Cheney (Washington), 278
Chiang-Kai-Shek, Madame, 92
Chief Joseph, 279
Chief Lawyer, 279
Chief Leschi, 279
Chief Seattle, 279
Child Alone, 181
Child of the Sun, 218
Chile, 164, 301, 303, 306
China
    government, 58
    images, 2, 13, 60–62, 65, 106, 108, 213
    main entry, 73–80
    multiformat resources, 61, 65, 182
    resources, 59, 65
China, People's Republic of, 8, 73–80
Chinese Communist Party, 75
Choijin Lama, 78
Christianity, 27, 97
Churchill, Winston, 4, 181
Civil Rights Movement (U.S.), 191–192, 197
Civil rights, 191, 197, 202, 222, 247
Clark, Henry Thurston, 230
Clark, William, 249
Clayton, Wilbur "Buck," 245, 246
Cleveland, Grover, 252, 256
Clinton, William, 186, 189
Cobb, Ty, 197
Codex Vindobonensis, 183
Coeur d'Alene, Idaho, 225,
Coleridge-Taylor, Samuel, 153, 247
Coles, Robert, 193
Colorado, 176, 190, 213–215
Columbia (space shuttle), 182, 204
Columbus, Christopher, 179, 182–184, 198
Commedia, La, 182
Comoro Islands, 24
Confederacy (Confederate States of
        America), The, 197
Confessions of St. Augustine, The, 9
Conseil d'Etat, 125–156
Cook, Captain James, 288
Cook, James, 51
Cooke, Roger, 280
Coos (tribe), 266
Copland, Aaron, 181
Coptic Museum, 27
Corelli, Marie, 243
Corpus Hermeticum, 31
Corse, Carita Doggett, 219
Cortazar, Julio, 304
Cortés, Hernán, 183
Covarrubias, Miguel, 190
Cow Creek Band of Umpqua (tribe), 266

Cowell, Herbert, 243
Craig, May (Elisabeth May Adams Craig),
        194
"Creating the Bill of Rights," 181
"Creating the Declaration of Independence,"
        181
"Creating the U.S. Constitution," 181
CSS Alabama, 206
Cuba, 168–170, 303
Curry, John, 245

D

da Vinci, Leonardo, 114, 154
Dagua River, 307
Dahlbergh, Erik, 150
Daily Worker, 188
Daisho-reki calendar, 94
Dali, Slavador, 147
Darling, Jay Norwood, 227
Darwin, Charles, 81, 243
d'Aulnoy, Marie-Catherine, 243
David Copperfield, 281
Davis, Jefferson, 243
Davis County Clipper, 274
Dawn, 181
Dawn at the Alamo, 272
de Gournay, Marie, 242
de Grandpre, Louis, 42, 112
de Ketham, Johannes, 204
de Montfaucon, Bernard, 15
de Navarre, Marguerite, 242
de Orellana de Chaves, Diego, 147
de Pizan, Christine, 242
de Poitiers, Diane, 242
de Scudéry, Madeleine, 242
Dead Sea Scrolls, xv, 31, 97
Declaration of Independence, 179, 181–182,
        197, 246
Denggi fever, 99
*Descripción geográfica y gobierno,
        administración y colonización de las
        colonias españolas del golfo de
        Guinea* (Geographical Description
        and Governmental Administration
        and Settlement of the Spanish
        Colonies in the Gulf of Guinea), 32
Desenberg, Edward, 241
DesiLu, 224
Detroit, Michigan, 237, 239
Detroit News, 239
Devil's Island, French Guiana (South
        America), 124
Dexheimer, Florence, 282

Dhaka, 71
Diaghilev, Serge, 106
Diario de la marina, 168
Dias del Diario de la marina en el exilio, 168
Dickens, Charles, 243, 281
DigiCULT, 7
Djibouti, 25
D-Lib Magazine, 7
Dobson, William Hervie, 62
Dominguez, Francisco, 190
Don Quixote, 2
Doonesbury, 189
Drepung Monastery, 79
Duggan, Margo, 291
Du Guillet, Pernette, 243
Dumas, Alexandre, 153
Dutch West India Company, 188

E

Eames, Charles, 194
Eames, Ray, 194
Earhart, Amelia, 182, 198, 208
East India Company, 150
East Timor, 61, 64, 81–82
Edo Era (Japan), 93–94
Educational Laws of Virginia, 193
Egan, Raymond B., 241
Egypt
    art, 158
    images, 10, 66, 103, 215
    main entry, 25–32
    periodicals, 128
    resources, 13, 236, 241
    texts, 112, 258
    video, 69
Ehon, 91, 95
Einstein, Albert, 4, 88
El Salvador, 171, 301
Election (U.S.), 198
Emancipation Proclamation, 179, 185, 197, 202
Emblem books, 126
England, 29, 94, 127, 155, 273
English Bible, 15
Enoch Scroll, 97
Entre Voces, 307
Epistolae, 235
Eskimos, 187
Ethiopia, 18, 33, 154
Europe in the Spring, 194

F

Fasiculo de Medicina, 204
Feather, Leonard, 225

Featherstonhaugh, George William, 282
Federal Writer's Project, 218
Federalist, The, 188
Fedorov, Ivan, 105
Fedorovich, Pakomov Alexey, 105
Fenian Brotherhood, 131
Fiji, 286, 290
Filchner Ice Shelf, 50
Filter, The, 7
Finding Katahdin, 230
First Monday, 7
Flanner, Janet, 194
Flight (aviation), 10, 53, 182, 198
Flora
    Canada, 167
    Japan, 93
    Liberia, 36
    North Carolina, 260
    Peru, 308
    Texas, 272
    Washington, 279
Florence, Italy, 29, 135
Florida, 163, 169, 175, 216–221
Florida Everglades, 217, 220
Folk Music, 58, 214
Ford, Henry, 239
Fourth of July, 246
Fraggle Rock, 233
*Framework of Guidance for Building Good
        Digital Collections, A*, 8
France
    and America, 195, 290
    and Congo Republic, 24
    and Cuba, 168
    images, 116
    main entry, 123–126
    posters, 119
    texts, 94, 126
    women writers, 242
    and World War II, 181
Frank, Leo, 221
Franklin, Benjamin, 179, 200, 267
French and Indian War, 267
Freud, Sigmund, 118
Frissell, Toni, 194
Fulbright, J.W., 209
Fungi, 167
Fürer-Haimendorf, Christoph von, 102

G

Gagarin, Yuri, 106
Gaines, Lloyd L., 247
Galapagos Islands, 92–93, 301, 307

Galdiano, Jose Lazaro, 147
Galilei, Galileo, 15, 133, 158
Gambia, 23, 33–34
Gamble, Sidney D., 76–77
Gandan (monastery), 78
Gandhi, Mohandas, 83, 103
General Magazine, The, 179
Geneva Bible, 187
Genius of Liberty, The, 191
Geographia, 97
Geologic Atlas of the United States, 273
George, David Lloyd, 157–158
German Antarctic Expedition, 53
German Antarctic Research Station, 52
Germany
    images, 116
    main entry, 126–128
    maps, 273
    posters, 119
    texts, 46, 94–95
Gershwin, George, 187
Getty Research Institute, 3
Gettysburg Address, The, 179, 185
Gettysburg, Battle of, 231, 267
Giambologna, 135
Gibran, Khalil, 99
Gillespie, Dizzy, 225
Giza, Egypt, 27, 29–30
Gnosticism, 31
Gold Rush, 61, 164, 207, 211, 226
Göttingen, Germany, 4, 127
Grant, Ulysses S., 244
Grapes of Wrath, The, 187
Grau, Polita, 169
Great Britain, 187, 231, 240
Great Chicago fire, 233
Great Depression
    and California, 211
    and Dorothea Lange, 194
    and Ethnic Groups, 198
    and Florida, 217–218
    and Pennsylvania, 267
    and sheep industry, 251
    and Utah, 273
Great Wall of China, 76
Greece, 31, 80, 128–129, 136
Green, Elizabeth Shippen, 189
Grenada, 170–171
Grey, Al, 225
Guatemala, 171–172, 303
Guinea, 18, 23, 34–35
Guinée, La, 35
Guitar, 212

Gutenberg Bible, 4, 153, 187
Gutiérrez, Dr. José Angel, 272

H
Hacivat and Karagöz Puppet Theater, 110
Haiti, 34, 163, 172, 241
Hamagid, 88
Hameliz, 88
Hamilton, Alexander, 188
Hampton, Lionel, 225
Hamy, Alfred, 282
Harper's Magazine, 189
Harper's Monthly, 281
Harper's Weekly, 180, 276
Harvard Classics, The, 9
Hats and headdresses, 139, 214–215
Havasupai (tribe), 208
Havazelet, 88
Hawaii, 8, 223, 246
Hay, John, 185
Hazevi/Haor/Hashkafa, 88
Heavenly Discourse, 265
Hebrew newspapers, 88
Helmasperger's Notarial Instrument, 4
Henry VIII, King of England, 153, 158
Hensley, Glenn S., 83
Henson, Jim, 233
Herblock, 183, 185
Heydar Aliev and National-Spiritual Values, 69
Hill, Abby Williams, 278
Himalayan culture, 61, 71, 79, 102
Hindu culture, 61
His Discourse of Old Age, 179
Hispanic culture, 198, 224, 302
HMS Endeavour, 288
Hodges, James, 270
Hollar, Wenceslaus, 168
Holocaust, 220–221, 228
Holy Land, 87–89, 103
Holy Roman Empire, 137
Homer, 158
Hong Kong. *See* China
Hoover, Herbert, 185
Hope, Bob, 180
Hopi (tribe), 208
Hopkins, Martha, 187
Hosea Commentary Scroll, 97
Hotel Colonial, 165
Houdetot, Frederic Christophe de, 125
Houphouet-Boigny, Felix, 25
Hualapai (tribe), 208
Hudson, Henry, 195

Human evolution, 11
Hupa (tribe), 211, 266
Hurricane Camille, 243
Hut Point, 51
Hyde, George, 214

I

I Remember Mama, 224
I Want to Go Back to Michigan; Down on the Farm, 239
Idaho, 224–225, 251, 279
International Federation of Library Associations and Institutions (IFLA), 4–5, 285–286, 301
Iliad, 158
Illingworth, Leslie, 157
Illustrators, 187, 189–190, 249
Immigration
    American, 199, 255–256
    Asian-American, 197
    Belgian-American, 118
    Chinese-American, 74
    Japanese-Brazilian, 94
    Jewish-American, 184
    Kansas Territory, 227
In the Know, 7
In the Loop, 11
Incas (tribe), 183
Incunabula, 89, 94, 113, 146, 235
Independent films, 304
India
    images, 14, 19, 60–62, 103, 108
    main entry, 82–84
    maps, 71–72
    resources, 4, 62, 64–65
    video, 102
Indian Coverts, 268
Indiana, 36, 226–227
Indians (native peoples)
    images, 208, 211, 224, 242, 265, 279
    resources, 183, 190, 249, 267–268
    texts, 263
    video, 120
Indochina, 67, 73, 98
Indonesia, 60, 61, 64–65, 84
Ingleby, John, 157
Ink and Blood, 179
Insulin, 168
International Military Tribunal for the Far East (Tokyo trial), 91–92
International Space Station, 10, 182
Internment camps, 211
Iran, 60, 63, 84–85, 90

Iraq, 62–63, 71, 85–86, 236
Ireland, 131–132, 155
Irish Republican Brotherhood. *See* Fenian Brotherhood
Isaacman, Allen, 39
Ishihara, Kuniko, 95
Islamic ceramics, 28
Islamic manuscripts, 6, 37
Israel, 29, 33, 86–90, 103
Italy
    images, 116, 137
    main entry, 132–135
    resources, 29
    texts, 126
Ivan Meštrović Museums, 120

J

Jackson, Andrew, 186
Jackson, Donald, 186
Jackson, Mississippi, 191
Jackson, Reverend James, 192
Jackson, William Henry, 83
Jacksonville Republican, 206
Jamaica Journal, 164, 173
Jamaica Times, 173
Jan Mayen Islands. *See* Norway
Japan
    art, 106, 143, 241
    images, 13–14, 60–62, 65, 75
    main entry, 90–96
    resources, 4, 58–59, 61–62, 65, 197
    texts, 62
Jay, John, 188
Jefferson, Thomas, 182, 188, 191, 199
Jenson, Nikolaus, 126
Johnson, Lyndon B., 192
Johnson, Virginia Wales, 144
Johnston, Frances Benjamin, 193
Johnstown Flood of 1889, 267
Jolson, Al, 190
Jordan, 66, 96–97
Journal of Magellan's Voyage, 137
Judaism, 97
Judge (magazine), 223
Juvonen, Helmi, 278

K

Kahn, Gus, 241
"Kalamazoo" (song), 241
Kansas, 193, 227, 250
Kantrowitz, Adrian, 204
Karuk (tribe), 211, 266

Keating, Bern, 192
Keaton, Buster, 283
Keenan, Joseph Berry, 91–92
Keller, Helen, 188
Kennedy, John F., 186, 283
Kenya, 33, 35
Ketubbot, 87–88
Khaan, Bogd, 77
Khafra, 27
Khan, Genghis, 78–79
Khrushchev, 106
Kierkegaard, Soren, 121
Kiewit, John S., 164
Khufu, 187
King, Dr. Martin Luther, 192, 239
Kingsley, Reverend Charles, 192
Kiplinger Magazine, 183
Kiribati, 286, 291
Klamath (tribe), 266
Köblitz, Urban, 126
Kononeko, Natalie, 152
Koop, C. Everett, 204
Koran, The, 15
Korean War, 184, 209, 288
Kulenovic, Rizah, 150
Kunz, Anita, 180

L
Labé, Louise, 242
Lady Janet, 239
Lagrange, Francis, 124
Lake Chad, 24
Landsat 7, 7, 182, 200
Lang, Herbert, 25
Lange, Dorothea, 194
Laos
    images, 60, 65, 106
    main entry, 98
    resources, 4, 61, 64, 112
Lapham, Increase Allen, 282
Laurel, Stan, 283
Laurents, Arthur, 192
Layla, 86
Lazarus, Emma, 184
Leaves of Grass, 190
Lee, Robert Cranston, 278
Lee, Robert E., 267
Lee, Russell, 192
Lewis and Clark
    images, 265
    resources, 162, 177, 190, 199
    texts, 276
Lhasa, Tibet, 66, 80

Liberation struggles—Africa, 18, 43
Liberia, 34, 36
Libya, 17, 36
Life Magazine, 112, 194
Lima, Jose Lezama, 169
Lincoln, Abraham
    images, 186, 267
    resources, 185, 193, 196, 226, 267
    texts, 179, 225
Lindbergh, Charles A., 182, 198, 208
Linnaeus, Carl, 149
Lithuania, 135–136
Litomerice, Czech Republic, 121
Little Cowpuncher, 208–209
Little Rock, Arkansas, 192, 209, 246
Livonia Region, Europe, 135
Llanystumdwy, Wales (UK), 158
Locomotive World, 237
London, England (UK), 29, 194, 200
Los Angeles, California, 188, 213
Los Angeles Examiner, 211
Lotter, Tobias Conrad, 136
Louvain, Belgium, 119
Louvre, The, 125
Low, David, 74
Luce, Clare Boothe, 194
Lummi (tribe), 279
Lumpkin, Ben Gray, 214
Luxor Temple, 27, 28
Lyceum and Lawn Tennis Club, 169

M
Macau. *See* China
MacDowell Colony, 181
Macedonia, 128, 136
Machado, Gerardo, 169
Machel, Samora, 39
Machi Picchu, 301
MacMeekin, Dan, 287
Madagascar, 24, 36–37
Madison, James, 188
Madras (Chennai), India, 83
Magalotti, Lorenzo, 133
Magna Carta, 114, 153–154, 202
Magnificent Ambersons, The, 224
Maine, 187, 230–231
Makah (tribe), 279
Malaysia, 59–65, 99–100
Maldives, 64, 101
Mali, 6, 19, 34, 37
Man for All Seasons, A, 190
Mandela, Nelson, 43–44
Manichaean Writings, 31

Manitoba, 167
Mantegna, 135
Manzanar (internment camp), 200, 211
Maori (tribe), 293–296
Maricopa (tribe), 208
Maris, Roger, 197
Marshall, George, 183
Marshall Islands, 286, 292
Marshall Plan, 183
Mary, Queen of Scots, 156
Maryland, 216, 231–233
Matsui, Robert T., 210
Mauritania, 20, 38
Maximilian zu Wied-Neuwied, Prince, 265
Maxwell, Ben, 266
McArdle, Henry, 272
McBeth, Kate, 224
McBeth, Sue, 224
McCallum, Jane, 271
Mead, Margaret, 189
Medieval texts
    anatomy/medicine, 14, 204, 260
    Bible, 186
    Icelandic, 131
    Islamic, 12
    Latin, 116
    Netherlands, 139
    Wales (UK), 157
    woodcut books, 116
Meir, Golda, 90
Memoirs of the Revolution in Bengal, 71
Memory Project
    American, 177, 21
    Arizona, 208
    Florida, 216, 218
    Indiana, 226–227
    Maryland, 232
    Montana, 248
    Ohio, 263
    Virginia, 277
    West Virginia, 281
    Wyoming, 283
Memphis, Tennessee, 246
Menkaure, 27
Mercati, Michele, 158
Meru Nyingpa Monastery, 79–80
Metallotheca, 158
Meuser, Caspar, 126
Mexico
    images, 235
    main entry, 173–174
    resources, 183
    texts, 164
    video, 34

Miami, Florida, 169, 217, 220
Micronesia, 285–286, 291
Middle Ages, 12, 121, 126
Middle East
    cartoons, 183
    images, 7, 62, 67–68, 85, 103
    resources, 4, 86, 103
Minsk, Belarus, 118
Mississippi, 191, 243–245, 264
Mississippi River, 243
Mississippi State Penitentiary, 243
Missouri, 245–247
Missouri River, 190, 265
Missouri State Fair, 246
Mitchel, John, 132
Mixtec (tribe), 183
Modoc (tribe), 266
Mohave (tribe), 208
Mohilla, Comoros Islands, 24
Moldavia, Romania, 144
Mongolia, 59, 66, 77–79
Montgomery, Alabama, 191–193
Monticello, 191
Montpensier, Anne-Marie-Louise, 243
Morgenstierne, George, 140
Morris, Lewis, 157
Morris, William, 157
Morrison, Hedda Hammer, 75
Morse, Lee, 225
Moscow Times, 105
Mount Vernon, 188
Mozambique, Liberation Front of
        (FRELIMO), 39
Mozambique Revolution, 39
Munch, Edvard, 140
Mundt, Karl, 270
Muppet Show, The, 233
Murray, William Vans, 290
Mushrooms, 167
Muslims, 37, 41, 61, 154
Myanmar, 61, 62, 64, 101

N
Nagasaki, 92–93
Nakatani, Sokiku, 96, 211
Namibia, 19, 40
Nast, Thomas, 74
National Aeronautics and Space
        Administration (NASA), 7, 10, 53
National Diet Library, 93, 95
National Estuarine Research Reserve System
        (NERR), 8

National Oceanic and Atmospheric
Administration (NOAA), 8
National Organization of Cypriot Fighters
(EOKA), 80
National Science Foundation (NSF), 5, 9, 50,
54
National Severe Storms Laboratory (NSSL), 8
Native Americans
contact with Europeans, 183–184
customs, 195
images, 74, 162, 179, 208, 231, 248–249,
255
maps, 214
multiformat resources, 199, 215, 256, 264,
268, 280
textual documents, 266
Nauru, 286, 292
Navajo (tribe), 208
Nefertari, 29
Nefertiti, 26
Nepal, 59–60, 64–66, 102
Netherlands
and America, 195
and European library, 115–116
and Indonesia, 84
exhibitions, 3, 6
images, 10
main entry, 138–139
New Hampshire, 181, 252
New Jersey, 216, 252–253
New Orleans, Louisiana, 229–230
New York, 29, 216, 252–258
New York City, 182, 196, 253, 256
New York Journal, 180
New York Times, 190
New York World's Fair, 70, 174, 307
New Zealand
and Antarctica, 49, 51, 52, 54
and Oceania, 285–286
main entry, 293–296
video, 10
Newton, Isaac, 89
Nez Percé (tribe), 224, 279
Niagara Falls, 166
Nicaragua, 174–175
Niger, 40
Nigeria, 21, 40–41
Nightingale, Florence, 154
Niiler, Eric, 204
Nijinsky, Vaslav, 106
NISO Newsline, 7
Nixon, Richard M., 73, 276
Norfolk, Virginia, 193, 276
Normandy, 194

North Africa, 64, 97, 116
North Dakota, 190, 261
North Korea, 60, 62–63, 66, 102
Northern Ireland, 155
Northern Larsen Ice Shelf, 50
Norway, 37, 135, 140–141
Nothiger, Andreas, 4
NOVA (television program), 54
Nubia Museum, 28, 31
Nunavut, 168
Nuremberg Mahzor, 89

O

Oakland County, Michigan, 241
Oaxaca, Mexico, 183
Obelisks, 29
OCLC. *See* Online Computer Library
Center (OCLC)
Ogai, Mori, 96
Oliphant, Pat, 189
Olson, Charles, 215
O'Mahony, John, 132
Oman, 103
O'Neill, Thomas P., 233
Online Archive of California, 169, 211
Online Computer Library Center (OCLC)
CONTENTdm, 14, 163, 221, 278
initiatives, 2
publications, 115
purpose and content, 9–10
Open Video Project, 10
Opium, 65
Oregon, 176, 264–266, 279
Oregon Territory, 279
Orinoco River, 307
Otago Institute, 295
Otovalo, Ecuador, 307
Ouaddai, 24

P

Pacific Islands, 287–289, 291, 295–297
Pacific Northwest, 104, 195, 265, 278
Pacific Railroad, 233, 280
Pacific Rim Region, 213
Pacific studies, 60
Pagodas, 76, 101
Paiute (tribe), 208
Pakistan, 4, 60, 64–65, 71, 83, 103
Palau, 286, 292
Palestine, 30, 90, 103
Palma, Tomas Estrada, 169
Panamint Shoshone (tribe), 211

Papago (tribe), 208
Paper God Prints, 74
Papua New Guinea, 285–286, 289, 295–297
Papyri, 17, 30, 68, 236, 258
Paraguay, 301, 303, 308
Paris, France, 29, 123, 194
Parker, Bonnie, 272
Parkinson, Sydney, 290
Parks, Rosa, 193
Parrish, Maxfield, 268
Patterson, Marvin Breckinridge, 194
Penn, William, 267
Pennsylvania, 184, 194, 216, 267–268
Pentagon, The, 194
Penvenne, Jeanne, 39–40
Persian Gulf War, 184
Peru, 301–303, 308–309
Pettus, Peter, 191
Philip II, King of Spain, 147, 273
Philippines, 60, 61, 64–65, 104
*Photographic Atlas of Selected Regions of the
    Milky Way, A*, 221
Piazza of San Marco, 137
Picasso, Pablo, 4, 147
Picturesque India, 84
Pima (tribe), 208
Pine Island Glacier, 50
Pippin, 190
Pitford Braddick Peticolas, Jane, 191
Pizarro, Francisco, 183
Platina, Bartolomeo, 158
Poe, Edgar Allan, 232
Poland, 135, 141, 179
Polar Bear Expedition, 239
Political campaign songs, 192
Pomo (tribe), 211
Portugal, 77, 94, 142
Portuguese Possessions in Oceania, 82
Posters
    African, 43
    Chinese, 74, 76
    Cuban, 179
    German, 119
    movie, 110
    Swedish, 149
    Swiss, 152
    Wilanów Poster Museum, 142
Preameneu, Bigot de, 125–126
Prokudin-Gorskii, Sergei Mikhailovich, 97,
    104, 111, 137
Prophet, The, 99
Provo, Utah, 273
Puck (magazine), 223
Puerto Rico, 303

Pushkin, Alexander, 153
Pyramids, 27, 29

Q
Qatar, 104, 112
Queensland, 8, 290
Quito, Ecuador, 307
Qumran (West Bank), 31, 97

R
Railroad
    images, 111, 232–233, 257, 280
    maps, 216, 240
    online resources, 211, 227
    periodicals, 237
    timetable, 230
Ramayana, 154
Ranfurly, Lord, 294
Rangiatea, 294
Raphael, 135, 159
Red Sea, 8, 32, 112
Reinhold, Ruth, 208
Rembrandt, 135, 139
Rhode Island, 268
Richmond, Virginia, 276
Rijksmuseum (Netherlands), 10, 139
Riley, Lewis, 245
RKO Pictures, 224
RLG DigiNews, 7
Robbins, Jerome, 192
Robinson, Jackie, 179, 197
Rock and roll, 187, 200
Rockwell, Norman, 268
Roman Auditorium, 27
Roman de la Rose, 126
Roman Forum, 9
Roman Nymphaeum, 81
Romania, 142–144
Rome, 29, 133, 158
Roosevelt, Eleanor, 226
Roosevelt, Franklin Delano, 4, 178, 181, 217,
    256
Roosevelt, Theodore, 201, 256, 258
Ross, James Clark, 51
Rossa, O'Donovan, 132
Rounds, Charles, 282
Rowlandson, Thomas, 157
Royal Society of New Zealand, 295
Rubens, 135
Rugg, Harold, 275
Ruiz, Enrique Labrador, 169
Rural Life in Bengal, 84

Russia
  and Alaska Frontier, 195
  famous persons, 243
  main entry, 104–107
  maps, 69, 135
  images, 90, 136–137, 179, 182
  and World War I, 239
Russian Empire, 104, 118, 136
Russian Far East, 104–105, 195
Russian Orthodox Church, 105, 186–187
Ruth, Babe, 197
Rwanda, 41, 69

S

Sacred Heart Review, 234
Saint Joan de Cassellas, Chapel of, 117
Salt Lake Telegram, 274
Salyut 1, 182
Sami, 141
Samoa, 286–287, 295, 297
San Fernando Valley, 212, 213
San Francisco, 74, 211, 212, 258
San Marino, 137, 144, 212
Sanctuary of Apollo Hylates, 81
Santa Anita (internment camp), 211
Santa Coloma, Andorra, 177
Saskatchewan, Canada, 167
Saudi Arabia, 62, 107
Scandinavia, 135, 242
Schwartz, Tony, 196
Scotland, 155–156
Scott, Robert Falcon, 51, 140
Second Nuremberg Haggada, 90
Senegal, 20, 23, 34, 41–42
September 11th, 193, 200
Sera Monastery, 79–80
Shackleton, Sir Ernest, 49, 52–53
Shaffer, Melvin C., 116, 125, 127, 134
Shakespeare, William, 163, 192, 199, 281
Shanksville, Pennsylvania, 194
Shasta (tribe), 211, 266
Shoeki, Ando, 96
Siberia, 4, 104–105, 195
Sierpc, Poland, 141
Sierra Leone, 18, 42
Silk Road, 90, 274
Simic, Charles, 265
Sinai, 30, 32, 103
Singapore, 60, 61, 64–65, 107
Sino-Japanese Conflict, 13, 62, 75
Siple, Paul, 51
Sistine Chapel, 159
Siuslaw (tribe), 266

Sixth Map of Asia, 97, 112
Skokomish (tribe), 279
Slavery
  abolition, 243
  African, 37
  American history, 178–179, 195, 197, 267
  civil rights, 192
  Civil War, 235, 238
  Kansas, 227
  New York, 254
Sloan, John, 190
Slovakia, 119, 145
Slovenia, 145–146
Smith, William V., 238
Smithsonian Institute, 11, 36, 162, 280
Society of American Archivists, 11
Socks Goes to Washington, 189
Sohon, Gustavus, 280
Solomon Islands, 286, 297–298
Somanatha (temple), 61
Sondheim, Stephen, 192
Soudan Underground Mine State Park, 242
South Africa
  images, 37
  interviews, 39
  main entry, 42–44
  resources, 17, 20
South Carolina, 269–270
South Dakota, 190, 270
South Korea, 60, 61, 108
South Pacific, 67, 285
Southeast Asia, 60, 61, 64–65, 67, 288
Soviet
  cartoons, 183, 200
  images, 67, 105–106, 136
  resources, 105–106
Spain
  images, 94
  main entry, 146–147
  resources, 13, 195
  texts, 127, 273
Spaulding, Albert G., 255
Sputnik 1, 182
Sri Lanka, 60, 63–65, 103, 108
St. John, Primus, 265
St. John the Theologian (monastery), 129
St. Petersburg, 105
Stafford, William, 265
Stalin, 78
Stanley, John Mix, 280
Stanwyck, Barbara, 224
Starkey, David, 153
State archives
  Arizona, 208

California, 210–211
Colorado, 213
Florida, 218
Georgia, 221
Hawaii, 223
Maine, 230
Maryland, 231
New York, 254, 256–257
North Carolina, 259
Oregon, 266
Pennsylvania, 268
Utah, 274
Virginia, 277
Washington, 279
West Virginia, 281
Wyoming, 283
State libraries
  Alaska, 206
  Bavarian, 113, 115, 128
  California, 212
  Connecticut, 215
  Florida, 218
  Nevada, 254
  North Carolina, 259
  Ohio, 262
  Pennsylvania, 267
  Russian, 104
  Saxon, 126
  Tennessee, 271
  Texas, 272
  Wyoming, 283–284
Statesman Journal, 266
Statue of Liberty, 184, 193
Steichen, Edward J., 193
Steinbeck, John, 187, 257
Stephens, James, 132
Stevens, Isaac, 280
Stevens, Roger Lacey, 190
Stevenson, Edward, 224
Stockholm, Sweden, 151
Stone Age, 44
Strother, David Hunter, 281
*Structure of the Heavens, A Poem on Islamic
    Law, Islamic Saints*, 19
Stryker, Deena (Boyer), 169
Studemeister, Margarita S., 6, 63
Sudan, 31, 44–45, 63
Sukuma Region, Tanzania, 35, 45
Suriname, 301, 309
Swaziland, 45
Sweden, 148–151
Switzerland, 40, 151

Syria, 31, 62, 68, 71, 108
Szyk, Arthur, 179

T
Tabakov, Igor, 105
Taiwan, 57, 60, 61, 65, 108
Tajikistan, 108–109
Takelma (tribe), 266
Talmudic literature, 88–89
Tampa, Florida, 219
Tanforan (internment camp), 211
Tanzania, 35, 39, 45
Taylor, Thomas, 157
Te Ao Hou, 294
Telnaes, Anne, 185–186, 200
Temples
  China, 76
  Egypt, 28–29, 31
  Japan, 94
  Mongolia, 78
  world, 14
Tennessee, 193, 270–271
Texas, 36, 271–273
Thailand
  images, 14, 60, 65–66, 106
  main entry, 109
  resources, 4, 58, 61, 64
Thomas, John, 157
Tibet, 61, 66, 79–80, 102
Timbuktu, Mali, 6, 19, 37
Tintern Abbey, 236
Tirana, Albania, 117
Tobey, Mark, 278
Togo, 17, 45–46
Tombs, 27, 29, 32, 99
Tonga, 37, 286, 295, 298
Tortuguero Box, 183
Toubou, 24
Transylvania, Romania, 144
Trott, Nicholas, 270
Trudeau, Garry, 189
Tryal of Spencer Cowper, Esq, The, 204
Tulalip (tribe), 279
Tule Lake (internment camp), 211
Tunisia, 46
Turkey, 14, 57, 62, 109–110
Turkmenistan, 111
Turner, J.M.W., 157
Tutankhamen, 26, 241
Tuvalu, 286, 298
Twain, Mark, 187, 281

Twiggy, 187
Two-Hatchet, Keith, 225

U

U.S. Capitol Building, 191
U.S. Constitution, 181, 188, 191, 197, 210
U.S. Geological Survey (USGS), 49–50, 54, 182, 273
U.S. National Library of Medicine (NLM), 2, 12, 202
Ubangi River, 23
Ucayali, Peru, 308
Uganda, 17, 46
Ukiyo-e, 91
Ukraine, 106, 152–153, 258
Ulaanbaatar, Mongolia, 78
Undset, Sigrid, 141
UNESCO
    and Africa, 17, 26, 31
    and Asia, 59, 64, 70, 79, 100
    and South America, 301–302
    scope and purpose, 1, 11
United Arab Emirates, 111
United Kingdom, 51, 153–154
United States Institute of Peace (USIP), 6, 63
United States Pacific Railroad Survey, 280
Upper Macedonia, 128
Urbino, Italy, 29, 158
Uruguay, 301, 309
Utah, 176, 190, 273–274
Uzbekistan, 111

V

Valley of the Kings. *See* Tombs
Vanuatu, 286, 299
Varmus, Harold, 204
Vatican, The, 158–159
Veléz de Escalante, Silvestre, 190
Venezuela, 301, 303, 310
Vermont, 274–275
Veterans
    Florida, 219
    Indiana, 226
    Library of Congress, 178, 184, 200–201
    Maryland, 233
    Michigan, 236, 238–239
    Pennsylvania, 268
    West Virginia, 281
Vicksburg, Mississippi, 246
Victorian Era, 192, 243

Vienna, Austria, 94, 135
Vietnam
    architecture, 60
    images, 65, 106, 183, 219
    resources, 60, 52, 64, 112
    Vietnam War, 111–112, 180, 184, 189, 226
Vihara at Paharur, 70
Vilnius, Lithuania, 136
Virginia, 182, 188, 193, 216, 275–277
Virginia Gazette, 275
Virginia Tech tragedy, 277
Von Wicht, John, 181
Voyage en Perse, 85
Voyage in the Indian Ocean and to Bengal, undertaken in the Years 1789 and 1790: Containing an Account of the Sechelles Islands and Trincomale, A, 112
Voyage to the East, A, 71

W

Wada, Makoto, 190
Walachia, Romania, 144
Waldseemüller, Martin, 182
Wales, 157, 236
Wallace, Idaho, 225
Walloon, 118
Wampanoag (tribe), 268
War of 1812, 239–240
War Illustrated, The, 76
War relocation camps, 91
Warren, Earl, Chief Justice, 185
Washington Post, 183, 185
Washington (state), 277–280
Washington, DC, 189, 191, 216, 280
Washington, George, 182, 186, 188, 191, 198, 290
Water Babies, 192
Watergate, 189
Watkins, Carleton E., 157
Watkins, Caroline Emma "Carrie," 245
Webster, Daniel, 231, 275
Welch, Holmes Hinkley, 75
Werntz, Carl, 193
West, Mae, 190
West, Philip, 147
West Africa, 19–20, 22–23, 41
West Side Story, 190, 192
West Virginia, 216, 280–281
Westermeier, Clifford P., 215
Western Canada, 164
Whillans Ice Stream, 50
Whiting, Richard A., 241

Whitman, Walt, 190, 258
Whittle, Frank, 182
Whole Works of Sir James Ware concerning Ireland, The, 132
Wilder, D.W., 227
Wilder, Thornton, 181, 199
Williams, Brian, 95
Williams, Joe, 225
Williamsburg, Virginia, 275
Winter's Journey from Milwaukee to Green Bay, A, 282
Wisconsin, 118, 282
Women's suffrage, 197, 201, 244, 270, 280
Women artists, 166, 187, 205
Wonderful Wizard of Oz, The, 194
Wood, Art, 180
Wood, C.E.S. (Charles Erskine Scott), 265
Wood, Grant, 245
Woodcuts, 116, 203, 235
Woodhouse, Herbert (Bert) C., 44
Woodhull, Victoria, 269
Woodruff, Hale, 181
Wordsworth, William, 236
Works Progress Administration (WPA), 178, 217, 241
World Monuments Fund, 14
World Trade Center, 194
World War I
    audio recordings, 206
    images, 104, 118, 136
    journals, 246, 288
    posters, 119, 213, 232
    resources, 86, 184, 200
    service records—Hawaii, 223
World War II
    audio recordings, 206
    Bob Hope and, 180
    cartoons, 183

documents, 127
images, 83, 116
Japanese internment, 210, 211
Jewish property, 87
journals, 288
posters, 232, 249
resources, 183–184, 200
women journalists, 194
Wrensted, Benedicte, 224
Wright, Frank Lloyd, 184, 218
Wright Brothers, 182, 198
Wyeth, N.C., 268
Wynn, Ed, 180
Wyoming, 248, 279, 282–284

Y

Yahooskin (tribe), 266
Yakama (tribe), 279
Yale Divinity Library, 24–25, 36, 74
Yale University, 2
Yaqui (tribe), 208
Yavapai (tribe), 208
Yellowstone National Park, 283
Yellowstone River, 190, 247
Yemen, 69, 112
Yorktown, Virginia, 275
Young, Chic, 180
Yugoslavia, 120, 146
Yukon, 164, 278
Yurok (tribe), 211, 266

Z

Zambia, 46
Zanabazar, 79
Zimbabwe, 19, 47

About the Authors

Michael J. Aloi is an Associate Professor and Technical Services Librarian at Dowling College in Oakdale, New York. He is the principal cataloger for Dowling College and has previously coauthored articles for *Technical Services Quarterly*, the *Journal of Web Librarianship*, and *Library Administration & Management*.

Marjorie Fusco is an Associate Professor and Reference Librarian at Dowling College in Oakdale, New York. She has done library research for many years and coauthored the book *Distance Learning for Higher Education: An Annotated Bibliography*, published in 2002.

Susan E. Ketcham is a Professor and Reference Librarian at Long Island University in Brentwood, New York. Prior to her current position, she was a cataloger for over 20 years. She coauthored the book *Distance Learning for Higher Education: An Annotated Bibliography*, published in 2002; contributed a chapter to the book *Introducing and Managing Academic Library Automation Projects* (1996); and writes book reviews for the *Library Journal*'s column Professional Media. She also teaches at the Long Island University Palmer School of Library and Information Science.

LaVergne, TN USA
13 February 2011

216278LV00002B/10/P

9 781555 707019